Charles George Walpole

A Short History of the Kingdom of Ireland

From the Earliest Times to the Union with Great Britain

Charles George Walpole

A Short History of the Kingdom of Ireland
From the Earliest Times to the Union with Great Britain

ISBN/EAN: 9783337170714

Printed in Europe, USA, Canada, Australia, Japan

Cover: Foto ©ninafisch / pixelio.de

More available books at **www.hansebooks.com**

A SHORT HISTORY

OF

THE KINGDOM OF IRELAND

From the Earliest Times to the Union with
Great Britain

WITH FIVE MAPS AND APPENDICES

BY

CHARLES GEORGE WALPOLE, M.A.
BARRISTER-AT-LAW; AUTHOR OF "A RUBRIC OF THE COMMON LAW"

NEW YORK
HARPER & BROTHERS, FRANKLIN SQUARE
1882

PREFACE.

The present volume is an attempt to lay before the reader an outline of the leading features of the history of Ireland down to the time when that country ceased to be a separate kingdom. Since the union of the two Parliaments, Irish history has become inextricably blended with the history of Great Britain; and any attempt to relate it would entail a task of far greater magnitude, and one beyond the scope of a popular work.

The author can take no credit for original research. The principal materials of which use has been made are the very numerous historical works bearing on the subject, written from very diverse points of view; the published state papers; the published correspondence of eminent statesmen; and the statutes of the realm. Wherever passages appear between inverted commas the quotations come from the three latter sources.

It is hoped that a full chronological table and a list of the chief governors of Ireland will to some extent supply the deficiencies in the text, which are almost unavoidable in such a sketch as is here presented.

C. G. W.

3 Dr. Johnson's Buildings, Temple.

CONTENTS.

	PAGE
CHRONOLOGICAL TABLE...	xi
LIST OF AUTHORITIES...	xxix

BOOK I.
INDEPENDENT IRELAND.

CHAPTER
I. CONDITION OF THE EARLY IRISH...	3
II. CHRISTIANITY AMONG THE EARLY IRISH...	10
III. THE SCANDINAVIAN TYRANNY...	15

BOOK II.
THE ANGLO-NORMAN SETTLEMENT.

I. THE FILIBUSTERS...	23
II. THE COLONISTS...	28
III. THE GREAT TERRITORIAL BARONS...	32
IV. THE ASSIMILATION OF THE SETTLERS...	39
V. THE RUIN OF THE ENGLISH COLONY...	44

BOOK III.
THE FIRST CONQUEST.

I. THE TURN OF THE TIDE...	53
II. THE REHABILITATION OF THE ENGLISH GOVERNMENT...	59
III. THE CONFISCATION OF THE CHURCH LANDS...	64
IV. THE WINNING OF THE CHIEFTAINS...	68
V. THE IMPOSITION OF THE NEW FAITH...	73
VI. THE PLANTATION OF LEIX AND OFFALY...	81
VII. THE WAR WITH SHANE O'NEIL...	84
VIII. THE PLANTATION SPIRIT ABROAD...	89
IX. THE DESMOND REBELLION...	95

CONTENTS.

CHAPTER	PAGE
X. The Plantation of Munster	103
XI. Sowing the Wind	107
XII. The War with Tyrone	114
XIII. The Introduction of English Ideas	122
XIV. The Plantation of Ulster	130
XV. The Muzzling of the Parliament	136
XVI. The Plantation of Leinster	140

BOOK IV.
THE SECOND CONQUEST.

I. Sowing the Wind Again	153
II. The Wentworth Scourge	156
III. Provincial Insurrections in 1641	165
IV. The Consolidation of the Revolt	175
V. Plots and Counterplots	180
VI. The Subjugation	189
VII. "The Curse o' Crummell"	195

BOOK V.
THE THIRD CONQUEST.

I. Restoration Compromises	205
II. Tolerance and Intolerance	212
III. The Secession	219
IV. The Reconquest	226
V. The Broken Treaty	232
VI. The Outlawry of the Roman Catholics	238

BOOK VI.
THE FOURTH CONQUEST.

I. The Shackling of the English Colony	251
II. The Statutory Destruction of Irish Trade	255
III. Protestant Ascendency and its Works	259
IV. The Results of Bondage	267
V. The Beginning of Corruption	275
VI. The Revolt of the Colony	281
VII. The Concession of Home Rule	288
VIII. The Demand for Parliamentary Reform	292
IX. Conflicts with the English Parliament	298
X. Local Riots and Agrarian Disturbances	304

CONTENTS.

CHAPTER		PAGE
XI.	The Agitation for Reform and Emancipation of the Roman Catholics	307
XII.	Partial Emancipation of the Roman Catholics	313
XIII.	Prosecutions	319
XIV.	Blighted Hopes	323
XV.	New Departures	329
XVI.	France at "England's Back Door"	334
XVII.	Martial Law	338
XVIII.	The Triumph of Coercion	342
XIX.	The Abortive Local Risings	348
XX.	The Irish Jacquerie	354
XXI.	Trampling Out the Fire	362
XXII.	The Last Flicker of the Flame	368
XXIII.	The Sale of the Constitution	371
XXIV.	Annexation	377

Appendices 383
Index 409

MAPS.

IRELAND BEFORE THE ANGLO-NORMAN INVASION..............*Frontispiece*
" THE ANGLO-NORMAN SETTLEMENT IN THE THIRTEENTH
　　CENTURY.................................*To face page* 20
" IN THE REIGN OF HENRY VII...................　　"　　50
" THE PLANTATIONS OF MARY, ELIZABETH, AND
　　JAMES I....................................　　"　　150
" THE PURITAN SETTLEMENT......................　　"　　202

CHRONOLOGICAL TABLE.*

A. D.
c. 432. Arrival in Ireland of St. Patrick.
c. 444. Foundation of the see and priory of Armagh by St. Patrick.
c. 450. Foundation of the abbeys of Inniscathery, Downpatrick, Saul, Trim, Ardagh, Duleek, Drumshallon, and Louth by St. Patrick.
c. 465. Death of St. Patrick.
c. 480. Foundation of an abbey at Antrim by Dartract, a disciple of St. Patrick.
Foundation of an abbey at Clogher by St. Aid.
c. 484. Foundation of the nunnery and abbey of Kildare by St. Brigid.
c. 500. Foundation of a monastery at Swords by St. Columb.
Foundation of a priory at Castle-Dermot by St. Dermot.
Foundation of the abbey of Lough Deary, Co. Donegal (St. Patrick's Purgatory), by St. Dabeoc.
c. 510. Foundation of the abbey of Emly by St. Ailbe.
c. 530. Foundation of the abbey of Glendalough by St. Kevin.
c. 540. Foundation of an abbey at Clones by St. Tigernach.
Foundation of the abbey of Roscommon by St. Colman.
c. 544. Foundation of the abbey of the island of All-Saints, in Loughrea, by St. Kieran.

A. D.
c. 546. Foundation of abbeys at Derry and Durrow by St. Columb.
c. 548. Foundation of the abbey of Clonmacnoise.
c. 549. Foundation of the abbey of Clonard by St. Kieran.
c. 550. Foundation of the abbey of Muckamore, Co. Antrim, by St. Colman.
Foundation of the abbey of Aghmacarte by O'Dempsey.
c. 555. Foundation of the abbey of Drumlane, Co. Cavan.
Foundation of the abbey of Kells by St. Columb.
Foundation of the abbey of Bangor by St. Comgall.
c. 563. St. Columbkill preaches Christianity in the Western Isles.
c. 570. Foundation of a monastery at Ardfert by St. Brendan.
Foundation of the abbey of Innisfallen by St. Finian the Leper.
Foundation of the abbey of Aghadoe by St. Canice.
c. 572. St. Columbanus.
590. *Gregory the Great Pope of Rome.*
Foundation of a monastery at Drumcliffe by St. Columb.
600. *St. Augustine converts Ethelbert, King of Kent.*
c. 620. Foundation of a monastery at Kilmacduagh, Co. Galway, by St. Colman.
627. *Conversion of Edwin, King of Northumbria, by St. Paulinus.*

* The events printed in *italics* are other than those occurring in Ireland.

CHRONOLOGICAL TABLE.

A. D.
630. Foundation of the abbey of Lismore by St. Mochuda.
Foundation of the priory at Fore, Westmeath, by St. Fechin.
634. *St. Aidan, from Iona, reintroduces Christianity at Lindisfarne.*
c. 650. *Irish missionaries on the Continent.*
660. Foundation of a monastery at Cong, Co. Mayo, by St. Fechan.
665. Foundation of a monastery at Mayo by St. Colman.
c. 745. Feargal (Virgilius) flourished.
787. *The Northmen invade England.*
795. The Northmen invade Ireland.
800. *Charles the Great Emperor of the West.*
Foundation of the abbey of Inistioge, Co. Kilkenny.
815. Arrival of Turges.
844. His death. Massacre of the Northmen by the Irish.
849. Fresh incursions of Northmen.
c. 850. Joannes Scotus Erigena flourished.
853. Arrival of Amlaf. Nose-money is collected.
872. The Northmen invade Scotland from Ireland.
879. *Peace of Wedmore between King Alfred and the Northmen.*
c. 900. Reign of Cormac McCulinan, King of Leinster.
937. *Amlaf with a contingent of Northmen from Ireland defeated at Brunanburgh by Athelstan.*
948. Conversion of the Northmen in Ireland.
St. Mary's Abbey, Dublin, founded by the Northmen.
968. Battle of Sulchoid.
Brian Born succeeds to the throne of Munster.
980. The Northmen defeated at Tara by Malachy, King of all Ireland.
Foundation of the priory of Holmpatrick, Co. Dublin, by Sitric.
983. Brian extends his rule over Leinster.
997. Struggle between Brian and Malachy.
1001. Seizure of the throne of Tara by Brian.
1002. *Massacre of Northmen in England by the Saxons.*
1003. *Invasion of England by Sweyne.*
1013. Rebellion of Leinster in conjunction with the Northmen.
1014. Battle of Clontarf. Death of Brian.
Restoration of Malachy.
1016. Malachy defeats the Northmen.
1017. *Canute King of England.*
1022. Death of Malachy.
1023. Teige and Donchad, sons of Brian, joint rulers of Munster.
Murder of Teige by Donchad.
1038. The priory of Christchurch, Dublin, founded by Sitric, Danish Prince of Dublin.
Donchad marries a daughter of Earl Godwin.
1051. Harold takes refuge with Donchad after his rebellion against Edward the Confessor.
1058. Donchad becomes titular king of all Ireland.
1063. Donchad defeated by Turlough, son of Teige.
1064. Turlough titular king of all Ireland.
1066. *Battle of Hastings.*
1086. Death of Turlough. He is succeeded by his son Murkertach.
1087. *William II. of England succeeds.*
1088. Tigernach, abbot of Clonmacnoise, writer of the "Annals of Tigernach," dies.
1100. *Henry I. of England succeeds.*
1106. Foundation of a monastery at Lispool by McNoel McKenless.

CHRONOLOGICAL TABLE.

A. D.
1111. Synod of Rath Bresail.
1119. Death of Murkertach.
1121. Death of Donald O'Loghlin.
1132. Struggle between Connor O'-Brien of Munster and Turlough O'Connor of Connaught.
1135. *Stephen of England succeeds.*
1142. Abbey of Mellifont founded by O'Carroll of Argiel.
1148. Abbey of Bective founded by O'Malachlin of Meath.
Abbey of Baltinglass founded by Dermot McMurrough.
Abbey of Monasternenagh, Limerick, founded by O'Brien.
1151. Foundation of a nunnery at Kilcleeheen, Co. Kilkenny, by Dermot McMurrough.
Battle of Moinmor.
Turlough O'Connor titular king of all Ireland.
1152. Synod of Kells.
A Cistercian monastery founded at Athlone.
1153. A Cistercian monastery founded at Newry by O'Lochlin.
Abduction of O'Rourke's wife by McMurrough.
1154. *Henry II. of England succeeds. Pope Adrian IV. grants Ireland to Henry II. of England.*
Conflict of Turlough O'Connor with O'Lochlin of Ulster.
Foundation of a monastery at Odorney in Kerry.
1156. Death of Turlough O'Connor.
1159. Foundation of the monastery of Inis Connagh, Tipperary, by Donnell O'Brien.
1161. O'Lochlin titular king of all Ireland.
Foundation of the abbey of Boyle, Roscommon, by Maurice O'Dubhay.
1166. Death of O'Lochlin.
Rory O'Connor titular king of all Ireland.
Foundation of the priory of All-Saints, Dublin, by Dermot McMurrough.

A. D.
1168. Flight of Dermot McMurrough.
1169. *His bargain with Strongbow.*
Arrival of Fitzstephen. Capture of Wexford.
Invasion of Ossory. Arrival of Raymond le Gros.
Capture of Waterford.
Arrival of Strongbow. His marriage with Eva McMurrough.
Capture of Dublin.
1170. Synod of Armagh and manumission of English slaves.
Death of Dermot McMurrough.
Siege of Dublin.
Strongbow returns to England and makes his peace with Henry.
Becket murdered.
Monastery founded at Fermoy.
1171. Henry II. arrives.
He receives the submission of the chieftains.
1172. Synod of Cashel.
Government organized by Henry at Dublin.
He returns to England.
Foundation of the abbey of St. Thomas, Dublin, by William Fitzaldelm.
1174. Capture of Limerick.
Foundation of the priory of Kilmainham by Strongbow.
1175. Treaty between Henry and Rory O'Connor.
1177. Prince John Lord of Ireland.
1178. Foundation of an abbey at Astrath, Co. Donegal, by Roderick O'Cananan.
Foundation of an abbey at Dunbrody, Co. Wexford, by Hervey Mountmorres.
1180. Foundation of an abbey at Jerpoint, Kilkenny, by McGilapatrick of Upper Ossory.
Foundation of an abbey at Middleton, Cork, by the Barrys.
Foundation of an abbey at Inniscourcy, Down, by Sir John De Courcy.

CHRONOLOGICAL TABLE.

A.D.
1181. Foundation of Holy Cross Abbey by Donnell O'Brien.
1183. Foundation of an abbey at Abbeyleix by Cuchry O'Moore.
1184. Prince John lands at Waterford.
Mutiny of the chieftains.
1185. Foundation of the priory of St. John at Waterford by Prince John.
1189. Foundation of a monastery at Monasterevan, Kildare, by O'Dempsy.
Death of Henry II.

RICHARD I., 1189-1199.

1190. Foundation of a monastery at Knockmoy, Galway, by Cathal O'Connor.
Foundation of the nunnery of Grace-Dieu, Co. Dublin, by John Comin, Archbishop of Dublin.
1193. Foundation of the priory of Kells, Co. Meath, by Walter De Lacy.
Foundation of the priory at Kells, Co. Kilkenny, by Geoffrey Fitz-Robert.
Foundation of the Gray Abbey, Down, by Africa De Courcy.
Foundation of the monastery of Corcumroe, Co. Clare, by Donogh O'Brien.
Death of Rory O'Connor.
1195. Foundation of the abbey of Clare by Donald O'Brien.

JOHN, 1199-1216.

1200. Foundation of Tintern Abbey, Wexford, by William, Earl Marshal.
Foundation of a nunnery at Grany by Walter de Riddlesford.
Foundation of a monastery at Kilcooly, Tipperary, by Donogh O'Brien.
Foundation of a monastery at Kilbeggan by the Daltons.
Foundation of the Commandery of St. John for Hospital-

A.D.
lers, at Wexford by William, Earl Marshal.
1202. Foundation of a priory of Great Connall, Kildare, by Meyler Fitz-Henry.
Foundation of the priory of St. Wolstans, Naas, by Adam de Hereford.
1205. Foundation of the abbey of Abingdon, Limerick, by Theobald Walter.
Surrender of two thirds of Connaught by Cathal O'Connor to King John.
Disgrace of De Courcy.
1206. Foundation of the priory at Newtown by Simon Rochford.
Foundation of the priory for Crouched Friars at Castle-Dermot by Walter de Riddlesford.
1207. Foundation of the Commandery of St. John for Hospitallers at Any, Co. Limerick, by Geoffrey De Marisco.
Foundation of the Crouched Friary at Ardee by Roger De Pipard.
1208. Foundation of the friary of St. Saviour's, Dublin, by William, Earl Marshal.
1210. King John in Ireland. He divides it into counties.
1211. Foundation of St. John's Abbey, Kilkenny, by William, Earl Marshal.
1213. Foundation of the monastery at Tralee by Lord John Fitz-Thomas Fitzgerald.
1214. Foundation of the Gray friary, Cork, by Dermot McCarthy Reagh.
1215. *The Great Charter signed in England by John.*

HENRY III., 1216-1272.

1216. The privileges of the Great Charter extended to Irish subjects.
1220. Foundation of the abbey of the Holy Trinity at Tuam by the De Burghs.

CHRONOLOGICAL TABLE. xv

A.D.
1221. Grant of Connaught to De Burgh by Henry III.
1224. Foundation of the abbey of Tracton by Maurice McCarthy.
Foundation of the Dominican friary at Drogheda by Luke Netterville, archbishop of Armagh.
Foundation of the priory of Aughrim by Theobald Butler.
Foundation of the priory of Ballybeg, Cork, by Philip De Barry.
Foundation of the priory of Athassal, Tipperary, by William Fitzaldelm.
Foundation of the priory of Nenagh, Tipperary, by the Butlers.
Foundation of a Franciscan friary at Youghal by Maurice Fitzgerald.
1225. Foundation of the Black Abbey, Kilkenny, by William, Earl Marshal.
1226. Foundation of the convent of St. Saviour's, Waterford, by the citizens.
1227. Foundation of the priory of Mullingar by Ralph le Petit, Bishop of Meath.
1229. Foundation of St. Mary's Convent, Cork, by Philip Barry.
1232. *Fall of Hubert De Burgh.*
Foundation of a convent at Carrickfergus by Hugh De Lacy.
1234. Foundation of the Franciscan friary at Kilkenny by Richard, Earl Marshal.
Richard, Earl Marshal, declared a traitor and treacherously killed.
1235. Foundation of the monastery of St. Francis, Dublin, by Ralph le Porter.
1236. Foundation of the monastery of Multifarnam, Westmeath, by William Delamare.
1237. Foundation of the monastery

A.D.
at Mullingar by the Nugents.
1240. Foundation of the Gray priory at Drogheda by the Plunkets.
Foundation of the Franciscan friary at Waterford by Sir Hugh Purcell.
Foundation of the Cistercian monastery at Ennis by Donough Carbreach O'Brien.
Foundation of a convent at Lismullen, Co. Meath, by Alicia De la Corner.
1241. Foundation of a convent at Athlone by Cathal O'Connor.
Foundation of the Dominican friary at Athenry by Meyler De Bermingham.
1244. Foundation of the Dominican friary at Coleraine by the McEvelins.
1252. Foundation of the Dominican friary at Sligo by Maurice Fitzgerald.
1253. Foundation of the Dominican friary of St. Mary, Roscommon, by Felim O'Connor.
Foundation of the Dominican friary at Athy by the Hogans.
Foundation of a monastery at Limerick by O'Brien.
Foundation of Hacket's Abbey, Cashel, by William Hacket.
Foundation of the Gray friary, Dundalk, by De Verdon.
Foundation of the Franciscan friary at Ardfert by Thomas, Lord of Kerry.
1257. Foundation of a monastery at Athy by the Hogans.
1258. *The Provisions of Oxford.*
1259. Rising of the McCarthys of Desmond.
Massacre of the Geraldines.
Foundation of monastery of Holy Trinity, Dublin, by the Talbots.
1260. Foundation of the Gray Abbey at Kildare by De Vesci.

CHRONOLOGICAL TABLE.

A.D.
1263. Foundation of the abbey of St. Mary Trim by Geoffrey De Genneville.
Foundation of a monastery at Armagh by Archbishop Scanlen.
1264. Foundation of a monastery at Arklow by Theobald Fitzwalter.
Battle of Lewes.
Contest between the Geraldines and the De Burghs.
1265. *Battle of Evesham.*
1268. Foundation of a monastery at Rossibercan, Kilkenny, by the Graces and Walshes.
Foundation of a monastery at Youghal by the Baron of Offaly.
1269. Foundation of a monastery at Leighlin Bridge by the Carews.
Foundation of a monastery at Lorrah, Tipperary, by Walter De Burgh.

EDWARD I., 1272-1307.

1272. The Irish petition for the extension to them of the English laws.
Foundation of Hore Abbey, Cashel, by Archbishop McCarvill.
1274. Foundation of the abbey of Rathbran, Mayo, by the Dexeters.
1277. De Clare invades Thomond.
1280. Feuds between the Geraldines and De Burghs.
1290. Quarrel between De Vesci and the Baron of Offaly.
Foundation of a monastery at Clare-Galway by John De Cogan.
Foundation of a monastery at Buttevant by David Oge Barry.
Foundation of a monastery at Galbally, Limerick, by O'Brien.
Foundation of a monastery at Ross, Wexford, by Sir John Devereux.

A.D.
Foundation of a monastery at Clonmines by the McMurroughs.
Foundation of a monastery at Dungarvan by John Fitz-Thomas Fitzgerald.
Foundation of the Carmelite convent at Dublin by Sir Richard Bagot.
Foundation of the Carmelite convent at Ardee by Ralph Peppard.
1291. Foundation of a Dominican friary at Kilmallock by Gilbert Fitzgerald.
1296. Foundation of the Franciscan friary at Galway by Sir William De Burgh.
Battle of Dunbar.
1298. *Battle of Falkirk.*
1300. Foundation of a monastery at Cavan by O'Reilly.
1302. Foundation of a Franciscan friary at Castle-Dermot by Lord Offaly.

EDWARD II., 1307-1327.

1307. Foundation of the Gray friary at Castle Lyons, Cork, by John De Barry.
1308. Piers Gaveston lord-lieutenant.
1312. Foundation of monastery at Tullow, Carlow, by Simon Lombard and Hugh Tallon.
1314. Robert Bruce takes refuge in Ireland.
Battle of Bannockburn.
1315. Foundation of an Augustinian friary at Adare, Limerick, by Earl of Kildare.
Edward Bruce lands at Carrickfergus.
Rising of the Ulster Irish and the discontented English of Meath.
Bruce's successes. Rising in Connaught.
Bruce is crowned at Dundalk.
1316. Battle of Athenry.
Arrival of Robert Bruce.

CHRONOLOGICAL TABLE. xvii

A.D.
He advances to Dublin. Famine.
He retires into Scotland.
1317. Foundation of a Carmelite convent at Athboy by William de Londres.
1318. Battle of Dundalk. Death of Edward Bruce.
1320. Foundation of a monastery at Bantry by O'Sullivan.
A university at Dublin projected by Archbishop Bicknor.

EDWARD, 1327–1377.

1327. Civil war between the De Burghs and the Butlers and the Fitzgeralds of Desmond.
Rising of the McMurroughs.
1329. Unsuccessful petition by the Irish for recognition by English law.
Risings in Thomond, Westmeath, and the south.
1330. Maurice Fitz-Thomas Fitzgerald created Earl of Desmond and granted the palatinate of Kerry.
He renders assistance to the lords justices against the Irish.
Risings in Leinster.
1331. Arrest of Desmond, De Birmingham, and Mandeville.
1333. Murder of the Earl of Ulster. Partition of his estates.
1336. Release of the Earl of Desmond.
1338. *Beginning of the war with France.*
1339. Risings in Munster subdued by Desmond.
1341. The king proposes to resume the estates of the great landowners.
1342. Parliament summoned to meet at Dublin.
Convention held at Kilkenny.
Petition to the king, who gives way.
1344. Sir Ralph Ufford seizes some of Desmond's estates.

A.D.
Desmond surrenders, and is bailed.
Kildare is arrested.
1346. *Battle of Crecy.*
Surrender of Calais.
1348. Kildare and Desmond pardoned.
1349. The black death.
1356. Foundation of a friary at Knocktopher by James, second Earl of Ormonde.
1361. Lionel, Duke of Clarence, lord-lieutenant.
Rising in Munster.
1367. Statute of Kilkenny.
1369. Risings in Wicklow and Limerick.

RICHARD II., 1377–1399.

1379. Ordinance against absentees.
1385. Robert De Vere, the king's favorite, made Marquis of Dublin and Duke of Ireland.
1387. The king comes of age.
1392. Rising of Art McMurrough in Leinster.
1394. Richard II. lands at Waterford. Submission of the chieftains.
1395. Richard at Dublin. Reforms the judicial bench. Returns to England, leaving the Earl of March lord-lieutenant.
Rising of McMurrough and the O'Byrnes of Wicklow.
Defeat and death of the Earl of March.
1399. Richard's second expedition to Ireland.
Landing of Bolingbroke at Ravenspur.
The king embarks for Milford Haven.

HENRY IV., 1399–1413.

1400. Immigration of Scots into Antrim.
Foundation of an abbey at Longford by O'Farrell.
1401. Risings in Wicklow.

HENRY V., 1413–1422.

1413. Fresh struggles between the

English and the natives.
1415. *War with France.*
An Irish contingent with the king in Normandy.
Battle of Agincourt.
1418. Art McMurrough captured.
1421. Risings in Leix.

HENRY VI., 1422-1461.
1433. Wars between the O'Neils and O'Donnels.
1438. Statutes against absentees.
The sixth Earl of Desmond marries Catharine McCormac, and is expelled from his estates by his uncle.
1439. Fitzstephen's moiety of the kingdom of Cork granted to the seventh Earl of Desmond.
1449. Richard, Duke of York, lord-lieutenant.
1450. Risings in Westmeath.
1454. *Duke of York appointed protector.*
1455. *First battle of St. Albans.*
1459. *The fight at Blore Heath.*
The panic at Ludlow and flight of the Yorkists.
Duke of York takes refuge in Ireland.
1460. *Battle of Wakefield.*
Battle of Towton.
Foundation of New Abbey, Naas, by Sir Rowland Eustace.
Foundation of the Franciscan friary, Enniscorthy, by Donald Kavenagh.

EDWARD IV., 1461-1483.
1461. The eighth Earl of Desmond founds the College of Youghal.
1465. Foundation of a monastery at Glenarm, Co. Antrim, by Robert Bissett.
Foundation of a Franciscan monastery at Kilcrea, Co. Cork, by McCarthy Mor.
1467. The Earl of Desmond is charged with treason, and executed.
1472. Institution of the Brotherhood of St. George.
1478. Gerald, eighth Earl of Kildare, lord deputy for fourteen years.

EDWARD V., 1483.

RICHARD III., 1483-1485.
1484. Foundation of the Augustinian friary at Naas.

HENRY VII., 1485-1509.
1487. Lambert Simnel crowned in Dublin.
Kildare suspected of treason.
Battle of Stoke.
1488. Kildare is pardoned.
1489. Fighting in Desmond.
Fighting in Ulster.
1490. Perkin Warbeck arrives in Cork.
1492. Fall of Kildare.
1494. Sir Edward Poynings lord deputy.
Crushes the adherents of Warbeck.
Parliament at Drogheda, Poynings's Act.
1496. Arrest of Kildare.
He is pardoned and made lord deputy, and governs Ireland till 1513.
1497. Warbeck again in Ireland.
Fighting between the natives and the Bourkes of Connaught.
Battle of Knocktow.

HENRY VIII., 1509-1547.
1513. Death of Kildare. His son is elected lord justice in his room.
1515. *Wolsey created a cardinal and made lord chancellor.*
1516. Feuds in Desmond.
Feuds in the Ormonde family.
Feuds between Ormonde and Kildare, and Ormonde and Desmond.

CHRONOLOGICAL TABLE.

A.D.
1519. Kildare summoned to London.
He marries a daughter of the Marquis of Dorset.
1520. *He is present at the Field of the Cloth of Gold.*
1521. Risings in Leix and Offaly.
1523. Kildare returns.
Wolsey begins a visitation of the English monasteries.
1524. Desmond holds a treasonable correspondence with Francis I. of France.
Kildare lord deputy. He is ordered to arrest Desmond, and fails to do so.
1526. Kildare again summoned to England, and lodged in the Tower.
He is released on bail.
1527. *Henry raises the question of the divorce.*
1528. Rising of O'Connor of Offaly. He captures Lord Delvin, the lord deputy.
1529. Desmond's treasonable correspondence with Charles V.
His death.
Fall of Wolsey.
1530. Kildare sent back to suppress O'Connor's rising.
1531. *The "submission" of the clergy in England.*
1532. *Henry marries Anne Boleyn.*
Kildare made lord deputy.
He makes a treaty with O'Connor and O'Carrol.
1534. He is summoned to England, and lodged in the Tower.
His son, Lord Thomas, rebels. Besieges Dublin Castle.
Kildare dies in the Tower.
1535. Skeffington captures Maynooth. Flight of Lord Thomas. Submission of O'Connor.
Lord Thomas surrenders.
Act of Supremacy (English).
Thomas Cromwell appointed vicar-general.
1536. Lord Leonard Gray lord deputy.
Suppression of the lesser monasteries (English).

1537. Lord Thomas Fitzgerald and his five uncles executed.
Lord Leonard Gray's campaign in Limerick.
He destroys O'Brien's Bridge.
The supremacy supported in Ireland by Archbishop Brown, and opposed by Archbishop Cromer.
The proctors are expelled from Parliament.
Act of Supremacy (Irish).
Act for Suppression of Religious Houses (Irish).
1538. Destruction of relics, etc.
1539. *Dissolution of the greater monasteries (English).*
Law of the Six Articles.
Lord Leonard Gray's expedition into Ulster.
Battle of Belahoe.
His campaign in Munster.
Commission for the suppression of religious houses.
1540. Sir Anthony St. Leger negotiates with the chieftains.
Submission of the Irish chieftains and Anglo-Irish lords.
Distribution of Church lands.
1541. Title of King of Ireland conferred on Henry.
1542. Submission of O'Neil and O'Donnel.
1544. *Irish contingent present at the siege of Boulogne.*
General peace in Ireland.

EDWARD VI., 1547–1553.

1547. *Duke of Somerset Protector.*
Disturbances in Leix and Offaly.
1548. O'Moore and O'Connor sent to England as prisoners.
Civil war between the chieftains and the Tanists in Tyrone, Tyrconnel, and Clanricarde.
1549. *First Prayer-book of Edward VI.*
1551. Introduction of the new liturgy.
Conference with the clergy in St. Mary's Abbey.

CHRONOLOGICAL TABLE.

A. D.
Pillage of Clonmacnoise.
1552. Arrest of the Earl of Tyrone (Con Mor).
War between the Baron of Dungannon and Shane O'Neil.
Second Prayer-book of Ed. VI.

MARY, 1553–1558.

1553. Archbishop Dowdal recalled.
Dismissal of the Conforming bishops.
Operations against Leix and Offaly.
Restoration of the young Earl of Kildare.
1555. Fighting in Thomond for the succession.
Continued immigrations of Scots into Antrim.
1556. Act in explanation of Poynings's Act.
1558. Death of the Baron of Dungannon.
Reduction and Plantation of Leix and Offaly.

ELIZABETH, 1558–1603.

1559. Death of Con Mor, Earl of Tyrone.
Shane O'Neil assumes the sovereignty of Ulster.
Sir Henry Sidney marches against him.
Negotiations ensue.
1560. Act of Uniformity (Irish).
Continued strife in Thomond.
Shane captures O'Donnel and his wife.
1561. Sussex is defeated by Shane.
Plots to secure his murder.
Shane goes to England.
Death of second Baron of Dungannon.
Elizabeth and Shane come to terms.
1562. Shane returns to Ireland.
1563. Peace signed between Elizabeth and Shane.
Shane massacres the Scots of Antrim.
Struggle between Desmond and Ormonde.

A. D.
Desmond is taken prisoner.
1566. Renewal of the war with Shane.
Hugh O'Donnel joins the English.
1567. Shane defeated at Letterkenny.
Is murdered by the McDonnels.
Turlongh Luinagh becomes "the O'Neil."
Sidney makes a progress through Munster and Connaught.
He arrests Desmond, and his brother, Sir John, and the sons of the Earl of Clanricarde.
Murder of Darnley; Mary Queen of Scots marries Bothwell.
She is compelled to abdicate.
1568. *She takes refuge in England.*
Scheme for planting Desmond.
Sir Peter Carew claims estates in Cork and Carlow.
Insurrection in the Netherlands begins.
Rising of Sir James Fitzmaurice Fitzgerald; Lord Clancarty; and Sir Edmund, Sir Piers, and Sir Edward Butler in Munster.
1569. Attainder of O'Neil and confiscation of his Ulster territory.
Ormonde detaches his brothers from the Munster insurgents.
Sir Edward Fitton President of Connaught.
1570. Rising of the Bourkes.
Sir James Fitzmaurice captures Kilmallock.
Ormonde reduces Munster.
Pope Pius V. releases Elizabeth's subjects from their allegiance.
Sir Thomas Smith endeavors to make a plantation in Down.
1571. Sir John Perrot hunts Fitzmaurice into the vale of Aberlow.
1572. Clanricarde is liberated and Connaught pacified.

CHRONOLOGICAL TABLE. xxi

A. D.
Surrender of Sir James Fitzmaurice.
Massacre of St. Bartholomew.
1573. Walter Devereux, Earl of Essex, obtains a grant of territory in Ulster, and endeavors to make a plantation.
1574. Massacre of Rathlin Island.
Escape of the Earl of Desmond from Dublin.
1575. *The Netherlanders offer the sovereignty to Elizabeth.*
1576. Death of Essex.
Sir William Drury President of Munster.
Sir Nicholas Malley President of Connaught.
1577. Sidney levies illegal taxes on the Pale.
Remonstrance of the loyal English.
Rory O'Moore, the outlaw, in Leix and Kildare.
Massacre of Mullaghmast.
1579. Sir James Fitzmaurice lands at Smerwick.
Rising of the southern Geraldines.
Death of Sir James Fitzmaurice.
Successes of the rebels.
Death of Sir William Drury.
Desmond joins the rebels.
Youghal is burned.
1580. *Campion and Parsons, the Jesuits, in England.*
Campaign of Ormonde and Sir William Pelham in Munster.
Risings in Wicklow.
Lord Gray de Wilton defeated at Glenmalure.
The Spaniards land at Smerwick.
Lord Gray's campaign in Munster.
Massacre of the Spaniards.
Risings in the Pale.
Executions in Dublin.
1581. Death of Dr. Saunders, the Pope's legate.
1582. Death of Sir John and Sir James of Desmond.

A. D.
Suppression of the Munster rebellion.
1583. Death of Desmond.
1585. *Treaty between Elizabeth and the Netherlanders.*
1586. Attainder of the Munster rebels and confiscation of their estates.
Plantation of Munster.
Seizure of Red Hugh.
1587. *Execution of Mary Queen of Scots.*
1588. *Destruction of the Spanish Armada.*
Arrest of Sir John O'Dogherty and Sir Owen McToole.
1589. Confiscation of Monaghan.
1591. Tyrone marries Bagnal's sister.
1592. Escape of Red Hugh.
1595. Confederation of the Ulster chieftains.
Death of Turlough Luinagh.
Tyrone assumes the title of the O'Neil.
1597. Fighting on the Blackwater.
Anarchy in Connaught.
Death of Lord Burgh.
1598. Blockade of the Blackwater fort.
Battle of the Yellow Ford.
General rising. The Sugan Earl in Munster.
1599. Lord Essex arrives with a large army.
His campaign in Munster.
Concludes a truce with Tyrone.
Is recalled.
1600. Mountjoy lord deputy. He reforms the army.
Sir George Carew President of Munster.
Sir Henry Docra occupies Derry.
1601. Capture of the Sugan Earl.
Arrival of the Spaniards at Kinsale.
Battle of Kinsale.
1602. Flight of O'Donnel.
Carew reduces Munster.
Famine brought on by the wholesale destruction of the crops.

A.D.
1603. Tyrone surrenders.
Death of Elizabeth.

JAMES I., 1600–1625.
1603. The Popish clergy ordered to leave Ireland.
Peace concluded with Spain.
1605. Abolition of the laws of Tanistry and gavelkind.
The Gunpowder Plot.
1607. Flight of Tyrone and Tyrconnel.
1608. Rising of Sir Cahir O'Dogherty.
Confiscation of six counties in Ulster.
1610. Abolition of the Brehon law.
1611. Persecution of Roman Catholics.
The plantation of Ulster.
Creation of the order of baronets.
1612. The plantation of Wexford.
1613. Parliament summoned. Creation of boroughs.
1614. Attainder of Tyrone and the Ulster chieftains.
Repeal of the old statutes against the Irish.
1619. Plantation of Longford and Ely O'Carroll.
Plantation of Westmeath.
1622. Plantation of Leitrim and parts of King's and Queen's counties.
1624. *War declared with Spain.*
Transplantation of native septs to Kerry.
Confiscations in Wicklow.
Projected planting of Connaught.

CHARLES I., 1625–1649.
1626. Composition made by the Connaught land-owners.
"The Graces" promised.
1628. *The Petition of Right supported by Wentworth and Pym.*
Wentworth is made president of the north.
Charles's third Parliament is dissolved. Sir John Eliot sent to the Tower.

A.D.
1632–1636. Compilation of the "Annals of Ireland" by the Four Masters.
1633. Wentworth is appointed lord deputy.
Laud is made Archbishop of Canterbury.
1634. Wentworth dragoons the Irish Parliament.
1635. Commission of "defective titles" in Connaught.
Sentence on Lord Mountnorris.
1636. Introduction of the linen manufacture.
1637. *The Scots resist the new liturgy.*
Decision of the English Court of Exchequer on ship-money.
1638. *The Covenanters prepare for war.*
1639. *The pacification of Berwick.*
The Scottish Parliament abolish episcopacy and prepare for war.
1640. Wentworth created Earl of Strafford and Lord-lieutenant of Ireland.
Augmentation of the Irish army.
The Scots invade England.
Battle of Newburn.
Negotiations at Ripon.
The Long Parliament commences sitting.
Strafford and Laud impeached.
1641. *Bill of attainder against Strafford. He is executed.*
Ormonde and Antrim plot to seize the Irish government in support of Charles.
Rory O'Moore's plot to seize the Castle.
Rising and massacres in Ulster.
The Roman Catholic Anglo-Irish join the rebels.
Siege of Drogheda.
1642. Risings in Connaught and Munster.
Charles raises his standard at Nottingham.
Arrival of Colonel Owen O'Neil and Colonel Preston.
Synod at Kells.

CHRONOLOGICAL TABLE. xxiii

A.D.
Battle of Kilrush.
Confederation of Kilkenny.
Battle of Edgehill.
The king in winter-quarters at Oxford.
1643. Battle of Ross.
Ormonde made a marquis.
Battle of Roundaway Down.
Essex relieves Gloucester.
Cessation agreed upon between Ormonde and the rebels.
First battle of Newbury.
Parliament take the Covenant.
The war continued on behalf of the Parliament by the Scots in Ulster, by Broghill and Inchiquin in the south, and by Sir Charles Coote in Sligo.
1644. Ormonde lord-lieutenant.
The Irish contingent cut off at Nantwich.
Deputations from the two parties in Ireland to the king at Oxford.
Battle of Marston Moor.
Second battle of Newbury.
Negotiations with the rebels.
1645. *Negotiations between the king and the Parliament at Uxbridge.*
Glamorgan despatched by Charles to make terms with the rebels.
Battle of Naseby.
Arrival of Rinucini, the Pope's legate.
Glamorgan concludes a secret treaty.
Its discovery. Glamorgan is arrested.
1646. He is liberated.
Divisions among the Confederates.
A treaty signed between Ormonde and the Confederates.
Charles surrenders to the Scots.
Battle of Benburb.
Rinucini and Owen Roe seize the government at Kilkenny.
1647. *Presbyterianism established in England.*

A.D.
Conflict between the Parliament and the army.
The king seized at Holmby.
Ormonde surrenders Dublin to the Parliament.
Battle of Dungan Hill.
Inchiquin takes Cashel.
Battle of Knocknanoss.
1648. Inchiquin deserts to the Confederates.
Rinucini takes refuge with Owen Roe's army.
Strife among the Confederates.
Royalist risings in Kent, Essex, and South Wales.
Return of Ormonde.
Rupert and his fleet arrive at Kinsale.
The Scottish army invades England, and is defeated at Preston and Wigan.
Colonel Pride expels the Presbyterian majority from the House of Commons.
1649. Peace published between the king and the Confederates.
Death of the king.

THE REPUBLIC, 1649-1653.
1649. Prince Charles proclaimed at Cork.
Flight of Rinucini.
Ormonde besieges Dublin.
Battle of Rathmines.
Arrival of Cromwell.
Capture of Drogheda.
Capture of Wexford.
Death of Owen Roe.
Campaign in the south.
Revolt of the southern garrisons to Parliament.
1650. Capture of Kilkenny and Clonmel.
Cromwell returns to England.
Battle of Dunbar.
Surrender of Waterford.
Flight of Ormonde and Inchiquin.
1651. Capture of Athlone.
Capture of Limerick.
Battle of Worcester.
Death of Ireton.

1652. Surrender of Galway.
   Act for the Settlement of Ireland.
   Survey of Ireland.
   Banishment of the Irish soldiery.
   Conflict between the army and the Rump.
1653. Transplantation of the Irish beyond the Shannon.
   Cromwell expels the Rump.

THE PROTECTORATE, 1653–1660.

1653. The "*Barebones Parliament.*"
1654. The plantation of Ireland continues.
   The first Protectorate Parliament. Thirty members sit representing Ireland.
1655. *Cromwell divides England into eleven military districts.*
1656. *The second Protectorate Parliament.*
   Henry Cromwell lord-lieutenant.
1658. *The third Protectorate Parliament.*
   Death of Cromwell. He is succeeded by Richard Cromwell.
1659. *The Rump restored by the army. Lambert ejects the Rump. Monk marches from Scotland.*
1660. *He declares for a "free Parliament."*
   Coote and Broghill seize the commissioners in Dublin Castle.
   Charles issues the Declaration of Breda.

CHARLES II., 1660–1685.

1660. Re-establishment of the Church.
   The king's declaration for the settlement of Ireland.
1661. *Corporation Act.*
1662. *Act of Uniformity.*
   Act of Settlement.
1663. Court of Claims opens in Dublin.
   Blood's plot.
   Ireland excluded from the Navigation Act.
1664. *The Conventicle Act.*

1665. Act of Explanation.
   The Five Mile Act.
1666. *The Fire of London.*
   Prohibition of export to England of Irish cattle and provisions.
1667. *The Cabal Ministry.*
1670. Toleration of Roman Catholics.
   Secret treaty of Dover.
1671. Petition to review the Act of Settlement.
1672. *Declaration of Indulgence.*
1673. *The English Parliament contemn the Irish petition.*
1678. The Popish plot.
   Arrest of Archbishop Talbot.
1679. Arrest of Archbishop Plunket.
1681. *Execution of Plunket.*
1685. Richard Talbot made lieutenant-general.

JAMES II., 1685–1691.

1685. Reconstruction of the army.
   Insurrection of Monmouth.
1687. Reconstruction of the corporations.
   Tyrconnel lord-lieutenant.
   Persecution of Trinity College, Dublin.
1688. *Acquittal of the seven bishops.*
   Flight of Protestants to England.
   William lands at Torbay.
   Flight of James.
   Closing of the gates of Derry and Enniskillen.
1689. Tyrconnel raises regiments for James.
   War is declared against France.
   William proclaimed at Derry.
   Siege of Derry and Enniskillen.
   James lands at Cork.
   Holds a Parliament at Dublin.
   Siege of Derry raised.
   Battle of Newtown Butler.
   Arrival of Schomberg.
   He is besieged at Dundalk.
1690. Charlemont captured.
   William lands at Carrickfergus.
   Battle of Beachy Head.
   Battle of the Boyne.
   Flight of James.

CHRONOLOGICAL TABLE. xxv

A.D.
Abortive siege of Limerick.
William returns to England.
Capture of Cork and Kinsale by Marlborough.
1691. Capture of Athlone.
Battle of Aughrim.
Surrender of Galway.
Second siege of Limerick.
Articles of Limerick.

WILLIAM III., 1691–1702.
1692. Emigration of Irish Roman Catholics.
Exclusion of Roman Catholics from Parliament.
The House of Commons resist the initiation of Money Bills by the Privy Council.
Battle of Steinkirk.
1693. Battle of Landen.
1696. Act for disarming the Roman Catholics.
Penal act against foreign education.
English act amending the Navigation Act unfavorably to Ireland.
1698. Molyneux's book on the independence of the Irish Parliament.
Penal act against mixed marriages.
1699. *William's grants of Irish forfeitures attacked in the English House of Commons.*
English act prohibiting the export of Irish wool.
Irish act laying prohibitive tariff on the export of wool.
1700. *The Resumption Act.*
1701. Act disqualifying Roman Catholic solicitors.

ANNE, 1702–1714.
1704. Penal act against the Roman Catholics.
1706. Increase of Jacobitism. Domination of the High Church party.
1708. *Battle of Almanza.*
Further act against Roman Catholic solicitors.

A.D.
1710. Penal act against the Roman Catholics.
Fall of the Whig ministry. Tory administrations of Harley and St. John.
1711. Agrarian disturbances. Ever Joyce. The Houghers.
Persecution of the Presbyterians.
Sir Constantine Phipps leader of the Jacobites.
Duke of Ormonde made commander-in-chief.
1713. *Treaty of Utrecht.*
1714. *Fall of the Tory ministry.*

GEORGE I., 1714–1727.
1715. *Flight of the Duke of Ormonde and Bolingbroke. They are attainted.*
Rebellion in Scotland.
1716. *The Septennial Act.*
1719. Conflict between the English and Irish Houses of Lords.
Act subjecting the Irish to the English legislature.
Toleration Act.
1723. Wood's patent granted.
1724. The Drapier's letters.
Prosecution of Swift's printer.
1725. The patent cancelled.
Potato famine.
1726. Archbishop Boulter lord justice.

GEORGE II., 1727–1760.
1727. Act disfranchising the Roman Catholics.
Tillage Act.
1734. Further stringent act against Roman Catholic solicitors.
1740. The Kellymount gang outrages.
1742. Death of Archbishop Boulter.
1744. Lord Chesterfield lord-lieutenant.
1745. *Battle of Fontenoy.*
The young Pretender in Scotland.
1746. *The battle of Culloden.*
1747. Death of Archbishop Hoadly.
1748. *Peace of Aix-la-Chapelle.*
1749. Lucas stands for Dublin.

B

CHRONOLOGICAL TABLE.

A.D.
Threatened with prosecution, he flies to England.
Rivalry between Primate Stone and Speaker Boyle.
Contest in Parliament about the appropriation of surpluses.
1753. Prosecution of Nevill.
Petition of the Earl of Kildare.
Death of Morty Oge O'Sullivan, the smuggler.
1755. Fall of Primate Stone.
1756. *Commencement of the Seven Years' War.*
Henry Boyle created Earl Shannon.
1757. Formation of the Roman Catholic Committee.
1759. Riots in Dublin on the rumor of a contemplated union.
1760. Thurot's descent on Carrickfergus. His defeat and death.

GEORGE III., 1760–1820.
1761. Insurrection of the Whiteboys.
1762. Insurrection of the Oakboys.
1763. Attacks on the pension list.
Peace of Paris.
1764. Roman Catholic Relief Bill thrown out.
1765. Act to Regulate the Law of Highways.
The Stamp Act for the American colonies.
1766. Execution of Father Sheehy for Whiteboyism.
Repeal of the Stamp Act.
1767. Lord Townshend lord-lieutenant.
Charles Townshend taxes American imports.
Octennial Act.
1768. Rising of the Steelboys.
1769. Contest about the Money Bills.
Augmentation Bill passed.
1771. Extensive emigration to America from Ulster.
Contest about the Money Bills.
1772. Resignation of Townshend.

A.D.
1773. *The people of Boston throw overboard the imported tea.*
The Irish national debt amounts to £1,000,000.
1774. *The Constitution of Massachusetts is annulled.*
1775. Continuation of the Whiteboy outrages.
Irish troops are sent to America.
Battle of Lexington.
Increase of the debt and of the pension list.
Flood is made a vice-treasurer.
1776. The embargo.
Declaration of American independence.
1777. *The English occupy Philadelphia.*
The surrender at Saratoga.
1778. *France recognizes the independence of the American colonies.*
First Roman Catholic Relief Bill passed.
1779. Agitation in favor of freedom of trade.
Efforts in the English Parliament to open Irish trade.
Formation of the volunteers.
Spain declares war against England.
1780. *Freedom of trade granted to Ireland.*
War declared against Holland.
1781. Agitation for legislative independence.
The Perpetual Mutiny Bill passed.
Surrender of Lord Cornwallis at Yorktown.
1782. Further Roman Catholic Relief Act.
Meeting of the volunteers at Dungannon.
Resignation of Lord North.
Repeal of 6 Geo. I.
Amendment of Poynings's Act.
Habeas Corpus Act.
Death of Lord Rockingham.
1783. *Declaratory Act.*
Peace of Versailles.

CHRONOLOGICAL TABLE.   xxvii

A.D.
  Coalition Ministry formed between Fox and Lord North.
  Agitation for parliamentary reform.
  The Volunteer National Convention.
  Rejection of Flood's Reform Bill.
  Fall of the Coalition Ministry.
  Pitt becomes prime-minister.
1784. Rise of the Peep-o'-day Boys and Defenders.
1785. Orde's commercial resolutions.
  Jealous opposition of the English manufacturers.
  Orde's Bill abandoned.
  Agitation for reform.
1786. Rightboy disturbances.
  Dublin Police Act passed.
1787. Growth of the Rightboy disturbances.
  Debates on the tithe question.
1788. Increase of Defenderism.
  The king's illness becomes serious.
  The Regency question in the English Parliament.
1789. The Regency question in the Irish Parliament.
  The king recovers.
  Meeting of the Estates-General at Versailles.
  Storming of the Bastile.
1790. Fox sympathizes with the French Revolution, which produces a breach between him and Burke.
1791. Agitation for Roman Catholic emancipation.
  Louis XVI. escapes and is captured at Varennes.
  Formation of the Society of the United Irishmen.
1792. Roman Catholic Relief Act.
  Accidental burning of the House of Commons.
  Austria and Prussia invade France.
  They are forced to retire from Valmy.
  Battle of Jemappes.
  Meeting of the Roman Catholic Convention.

A.D.
1793. Petition of the Roman Catholics presented to the king.
  Increase of Defenderism.
  Execution of Louis XVI.
  War declared by France against England.
  Further Roman Catholic Relief Act.
  Convention Act.
  Gunpowder Act.
  Ponsonby's motion on reform rejected.
  Activity of the United Irishmen.
  Secret committee of the House of Lords to inquire into the disturbed state of the country.
  Flight of Napper Tandy.
1794. Prosecution of Hamilton Rowan and imprisonment of Simon Butler and Oliver Bond.
  The Duke of Portland and some of the old Whigs join the ministry.
  Arrest of Jackson.
  Suppression of the United Irishmen.
  The society is reconstructed as a secret association.
1795. Arrival of Lord Fitzwilliam as Viceroy.
  Grattan's bill for complete emancipation of the Roman Catholics.
  Recall of Lord Fitzwilliam.
  Trial and death of Jackson.
  Rejection of Grattan's Bill.
  Tone goes to America.
  Battle of the Diamond.
  Formation of Orange lodges.
  Spain declares war against England.
  Establishment of the French Directory.
1796. The Insurrection Act.
  Tone at Paris.
  Fitzgerald and O'Connor at Basle.
  Extension of the United Irishmen to Leinster.
  French expedition to Bantry.

CHRONOLOGICAL TABLE.

A.D.
1797. Arthur O'Connor is arrested, and released on bail.
Lord Moira attacks the government in the English House of Lords.
Martial law in Ulster.
Grattan's Reform Bill rejected.
Secession of the opposition.
Increase of the United Irishmen.
Mutiny at the Nore and Spithead.
Battle of Camperdown.
Execution of Orr.
Lord Moira again attacks the government in the English House of Lords.
Grattan retires from public life.
1798. Sir Ralph Abercrombie succeeds Lord Carhampton as commander-in-chief in Ireland.
He resigns his command.
Martial law in Leinster.
O'Connor is arrested at Margate.

A.D.
Mar. 11. Arrest of the executive committee of the United Irishmen at Oliver Bond's.
May 19. Arrest of Lord Edward Fitzgerald.
" 23. Risings round Dublin and in Kildare and Carlow.
" 25. Risings in Wicklow.
" 27. Risings in Wexford.
June 4. Battle of New Ross.
" 7. Risings in Down and Antrim.
" 9. Battle of Arklow.
" 21. Capture of Vinegar Hill.
Aug. 22. The French at Killala.
" 26. Battle of Castlebar.
Sept. 8. Battle of Ballinamuck.
Oct. 10. French expedition to Lough Swilly. Capture of Tone.
Proposal of the Union.
1799. Opposition to the Union.
Defeat of the government.
The English Parliament agree to Pitt's resolutions on the Union.
1800. The Act of Union.

LIST OF AUTHORITIES.

Alison ....Life of Lord Castlereagh.
Archdall........................Monasticon Hibern.

Baratariana.
Barrington.....................Rise and Fall of the Irish Nation.
Betham, Sir William............Dignities Feudal, etc.
Brewer.........................Introduction to the Carew State Papers.
Burke's Works.

Camden.........................Britannia.
Carew..........................State Papers.
Carlyle........................Letters of Cromwell.
Carte..........................Life of the Duke of Ormonde.
Castlehaven, Lord..............Memoirs.
Castlereagh....................Correspondence.
Connellan and McDermot.........Annals of the Four Masters.
Cornwallis.....................Correspondence.
Cox, Sir Richard...............Hibern. Anglicana.
Curry..........................Review of Civil Wars in Ireland.
Cusack, Miss M. F..............History of the Irish Nation.

Davis, Sir John................Discoverie of the True Causes, etc.
   "   "   ....Historical Tracts.
   "   "   ....Reports.
Desiderata Curiosa.

Fitzgibbon, Lord Clare.........Speech on the Union.
Fitzmaurice, Lord E. ....Life of Lord Shelburne.
Foster.........................Life of Strafford.
Froude.........................English in Ireland.
   "   ....History of England.

Gilbert........................History of Dublin.
Godkin.........................Irish Land War.
Gordon.........................History of the Irish Rebellion.

LIST OF AUTHORITIES.

Grattan.................Memoir of Right Hon. Henry Grattan.
Grattan's Speeches.
Green..................Short History of the English People.

Hallam.................Constitutional History.
Hancock, W. Neilson.....Ancient Laws of Ireland.
Hardy..................Life of Lord Charlemont.
Haverty................History of Ireland.
Hay....................History of the Insurrection in Wexford.
History of Roger.
Hutchinson.............Commercial Restraints of Ireland.

Irish Commons Journals.

Joyce..................Origin and History of Irish Names.

King...................Estate of the Protestants of Ireland under James II.

Langrishe, Sir Hercules...Bataria.
Lanigan................Ecclesiastical History of Ireland.
Lascelles..............Liber Munerum pub. Hibern.
Lawless (Lord Cloncurry)..Personal Recollections.
Lecky..................History of England during Eighteenth Century.
"   ....Leaders of Public Opinion in Ireland.
Leland.................History of Ireland.
Leslie.................Answer to King's Estate of the Protestants.
Lingard................History of England.
Lodge..................Irish Peerage.
Ludlow.................Memoirs.
Lynch..................View of Legal Institutions, etc., in Ireland.

Macaulay...............History of England.
McGee..................Popular History of Ireland.
McNevin................Confiscation of Ulster.
Madden.................History of the United Irishmen.
Maine..................Village Communities.
"   ....Early History of Institutions.
Mason..................Essay on the Irish Parliament.
Mahon, Lord............History of England.
Massey.................History of England.
May....................Constitutional History.
Meehan.................Confederation of Kilkenny.
Moore..................History of Ireland.
"   ....Life of Lord Edward Fitzgerald.
Moryson................History of Ireland.

LIST OF AUTHORITIES. xxxi

Mountmorres .... History of the Irish Parliament.
Musgrave .... History of the Irish Rebellion.

O'Callaghan .... History of the Irish Brigades.
O'Connell .... Memoir of Ireland.
O'Connor .... History of the Irish Catholics.
O'Conor .... Military History of the Irish Nation.
O'Donovan .... Annals of the Four Masters.
O'Halloran .... History of Ireland.
O'Mahony, J. .... Keating's History of Ireland.
O'Mahony, Rev. F. .... Ancient Laws of Ireland.
O'Sullivan .... Historia Cath. Ib. Comp.

Parliamentary History.
Petty, Sir William .... History of the Down Survey.
"   "   .... Political Anatomy of Ireland.
Playfair .... British Family Antiquities.
Plowden .... Historical Review.
"   .... History of Ireland.
Prendergast .... Cromwellian Settlement.

Reid .... History of the Presbyterian Church in Ireland.
Richey .... Lectures on the History of Ireland.
"   .... Ancient Laws of Ireland, Brehon Tracts.
Russell, Lord .... Life of Fox.

Scobell .... Acts and Ordinances of the Long Parliament.
Shirley .... Some Account of the Territory of Farney.
"   .... History of Monaghan.
Smith, Charles .... History of Cork.
"   "   .... History of Kerry.
"   "   .... History of Waterford.
Spenser, Edmund .... View of the State of Ireland.
Stanhope, Lord .... Life of Pitt.
State Papers (Henry VIII.).
"   "   (James I.).
State Trials.
Statutes at Large (English).
"   "   (Irish).
Strafford Papers.

Todd .... Life of St. Patrick.
Tone .... Autobiography.
Transactions of the Royal Irish Academy, vols. xiv., xvi.

Wakeman .... Archæologia Hibern.
Warner..................... History of the Irish Rebellion.
Wills...................... Irish Nation.
Wood, Anthony.............. Diary of, in Athenæ Oxonienses.
Wright..................... History of Ireland.

Young .... Tour in Ireland.

Book I.
INDEPENDENT IRELAND

A SHORT HISTORY
OF
THE KINGDOM OF IRELAND.

CHAPTER I.
CONDITION OF THE EARLY IRISH.

THE earliest colonization of Ireland, like that of most other countries, is wrapped in a cloud of myth. Ancient legends tell us of immigrations of "Nemedians," "Firbolgs," and "Tuath da Danaan;" of a niece of Noah, and a near descendant of Japhet. But all that can be gathered from such mention as is made of the island by ancient writers, from the etymology of local names, and from antiquarian research, enables us to affirm that Ireland was originally inhabited by a people of Turanian origin, which gave way before parties of immigrant Celts from Western Europe. The latter passed over partly from Britain and partly from the shores of Spain, in the population of which locality there was a considerable Phœnician element.

This Celtic stock was from time to time supplemented by the arrival of more Celts, and subsequently by the incursion of a Teutonic people, the "Scoti," who appear to have acquired the dominion of the island, but, while retaining the mastery, to have been eventually absorbed and assimilated by the more numerous native population.

Society was based on the tribal system. Each tribe, or clan, or, as the Irish called it, "sept," consisted of a number of families, bearing the same name as the original founder of the tribe. The head of each family was autocratic, but owed allegiance to the chief of the tribe. And the chief of the tribe acknowledged the overlordship of a superior chieftain, to whom he paid a tribute. In some cases a group of tribes accepted as their chieftain the head of what was believed to be the primary tribe; in others they formed a confederacy, and chose one of the tribe chiefs to be their head.

The tribes had each their respective territory, part of which was enjoyed in common, as common tillage, meadow, wood, or pasture-land; part was occupied by the dwellings of the members of the tribe, with their curtilages; part was devoted to the use of the chief for the time being; and part was occupied by separate families of the noble class, who had contrived to appropriate a portion of the public lands. The sovereign chieftain held his own royal demesne lands, carved out of the territories of the various tribes which formed the group or confederacy. The chiefship of the tribe, or the chieftainship of the group of tribes, was elective; and during the lifetime of each such chief or chieftain, his successor, called the "Tanist," was chosen by the tribesmen. The Tanist was always taken from the same family as the chief; and was the most serviceable member of the family for the time being that could be found—perhaps the son, perhaps the brother, or perhaps some one less near in blood, according to his age and capacity. The other officers of the tribe were the Druid, the Bard, and the Brehon, all hereditary officers.

The Brehon, as the depositary of knowledge to which few could attain, was a person of great consideration. He was the general professional arbitrator in all disputes. Submission to his jurisdiction and decision could not indeed be compelled by the suitor; but in practice, through the force of public opinion, neither the one nor the other was questioned. He was remunerated in each case which he was called upon to decide, by payment of his dues, consisting of fifteen cows and ten days' entertainment. If convicted of giving a partial decision, he was branded on the cheek.

The law administered by the Brehon was the common-law of the Celtic people, which had grown up in course of time by the crystallization of various local customs. At first it was handed down by oral tradition ; but subsequently these customs were collected, and written down, at a comparatively early date ; and, after the introduction of Christianity, to some extent supplemented by the canon-law. The manuscript fragments of ancient law-tracts which remain to us, and the great Irish code the "Senchus Mor," which claims the middle of the fifth century for the date of its compilation under the auspices of St. Patrick, exhibit an elaborate system of jurisprudence, which regulated the dealings between man and man so lately, in some parts of Ireland, as the reign of James I. The character and origin of the "Senchus Mor" are best described in a passage in the introduction of the work itself. "How the judgment of true nature," we read, "which the Holy Ghost had spoken through the mouths of the Brehons and just poets of the men of Erin, from the first occupation of the island down to the reception of the faith, were all exhibited by Dubhtach * to Patrick, what did not clash with the word of God in the written law and in the New Testament, and with the consciences of the believers, was confirmed in the law of the Brehons by Patrick, and by the ecclesiastics and the chieftains of Erin. For the law of nature had been quite right, except the faith and its obligations, and the harmony of the Church and the people."

We can form some idea of the criminal branch of the Brehon law from its digested form in the "Book of Aicill," which is believed to have been put together about the middle of the third century. The distinction between a crime and a civil wrong was not very clearly defined, the former being to a great extent treated as "a tort," and compensated by damages. This was mainly due to the tribal character of society, in which every illegal act was a personal injury, but could not be an offence against the state, when there was no state to take cognizance of it. The law was enforced by the levying of "erics," or fines, of so many cows upon the offender by the process of distress · and, if he was unable to pay, upon the whole family of which he was a member. If the right to take the distress was disputed, the Brehon settled the point in an arbitration. One of the

---

* The chief Brehon of that day.

principal provisions, and one common to the early Teutonic peoples of Britain and Germany, was the law of compensation for murder. The family of the slain bread-winner was entitled to receive a fine from the slayer; and if his family were compelled to liquidate the fine on his behalf, he was deprived of the enjoyment of his civil rights, and his share of the tribal allotments was appropriated to the satisfaction of the damages paid on his account. Injuries to women were atoned for in the same way. And various penalties were inflicted for the offences of incest, rape, adultery, perjury, theft, receiving of stolen goods, and all acts of dishonesty. Fines were also levied for various "wrongs" in the truer sense of the word, and also for breaches of contract, such as trespass, slander, fraud, negligence in regard to bailments, the non-payment of their liabilities by debtors or their sureties. The law relating to husband and wife was of a singularly enlightened character. Where the husband and the wife had each property of their own, the wife was called "the wife of equal dignity." She was in all respects recognized as equal to her husband, and neither party could contract without the consent of the other. A number of provisions regulated the boundaries of land, the preservation of roads, woods, and watercourses, the property in swarms of bees, and the bartering of goods. Hospitality to strangers was strictly enjoined; and there were many sumptuary laws with respect to the wearing of apparel.

With regard to the tenure of land, the common land of the tribe was enjoyed by all the members. Part was used for grazing purposes, and part was allotted in tracts, for the purpose of cultivation, to the various heads of households. The ownership of the common land was vested in the tribe, and the right of user was based upon tribe-membership only. The leading idea with respect to the specifically appropriated land was that of a partnership among the male members of the *stirps*. The law of primogeniture was unknown. On the death of any member of a family, his sons who were householders, both legitimate and illegitimate, took an equal share of his holding by the Irish custom of gavelkind. They were partners with him during his lifetime, and on his death the property survived to

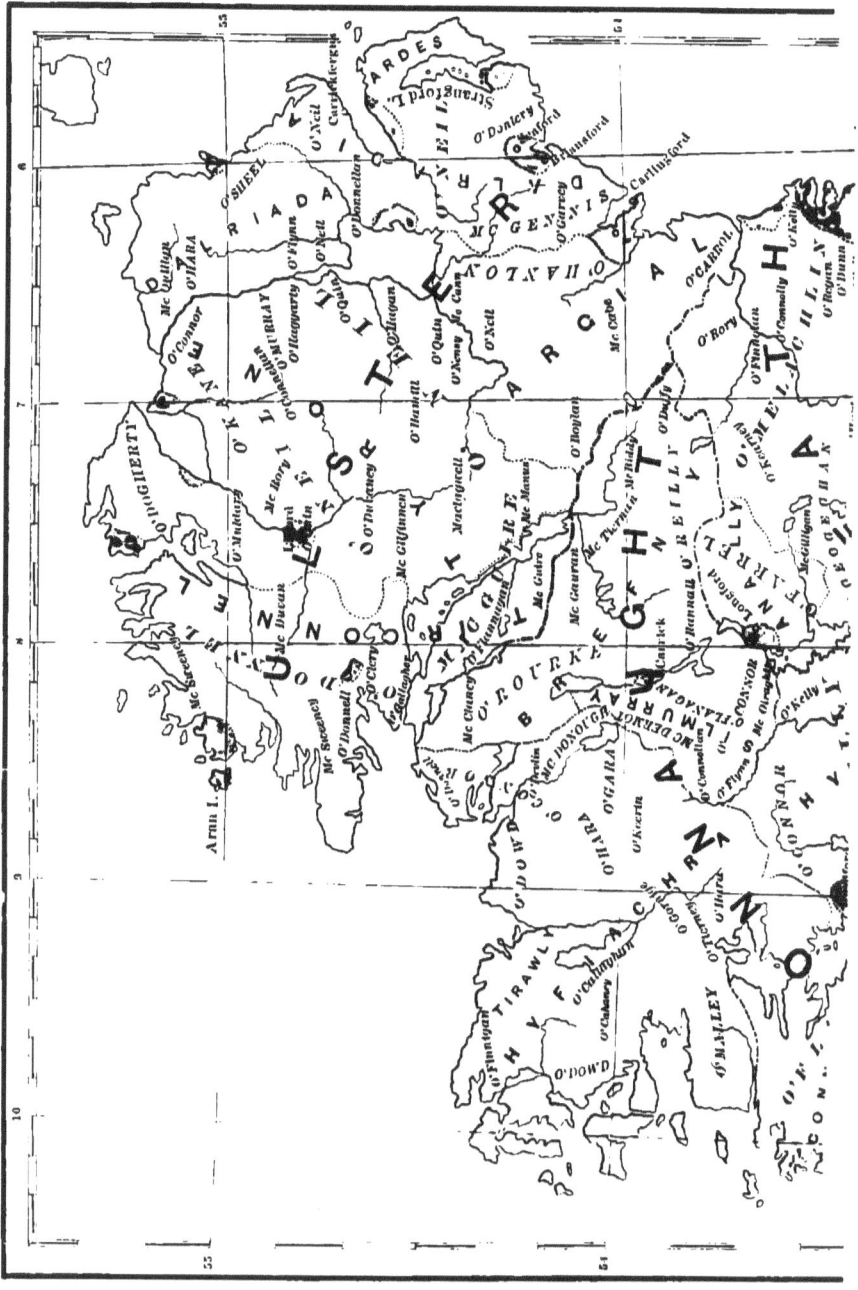

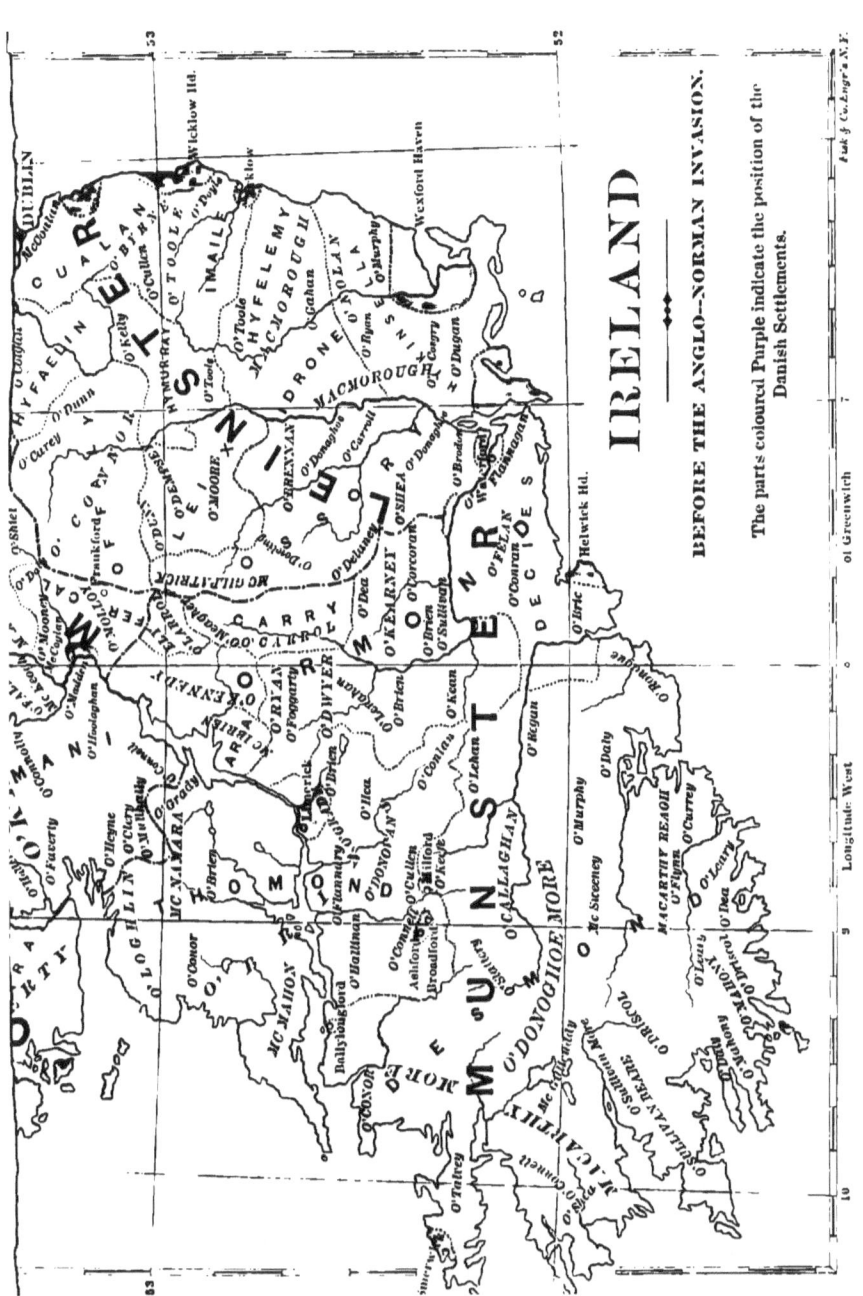

them as co-owners in undivided shares. In later times a quit-rent was demanded on each holding by the chief; but the land was never held on the condition of the rendering of anything in the nature of feudal service. A very curious custom sometimes prevailed in the distribution of the appropriated lands, under which, where circumstances would permit of it, an organization sprang up known as the "*Geilfine* system." The original acquirer of the land, as each of his sons grew up and was ready to leave the home, gave him his share in the paternal acres, and planted him out to maintain a household of his own. This was done successively to the number of four sons, if he had as many; the fifth and youngest remained with his father, and inherited the original home. The father and the four sons formed a family group of five households, which went by the name of the *Geilfine*,* or "right-hand group," from the five fingers on the hand (*gilla*). The youngest son, in his turn, when he had succeeded to the residue of the property and his sons grew up, planted them out one by one on portions of the remainder of the family land. He and his four sons then became the *Geilfine*, and his brothers' four households were in this way pushed further off from the household of the *stirps*, and were known as the *Deirbhfine*, † or "particular group." The youngest and fifth son of the new *Geilfine* chief, in his turn, repeated the process, forming for himself and his sons a fresh *Geilfine* on his own account. The last *Geilfine* then became the *Deirbhfine* in its turn, and the old *Deirbhfine* became the *Iarfine*, ‡ or "after-group." Again the process was repeated, and yet another and newer *Geilfine* was formed; each group, as before, took the place of the group more remotely related, and the *Iarfine* became the *Indfine*, § or "end group." Here the process ceased, and no further subdivision was made. Each group acquired a separate instead of an undivided share in the paternal acres, and became a fresh *stirps*, retaining the tract allotted

---

* Quære *geil* or *geal*, "white" or "fair"? *fine*, a "family."
† *Deirbh*, also "true," "handsome."
‡ *Iar*, adverb, "after;" adjective, "black;" substantive, "the end."
§ *In* (quære *inne*, "the middle"?), "small;" in compounds, "proper," "fit." (Quære *ind*, the head or *end* of an arrow?)

to it, and repeating the plotting-out of its own share in its own way. Each family worked out on this plan consisted of seventeen households—four in each of the four groups plus the original home. Where a group became extinct, the lands were taken *per stirpes* by the other groups of the family. On failure of a male representative, the land reverted to the tribe; though in later days, when the tribe system was becoming weakened, the daughters were in such cases permitted to inherit.

Agriculture was very much in its infancy. A little grain was grown by each family for its own support. The principal source of wealth, and the measure of value, as among primitive nations it always has been, and still is, was cattle. The fines were calculated in cows. The cow was the unit of value in all trade dealings. The square measurement of land was based upon the number of cows which could be supported on a given piece of ground of a given quality. Besides cows, another valuable property were the droves of pigs, which were turned out to get their living on the common forest-land; the flocks of sheep, which were depastured on the uplands of the tribe; and last, though not least, a breed of small horses remarkable for their fleetness. The ordinary dwellings of the tribesmen were small buildings, made of wood and wattles, about seventeen feet in length, with sometimes a detached kitchen in the rear. Their chiefs' houses were considerably larger, the average length being thirty-seven feet. But though these rude habitations were sufficient for ordinary purposes, we can judge from their stupendous sepulchral chambers, built of uncemented stones, such as the cairn of Newgrange and the hill of Dowth,* that when occasion required they could produce something demanding no mean architectural skill. The tribal dwellings were generally built in groups: sometimes perched upon an island in a landlocked mere; sometimes standing out of the water upon rough-hewn, well-driven piles; sometimes comprising a strong natural position upon the high ground, and protected with artificially constructed earthworks. The strength and size of their hill forts, the raths and duns, must have been very considerable. A

---

* Works of this character are believed to be pre-Celtic.

strong earthwork, including a large area, contained the huts of the tribal garrison, and the towering central mound occupied by the chief, with excavated storehouses for the reception of grain; or a formidable wall of irregular unmortared masonry, ten, twelve, or fourteen feet in thickness, formed a circular fortress, which in those days must have been well-nigh impregnable.

Trade had been carried on between Ireland and the countries lying round the Mediterranean basin from the earliest times. The staple of the export trade was ores. There was also some traffic in slaves, which were brought over from Britain and the continent. The great walled road from Dublin to Galway was the trade highway which opened up the west. The unalloyed gold ornaments, torques, rings, fibulæ, bracelets, and the bronze swords, skeens, and spearheads, with articles of domestic use, found in the bogs and tumuli, or ploughed up in newly broken land, give us evidence of a considerable acquaintance with the working of the precious metals.

The religion of the people was akin to the ancient Mithraic cult. The Celtic names of places bear strong indications of the existence of fire-worship, introduced by the Phœnician colonists, when the phallic dances sped round the venerated pillar-stones, and the Druids, priests of the sun, offered human sacrifices on the huge altar-stones, and laid to rest in the cromlech tombs the ashes of the dead warrior. A trace of serpent-worship still survives in the legend of the expulsion of the snakes from Ireland by St. Patrick.

CHAPTER II.
CHRISTIANITY AMONG THE EARLY IRISH. A.D. 450-1150.

WE can depend on nothing in the nature of authentic history prior to the early part of the fifth century. Were we to take upon trust all that is told us by the bardic historians who flourished between A.D. 800 and A.D. 1000, or even in the more trustworthy compilation of ancient chronicles made in the seventeenth century by Michael O'Clery, a Franciscan monk, from original documents no longer existing, and known as the "Annals of the Four Masters," we should have, apart from innumerable stories of giants and necromancers, to go back to the Deluge, and to record the doings of a hundred and eighteen kings of Ireland of pure Milesian or Scotic race. We should learn how Heber and Heremon, the two sons of Milesius, took each a share of the island—the former the southern, and the latter the northern, half; how Ollam Fohdla instituted a triennial assembly of chiefs, Druids, and Bards at Tara; how Kimbaoth, King of Ulster, built a palace at Emania, near Armagh; how Cormac Ulphada founded three academies for the study of war, literature, and jurisprudence at Tara; how a rebellion of the subject races was for a time successful against their Scotic masters, and how they were crushed by the Milesian prince Tuathal; how this same Tuathal, the king of the north, imposed a grievous tribute upon the south, which was paid for five hundred years; how Finn McCumhal, the mighty warrior— the Irish King Arthur, better known in Scotland as Fingal, or Fin the Stranger—was the leader of the Fenian heroes and the national militia; and how "Nial of the Nine Hostages," so called from the pledges which he wrung from nine different nations, invaded Britain and Gaul in the declining years of the Roman occupation.

Patricius was a Christian Gaul, born at Boulogne, about A.D.

400, of which town his father was a burgess of substance. When Nial of the Nine Hostages invaded Gaul, Patricius was taken captive, and at the age of sixteen carried into Ireland, where he became a slave, and tended the cattle of his master in the County of Antrim. After six years' captivity he ran away from his master, got on board a ship, and escaped to his own country. Some years later, having been greatly moved by certain dreams, in which he believed that he had received a direct commission from the Almighty to preach the gospel in the land of his captivity, he devoted himself to a missionary life, received holy orders from the Gallican Church, and reached the coast of Wicklow about the year A.D. 445.

Christianity had not been absolutely unheard of in Ireland when St. Patrick arrived. A few converts had probably been made either by imported slaves, or the efforts of Palladius, who some years before had attempted to conduct a mission there and had failed; but substantially the whole people were pagans, and there was no foundation at all for St. Patrick to work upon. The missionary, finding no encouragement on the Dublin coast, proceeded northward, and landed at the entrance to Strangford Lough. He remained some time in this part of the country, and was well received, and made some important converts. He then moved into Meath, and found King Leoghaire, the son of Nial, presiding over the great council at Tara. The monkish legends tell us of how the saint disturbed the assembly by lighting a great fire on the Hill of Slane, and how the king and all his company came forth to punish him for his audacity; how a contest took place between the saint and the Druids, and how the latter were worsted by St. Patrick's miraculous powers; the consequence of which was that the king was baptized, and all his chiefs. Discounting this liberally, however, we may conclude that St. Patrick's missionary efforts were successful with the chiefs of the people, and that the latter, following the lead of the heads of their tribes, willingly received the new doctrine which was brought to them.

St. Patrick then proceeded through Connaught and Ulster, winning a conspicuous success at the "field of slaughter" in Leitrim, where he overthrew the sacred monolith, and denounced the bloody idolatry practised in honor of the sun. Subsequently his missionary journeys took him through Munster and Leinster, and he eventually returned to his starting-place in County Down, to found the neighboring bishopric of Armagh, and consolidate the Church of which he had laid the foundations in all quarters of the island.

Wherever St. Patrick went, he seems to have been received with very little opposition; what there was, coming chiefly from the Druid establishment, which it was his object to destroy. He passed from place to place, seizing every opportunity afforded by any local gathering, and, after baptizing his converts, erected rude places of worship, constructed of wood and wattles—the fashion of building then prevailing in the country. Occasionally he went with his life in his hand, where the influence of the old cult was active in its own defence; but the bulk of the people accepted his teaching with readiness, and left their old superstitions without regret.

His first step seems always to have been to secure the chief of the clan, and the tribal instincts of the rest of the community made thousands of converts to the religion adopted by their lords. The conversion of the multitude was at first, of course, to a great extent nominal; but St. Patrick had the wisdom to ordain priests from among the people themselves, and to plant them, wherever he had the opportunity, in groups, which subsequently developed into monasteries, within the territory of each clan, thereby creating, besides a network of missionary outposts, a system which was at once both civilizing and educational. He also adapted the pagan superstitions to Christian uses, and absorbed the heathen holydays into the festivals of the Church.

The Church in Ireland, as constituted by St. Patrick and his successors, partook considerably of the tribal character of the country. Land was granted by the tribes for the support of religious houses, whose abbots dropped into the position of chiefs, to whom the occupiers of the lands owed a sort of tribal allegiance. The lands themselves descended to the successor-designate of the abbot, who was called a "co-arb," and elected by the members of the brotherhood and the tribesmen, in analogy with the law of Tanistry. The smaller ecclesiastical establishments owed allegiance to the parent monastery, and paid a tax or tribute to its support. On the other hand, the bishops, except in the cases of the sees of Armagh and Trim, were not necessarily attached to any diocese, but were subordinate to the abbots, and were in the nature of suffragans of the parent house.

After Christianity had become well established in Ireland, the monastic schools of learning, which in their halcyon days produced Virgilius, Bishop of Salzburg, and Joannes Scotus, grew to be in advance of those on the Continent; and were much frequented by foreign ecclesiastics amid the troubles of the sixth and seventh centuries, not only for the sake of their teaching and their libraries, but also for the peace and security which they were there able to enjoy. A great missionary spirit also arose in the Church. The unattached bishops wandered into Scotland, Britain, and Gaul, and even farther afield in Europe; but though the spread of Christianity in the sister isle among the pagan Scandinavian settlers was largely due to the efforts of Columbanus and Columba and others, the Irish missionaries on the Continent in the seventh century, and later, caused considerable scandal and indignation by reason of the roving commission under which they intruded into the dioceses of other bishops.

As the outcome of the tribal system, the areas of ecclesiastical jurisdiction grew to be coincident with the territories of the tribes or groups of tribes; and as intercourse with the Continent grew, and the influence of Rome became felt in the island, the bishops, who were at first the officials of the abbots, came gradually to the front; the tribal district of the monastery grew into the diocese, and at a synod held at Rath Bresail, in A.D. 1111, the boundaries of twenty-four dioceses were defined, exclusive of the Danish bishopric of Dublin.

Though not refusing to acknowledge the supremacy of the Pope, the Irish Church had all along been connected with Rome by the loosest ties. The clergy at length seem to have become impressed by the reiterated charges of irregularity in their organization, and to have consented to be reconstituted according to Roman ideas. A synod was accordingly held at Kells, in A.D. 1152, under the auspices of Bishop Malachy, and a rearrangement of the sees effected. Cardinal Paparo, the Pope's legate, presided. He distributed four pallia among the four archiepiscopal sees of Armagh, Cashel, Dublin, and Tuam, and affiliated ten, twelve, five, and seven suffragan sees to each of the four metropolitans respectively. He constituted the Archbishop of Armagh primate of all Ireland; and where bishoprics and parishes were not maintained by any allocated lands, he ordained the payment of tithes to the clergy by the individual members of the tribe. The submission of the Church of Ireland to the Bishop of Rome, who claimed a right of disposition over "the isles of the sea," became subsequently a link in the fanciful title to the lordship of Ireland put forward by the English kings.

CHAPTER III.

THE SCANDINAVIAN TYRANNY. A.D. 795–1014.

THE strictly historical period can hardly be said to begin much before the introduction of Christianity into the island by St. Patrick, in the middle of the fifth century. We find that by that time there had grown up four confederations of tribes, corresponding pretty nearly to the four provinces into which the island is now divided. These confederacies each acknowledged a royal family of its own: Ulster that of the O'Neils, Connaught that of the O'Connors, Munster that of the O'Briens, and Leinster that of the McMurroughs. It is convenient to make use of the names by which the four provinces are now known; but it must be remembered that the Norse termination of "ster," or *stad*, a place, shows that, with the exception of that of Connaught, they could not have been in use before the ninth century. These four kingdoms again, in theory, recognized a branch of the Ulster family of O'Neil as lords paramount, of sacred and royal race. But this overlordship was really only maintained by force; it was the source of constant wars and disturbances; and the right to it was frequently disputed by the formidable kingdom of Munster. The royal demesne of Meath, the appanage of the Ulster family, which included Westmeath, Longford, and part of King's County, was sometimes reckoned as a fifth kingdom. The kingdom of Munster was divided into the two districts of Desmond and Thomond, whose leading families, the McCarthys and the O'Briens, claimed to occupy alternately the throne of Cashel.

While the Church was developing in strength and influence, and learning and civilization were being fostered within the walls of the religious houses, the civil history of Ireland is barren of everything but quarrels and "hostings;" and we find but little if any improvement in the condition of the people, though it is noteworthy that women had been prohibited from fighting in the ranks in battle. The condition of society was changing. The tribe system was decaying; the tribe lands were becoming monopolized by the noble class; the free tribesmen were deteriorating, while the chiefs and great men were absorbing all political and social power. As the chieftains became more absolute, they assumed the privilege of quartering themselves and their retinue upon their subjects at their own pleasure, and extracting from them both food and forage. This oppressive custom was known as "coshering," and in later times was commuted for a tribute which was called "bonaght." As the tribal land became occupied, and the population grew, the tribes, always jealous of each other, became aggressive. Lands were seized and cattle were lifted; laws were set at defiance; and ambition prompted the chieftains to encourage the tribal strife. The great southern kingdom grew in importance; the supremacy of the royal house was called in question; and internal dissensions were gradually paving the way for foreign invasion.

Until the end of the eighth century, Ireland had been free from the Scandinavian scourge, which for four hundred years had swept over Britain and the coasts of Gaul. But she suffered, in common with those countries, from the later incursion of pagan vikings, popularly known as the Danes. The Northmen made lodgements on various parts of the coast, more particularly on the east side of the island. Their attack was fierce and sudden. They burned, they plundered, they ravished, they massacred, and struck terror into the hearts of the native Irish. The disunited tribes, though at first checking the earlier settlers, were unable, upon the arrival of reinforcements under Turges, to offer any effectual resistance; the foreigners overran the whole island, and brought it into complete subjection. The pagan invaders particularly expended their fury upon the Church; breaking down the stone oratories, and destroying the religious houses and schools of learning; burning the ancient books and manuscripts, melting down the bells, breaking up the crosiers and pastoral staves, and driving the monks and scholars into the mountains. They exacted heavy tributes on the tribesmen in kind and money, and those who were unable to pay were reduced to slavery.

Driven to revolt, the Irish rose on their oppressors, a general massacre took place, and Turges was put to death. But the reaction was only transient. More Northmen arrived upon the coast; Amlaff, Sitric, and Imar, with countless crews of fierce warriors, swarmed over from the North Sea and enslaved the island. The Irish, still divided among themselves, were easily broken; and colonies of the enemy were planted at the mouths of all the principal rivers. At Carlingford, at Dublin, at Wexford, at Waterford, at Limerick, the Norse immigrants firmly established themselves. They built fortified towns, and formed active trading communities; numerous settlements were made on every part of the coast, and were even occasionally pushed into the interior of the country.

At length, a master spirit arose to rescue the Irish from their oppressors. The Danes of Limerick held the district of Thomond in cruel bondage, and had brought to his knees the King of Munster, who then happened, by the rule of alternate succession, to be of the Dalcassian race of O'Brien.

The king's brother, Brian Borumha, or Boru, had scorned to make his peace with the foreigner, and had taken to the mountains. He became the head of a desperate band, and at length roused his brother to renew the contest. A great battle was fought at Sulchoid, near Limerick (A.D. 968). The Danes were driven pell-mell into the city, the victorious Irish entering with them; Limerick was sacked and burned, and its inhabitants put to the sword or enslaved.

Having crushed the Northmen in this part of the country, Brian, upon the death of his brother, who was murdered by some discontented chieftains, although it was the turn of the Euganian line of Desmond to reign, seized on the throne of Cashel. He soon established himself as ruler of all Munster, overran Ossory and subdued Leinster, and began to turn his mind to the more ambitious scheme of laying hands on the sovereignty of the whole island. The Danes of Dublin and the east coast had about this time received a severe check, at the battle of Tara, from Melachlin, the hereditary King of Ireland; but they obtained a short respite, by reason of the rivalry of Melachlin and Brian. The latter, for thirty years after the fall of Limerick, was exerting his supremacy over an extending area. He laid waste Connaught and Meath, and burned the royal stronghold at Tara, but he had not yet ventured to seize upon the throne. In A.D. 1001 he consummated his ambitious scheme, deposed Melachlin, received the submission of, and took hostages from, the chieftains of the north, and, gathering all the power into his own hands, was acknowledged sovereign of all Ireland.

The vigorous action of Brian restored tranquillity to the distracted island, and for twelve years he reigned in uninterrupted peace. The Danes, however, who had been reduced under his determined rule into quiet traders in the seaport towns, began to be astir. They concerted a rebellion with the people of Leinster, and begged for aid from their kinsmen in the Orkneys and in Norway, who sent a large fleet to their assistance, under Sigurd.

King Brian was now stricken in years, but his spirit and judgment were as keen as ever. He opposed to the confederate forces an army of Munster men, of Connaught men, and of the men of Meath, under his five sons and the deposed King Melachlin, and joined battle at Clontarf, on Good Friday, A.D. 1014.

From dawn till eve the death-struggle was maintained. There was great slaughter on both sides. The Northmen were finally driven back upon the sea, and the remnant of the army took refuge in Dublin. But the victory was dearly bought. The old king, too weak to go into the battle, was lying in his tent, when some Danish fugitives, taking advantage of his being poorly guarded, broke in and put him to death.

With his death his whole system of a united government melted away. The subjugated provinces reasserted their independence, and the deposed Melachlin again became titular king of all Ireland. The Northmen, who for two centuries had been a formidable and at times a dominant power in the island, were so broken by the overthrow at Clontarf that they never again became dangerous. They never, indeed, seem at any time to have mastered the country so completely as they did in the days of Turges; and then success was probably due to the disunion of the native princes, whom they were careful to play off against each other, frequently taking sides with one or other of the provincial kings, for their own security, or for purposes of plunder. After the lapse of more than a hundred years following on their first arrival, they had embraced Christianity, not so much through their intercourse with the Irish as with their kinsmen in Britain; for they received their orders, and their Bishops of Waterford and Dublin were ordained, from Canterbury. Remaining in their old settlements, they never were completely driven out of the island, but were at length absorbed among the Anglo-Irish of the Pale.

Brian's usurpation of the throne of Tara opened the door to anarchy. The supremacy of the old royal race had been hitherto acquiesced in, at any rate in theory, without question. But the example set by the King of Munster encouraged the other provincial kings to thrust rudely aside the ancient rule; and from this time till the days of Strongbow we have little else to record but a constant struggle, with varying success, of ambitious princes for the sovereignty, with occasional efforts on the part of the Church to restore peace and order by the interposition of its pacific influence.

The restored Melachlin reigned for eight years with some vigor till his death. The Dalcassian house then again pushed to the front; Donchad, the son of Brian, and his rival Turlough, the son of Teige, another of Brian's sons, successively becoming *de facto* rulers of the greater part of the island. Murkertach succeeded Turlough, and maintained the ascendency of the Munster dynasty; and then Donald O'Lochlin, of the royal house of Nial, became for two years titular king, until his death, in A.D. 1121. After him the kings of Connaught put in a claim, and Turlough O'Connor wrested the sovereignty from the house of Brian by sowing dissension among the rival claimants to the throne of Cashel. The struggle with the house of Thomond was put an end to by the battle of Moinmor, in which Turlough O'Brien was killed and his army routed. The King of Connaught had now, however, to reckon with an Ulster prince, Murtough O'Lochlin or O'Neil, and the conflict continued till A.D. 1156, when Turlough died, and Murtough O'Lochlin succeeded to the overlordship of the whole island. On the death of Murtough O'Lochlin, Turlough's son, Rory O'Connor, whose violent pretensions the late King of Ulster had effectually disposed of, succeeded to the supreme sovereignty without opposition. He was the last king of independent Ireland.

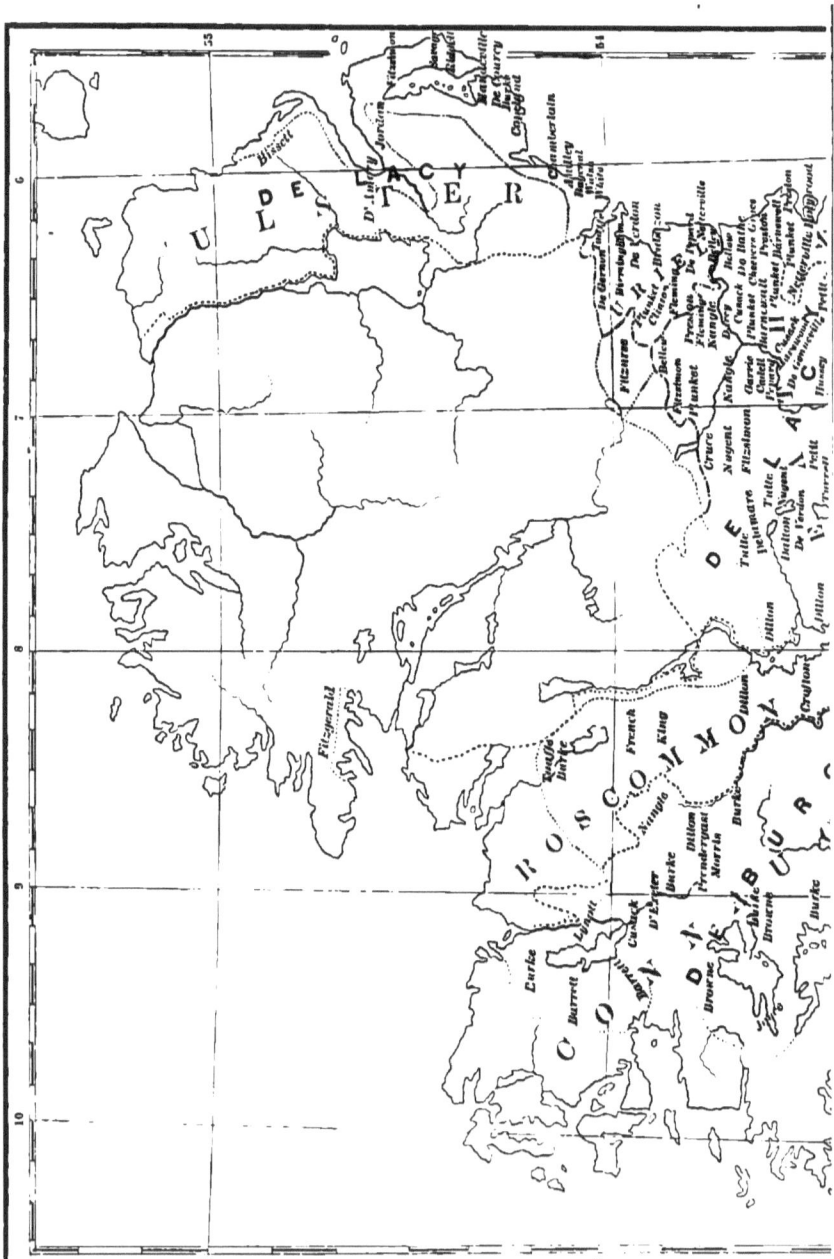

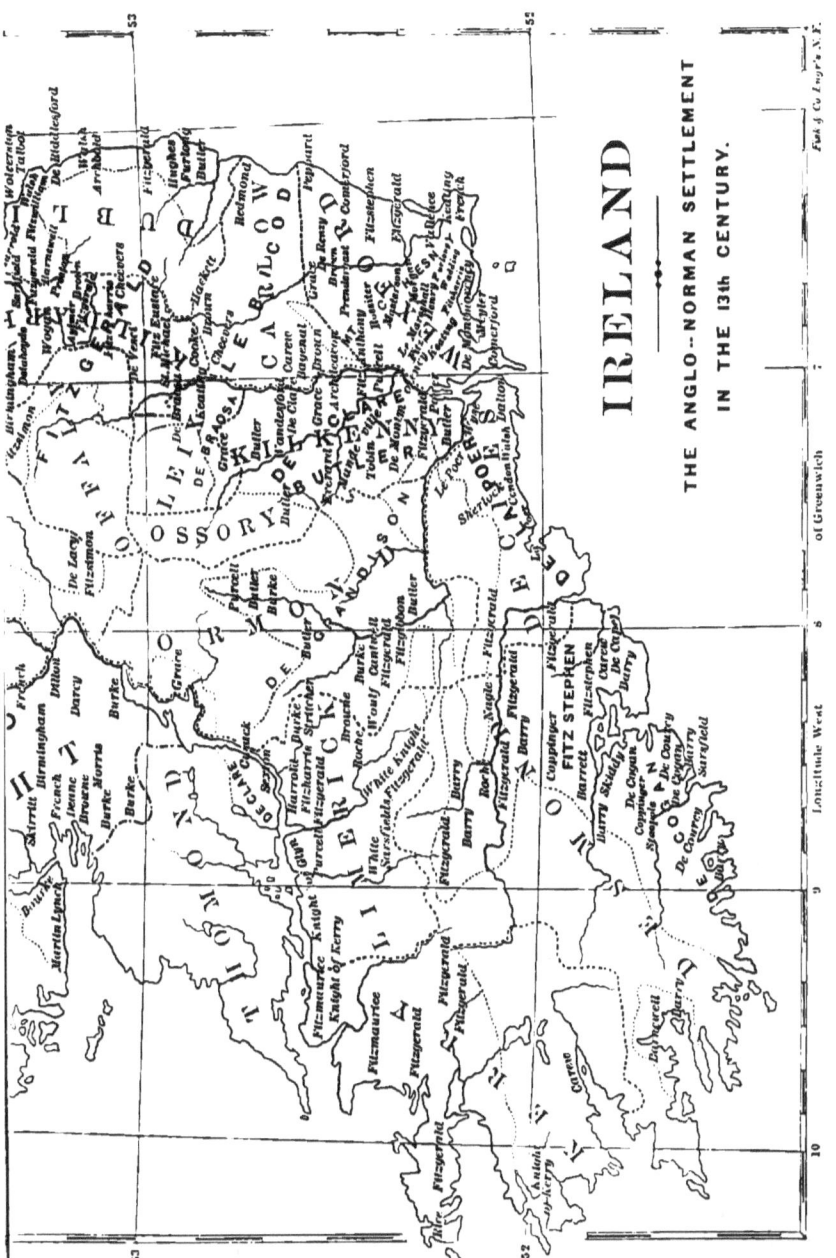

Book II.
THE ANGLO-NORMAN SETTLEMENT

CHAPTER I.
THE FILIBUSTERS. A.D. 1169–1172.

RORY O'CONNOR was fierce and brutal; he was brave, but unstable. There was nothing in him in the nature of a leader of men. The allegiance of Ulster and Munster was little more than nominal; and he had an open quarrel with Dermot McMurrough, the King of Leinster. Dermot was equally brutal and unscrupulous. He had incurred the displeasure of Rory's father, Turlough, by the abduction of the wife of Tiernan O'Rourke, Lord of Brefny and a chieftain of the kingdom of Connaught; and though protected during the reign of O'Lochlin, on the accession of Rory he found that he had to confront not only the anger of the new monarch and his client O'Rourke, but also the disaffection of his own kingdom of Leinster and the Danes of Dublin, whom he had by his cruel tyranny driven into revolt. Dermot, unable to meet the storm, fled from his kingdom in 1168, and sought protection of the Angevin King of England, who was then in Aquitaine.

The Norman kings had already marked Ireland for conquest, as a house divided against itself. And Henry Plantagenet had obtained from Pope Adrian IV., the only Englishman who ever occupied the chair of St. Peter, an extraordinary document, which purported, "for the purposes of enlarging the borders of the Church, setting bounds to the progress of wickedness, reforming evil manners, planting virtue, and increasing the Christian religion," and, in consideration of the payment from Ireland to Rome of "the annual pension of one penny from each house," to make a grant of the whole island to the king. Henry, however, was too busy with other matters to take advantage of the papal bull, and allowed his designs to slumber until the arrival of the King of Leinster. He was not inclined even then to offer Dermot any substantial help, but gave him letters-patent recommending his own subjects to undertake the adventure, in return for which Dermot did homage and swore fealty.

Dermot went to England to beat up recruits. He came to a bargain with Robert De Clare, Earl of Pembroke and Chepstow, a broken-down Norman noble of good family; and with a group of Norman-Welsh gentlemen, the descendants—some legitimate, some illegitimate—of Nesta, the daughter of the prince of South Wales, by Henry I., Gerald De Windsor, the Lord of Carew, and Stephen De Marisco, the Constable of Abertivy. Of these the most conspicuous were Maurice Fitzgerald, Robert Fitzstephen, Raymond le Gros, and Hervey Mountmorres, Fitzgerald's son-in-law.

Fitzstephen and Mountmorres first crossed with a few followers, seized the Danish town of Wexford, and made a bloody raid into Ossory. Raymond soon followed. Landing at Waterford, he defeated the men of Decies with great slaughter, and, having captured seventy of the principal citizens, broke their limbs and cast them over the cliffs into the sea. Strongbow himself arrived shortly afterwards with reinforcements. Waterford was taken and sacked, and the earl's marriage was celebrated with Dermot's daughter, Eva, amid the smoking ruins of the town.

The adventurers then turned to the northward, captured and plundered Dublin, the leading Danes of the city escaping in their ships to the Orkneys; and carried fire and sword into Meath and Brefny.

The success of these pioneers had a disturbing effect on King Henry. The latter was glad enough to get a foothold in Ireland, but there was the danger lest these lawless Normans, having won a kingdom by their swords, should keep it for themselves. He accordingly commanded Strongbow to return with all his men, and forbade all intercourse between Ireland and his own subjects. To return, however, was not so easy. Dermot died suddenly, and thereupon every Irishman turned upon the foreigners, and the handful of English found themselves blockaded in Wexford and Waterford by the natives, and in

Dublin by the Danes, who had returned from the north with reinforcements.

No sooner had the Northmen been driven into the sea than Rory O'Connor, who had stirred himself but little to protect his kingdom, roused himself to action, and having been joined by the King of Thomond, O'Rourke of Brefny, and Lawrence, the warlike archbishop, invested Dublin with a large Irish force. But the effort was unsuccessful. After a siege of two months, a desperate sally was made by the besieged, and the undisciplined Irish, unable to withstand the marshalled attack of the Norman knights, were dispersed in terror and confusion. Wexford in the meantime had fallen, and Strongbow, too late to relieve it, proceeded to Waterford, and, having re-established his authority over the neighboring district, crossed from thence to England to make his submission to the king. Henry, having accorded him his tardy forgiveness, proceeded in 1171, in a fleet of 240 ships, with 400 knights and 4000 men-at-arms, to Waterford. This conspicuous display of force seems to have impressed the Irish chieftains with the idea that Henry was irresistible. Without a master spirit to subdue their tribal jealousies and to cement the discordant elements together, united resistance was impossible. The King of Leinster had been a puppet in the hands of the English, and Strongbow was now posing as his successor. Rory was more intent upon coercing the King of Ulster than upon performing his duties as overlord by affording protection to the princes of the south. Accordingly, the Munster chieftains "came in." First, McCarthy of Desmond, who surrendered Cork, and received therein an English garrison; then O'Brien of Thomond, who similarly surrendered Limerick; next Donchad of Ossory, and O'Phelan of Decies, and all the petty chiefs of Munster. Henry made a royal progress to Cashel and Tipperary, and then proceeded to Dublin. The Danes swore allegiance, as did O'Carrol of Argial and O'Rourke of Brefny; and Rory at length turned to bay behind the Shannon. Negotiations with him were opened, but nothing came of them, and he and Henry tacitly agreed to leave one another alone. The kingdom of Ulster also held aloof.

Henry kept Christmas at Dublin, entertaining all the Irish chiefs right royally. He occupied the winter in organizing a government upon the English model. His first object was to plant the feudal system on Irish soil. Dermot had pretended to appoint his son-in-law Strongbow as his successor to the kingdom of Leinster, and had granted large tracts of land to him and to his fellow-adventurers. Henry compelled them all to surrender their grants, and to receive them again from himself on the condition of their rendering him homage and military service. He decreed that his English subjects should be governed by English law; but he did not interfere with the natives, who continued, as before, to regulate their affairs by the Brehon law. He instituted the hereditary offices of marshal, justiciary, constable, seneschal, chamberlain, butler, standard-bearer, etc., which had been attached to the king's court, since the Conquest, in England. He roughly divided the ceded districts into counties, and pricked sheriffs. He set up the three royal law courts of Bench, Pleas, and Exchequer in Dublin, and provided for the going of circuit by the judges. He appointed a chief governor of the kingdom to act as his viceroy in his absence, the king's justiciary, or lord justice. He held a council of nobles, in which it was enacted* that, if the chief governor should die in office, his functions should be exercised by one (afterwards two and three†) of the principal officers of state, to be chosen by the chancellor, the treasurer, and the rest of the king's council of state, until the king should make a fresh appointment.

His next step was to place the most reliable of his followers in responsible posts, for the due security of his new dominions, to reward them for their services, and to strengthen his hold on the seaports.

Meath had always been an appanage of the sovereign; he accordingly granted the whole of it to his new constable, Hugh De Lacy, and his heirs. He granted to John De Courcy the province of Ulster, provided he could succeed in subduing it.

---

* Statute of Henry Fitzempress. 18 Hen. II.
† 33 Hen. VIII. c. 2.

He confirmed the grants in Wexford to Maurice Fitzgerald, to Hervey Mountmorres, and to Robert Fitzstephen. He stationed William Fitzaldelm, Philip De Braosa, and Philip of Hastings in Wexford. He granted the city of Dublin by royal charter to the citizens of Bristol, giving them the right of free trade with the rest of his dominions; and confirmed the city of Waterford to the Danes.

He next proceeded to win over the Church to his side. The clergy, on the first invasion of the English, had held a council at Armagh, whereat they had decided that the imminent enslavement of their country was a just judgment from heaven upon the traffic with Bristol in English slaves, and had promptly ordered the manumission of every English bondman in the island. They seem to have been greatly impressed with Adrian's bull; and made their peace with Henry, and accepted him as their temporal head without reserve. Henry held a synod at Cashel, at which the Bishop of Lismore presided as Pope's legate, and promulgated some decrees, which purported to reform certain alleged irregularities of Church discipline. He declared that the Church lands should thenceforth be freed from all exactions of the laity; relieved the ecclesiastics from the payment of erics in respect of crimes committed by their relations; and confirmed the claim of the clergy to the payment by the laity of tithes.

The work of organization was suddenly arrested. Henry was summoned by the papal legates in Normandy to appear before them and render an account in respect of Becket's murder; and in April, 1172, he sailed from Wexford for St. David's.

CHAPTER II.

THE COLONISTS. A.D. 1172–1189.

In the introduction of the feudal system into Ireland we recognize the germ of the "Land Question," which has proved the stumbling-block to its tranquillity for seven hundred years. The theory of the feudal system was that all the soil belonged to the king, who had accordingly the right to make grants of tracts of land in his discretion to his followers, to be held by them upon the condition of their rendering him the services of themselves and their retainers in the field whenever he should require them. The grant, though not so at first, soon became hereditary, and the land passed to the heirs of the grantee by descent, without reference to the consent of the tenants whom he had permitted to occupy and cultivate subdivisions of his domain. The land, too, was inalienable, and reverted to the king if the heirs of the grantee failed, or he became attainted for treason; but, though inalienable, the tenant in chief from the crown could make sub-grants of portions of his land to smaller men, who were bound to him in the same way as he was bound to the king; and these again could repeat the process with still smaller men—the process being known as subinfeudation. This system could not be applied to Ireland, where the tribal system prevailed, without revolutionizing the whole structure of society; and its application was, in the eyes of the Irish, nothing but a high-handed invasion of the rights of property, and an act of shameful injustice.

We find the thin end of the wedge introduced by Dermot surrendering to Henry and his heirs a kingdom of which he was only the elected monarch; to which no ruler, according to the law of the land, could have any rightful claim but through the free suffrages of the tribal chiefs. We find him again making grants of territory to Strongbow, Fitzstephen, and others, over which he had not the shadow of a right: lands which belonged to various native septs, whose chosen overlord he was, but over whose lands he had no right of control. The lands thus illegally granted were occupied by the Norman adventurers, who held them by force, the tribes who dwelt thereon either being expropriated or reduced to the position of tenants. Again, Henry based his title to be lord paramount over the island on the papal bull, which was obviously no title at all; and he affected to treat those who opposed him as rebels, and claimed to escheat their lands by branding them with treason, and to re-enjoy that which he never possessed, and to which he could have no claim.

The Normans had as yet made but slight lodgements on the coasts; but the time was coming when this fiction of feudal tenure was to be forced gradually upon the whole island, and to be converted into an engine for the transfer of the soil from the native Celt to the colonizing Norman. Every effort of the people to assert its independence was to be punished as treasonable offence, entailing the resulting penalty of a forfeiture of the land. When the owners were dispossessed, they might be permitted to occupy as tenants at will, to support themselves by tilling the ground, and to pay for the privilege in rent to the new land-owner. What was begun in 1170 was continued in after-generations, until the whole island came into the possession either of English immigrants, or those natives who accepted the new order of things, and received again their lands as grants from the English crown.

It should also be remembered that the invasion of Ireland in the twelfth century was not an invasion by England, but by the Normans of the Continent. Henry was Duke of Normandy and Count of Anjou, and he also happened to be King of England. His ancestors had reduced England to a dependency of the Norman duchy, and in like manner the Normans of his day proceeded to spread through England over to Ireland. England had been occupied by the penniless riffraff of Normandy; after a hundred years' occupation of England, the Norman adventurers of that day swarmed upon the coasts of Ireland, in order to win a kingdom after the manner of their forefathers. It was a fresh invasion of Northmen by a circuitous route through Normandy and Britain.

Henry had accomplished his primary object, that of securing his authority over the colonists. He left it to them to maintain themselves, and to extend their borders as best they could, relying on the incentives of self-preservation and rapacity. The grants of territory he had made were to a great extent of a nominal character. Most of what he gave was in the hands of the native Irish, and, if to be enjoyed, would have to be won and held by the sword. The colonists lost no time in carrying out this programme. The island was densely wooded; it was traversed by mountainous ridges, running in Leinster and Munster for the most part from N.E. to S.W., through which burst numerous rivers, which broadened at their outfall into estuaries. The interior was broken with chains of lakes and huge tracts of morass. There was hardly a road in the country, and the only accessible portions were the river-valleys and the coast. These were the points of attack in the time of the incursions, of the Northmen, in whose footsteps the Normans followed. Settlements of their followers were made, and forts were built for their protection in the open lands of Meath and Leinster, the tribes retiring into the hill country and the bogs. They peopled the lower valleys of the Shannon, the Slaney, the Suir, the Barrow, and the Blackwater; they settled down upon the lowlands of Louth and the coastline of Down. Marauding expeditions were made to satisfy the rapacious soldiery. Ulster was attacked by De Courcy, who seized Downpatrick and overran Dalradia; Milo De Cogan made a raid across the Shannon, but the men of Connaught had laid waste their land, and he was forced to beat a retreat. Raymond le Gros captured the town of Limerick; and, in return for reinstating McCarthy King of Desmond, who had been imprisoned by his rebellious son, received large grants of land in Kerry. From time to time fresh parties of adventurers arrived, and received allotments. Subinfeudation was carried on briskly, and both the new and the old comers were planted in freeholds by those who had received grants from the king.

Henry never returned to Ireland to complete his conquest, but he proceeded to make further grants of Irish territory to his friends: giving all Connaught to Fitzaldelm; the kingdom of Cork to De Cogan and Fitzstephen, who partitioned it east and west of the city; the kingdom of Limerick to Philip De Braosa, and the Decies to Le Poer; but reserving the cities of Cork and Limerick to himself. He then created his son Prince John lord of Ireland; and that youth, when the chieftains of Leinster came to do him honor, insulted them by his insolent conduct and levity, plucking them by the beard and ridiculing their fashion of dress. John's conduct put the match to a train which was ready to be fired. The Irish who had been driven from their own lands were ready to rise, and those who had become English subjects were alienated by the brutality and profligacy of the Normans. A confederacy was formed, and the English were attacked at all points and driven out of Munster. No sooner, however, was success apparently in the hands of the Irish than they fell to quarrelling: the rebellion died out, the English regained all that they had lost, and the chieftains again acknowledged the suzerainty of the king.

But the submission of the Irish chieftains was mainly a sham: they had been ready enough to swear allegiance to Henry as lord paramount; they had professed to recognize the suzerainty of Rory, and they were not unwilling to do the same to a king against whom Rory was unable to protect them. Rory himself, in 1175, after having overrun Meath in a raid out of Connaught, was frightened by a victory of Raymond over the Prince of Thomond into making a treaty with Henry; the substance of which was that he should recognize Henry as sovereign prince, and himself continue King of Ireland beyond the English border, yielding a tribute of hides, which he never paid. But this was all! Henry pretended that the Irish chieftains had become his vassals, subject to all the attending feudal liabilities. Of this they had no conception; and as soon as his back was turned they set him at defiance, and asserted their independence at the first moment at which it suited their convenience. As for the English settlers, they were looked upon by the Irish as interlopers. They were not safe in their own forts; the natives were constantly on the watch to attack and expel them; and in consequence there was perpetual though desultory warfare going on within the English precincts even to the walls of the sea-coast cities.

CHAPTER III.

THE GREAT TERRITORIAL BARONS. A.D. 1200–1300.

HENRY was dead; and John had succeeded his brother Richard. He returned in A.D. 1210 to Ireland with a considerable force, a wiser if not a better man than when he had first landed at Waterford. Upon his arrival the chiefs promptly made their submission: O'Donnel and O'Neil from the north; Cathal of the Bloody Hand, of the house of O'Connor, from the west. Hostages were taken as well from the turbulent Norman barons as from the natives. The civil administration was attended to; and Leinster and Munster were divided into twelve counties, corresponding very much to those existing at the present day.*

This second visit of John to Ireland, who soon had his hands full both in England and on the Continent, was of short duration. During his reign, and also the long reigns of Henry III. and Edward I., the history of Ireland maintains one monotonous character: a quick succession of lieutenant-governors; a constant border warfare between the natives and the settlers, characterized by bloody insurrections on the one hand, and bloody reprisals on the other; bitter feuds between the Irish themselves; jealous warfare between the rival Anglo-Irish houses; frequent submissions of the chieftains to the crown in return for promises of protection against the barons, which the king was unable or unwilling to afford; and a constant balancing by the crown of the former against the increasing power of the latter.

The more prominent events which catch the eye in this monotonous record of lawless brigandage are, a rising of the McCarthys of Desmond against the Geraldines; an intermittent

---

* Dublin (including Wicklow), Meath (including Westmeath), Kildare, Argial (Louth), Katherlagh (Carlow), Kilkenny, Wexford, Waterford, Cork, Kerry, Limerick, and Tipperary.

but bitter struggle between the latter and the De Burgos; a rising of the natives in Connaught and Offaly; a discreditable invasion and occupation of part of Thomond by Thomas De Clare, Earl of Gloucester; and a quarrel between De Vesci and Fitzgerald, Baron of Offaly, which ended in the ruin of the former, and the translation of the latter into Earl of Kildare.

The whole island had been nominally parcelled out in enormous grants among a few individuals. The larger portions were at different times erected into "counties palatine." The great barons on whom the crown had conferred these tremendous privileges accordingly occupied the position of independent princes. They planned and built fortified towns; they endowed them with land; they granted them charters of incorporation, and established markets. The franchise of a county palatine gave exclusive civil and criminal jurisdiction. There was a palatinate court, with its own judges, seneschal, sheriff, coroner, and escheator. The jurisdiction of the crown was ousted, and the king's writs did not run within the palatinate borders. The lord had all the powers and rights of the crown to make barons and knights, to grant lands to subtenants to be held by knights' service, and to retake such lands in case of forfeiture. Richard, Earl of Ulster, before starting with his contingent for the Scottish wars in 1303, made no less than thirty-three knights in Dublin Castle.

The original number of counties palatine created was three: the lordship of Meath, granted to De Lacy; the lordship of Ulster, to De Burgo; and the lordship of Leinster, to Strongbow. Strongbow's daughter and heiress married William Marshal, Earl of Pembroke, who left five daughters co-heiresses. Maud, who married Le Bigod, Earl Warrenne, inherited Carlow; Joan, who married Mountchesny, Wexford; Isabel, who married De Clare, Earl of Gloucester, Kilkenny; Sibyl, who married De Vesci, Kildare; and Eva, who married De Braosa, Leix. The king partitioned the lordship of Leinster among the five sisters, and Strongbow's single palatinate was resolved into five. In the reign of Edward III., the Earl of Desmond's territory in Kerry was erected into a county palatine; as also was Ormonde's country, the County of Tipperary. So that in all

2*

there were no less than nine independent princes in Ireland exercising regalian rights.

The estates of Strongbow's granddaughters passed by marriage into the hands of English noblemen, who drew their rents, and lived away in England. They eventually became forfeited to the crown under the statute against absentees.

The most powerful and most numerous of the Norman families was that of the Geraldines. They were all descended from Gerald Fitzwalter and Nesta, the Princess of South Wales. Maurice Fitzgerald, the elder of the brother-adventurers, was the ancestor of the earls of Kildare and Desmond and the Fitzgeralds of Leinster and Munster. William, Maurice's younger brother, and the father of Raymond le Gros, the grantee of the broad lands in Kerry, which he obtained from McCarthy of Desmond, was the ancestor of the Fitzmaurices, earls of Kerry, and is now represented by the Marquis of Lansdowne.

The head of the Leinster Fitzgeralds, the Baron of Offaly, received his estates by subinfeudation from the lords of Leinster. In the eighteenth year of King Edward I., De Vesci (one of the five representatives of Strongbow) and the seventh Earl of Offaly accused each other of treason. They were directed by the king to sustain their mutual charges in single combat; and when De Vesci, in preference, fled to the Continent, the king granted to the Baron of Offaly De Vesci's estates. His eldest son John was created Earl of Kildare, and was the ancestor of the marquises of Kildare and dukes of Leinster. The estates of this family lay in the counties adjacent to the capital. They became extremely influential by reason of this proximity; their castles threatened and overawed the government; and the house of Kildare became the most powerful in the island.

The Munster Geraldines received immense grants of land in the counties of Limerick, Cork, and Kerry from Henry II., which they held immediately from the crown. In Limerick alone the barony of Connell, which was ceded to them by the tribe of O'Connell, contained upwards of one hundred thousand acres. The founder of the house was Thomas, the second son of Maurice Fitzgerald, Lord of Offaly; the heads of the younger branches were afterwards known as the White Knight, the Knight of Kerry or the Black Knight, and the Knight of Glin. The huge territory of which Thomas was lord was added to in the time of his son, John of Callan, by the grant of the lordships of the Decies and Desmond and the castle of Dungarvan by Edward I. And Robert Fitzstephen's moiety of the kingdom of Cork passed by enfeoffment to Lord Thomas's greatgrandson, the first earl. The Desmond family intermarried with the native nobility, and encouraged social alliances between the settlers and the Irish. Their territory was so extensive that both settlers and natives grew to look upon the heads of the house as the chieftains of a powerful clan, who claimed and were accorded a suzerainty over the greater part of the southern province.

The great inland territory of Ormonde, or East Munster, and the fertile basin of the three rivers which fall into the sea at Waterford, became the possession of the great house of Butler, whose branches spread all over the counties of Tipperary and Kilkenny. They divided the northern from the southern Geraldines, and acted as a counterpoise to the overwhelming influence of both. The family of the Botilers, or Butlers, is descended from Theobald Walter, a nephew of St. Thomas of Canterbury, who was made hereditary chief butler or cupbearer to King Henry II. The chief butler, among other privileges, received a grant of the prisage of wines; that is, the right of taking from every ship importing twenty or more tuns of wine one tun from before, and one from behind, the mast. Theobald Walter obtained large grants of land in Kilkenny and Tipperary, besides the barony of Arklow. In 1391, the heirs of Strongbow's granddaughter Isabel sold Kilkenny Castle to the Earl of Ormonde. Seven of Theobald's descendants in afteryears obtained peerages: the barony of Dunboyne, the viscounties of Cahir, Mountgarret, Galmoy, and Tulleophelim, and the earldoms of Arran and Gouran, besides those of the elder *stirps* of the house of Butler who subsequently became viscounts Thurles, earls of Carrick, earls of Ossory, and earls, marquises, and dukes of Ormonde.

De Lacy's grant, the province of Meath, containing some

800,000 acres, vested in his two great-granddaughters, one of whom, Matilda, married Geoffrey de Genneville, and the other, Margaret, married John de Verdon, who held the barony of Dundalk. The lordship of Meath accordingly passed in moieties to these two families. De Genneville's portion, the lordship of Trim, was eventually carried into the family of Mortimer, Earl of March, and vested in the crown. The De Verdons continued a powerful family for many generations, and their moiety finally passed to the Talbots, earls of Shrewsbury.

Cathal, the King of Connaught, had in 1206 surrendered two thirds of his kingdom to the crown, on condition of his being secured in the remaining third as the king's vassal; and the Irish of that province had, upon his death, elected his brother king in his place. But, notwithstanding this, the compromise was wholly disregarded by the king, and on Cathal's death John granted the whole of the lordship of Connaught to William Fitzaldelm, a first-cousin of the great Hubert De Burgh, and his son Richard. Connaught was soon overrun. The new king's succession was disputed. The rival princes of the house of O'Connor were blindly rushing at each other's throats in bloody civil strife. The De Burghs, posted at Athlone, the fortress built by John upon the Shannon, now helping one of the combatants, and now another, watched their opportunity till the country was desolate and exhausted, then occupied the best of the land, drove out the native chiefs, and built themselves forts and castles from Galway in the south to Sligo in the north. Fitzaldelm was the head of the family of the De Burghs, or Bourkes, and ancestor of the earls and marquises of Clanricarde and the earls of Mayo. The lords of Connaught also became lords, and afterwards earls, of Ulster. Ulster had originally been granted to De Courcy; but he got into trouble with King John, who resumed his grant and gave it to Hugh De Lacy, the youngest son of the Lord of Meath. The whole of this vast territory afterwards passed to the De Burgh family, through Hugh's daughter Maud, who married Fitzaldelm's son Richard, the Lord of Connaught. But the lordship of Ulster was never much more than a nominal possession. The greater portion of that province was never subdued, and remained in the hands of the untamable peoples of the north; the great O'Neil and O'Donnel tribes, into which the sovereign clan had become divided, and the lesser septs, the McGuires of Fermanagh, the O'Rourkes of Brefny, the O'Reillys of Cavan, the McGennisses of Southern Dalradia, and the O'Kanes of Coleraine. The only portions which owned obedience to the De Burghs were the fringes of Down and Antrim, the southern border of Monaghan, and a few lodgements of Norman settlers on the coast of Donegal. After the murder of William, the third Earl of Ulster, his only daughter and heiress married Lionel, Duke of Clarence; and the earldom of Ulster and the lordship of Connaught passed in this way through females to Edmond and Roger Mortimer, and finally to Richard, Earl of Cambridge, the grandfather of Edward IV.; and so became vested in the crown.

Among the smaller grants were the seigniory of Bray, given to De Riddlesford; of Dangen and Tadhoyle to Robert De St. Michael; of Howth to Almaric St. Lawrence, the ancestor of the barons and earls of Howth; and "the honor of Limerick" to Braosa.

The subinfeudations created by these great tenants *in capite* gave rise to a number of barons holding large estates hardly less powerful than their immediate overlords. Large tracts of the province of Meath in this way estated the Nugents, barons of Delvin, the Flemings of Slane, the Petits of Dunboyne, the Tuites of Killallon, the Prestons of Gormanston, and others; while in Cork the Roches became barons of Fermoy, and the Barrys lords of Barrymore.

The great territorial barons had consolidated their power. The castles which they built with towering keep and inner and outer wards, guarded with frequent bastion towers and curtain walls, frowned over the surrounding country, and bade defiance to the ill-armed, ill-accoutred kerns whom the native chieftains led to battle. The Norman baron lived a life of rough self-reliance. He was a law unto himself, and dealt out rough justice to his tenants in the court-baron, according to a curious mixture of the Brehon law and the common-law of England. He was a border chieftain, ever watchful to protect the herds of himself and his retainers, to sally forth and chastise the cattle-lifters, or revenge an affront from a neighbor. When years began to tell upon him, and he thought with some remorse over the wild, lawless acts of which he had been guilty, his superstitious piety prompted him to bring over Norman builders and craftsmen, and to erect an abbey or a priory, which he endowed with a slice of his broad acres, to satisfy the clamorings of his conscience, and perhaps to afford a spiritual retreat for himself in his declining years.

CHAPTER IV.
THE ASSIMILATION OF THE SETTLERS. A.D. 1272-1335.

THE English system of government was confined to the English settlements. The Irish districts were outside the law. The law did not, in fact, recognize them: no Irishman could plead in the English courts, unless he was a member of the families of O'Neil, O'Brien, O'Connor, O'Melaghlin, or McMurrough— "the five bloods," as they were called, who enjoyed by royal grant the privilege of being the king's freemen. To kill an Irishman was not murder; they existed, in fact, as a separate nation, and were governed by their ancient Brehon law. On the accession of Edward I., the Irish who lived on English ground petitioned the crown for an equal recognition with the English by the English law, and offered to pay eight thousand marks for the privilege. But though the king was favorable to the concession, the English settlers would not consent, and so the claim slumbered.

The Irish chieftains, whose territories had been granted to the English, effected a sort of tacit compromise with the new grantees, retiring within the reduced limits of the more worthless land, and permitting the settlers to occupy the richer portions. Their lands lay interspersed among and dovetailed between the lands of the settlers in accordance with the configuration of the ground, their narrowed borders lying more in the heart of the country and in the less accessible districts. What was won from them by the sword was in effect surrendered; and though the natives were ever ready to lift the cattle of their Norman neighbors, and to reoccupy territories where the owners might have been left minors, and so less able to protect themselves, or where estates had devolved on females who had married husbands living away in England; though a deep race-hatred lay beneath the surface, which on occasions could burst forth, still time and convenience gradually drew the English and the Irish lords into mutual toleration, and at times combined them in a common resistance to the English crown.

The social condition of the settlers in course of time underwent a curious change. They lived isolated in their strongholds; they intermarried with the daughters of the native chiefs, and the native chiefs intermarried with their daughters; they fell into the singular Irish practice of fosterage, under which the children of the lord were drafted out to nurse with the family of his retainer. They employed the natives both for domestic and military service; they made alliances with the native tribes in their quarrels with their Norman neighbors. The consequence was that they became gradually weaned away from English ideas, habits, customs, and manners. They let their hair grow long and cultivated the mustache; they adopted the Irish dress, the Irish mode of riding bareback—even the Irish language and the Irish law; they aspired to be independent princes, like the Irish chieftains, whose will was law and whose law was license. "They became more Irish than the Irish themselves."

To check the growing degeneracy of the settlers, a Parliament was held in A.D. 1295, and a statute* passed embodying an ordinance given by the king at Westminster to compel the lords marchers, who had abandoned their tenants on their border estates to the tender mercies of the Irish, to return and protect them on pain of forfeiture; to compel absentees in England [for this curse of the country is as old as the thirteenth century] to assign a portion of their Irish revenues to the support of a military force for the common security; to restrain the number of mercenaries, or kerns, kept by the great lords; to enforce the making and repairing of roads and bridges; and to prohibit the use, by the English, of the native garb, mustache, and "culan."

The Norman supremacy in Ireland was at its zenith at the end of the thirteenth century; but a subtle decay was extending through the whole system. The king's Welsh and Scot-

---

* 23 Edw. I., Irish Statutes.

tish wars prevented him from bestowing much care on his Irish dominions; the revenue he derived from them barely paid the expenses of the government. They were a good recruiting-ground for the armies of the Welsh marches and the Scottish border; but apart from this they were a source of more anxiety than profit. Paralysis, therefore, having seized the heart of the English government in Dublin, all control began to fail over the trunk and the extremities; the whole was ripe for dissolution at the touch of an external solvent.

The overthrow of the English at Bannockburn, in A.D. 1314, was the signal for revolt among the native Irish. They had afforded a sanctuary to Bruce in his hour of adversity, and had watched with much anxiety the struggle between their masters and their Scottish kinsmen; and now the tide had turned against the former. The movement began in the north—the O'Neils being the first to stir; and overtures were made to Robert Bruce for the despatch to them of his brother Edward, to whom they were willing to offer the crown of Ireland. A petition from the Irish chieftains was sent to the Pope, setting forth their complaints against the English, and praying him to interfere and restrain the King of England from molesting them. But the Irish clergy were true to the English cause, and the only answer vouchsafed was the excommunication of the Bruces and all who took up arms against the English.

Edward Bruce landed near Carrickfergus with 6000 Scots, in A.D. 1315. He was at once joined by the Irish of the north, and presently by Fedlim O'Connor, King of Connaught. The Earl of Ulster was driven in upon Dublin. O'Brien of Thomond rose, and the chiefs of Munster and Meath; even the De Lacys, and many of the Anglo-Irish settlers, threw in their lot with the Irish; and Edward Bruce was crowned at Dundalk.

A struggle for existence now began on the part of the Desmonds, the Butlers, and the Kildares. Troops were collected and sent to co-operate with the helpless English government at Dublin, and to make a diversion in O'Connor's country. The latter and all his tribe were exterminated in the battle of Athenry; but the English were not strong enough to oppose

Bruce in the field. The Scots marched into Meath and Munster, laying waste the country with fire and sword, routing the English, and capturing their strongholds. Robert Bruce arrived with reinforcements; and the burning and plundering of towns, castles, and churches was carried into Tipperary and Kildare, and even to the walls of Dublin. But Bruce's excesses were the cause of his destruction: the desolated country had nothing left wherewith to support his army; famine and pestilence, the consequences of his ravages, thinned his numbers, so that, it is said, the survivors were reduced to eating the carcasses of the dead; the indiscriminate plunder of friends and foes caused his Irish allies to fall away; and the King of the Scots was summoned back to Scotland. Meanwhile, the Geraldines had collected an irregular force of 30,000 men. Roger Mortimer of Wigmore, the new lieutenant-governor, was reorganizing the government at Dublin. Leinster was reduced; and the opportunity for striking was not missed by the English. Sir John de Bermingham, having been appointed to the command of 1500 chosen troops, pushed his way northward, and met the enemy at Dundalk. A short sharp conflict ensued: the Scottish army was overthrown; the remnant escaped to Scotland; but Edward Bruce was among the slain.

The Scottish invasion was at an end; but the shock to the English system was severe, and the consequences far-reaching. The inability of the English government to afford protection to its Anglo-Irish subjects had been painfully demonstrated; and the result was a falling-away of the Anglo-Irish from their allegiance. The causes of estrangement had long been silently at work, and, now that the opportunity had come, the Norman baron became an Irish chief. The consequences to the English yeomen, who held the land as tenants to the territorial owners, were equally serious. Many were utterly ruined by the Scottish raid; many had suffered from the military requisitions of their own lords, who had adopted the Irish practice, for the support of their troops, of "coyne and livery," or free quartering of the soldiery for food and fodder. The total want of security for life and property compelled large bodies of them to quit the country. Those who remained sank into the condition of

THE ASSIMILATION OF THE SETTLERS. 43

the tribal Irish; and the deserted lands were reoccupied by the native clans.

All Desmond was in this way cleared of its English yeoman population. Large portions of Leinster suffered a like fate. The O'Moores and O'Connors swarmed out of the Slievebloom mountains, and reoccupied Leix and Offaly; the McMurroughs recovered Carlow and half the County of Wexford; while the O'Tooles and O'Byrnes were raiding from the Wicklow hills upon the fertile plains of Kildare. In A.D. 1333, William De Burgh, third Earl of Ulster, was murdered by Richard De Manneville, his own uncle by marriage; and his estates of right passed to his only daughter and heiress, who afterwards married Lionel, Duke of Clarence. The broad lands, therefore, of the lordships of Connaught and Ulster being in the feeble hands of a defenceless girl, O'Neil seized upon the Ulster territory; and two collaterals of the house of Bourke, Ulick and Edmund, sons of Sir William, divided Connaught, one taking Galway, and the other taking Mayo. The two Bourkes then threw off all allegiance to the English crown, adopted the Irish dress and manners, and took the names of McWilliam Uachtar and McWilliam Iochtar, the "Nether" and "Further" McWilliam. Two of their cousins became McHubbard and McDavid. Other "degenerate" English followed their example and affected the Irish nomenclature. Bermingham of Athenry called himself McYorris; D'Exester became McJordan; and Nangle, McCostelo. The White Knight took the name of McGibbon; the Baron of Dunboyne, McPheris; Fitzmaurice of Lixnaw, McMorice; while the Condons of Waterford became McMajoge, and the Fitzurses of Louth became McMahon.

CHAPTER V.

THE RUIN OF THE ENGLISH COLONY. A.D. 1320–1485.

ULSTER had been lost, and Connaught had revolted. Desmond, though acknowledging a bare allegiance to the king, was virtually independent. Thomond had never been regularly colonized. Only Leinster and Meath remained. Even Leinster was so honeycombed with Irish tribes that little more remained English than the walled towns, and the territories of the great earls of Kildare, and of the earls of Ormonde, who were almost as independent as the earls of Desmond. Of Meath not more than half had survived the encroachments of the McGeoghans and O'Melaghlins. So that we find the actual country where the king's writ ran was an undefined and decreasing district, which became known as "the English land," and which at this time consisted of the counties of Louth, Dublin, and Kildare, and parts of Meath, Tipperary, and Wexford.

The crown had by this time given up the idea of subduing the native Irish as hopeless; and, as it found the Anglo-Irish slipping away from its grasp, its policy became one of self-defence, and developed in two directions. One course pursued was to weaken the great lords, who had grown be-Irished; and to play off one against the other. The second was to prevent the English of the towns and the marches from being absorbed like the English of the outlying country. With the first object in view, the barons were alternately coerced and petted. Sir Anthony Lucy, the lord justice, arrested the young Earl of Desmond and flung him into Dublin Castle, from which he was not liberated till he had undergone eighteen months' imprisonment. Some portions of the Desmond estates were confiscated; and shortly afterwards Edward III., with still larger designs, coolly proposed to resume all royal grants in lieu of certain alleged arrears of debts due to the crown. The outraged Desmond roused the threatened nobility, and held a convention at Kilkenny of the "prelates, earls, barons, and community of Ireland," in opposition to the Parliament which had been summoned to meet at Dublin. In the convention a vigorous protest was made against the king's injustice, and charges of incompetence and dishonesty were launched against the royal officers. Whereupon the king, full of his Continental wars, thought better of his purpose, and let the matter drop. Stronger measures were undertaken under Sir Ralph Ufford, the lord justice, in A.D. 1344, who seized Desmond's estates, treacherously got possession of the castles of Castle-island and Iniskisty in Kerry, and hanged Sir Eustace De la Poer, Sir William Grant, and Sir John Cottrel. But later, when the king was glad to have an Irish contingent in France, we find him conferring knighthood on the Earl of Kildare for his services at the siege of Calais, and Desmond made lord justice.

In pursuance of the other course, it became a ruling principle to fill the offices of state with imported English to the exclusion of the native Anglo-Irish; a proclamation was issued (A.D. 1356) announcing that no one born in Ireland should thenceforth hold a command in any of the king's towns or castles. A distinction is drawn between "the English by birth" and "the English by descent," in favor of the former. The native Irish are "the Irish enemies," the Anglo-Irish are "the Irish rebels." The Anglo-Irish had no part or lot in the government of their own country, and the nominees of the English court absorbed every place of honor or emolument. Edward, in 1361, sent over his third son, Lionel, Duke of Clarence, the titular Earl of Ulster, to fill the office of lord-lieutenant. He treated the nobles with studied disrespect. In his hostings against the tribes, no colonist was permitted to approach his camp. On his third visit to Ireland, in 1367, he held a Parliament at Kilkenny, and passed the act known as "the Statute of Kilkenny,"* with the object of more effectually securing the loyal English from the contagion of Irish manners. The provisions of this statute, which applied only to the "English

---

* 40 Edw. III., Irish Statutes.

land," are a re-enactment and extension of Edward I.'s act of A.D. 1295. Intermarriage, fosterage, gossipred (the practice of standing sponsor), and sale and barter in time of war between the two races, were to be dealt with as felony; as also were submission to the Brehon law, and the practice of coyne and livery. The adoption by an Englishman of the Irish dress, language, and mode of riding entailed a forfeiture of his lands. Creditors were to look to the debtor alone for the payment of his due, and not to all the members of his family, as was the custom of the Irish. The cattle of the Irish pastured on English land without leave of the lord were to be liable to be distrained *damage feasant.* No Irishman was to be inducted into a living, or received into an English monastery. The Irish bards, who were regarded as spies, were forbidden, under pain of imprisonment, to be entertained by the English. The English were prohibited from keeping Irish mercenary troops, or to make war on the natives without leave of the government. Two years later, another act * commanded the return of all absentees on pain of forfeiture of their lands to the crown. These statutes were strong ones, but to have been effectual they required a powerful executive to enforce them; and, as this was wanting, like others of the same character they became a dead letter.

The natives were now assuming the offensive in all parts of the country. Newcastle was assailed by the tribes of Wicklow; the O'Briens threatened Limerick; the McMurroughs, who had been devastating Leinster, were bought off by the payment of a ransom of a hundred marks. The northern barrier, which had already receded from Carrickfergus to Downpatrick, was now found only in the frontier fortress of Dundalk, and New Ross had been captured by Art Kavenagh. Things were going hard with the English land, when Richard II. arrived in Waterford harbor with 30,000 archers and 4000 men-at-arms.

Richard was a person gifted with magnificent conceptions, which it was not given him to realize. He had made up his mind to go in for military glory, and he determined to begin

---

* 42 Edw. III., Irish Statutes.

with Ireland. His policy was, however, one of conciliation tempered with force—force to compel the " Irish enemies " to acknowledge his authority; and conciliation to the " Irish rebels," whom he believed, and not unjustly, to have been alienated by bad government. After some difficulty, he reached Dublin by way of the sea-coast, and summoned all the Irish chieftains to meet him there. Alarmed at the strength of the English army, as their forefathers had been at Henry II.'s display of force, the great chiefs came in — O'Neil, O'Brien, O'Connor, McMurrough, and many others, seventy-five in all. Richard entertained them with great magnificence, and received their submission. They bound themselves by their bonds to be loyal subjects, and to answer for the good behavior of their dependents. The Wicklow chiefs, in consideration of a pension to be paid to them, agreed to remove to other territories which the king undertook to provide; Richard intending to settle a colony in that stronghold of turbulence—and in this way the first idea of a "plantation" was formulated. The king published a free pardon to all the disaffected Anglo-Irish; and took vigorous steps to reform both the corrupt bench and the complicated civil procedure. Suspicions, however, being entertained with respect to McMurrough, the most daring and dangerous of the chieftains, he was thrown into prison; and, though soon set at liberty on giving hostages for his good behavior, he conceived a determined hatred of the English, which was not lessened by a subsequent attempt to entrap him. The king, conceiving that he had come, seen, and conquered, shortly returned to England to deal with the Lollard movement; leaving Roger Mortimer, the young Earl of March, his cousin and heir-apparent, at the head of the government. No sooner was Richard's back turned, and the government proceeded to carry out the plantation of Wicklow, than McMurrough rose in rebellion, captured Carlow, and defeated the royal troops at Kells; the young Earl of March being among the slain.

Richard's anger was now thoroughly roused. He perceived that the submission of the chiefs was nothing but a blind; and he at once determined to begin his work all over again. He sailed from Milford with a magnificent army and a fleet of two hundred sail, in A.D. 1399, and again landed at Waterford. He marched to Kilkenny; and thence plunged into McMurrough's country, in hopes of inducing him to give battle. But the wary chief knew better than to risk an engagement, and, retreating into the forests of Carlow, confined himself to harassing the royal army and cutting off stragglers. Richard now found himself in difficulties. In the midst of a hostile country, with no transport and no commissariat, he endeavored to cut his way to the coast. After a weary march, in which his troops suffered terribly from hunger, he at length reached the seashore, where his famished soldiers were relieved by the approach of his provision ships. Having narrowly escaped disaster, he a second time made his way to Dublin by way of the coast, and at once set to work to reduce Leinster to submission by the despatch of flying columns to scour the country. But before he had time to carry out his designs, the fatal news reached him of Bolingbroke's landing at Ravenspur, and he hurried back to England, and left Ireland to take care of itself.

The latest attempt to subdue Ireland by means of an English army had signally failed. England, which had for the last hundred years been occupied with foreign and border wars, was now about to be plunged into the bloody civil broils raised by the rival houses of York and Lancaster. No attention could be paid to Ireland; much less could expense be incurred on its account. And so the remnant of the English settlement was allowed to struggle on alone against the insurgent tribes. The "English land," or the "English Pale," as it grew to be called, was now reduced to the county of Dublin, and parts of Meath, Louth, and Kildare; and dikes and forts were built round its borders for the protection of the inhabitants. The sea-coast towns were isolated; and the great earls of Desmond and Ormonde received licenses to absent themselves from the Parliament at Dublin by reason of the danger and difficulty of passing through the Irish enemy's country. The native Irish had recovered the greater portion of the island: exacting tribute from the few English settlers who remained, and demanding and receiving "black rent" from the surviving English counties.

THE RUIN OF THE ENGLISH COLONY.

The houses of the Red and White Roses found keen partisans among both the Anglo-Irish and the natives. Richard, Duke of York, was lord-lieutenant for ten years, and during that time had become popular with both the one and the other. The house of Ormonde adhered to the Red Rose; the two great branches of the Geraldines, the earls of Desmond and Kildare, sided with the White. Many of both races fought in England during the civil war, as their forefathers had fought under the English flag in Wales and Scotland; and several Irish chiefs fell with Richard at Wakefield. This drain on the English of the Pale still further diminished their power to resist the raids of the natives. Left to themselves, they struggled for a bare existence. The government was in such low water in A.D. 1480 that the whole military establishment consisted of but eighty mounted archers and forty mounted "spears;" while the exchequer could barely show an annual revenue of £600. In self-defence, the colonists, finding the government unable to protect them, formed themselves into a fraternity of arms called "The Brotherhood of Saint George." Thirteen gentlemen were chosen from the four counties of the Pale, who met annually to choose a captain, and maintained a hundred and twenty mounted archers, forty horsemen, and forty pages for the protection of the English border. Panic legislation was also resorted to in the hopes of carrying out the intention of the Statute of Kilkenny, an act perpetually renewed, habitually set at nought, and constantly evaded by licenses of exemption. The colonists were empowered * to take the law into their own hands; and to take, kill, and behead all persons found thieving or robbing by night or by day, or suspected of that intent; to treat as Irish enemies, and to take the goods of, imprison, and demand a ransom for, all persons who did not shave the upper lip at least once a fortnight. To trade with the native Irish was made felony,† and natives who had dealings with the "English lieges" within the Pale were to be treated as the king's enemies.‡ All Irish who dwelt within the Pale were

---

* 5 Edw. IV. c. 2, Irish Statutes.   † 25 Hen. VI. c. 24, Irish Statutes.
‡ 10 Hen. VI. c. 5, Irish Statutes.

to assume English names, dress, and growth of hair, on pain of forfeiture of their goods.*

The spirit of these acts sufficiently indicates the helpless feebleness of the English government; and the powerlessness of the executive is apparent when we find a precarious respite allowed to the four shires by the Irish chieftains upon the payment of an annual tribute. O'Neil received £20 from the barony of Lecale and £40 from the County of Louth; O'Connor of Offaly received £60 from the County of Meath and £20 from the County of Kildare; McMurrough of Leinster received eighty marks from the crown. Even the walled towns, which had hitherto maintained their independence, now purchased protection by the payment of an annual cess: Dundalk attorning to O'Neil; Wexford to McMurrough; Limerick to O'Brien of Thomond; Galway to O'Connor; Cork to Cormac McTeig; and Kilkenny and Tipperary to O'Carrol of Ely. The lord deputy was within a measurable distance of being driven into the sea.

---

* 5 Edw. IV. c. 3, Irish Statutes.

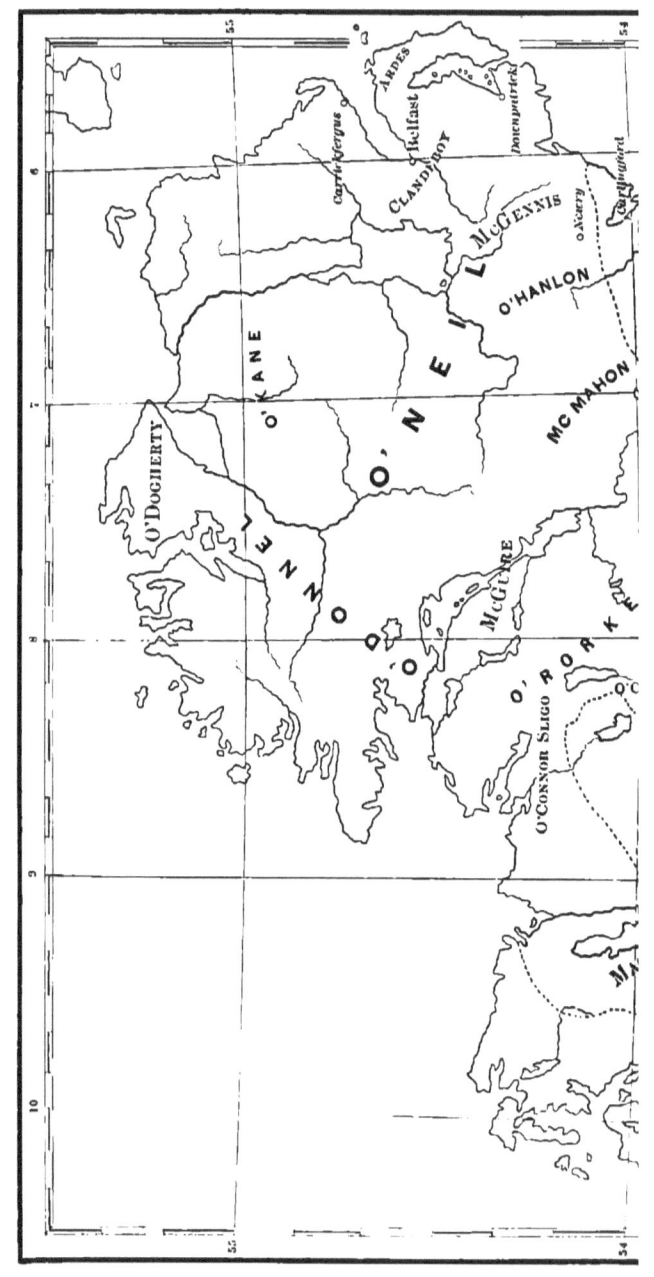

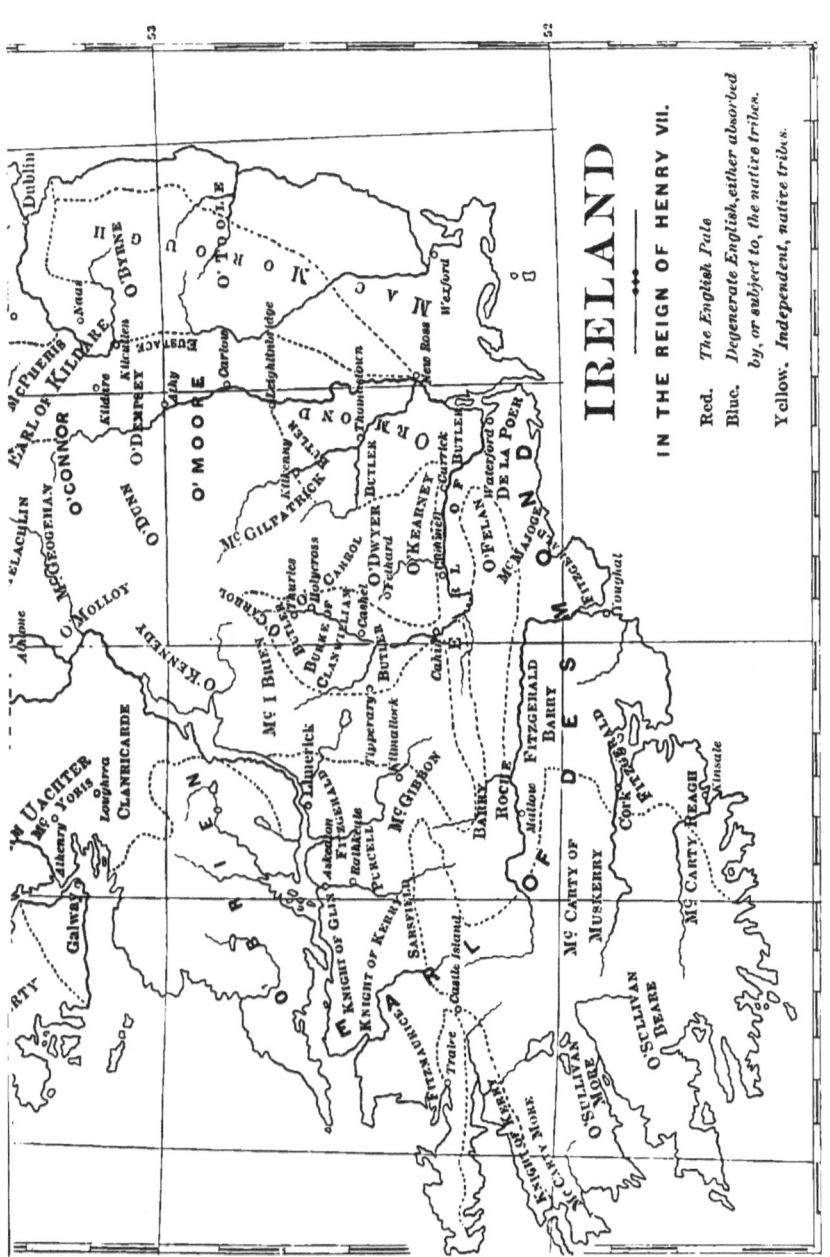

Book III.
THE FIRST CONQUEST

CHAPTER I.
THE TURN OF THE TIDE. A.D. 1485-1509.

THE English government had now almost reached its lowest pitch of disaster; and with the rise of the Tudor dynasty we find indications that the tide was beginning to turn. England, distracted with foreign wars and civil strife, had for two hundred years allowed the Irish question to drift. She was now about to take matters seriously in hand, and to carry out a stern policy of repression and extermination, not only against the Celtic race, but against the Anglo-Irish also. Henceforth we shall find but little distinction made between the natives and the old colonists—if any, it was in favor of the former—and a disposition to make a fresh conquest and a fresh settlement, and to subordinate the old blood to the new. "The English by birth" were to be the children of promise; "the English by descent" were to be the sons of Ishmael.

Henry VII. did not at first pay much attention to his Irish dominions. He left the government in the hands of the Earl of Kildare, notwithstanding the strong Yorkist proclivities of the family of the Geraldines. It was true that he was as much an Irish chief as an English peer, but from his influence with the native tribes he was too useful as well as too powerful to strike at at present. It was when Ireland had become a source of danger in being the rallying-point of every impostor started by the Duchess of Burgundy, that the king began to tighten his grasp.

Lambert Simnel had been crowned in the capital, by the Bishop of Meath, with a diadem taken from the head of an image of the Virgin in the nunnery of St. Mary les Dames. Two thousand Germans, under Marshal Schwartz, had landed at Dublin with the earls of Lincoln and Lovell. Kildare had openly espoused the pretender's cause. Kildare's brother had resigned the office of chancellor to accompany the *soi-disant* Earl of Warwick to England, and had fallen in the overthrow of Stoke. But Kildare was forgiven for the present, and confirmed for a time in his office of lord deputy. Four years later Perkin Warbeck had landed at Cork, and had been patronized by the Earl of Desmond. The earl and the Flemish Jew had beleaguered Waterford. They had been compelled to raise the siege; and this time Kildare did not commit himself; but the suspicious king had dismissed him from office, and raised up his rival Ormonde in his room.

The Parliament of Dublin, a packed body representing nothing, had been the pliant instrument of Kildare's treason. As long ago as Henry VI.'s reign this same Parliament, in A.D. 1459—when Richard, Duke of York, had fled from England, after the fight at Blore Heath, and resumed his position of lord-lieutenant—had presumed to act independently of England: to choose its own viceroy in the person of Richard; to assert its right to be bound only by its own laws;* to declare that writs could issue only under the great seal of Ireland; and to extend shelter to English political refugees. Such possibilities were to be put an end to, and all danger of independent action set at rest forever. Parliament was to become the convenient tool of the crown, instead of that of the earls of Kildare.

The Parliament of Ireland, which, before the ruin of the settlement, was summoned with great formality and sat with tolerable regularity, had degenerated into a somewhat anomalous body. The Upper House consisted of the lay peers, many of whom, like the earls of Desmond and Ormonde, claimed and received exemptions from attendance; the abbots and priors, who preferred generally to abide in their ecclesiastical quarters; and the bishops, most of whom were absentees from their dioceses. The Lower House consisted of the knights of the shires, which, with the exception of those within the Pale, were in the hands of the Irish enemy, and returned no members; and burgesses from a few of the towns, who were summoned, much against their will, for the purpose of packing the

---

* 37 Hen. VI., Irish Statutes.

assembly, or of being squeezed into giving a money grant. Many were not elected by the freemen of the city at all, but received the royal writ directed to them personally by name. When the bishops and abbots were unable to attend, they sent their proctors to represent them; and a practice grew up of summoning two proctors regularly from each diocese, who sat with the knights and burgesses, and claimed to be members of the legislature, and to have a free right of suffrage on every question as representatives of the clergy in the Lower House.

Parliament was originally a great council of the barons, the prelates, and "the faithful,"* who met to deal with matters of state, to advise upon the raising of money, and to register the king's decrees, which, upon enrolment, had the force of statutes. The obligation to be summoned and the privilege of sitting, in the case of the temporal peers, was originally founded on the feudal tenure of their baronies; and in the case of the spiritual peers on that of their lay fees. Knights of the shire were first summoned about the middle,† and burgesses towards the end,‡ of the thirteenth century. The lords spiritual and temporal all sat together until the reign of Henry IV. They met at irregular intervals when summoned by the king's lieutenant or his deputy, or the lord justice for the time being, in times of emergency, and for the purpose of granting subsidies. Sometimes they met at Dublin, sometimes at Kilkenny or Drogheda; and in the thirty-third year of Edward III.§ (1359) we find the peers, abbots, bishops, and commons of Leinster summoned to Dublin on December 7th, and those of Munster summoned to Waterford on December 14th.

A scratch assembly, as the Irish Parliament in effect was, might in time have grown into a constitutional body. It was, in fact, the nucleus of a representative system. Its vitality, usefulness, and power of development were effectually stunted by the policy of Henry VII.

That monarch sent over to Ireland, in 1494, Sir Edward

---
* King's writ, 6 John.
† King's writ, 37 Hen. III.; Irish Statutes, 48 Hen. III., and 53 Hen. III.
‡ King's writ, 10 Edw. I.; Irish Statutes, 23 Edw. I., 28 Edw. I.
§ King's writ, 33 Edw. III.

Poynings as lord deputy, and several eminent lawyers, with a thousand men-at-arms. His avowed intention was to thrust back the native Irish; his real object was to crush the adherents of Warbeck. With this purpose in view, he marched, with both Ormonde and Kildare in his train, against O'Hanlon and McGennis in Ulster. Meantime a brother of Kildare seized the castle of Carlow and raised the Yorkist flag. Poynings patched up matters with the native chiefs, and turned on the mutinous Geraldine. Short shrift was made with the rebels, and the victorious deputy proceeded to summon a Parliament at Drogheda.

The first branch of the legislation here initiated was for the benefit of the natives, and the protection of the inhabitants of the Pale from the exactions of the great lords. It was declared to be high-treason to excite the natives to war. Private hostilities were forbidden unless with the license of the lord deputy, as was also the practice of coyne and livery. The owners of march lands were to reside on their estates; and it was made felony to permit the Irish enemy or Irish rebels to pass the borders. The citizens and freemen of the towns were forbidden to become the retainers of the lords; and apprentices only were to be admitted to be freemen of the corporations. The judges and chief officers of state were henceforth to hold office only during the king's pleasure, instead of for life. And the Statute of Kilkenny was re-enacted, with the exception of the provisions relating to the use of the Irish language, and the non-use of saddles, both of which practices had become so universal that it was thought to be hopeless to forbid them.*

The next branch of legislation was directed against the independence of the Irish legislature, and effectually subordinated it to that of England. The intention was that a benevolent monarch should be able to curb the enterprise of a lawless nobility. The real effect of it was to enslave the Parliament. It was provided† that all statutes which had up to that date

---

* 10 Hen. VII. cc. 13, 17, Irish Statutes.
† cc. 4, 22, Irish Statutes.

been passed by the English legislature should thenceforward be binding and effectual in Ireland; that no Parliament should in future be summoned in Ireland till the lord deputy had first obtained the king's license for its being held, and had submitted to the king and the privy council the heads of all bills which it was proposed should be brought in; and that the consent of the king and the council to such bills should be obtained before they could be proceeded with. Thus, in effect, making all legislation to come cut and dried from the crown, and to be merely *pro formâ* registered by the Irish Houses of Parliament.

The opportunity was now taken of aiming a blow at the lords of the Pale, and to make an example of the Earl of Kildare. The last act of the Parliament of Drogheda was to attaint him for high-treason, on the ground of his intimacy with the native Irish, and his being privy to his brother James's exploits at Carlow. He was then sent in custody to England. His blunt boldness, however, seems to have disarmed Henry's suspicions, and to have persuaded him that an act of clemency would convert him into a useful adherent. The earl was therefore set at liberty in August, 1496, and sent back to Ireland as lord deputy. This policy of turning the poacher into a keeper was eminently successful. Thenceforth Kildare continued Henry's faithful retainer, and his energy and influence over the native Irish maintained the power of the crown within the marches of the Pale as it had not been for two generations. He rebuilt the ruined towns of Leinster, and built castles on the borders of the Pale; he made raids into Desmond, and forced garrisons upon the cities of Cork and Kinsale, which had shown a disposition to support Warbeck. He penetrated into Connaught to curb the growing power of the Bourkes, and into Ulster to support his nephew, Turlough O'Neil, in a quarrel with another of the O'Neil family,* capturing the castles of Athleague, Roscommon, Castlereagh, and Kinard, and handing them over to his Irish allies. Ulick Bourke, Lord of Clan-

---

* Turlough's father, Henry O'Neil, had married Kildare's sister, the Lady Eleanora Fitzgerald.

ricarde, who had a private quarrel with the lord deputy, then formed a league against him, with O'Brien of Thomond and other Munster chieftains. Kildare marched against them with the men of the Pale and the trained bands of Dublin, and a strong native contingent sent by Turlough O'Neil. The two armies met at Knocktow, near Galway, and the lord deputy defeated the leaguers with great slaughter.

Though originating in a family feud, which developed into a struggle between the confederate tribes of the northeast and those of the southwest, the battle of Knocktow marks the turning of the tide in favor of the crown. It indicated the disposition and ability of the English to take the offensive, and taught the Irish, both "enemies" and "rebels," that in their intestine conflicts victory was found on the side where the English sword was thrown into the scale. It displayed the assumption of new vigor on the part of the executive, and sent forth a warning note that the days of English impotence were drawing to a close.

CHAPTER II.

THE REHABILITATION OF THE ENGLISH GOVERNMENT.
A.D. 1509-1540.

HENRY VIII. was now King of England, and he and his astute minister Wolsey were busy evolving a Tudor policy for Ireland. In England the old nobility had been decimated by the civil war, and a new nobility was springing up more dependent upon the royal favor. Parliament, under Wolsey's advice summoned but seldom, was becoming discredited and harmless. The atmosphere of domestic affairs was at present clear, and Henry's foreign policy was to balance the French king against the Hispano-German emperor. England had now leisure to turn her attention to Ireland. The time was come for the struggle to begin between the crown and the great Anglo-Irish lords.

Henry was determined that the Irish scandal should continue no longer. The same reports were made to him of the prevailing anarchy, by council, judges, and agents. The times were urgent, and the drifting system had been too long permitted. Two distinct courses were the constant subject of discussion between the king and the Irish government. The latter warmly advocated a policy of extermination and plantation. The Irish were to be driven from their lands; the chiefs deposed; the cattle, their principal source of wealth and subsistence, driven off or slaughtered; and the whole native population decimated by starvation. The land was then to be granted out to English freeholders, who should pay a head rent to the crown. Henry shrank from the expense, if not from the brutality, of such a course. His plan was coercion and conciliation. The power of the crown was to be exerted, and order maintained. Overtures were then to be made to the native chiefs, to induce them to give allegiance to the king;

and the prospect of royal favors was to be held out to them. "Sober ways, politic drifts, and amiable persuasions, founded on law and reason," were to be used to draw them gradually into the appreciation of English laws, manners, and habits; and to convince them of the material benefits they would derive from holding their land in fee as grantees from the crown instead of by the shadowy, elective life tenure which was given them by the Brehon law. Henry, as was his way, chose his own line, and the extermination and plantation policy was shelved for the present.

Wolsey hated the Geraldines. He saw them setting the crown at defiance through their powerful Irish connection, having intermarried with the families of half the native princes in the island. He saw them, through their power to raise or quell at their pleasure the turbulence of the Irish, force themselves upon the crown as the only persons able to carry on the government. Henry VII., it was said, when told that all Ireland could not govern the Earl of Kildare, had exclaimed, "Then shall he govern all Ireland," and promptly made him lord deputy. This great Geraldine had died in 1513, in the midst of a campaign against the O'Carrols of Ely. His son and successor Gerald, the ninth earl, had stepped into his father's shoes. The council had elected him lord justice on his father's death, and he had shortly afterwards been appointed by letters-patent from the crown. He inherited all his father's popularity with the natives; and for several years was, like him, at once a necessity and a source of anxiety to the English government.

Henry began to feel his way by aiming several tentative strokes at Kildare. The house of Butler had always been firmly attached to the Red Rose and the Tudor cause; and was traditionally a rival of the Geraldine house. The earls of Ormonde had never fallen away from English habits and cultivated the natives to the same extent as the Kildares, or the still more degenerate Fitzgeralds of Desmond. The king accordingly summoned the lord deputy to England to answer certain charges of allying himself with the " Irish enemies;" and first the Earl of Surrey, who was connected with the house of Ormonde by marriage, and shortly afterwards Sir Piers Butler, the head of the house, was put in his place. Kildare, after a three years' sojourn at the English court, during which he secured influential friends by marrying the Lady Elizabeth Gray, a daughter of the Marquis of Dorset, succeeded in exculpating himself, and returned to his government. Again was he charged with treasonable practices—this time for neglecting to arrest the Desmond, who was coquetting with Francis I.—was summoned to England, and thrown into the Tower. Enlarged through the intrigues of his high connections, he again returned to Ireland, as adviser to the new lord deputy Sir William Skeffington, whom he shortly superseded.

A third time the attack was made, and charges of treason preferred; and this time the blow fell heavily. He reluctantly passed over to England, leaving his son Lord Thomas to act as vice-deputy, and was a second time lodged in the Tower. But this stroke was not aimed at the earl alone: the whole Fitzgerald family were to feel the weight of the king's arm. With the view of forcing the hand of the Geraldines, letters were written and conveyed to Dublin stating that Kildare had been executed. His son Lord Thomas—Silken Thomas, as he was popularly called, on account of the richness of his apparel—on hearing the news, rushed before the council sitting in St. Mary's Abbey, threw down the sword of state, with which, as vice-deputy, he had been invested, and renounced his allegiance to the king. A futile revolt was sprung. An attempt was made, and failed, to represent it as raised in defence of the Catholic faith. The Pale was overrun with the retainers of the house of Fitzgerald, and a desultory siege of Dublin was begun, and raised, twice over. The royalist archbishop Allen, who had been Wolsey's chaplain, was caught in an attempt to escape to England, and ruthlessly murdered. Ormonde marched from the south. The tardy reinforcements under Skeffington arrived from England; and, throwing a garrison into his castle of Maynooth, Lord Thomas retired into the country of the Irish enemy to stir up the O'Moores of Leix and the O'Connors of Offaly to his assistance, and to intrigue with Spain and Rome.

And now there came into play a circumstance which marks the change from the old to the new order of things. Skeffington had brought with him a train of artillery, with which he laid siege to the castle of Maynooth. This fortress was believed to be impregnable, and no doubt, if sufficiently provisioned, under the old system of warfare it was so. Skeffington's guns breached the walls in twelve days, an assault was made, and the castle was taken. Hitherto the English and the Irish had been pretty evenly matched in point of fighting power. The more disciplined troops of the former had perhaps the best of it in the field; but the tactics of the Irish, mounted on their fleeter and more wiry horses, were to retire into the more difficult country, and to close up in the rear of the enemy and harass them with intermittent attacks. When there was fighting, it was hand to hand. The sword and the spear were the ordinary weapons on both sides. The skill in archery, which had made the English infantry so formidable, had been to a great extent lost, even in the four shires, notwithstanding repeated statutes* which enjoined the constant use of the bow. The great lords, secure in their stone castles, could defy both the Irish enemy and the royal troops, and laugh at a besieging force, till it was compelled from want of supplies to raise the siege and give up the raid. The invention of gunpowder put an end to the old fashion of warfare, and changed the relative position of the parties. The siege train of the lord deputy battered down the Norman castles about the ears of their owners. The introduction of hand-guns and field-cannon gave a small force of the king's troops a tremendous advantage over the half-naked and ill-armed kerns and gallowglasses. These terrible engines of destruction were necessarily a monopoly in the hands of the English government; the Irish having no such thing as an arsenal, or factory for arms and ammunition.

The fall of Maynooth crushed the rebellion. Silken Thomas, unable to raise the native tribes, surrendered on condition that his life was spared, and was sent to the Tower, where his father, on hearing of his son's revolt, had already died of a

---

* Irish Statutes, 5 Edw. IV. cc. 4, 5; 12 Edw. IV. c. 2; 10 Hen. VII. c. 9.

broken heart. The late earl had five brothers, three of whom it was known had strongly discountenanced the rebellion. But the ruin of the Geraldines was to be achieved by no half-measures. The five brothers were invited to a feast given by the lord-deputy, where they were treacherously made prisoners, and forwarded to the same prison-house as their unfortunate nephew. After lingering in prison for a twelvemonth, both they and Silken Thomas, notwithstanding the terms of his surrender, were all of them hanged at Tyburn; and the heir to the house of Fitzgerald, a boy of twelve, and son of the late earl by his second wife, found a refuge with Cardinal Pole at the Roman court.

The long-meditated blow at the house of Kildare had fallen at last. The effect was prodigious; the consternation of both Irish enemies and Irish rebels was complete. If not Kildare, who could withstand the crown? Nor was Ireland left in doubt upon the point. Lord Leonard Gray, who, on Skeffington's death, was made lord deputy, at once proceeded to enforce his authority upon the country. He reduced O'Connor of Offaly, and burned his stronghold; he marched upon the Shannon, and destroyed O'Brien's bridge, which was protected at each end by a tower of hewn marble, and had laid the Pale at the mercy of every raid from Thomond; he dashed into County Cork, and reduced the Munster Geraldines and the rebellious Barrys; he captured the important castle of Athlone, the key of the west, and overawed the Bourkes; he broke the power of the north by giving O'Neil a crushing defeat at Belahoe, in the barony of Farney, in Monaghan.

Such was the reputation of Lord Leonard Gray; and so rigorously did he enforce respect for the authority of the crown that in the two years during which he governed Ireland, prior to his departure for England in 1540, tranquillity hitherto unexampled reigned over the whole island, and a cessation prevailed both from rebellion and from internecine bloodshed.

CHAPTER III.

THE CONFISCATION OF THE CHURCH LANDS. A.D. 1527–1537.

In the meantime, Henry had quarrelled with the Pope, and was compelling with a high hand a reform in the discipline of the Church of England. His quarrel with the Pope, it will be remembered, arose from the refusal of the latter to allow Henry to divorce his wife, with whom for twenty years he had lived in conjugal felicity, but who was now middle-aged, and the mother of but one surviving child, and that a daughter. Wolsey had fallen a victim to the interests of the Boleyn faction, who believed him to be adverse to the divorce, and to Henry's impatience at his inability to influence Clement VII.

The inflexible will of Henry's new minister, Thomas Cromwell, was now guiding the royal counsels. At his suggestion, the king had declared himself "the only supreme lord and head of the Church and clergy in England." Convocation had been coerced into tendering its "submission," and the Pope's jurisdiction was ousted from the country.

A reform in the manners, morals, and discipline of the clergy had been called for by public opinion; a commission of inquiry into the condition of the religious houses had before been issued by Wolsey, who had himself suppressed some of the lesser monasteries. Cromwell, the king's "vicar-general," had relentlessly carried out the course initiated by Wolsey. One thousand religious houses, both great and small, were dissolved within the space of four years, and their lands and revenues appropriated by the crown. There were two parties in England who advocated Church reform, whose notions of what constituted reform were widely different. There were those who wished to wipe out abuses, and to remain in communion with Rome; there was the more advanced party, which protested against Romish heresies, and was determined to break away from Rome altogether. Henry, however, though he held strong opinions on purgatory, indulgences, and the worship of relics and images, hated the "Lutheran heresy," and lived and died a "good Catholic." And though both Cromwell and many of the bishops in heart sympathized with, and promoted, the interests of the Protestants, the king put to death Protestants and Romanists alike for denying the old doctrine of transubstantiation and the new doctrine of the royal supremacy.

Henry, having carried his point in England, proceeded to do the same in the sister isle. The only opposition likely to be met with was from the clergy, who smelt heresy afar off. But the mass of the Irish people, both natives and colonists, had hardly so much as heard of Lutheranism. The English lords and Irish chiefs looked on the king's usurpation of the headship of the Church as a matter of complete indifference, only concerning himself and the Pope; and, never having had the smallest scruple themselves in burning and plundering churches, cathedrals, and monasteries, were ready enough to see the Church lands appropriated when there was a prospect of having a share in the spoil.

There was considerably less ground for dissolving the religious houses in Ireland than those in England. The charge of immoral and sumptuous living was not even attempted. It was true that, as in England, they were corporations holding large tracts of land in mortmain; but, in the hideous condition of turbulence and poverty in which society in Ireland then groaned, the religious houses, like those on the Continent in the Middle Ages, were as lamps in the darkness and as rivers in a thirsty land. Though frequently plundered by all contending parties, they held together the fragments of learning and enlightenment, which would otherwise have died out. They, to some extent, occupied the position of universities and schools, being the only places where any education could be obtained. They served as inns and hostelries, where any who travelled from place to place could obtain accommodation, and frequently provided the lord deputy himself with food, forage, and lodging. Like the houses in England, they dispensed charity to the needy, and, unlike the houses in England, themselves served the ruined parish churches instead of absorbing the revenue and appointing a vicar on a pittance to do the work. These pleas, however, were not considered by Henry. He had abolished the abbeys, the priories, the monasteries, and the nunneries in England, and he would do the same in Ireland. Besides, he wanted their property for purposes of his own.

In the year 1537, Lord Leonard Gray summoned a Parliament for the purpose of carrying the Act of Supremacy. The lay element was pliant enough; but a sturdy resistance was met with from the clergy. The abbots and priors firmly opposed the bill in the Upper House; the proctors used every artifice of obstruction to prevent its passing in the Lower. So persevering were they in their efforts to defeat the measure that the lord deputy was compelled to prorogue the Parliament in order to deal with the obstructionists. During the recess the privy council determined that the proctors had usurped the right of speaking and voting; that they were only summoned as counsellors and assistants, and were "neither members nor parcel of the body of Parliament." On the reassembling of the Houses, a short bill* was run through, excluding them from all "voice and suffrage" in the legislature; and the mouth of the proctors being stopped—though the argument of usurpation of privileges by long custom would have applied equally to the English House of Commons to do more than vote a subsidy—matters went on swimmingly enough. The Act of Supremacy † was passed; and others which prohibited appeals to Rome, ‡ which gave the first-fruits of the clergy to the king instead of to the Pope, § which suppressed thirteen abbeys, ‖ and resumed to the crown the estates of absentees. ¶

By the act ** of 1537, and by a subsequent statute in 1542, †† all the property of the religious houses which had been or "ought to" be "surrendered" to his majesty was vested in the crown. The houses confiscated numbered upwards of four hundred. The personalty was valued at £100,000, and the land yielded an annual revenue of £32,000. Pensions of va-

---

* 28 Hen. VIII. c. 12.   † c. 5.   ‡ c. 6.   § cc. 8, 26.
‖ c. 16.   ¶ c. 3.   ** c. 16.   †† 33 Hen. VIII. c. 5.

rious amounts were given to the heads of houses and to most of the brethren, in consideration of orderly self-effacement. The "surrendering" was, of course, compulsory. Opposition was met by imprisonment, as in the case of the abbot of St. Mary's, Thurles. Many of the smaller houses became parish churches; the revenues of a few of the larger were transferred to the bishoprics in connection with them. The bulk of the land surveyed in Henry's reign was granted, either for a real or a nominal price, to the Englishmen composing the king's council in Dublin, the corporate towns, and some of the Irish and Anglo-Irish chiefs; the principal recipients being the judges, the lords of the Pale, and a few officers of the army.

CHAPTER IV.

THE WINNING OF THE CHIEFTAINS. A.D. 1540–1550.

HENRY had imposed his will upon the Church, and upon the Parliament of the Pale. He had overawed the great lords; he had exhibited his strength to the native Irish tribes; and to some extent had re-established order. It remained for him to carry out his policy of conciliation. Overtures were now made to the native chiefs; to the Earl of Desmond, who had been in open revolt, and had endeavored to strike up an alliance with Charles V.; and to other recalcitrant nobles of Munster. Both Irish enemies and Irish rebels were half ruined with their everlasting petty warfare. They had learned to dread the strong arm of the king; and they had before their eyes the example of the Earl of Ormonde, who had been promised, and had obtained, a portion of the plunder of the Church lands, on his engaging to uphold the king's supremacy against the pope. Sir Anthony St. Leger was now lord deputy; and he conducted the negotiations with great address. McMurrough of Carlow sent in his submission; the O'Dempsys, the O'Duns, and O'Moores, of Leix, followed; so did O'Connor of Offaly; so did the O'Molloys, the O'Melaghlins, and the McGeoghans, of Meath. Then came the O'Carrols of Tipperary, the O'Tooles and the O'Byrnes of Wicklow. The Earl of Desmond came in, and McYoris of Athenry, and McWilliam, Lord of Clanricarde. O'Brien of Thomond at first held back, and so did the chiefs of the north.

St. Leger summoned a parliament at Dublin; and then was seen a sight which had never been witnessed in Ireland before—the English lords and the Irish chiefs sitting beside each other in a national assembly. The Earl of Ormonde with McGilapatrick of Upper Ossory; the Earl of Desmond, and the lords Barry, Roche, and Fitzmaurice, with the Tanist of Thomond;

the barons of the Pale with O'Moore, O'Reilly, and McMurrough; Lord Bermingham of Athenry, and McWilliam Bourke. The speaker's address concerning the business of the session was translated into Irish by Ormonde. The Act of Supremacy was accepted and confirmed; and a bill* was passed conferring on Henry and his heirs the title of King, instead of Lord, of Ireland. The chiefs flung down their girdles, skenes, and caps in acknowledgment of Henry as their liege lord. Dublin was *en fête*: bonfires were lit, guns fired, wine flowed in the street; all prisoners, except those detained on capital charges, were set at liberty; and a general pardon was published by the king throughout all his dominions.

Soon O'Brien of Thomond and O'Neil and O'Donnel agreed, by indenture, to be faithful to Henry. The royal favors were then distributed; many of the leading chiefs being persuaded to pay a visit to the English court, that they might be impressed with the king's might and the resources of England, and be convinced of the futility of a struggle with their neighbor should she choose to put forth her strength.

Under the commission for the suppression of the religious houses, issued in 1538, twenty-four abbeys and priories were compulsorily surrendered to the crown. The first attacked were those of the Pale, which were the only ones which could be reached. But it was in Leinster and Munster that by far the largest proportion were situated. Those which were beyond the practical extent of the English jurisdiction were left to a more convenient season, and many of these were not surveyed till the reigns of Elizabeth and James, a few escaping the notice of the commissioners altogether. The Church lands which had not, up to this time, fallen within the king's grasp, by reason of their being situated in the Irish and Anglo-Irish country, were, on the submission of the chieftains of these territories, handed over to them as a reward for their newly found loyalty. All the abbeys and benefices in Thomond, excepting bishoprics, were granted to O'Brien, who was created Earl of Thomond for life and Baron Inchiquin. The great Abbey of

---

* 33 Hen. VIII. c. 1.

Clare was given to the Tanist of Thomond, who was made Baron Ibrackan, and granted the earldom of Thomond in reversion, on the death of his uncle, the chieftain of the tribe. The monasteries of Aghadoe and Aghmacarte were given to McGilapatrick, who took the name of Fitzpatrick, and was created Baron of Upper Ossory. McWilliam Bourke was made Earl of Clanricarde, and received extensive Church lands in Galway. McMurrough took the name of Kavenagh, and became Baron of Ballyan. It was arranged that O'Connor should become Baron of Offaly, and O'Donnel was promised the earldom of Tyrconnel; but their patents were never made out. Con O'Neil was created Earl of Tyrone, and his bastard son Baron of Dungannon. Large sums of money were also distributed among the Irish chiefs, and to each was assigned a house in Dublin for his occupation during the sitting of Parliament, "that they might suck in civility with the court air."

Formal indentures were entered into between the king and the tribal chieftains. The greater chiefs agreed to hold their lands of the king according to English law, to encourage agriculture, and to conform to English habits. They were to come to the king's courts for justice, to attend in their places in Parliament, and to provide a contingent to the lord deputy's forces when required; to send their sons to be educated at the English court, and to renounce the authority of the Pope. The lesser chiefs promised allegiance, agreed to pay a head rent for their cattle, and to turn out with all their men to assist the lord deputy in his wars. The king in return engaged to protect their lands from invasion, and to permit them to manage their own affairs within their own territory.

The principal inducement, however, to the greater chieftains to accept the king's suzerainty was the alteration in the tenure of the land. Henry insisted on the old fraud practised by the Plantagenets of recognizing the feudal laws as the laws of the country, and shutting his eyes to the Irish system of tenure. The chief surrendered his territory to the king, and the king regranted it to him to hold of the crown by knight's service. The king was benefited by obtaining a recognition of his sovereign rights, and the invaluable leverage of the law of forfeiture for treason incident to the English tenure. The chief was benefited by getting a grant in fee to himself and his heirs of the land, which never was his, which belonged to his tribe, and of which he was only the demesne lord for life by virtue of the will of the tribesmen. The arrangement was colorable and collusive, and in effect confiscated every acre in the island. Though the practical effect was not at first apparent, the foundation was laid for a huge future injustice.

The tribesmen themselves were wholly ignorant of the effect of what had taken place; but the submission of their lords was unpopular, and grudgingly acquiesced in. In many cases the newly created peers found the tribal dissatisfaction forcibly brought home to them. The new Earls of Thomond and Clanricarde, and the new Baron Ibrackan, on their return from the ceremony of inauguration at Greenwich, found portions of their countries in revolt. And the sons of O'Neil and O'Donnel, who had got some inkling of the juggle which was being played about the property of the tribe, headed the clansmen in a refusal to accept the new order of things. Fighting followed, and the peace was only restored in Thomond and Galway by the intervention of the deputy, who led his troops to support his fledgling nobility, and in the north by the overthrow of young O'Donnel by his father; while the schism in the O'Neil family was fought out between the new Baron of Dungannon, Mathew the bastard, and John or Shane O'Neil the legitimate son, who was clear-sighted enough to contend that by the law of Tanistry his father had nothing but a life-interest in the chieftaincy, and that the king had no power to settle the inheritance by the feudal laws.

The success of Henry's policy was greater and more immediate than could have been expected. Both Irish chiefs and Anglo-Irish lords kept to their bargain; and there seemed a fair prospect of Ireland becoming a united and loyal portion of the dominions of the crown. In ten years' time we find the lord chancellor, Sir Thomas Cusacke, reporting to the Duke of Northumberland that the king's circuits were held in the counties of Cork, Limerick, and Kerry; that the sheriffs were obeyed; and that Desmond, Roche, Barry, and Fitzmaurice were sitting as magistrates in petty sessions. The new peers were quiet, and studying to conform to the law; and were each prepared with their contingent for the support of order. Where depredations had been made by the natives, fines had been paid by the chiefs. In Fercal, roads were being cut through the forests; in Clanricarde, lands were coming under the plough; in Tipperary, the lives and property of travellers were respected, and cattle and agricultural implements could safely be left unguarded in the fields. It seemed as if the old days of lawlessness and tumult were passing away, and that those of progress and civilization were about to take their place.

CHAPTER V.
THE IMPOSITION OF THE NEW FAITH. A.D. 1547–1560.

HENRY's great object throughout was to rule in Ireland as he ruled in England; and, with this object in view, he strove in his ecclesiastical policy to destroy the pretensions of the Bishop of Rome, and to improve the religious houses off the face of the earth: beyond this he had no intention to go; and it is to be observed that the accepting of both these courses in no way necessitated a breach of religious communion with the Holy See. But it was otherwise with those into whose hands, upon Henry's death, the reins of government came. In England, Henry's new nobility, the Seymours, the Russells, the Cavendishes, had profited by the plunder of the Church lands, and were greatly concerned to keep what they had got, and prevent anything like a reaction. The interests of the advanced party of the reformers lay in the same direction, and many of those whom Henry had used as his instruments were inclined to the forward course. Accordingly, we find the new doctrines directly encouraged; the Law of the Six Articles repealed; the clergy permitted to marry; the mass displaced by the Lord's supper; first one new liturgy introduced, and then a second of a more advanced character; and the pulpits "tuned" by authorized preachers. The reforming tide was flowing strongly, and the new ideas prevailed. The secret of the success of the Reformation in England lay in its not being a movement in advance of its time. Large numbers of the people, especially those who dwelt in the cities and towns, were ready to entertain it. The impulse came from within, and not from without. All the acts of Parliament passed to promote it would have been of no avail had not large sections of the community been ready to receive it. The movement had been at work upwards of two centuries. The ground had been broken by

4

Wycliffe and the Lollards. The former had translated the Bible into English, so that people were in a position to form their own opinions, and to criticise freely what they had hitherto taken on trust; the latter were bitterly persecuted by the Church, and, being scattered through the country, continued secretly to spread their opinions far and wide. The recent discovery of the printing-press had led to the rapid increase of general knowledge by the ready multiplication of the vehicle for its transmission. A keen spirit of inquiry had grown up, which fearlessly probed into all subjects. The Church itself had become discredited by the undisguised worldliness of its servants and officers; and from the days of Chaucer onward had suffered from the satirical attacks to which it had laid itself open.

In Ireland the case was wholly different: no breath of the "Lutheran" or any other "heresy" had reached its shores; no scattered remnant had preached of doubt and invited inquiry; no translation of the Scriptures had reached the English of the Pale, much less had an Irish version been given to the natives. The "Englishry" and the "Irishry" were both devout followers of the orthodox faith; but they had all along existed as two peoples, each with its distinct religious system. The Anglo-Normans, on their arrival, found the island divided into bishoprics and parishes, and sprinkled with monastic institutions. Where they settled they made use of the existing local divisions; and, Norman fashion, lavishly endowed fresh religious houses of their own. Henry II. had been acknowledged by the Irish clergy. Where the crown had power to enforce its will it appointed bishops to the vacant sees; where the natives were independent the Pope appointed, sometimes on the king's nomination, and sometimes of his own motion. As the Irish were outlaws, there could be no lawful intercourse between the two races. As it was felony to introduce an Irishman into an English monastery, so was it as much as an Englishman's life was worth for him to enter an Irish one. No bishop or parish priest could remain in Irish territory without the approval of the chieftain, who frequently rejected even the Pope's nominee if he happened to want the appointment for any friend of his own. If the king appointed a bishop to a see in the Irish country, the appointment was a farce : the bishop was simply an absentee, living in Dublin, and dealing actively in politics. There were, in fact, though unrecognized as such, two distinct orthodox churches in the island, one in the English and one in the Irish land. As anarchy increased, religion suffered. The English plundered and burned the Irish abbeys, and the Irish retaliated on those of the Pale. Many of the border monasteries were little better than fortresses, with monks for garrisons, who fought and plundered like the rest of society. The dioceses were frequently left vacant for years. The parish churches and cathedrals beyond the ramparts of the walled towns were despoiled of their furniture and vestments, and fell into utter ruin. The country was desolate, and the population decimated. No tithe could be collected ; and the wretched incumbents, without parishioners and without stipends, ceased to fulfil their functions, and withdrew into the religious houses. Everywhere was misery and ignorance ; and the spark of religion was only kept alive by the begging friars, Spanish, French, and English, who, at the risk of their lives, continued their mission work, and shared in their wanderings the dangers and poverty of the people.

The clergy themselves were nearly as ignorant as their flocks. There was not a university in all the island. Few natives, either English or Irish, were fit for the office of bishop. The sees among the Irishry were filled with monks from the monasteries, who took no interest in the parishes within their dioceses ; those within reach of the royal arm were filled with imported Englishmen—not always of the best characters, for it was no easy matter to induce the more worthy sort and the scholars to consent to expatriation. To hope, by means of statutes and arbitrary acts, to force out of the grooves in which they had run for centuries a priesthood and a nation blindly wedded to an ancient faith was little short of madness ; yet this was what the forward party proposed to do when set free from the iron grasp of Henry. What wonder that the whole population of the island, both English and Irish, became united in one common bond and one common cause to resist an innovation which they looked upon at once as blasphemous and tyrannical, and was stamped with the detested policy of Anglicizing the Irish nation. A common platform had been found whereon the people of both bloods could meet. They could sink their mutual jealousies in their enthusiasm for their common belief. Henceforth Anglo-Norman and Celt were to be as one nation. The war of races was passing, the wars of religion were to begin.

These consequences were not, however, at first apparent. The seed was sown, and the crop was to follow; but some time was yet required for its full development. The passing of the Act of Supremacy had not roused the susceptibilities of the nation. In order to carry out his plans Cromwell had, in 1535, appointed George Brown, an Augustinian friar, and a strenuous supporter of the divorce, to be Archbishop of Dublin on the murder of Allen by Silken Thomas. The new prelate was consecrated by Cranmer. He strove, like a faithful servant, to carry out the Supremacy policy, and readily threw himself into his patron's designs for the suppression of image-worship. He amended the liturgy by substituting the king's name for that of the Pope; and, where he was able, pulled down the roods from the rood-lofts, and destroyed the shrines and images of the Virgin and other saints. He was strongly opposed by Cromer, Archbishop of Armagh, and the great bulk of the clergy of the Pale. But Cromwell's answer to obstruction was imprisonment; and, though many resigned their benefices, a sullen compliance was secured. On the death of Cromer, Henry appointed Dowdai to the primacy; but he was as stern an opponent to the new order of things as his predecessor. Only one other bishop supported Brown—Staples, Bishop of Meath, a moderate man, and one of Henry's recent appointments.

Cranmer and Northumberland had determined to introduce the new liturgy into Ireland; and Sir Anthony St. Leger, who, in consequence of the intrigues of Lord Chancellor Allen and the Irish Council, had been replaced by Sir Edward Bellingham, was sent again to Ireland with instructions to introduce the new service-book. An English version was ordered to be used where English was spoken, and an Irish one where otherwise; but it does not appear that any steps were taken for the making of an Irish translation. St. Leger addressed himself at once to the object of his mission, and summoned a meeting of the Irish clergy in Dublin Castle. On the production of the new liturgy, which was described by the royal proclamation as a translation of the prayers of the Church into the mother tongue, Archbishop Dowdal scornfully refused to receive it, and rose up with the main body of the clergy and retired from the conference. Archbishop Brown only remained, with Staples, Bishop of Meath; Quin, Bishop of Limerick; Lancaster, Bishop of Kildare; and Travers, Bishop of Leighlin. These five humbly accepted the king's orders; and the new form of prayer in English and the Bible in English were shortly after read in Christchurch Cathedral. The primacy of all Ireland was next transferred to Dublin from Armagh, which, being situated in O'Neil's country, was beyond the reach of the crown, and Dowdal retired to the Continent. An Englishman named Goodacre was elevated to the vacant archbishopric; and at the same time John Bale, a fiery and bigoted reformer, was advanced to the see of Ossory.

Some conception of the projects of the Reformers was now beginning to dawn upon the people. Their attention had been aroused by the interruption of their beneficial relation to the religious houses, and the casting-forth from their homes of the begging friars. Their wonder and indignation had been excited by the destruction of the wonder-working image of " Our Lady of Trim," and of the holy rood of Ballybogan; by the burning in High Street, Dublin, of the sacred " Baculus Jesu," which was believed to have been used by Christ himself, and to have been converted into a crosier by St. Patrick. They were struck with horror at the sacrilegious pillage, by the soldiers in Down, of the shrines and tombs of St. Patrick, St. Bridget, and St. Columbkill; and the atrocious act of vandalism committed by the garrison of Athlone in sacking and razing the ancient and magnificent abbey of Clonmacnoise. They had turned on Bishop Bale and stoned his servants, and besieged him in his palace, on his attempting to overturn the market-cross at Kilkenny.

But a brief respite was yet given before the Reformation became identified in their eyes with Anglicizing aggression, and Protestantism with a war to the knife. On the accession of Mary, the old order of things was restored for a brief season; and St. Leger, a kind of Gallio as far as articles of faith were concerned, was again the instrument of the royal will. Armagh was restored to its former privileges; and Dowdal, who had acknowledged the royal supremacy but rejected the new liturgy, was recalled from banishment. Archbishop Brown and his conforming bishops, with all the clergy who had taken to themselves wives, were formally deprived, and their children bastardized; while Bale and the Bishop of Limerick fled oversea to Geneva.

There was no persecution on account of the new faith, for the simple reason that there had been no converts. Those who filled the state offices had easy consciences, and took their religion from the crown. The great Earl of Ormonde conformed with the rest; and Gerald, the young heir of the house of Kildare, who was bound up with the Roman Catholic faction, and had been brought up by Cardinal Pole, was restored to his estates and to his earldom. The queen did not renounce the supreme headship of the Church. She continued to appoint bishops by the transmission of writs of *congé d'élire*, though she restored the jurisdiction of the Pope in things spiritual.* The Church lands which had been granted to the laity were not relinquished any more than they were in England; for both Mary and the Pope knew well enough that their new possessors, though they might be indifferent to their faith, were tenacious of their acquisitions; and, far from restoring those which were still vested in the crown, the queen continued to make fresh grants to whom she pleased, "with their appurtenances both spiritual and temporal." But King Edward's prayer-books were set aside, the sacrifice of the mass restored: in effect, matters in Ireland reverted very much to the position in which they were at the end of the reign of Henry VIII.; and the Pope, on the principle of half a loaf being better than no bread, consented to receive back his erring children upon these terms.

---

* 3, 4, P. and M. c. 8.

Elizabeth's first act in Ireland was to reverse all that her sister had done in Church matters. Edward's government had not ventured to summon a Parliament all through his reign for the purpose of registering the English Act of Uniformity; and the new liturgy had been introduced by an order in council. Elizabeth proceeded differently. She directed a Parliament to be summoned on January 11th, 1560, and care was taken that its composition should be of a satisfactory character. Representatives were summoned from ten only of the nineteen counties, and the burgesses were carefully selected from those boroughs where the royal influence was paramount; while none of the newly created peers were invited to attend. This deliberately packed body repealed the acts of Philip and Mary relating to the Pope's jurisdiction, and passed the Act of Uniformity * as it stood on the English statute-book, ordering all persons, on pain of fine and imprisonment, to attend church and hear the new liturgy. The only addition was a clause empowering those clergy who could not read English to read the service in Latin, and not in their native language, "as well in the difficulty to get it printed, as that few in the whole realm can read the Irish letters." A new oath of supremacy was also imposed, to be taken by all persons, on pain of forfeiture of office and promotion during life. The gift of first-fruits from the clergy was restored to the crown; † and the writ of *congé d'élire* was abolished, the queen being empowered to collate to benefices by letters-patent.‡

There seems to have been no difficulty in inducing the bishops to accept the change, at any rate those who came within reach of the arm of the law. The see of Armagh, which was situated beyond the Pale, was vacant by the death of Dowdal. It already had two pretenders—one in possession, a relative of O'Neil's, and one appointed by the Pope. Elizabeth appointed Adam Loftus, who resided in Dublin as an absentee. Curwin, whom Mary had installed in Dublin, and Bodkin, Archbishop of Tuam, who had complied under Edward VI., both continued in possession of their sees. Only three were deprived for dis-

---

* 2 Eliz. c. 2.   † Ib. c. 1.   ‡ Ib. c. 4.

obedience—Walsh, Bishop of Meath; Devereux, Bishop of Kildare; and Thonery, Bishop of Ossory.

It is difficult to tell how far the parish clergy complied, for even in the most populous parts of the country they had almost ceased to exist. True, the skeleton of the system remained; that is to say, the parochial divisions were undisturbed, and the ruins of the battered churches were to be found *in situ;* but no one remained to do the duty. The great tithes, and in many cases even the lesser tithes, had long ago been absorbed by the monasteries, and were transferred, with the rest of the Church property, to the landholders. The result was that in most cases there was nothing wherewith to pay the parson; and where, as frequently happened, the parish church had been served by an inmate of its tutelary religious house, on the abolition of the religious house the parish priest went too. So poor were the benefices that Elizabeth, in 1579, expressly authorized Archbishop Loftus to combine three or four livings into one, in order to bring the united annual income up to £40. And Sir Henry Sidney, writing to the queen in 1566, says that in Meath, which he calls "the best inhabited part of the diocese and the best governed country," out of 224 parish churches "105 are now impropriated to sundry possessions now of your highness, and now leased out for years; no parson or vicar resident upon any of them, and a very simple or sorry curate for the most part appointed to serve them, among which number of curates only eighteen were found able to speak English, the rest Irish priests—or rather Irish rogues, having very little Latin, and less learning and civility. In many places, the very walls of the churches down, very few chancels covered, windows and doors ruined or spoiled."

Within the English Pale, English ministers, professing the Reformed faith and wholly ignorant of the Irish language, were largely intruded, with the consequence that their congregations refused to attend church. It is not surprising that the mass of the people were driven into the arms of the begging friars, who preached the ancient faith in the native tongue upon the bare hill-sides, and enjoined an undying hatred of the Anglicizing Church of the Establishment.

CHAPTER VI.

THE PLANTATION OF LEIX AND OFFALY. A.D. 1547–1559.

HENRY VIII. had, in spite of the Irish council, carried out his plan of conciliating the Irish by "sober ways, politic drifts, and amiable persuasions of law and reason," and the fruits of his system promised well for the future. Upon his death the contrary counsels prevailed: it was believed to be better to drive the Irish than to lead them. The timorous counsels of the Dublin oligarchy could look for safety only in harsh and cruel measures, and little by little a course was entered upon of extermination and plantation, which was pursued for two centuries, and which, when combined with the policy of forcing a novel form of faith upon a reluctant people, has imbued the Irish nation with a hatred of English government which bids fair to be ineffaceable for generations to come.

The territories of Leix, Offaly, Fercal, and Ely lay in the centre of Ireland. They marched upon Ormonde's territory on the south, and upon Meath and Kildare on the north and east. They consisted chiefly of trackless forest and impenetrable morass, interspersed with tracts of profitable land, and were occupied by the warlike tribes of O'Moore, O'Connor, O'Dempsey, O'Dunn, O'Molloy, and O'Carrol. Thus situated and thus tenanted, they were the source of constant danger to the English settlement. They had in their time done more than their share in the constant harryings of the Pale, and they were a standing menace to the line of communication between Dublin and Kilkenny, which lay through Kildare and over Leighlin Bridge.

The chiefs of these tribes had been indentured by Henry; and though since then they had, on the whole, been pretty quiet, they showed some signs of turbulence on Henry's death. The government acted with prompt severity. They at once

4*

sent Sir Edward Bellingham, with six hundred horse and four hundred foot, to the spot, in conjunction with St. Leger's forces. Resistance there was none; O'Connor and O'Moore were captured, and sent over as prisoners to England; the strongholds of Dangen and Campa were taken; the tribes were thrust from their homes and dispersed, their cattle driven off, and their land laid waste. The rightful owners of the soil having been ejected, the next step was to repeople it with English colonists. This was accomplished, and a revenue of £500 per annum secured to the crown by the granting of leases of twenty-one years in the confiscated lands to various English colonists: notably to Sir Francis Bryan, who had married the Dowager Countess of Ormonde, and to other families which came over from England — the Barringtons, the Cosbies, the Berretons, and the Hovendens, the Harpools, the Deavils, the Grahams, the Pigotts, and the Bowens.

For nine years a guerilla warfare was kept up between the dispossessed tribesmen and the settlers of a most fierce and bloody character, which ended in the almost total expulsion of the latter. Again the government stepped in, and this time proceeded to do its work more thoroughly. The natives were either shot down in the field, or executed by martial law, and the remnant driven into the neighboring bogs and mountains, where for a few years longer they preyed upon and spoiled the settlers, and in their turn were hunted as brigands, and put to death as outlaws. The confiscated territories were converted into "shireland;"* the greater part of Offaly, Fereal, and Ely, being denominated King's County, and its stronghold Dangen converted into a fort, and constituted a market-town under the name of Philips-town, in honor of the queen's husband; while Leix, a portion of Offaly, and the barony of Upper Ossory, became Queen's County; and Campa was rechristened Maryborough, in honor of her majesty. The reinstated settlers were called upon to adhere to the English language and habits, to subscribe to the English laws, and to abjure Irish marriages and fosterage; to clear the country and maintain the fords

---

* 3, 4, P. and M. cc. 1, 2, 3.

and highways, and to build a church in every town within three years. These were the first counties which had been set out since the days of King John, unless the division of the County of Meath into Meath and Westmeath by Henry VIII. be taken into account.*

There is evidence in the correspondence between Elizabeth and the Earl of Sussex that, quite in the early part of her reign, the former had adopted in her own mind the plantation scheme, and looked forward to the possible destruction of the Ulster chieftains as affording the means of carrying it out. Sussex had also a plan for the more efficient governing of the island, by putting the provinces under responsible presidents, with a chief-justice and council, and a force of eight hundred men, and converting the queen's alleged rights to take "bonaght" into an annual tribute, all of which schemes were eventually carried out by succeeding deputies. Elizabeth was not, however, on her accession in 1558, prepared to enter upon an heroic treatment of the Irish question. On the death of her sister, she found England in a state bordering on revolution; plunged in a war with France, which had resulted in the loss of Calais; and threatened by Scotland, whose queen was married to the French king, and had assumed the arms of England. She could spare neither men nor money at present for schemes of aggression. It was only when driven by the intrigues of her foreign enemies, who endeavored to strike at her through Ireland, that she set herself the task of pursuing that policy to the bitter end.

---

* 34 Hen. VIII. c. 1.

CHAPTER VII.

THE WAR WITH SHANE O'NEIL. A.D. 1559-1569.

ELIZABETH's troubles soon began; and they arose out of her father's endeavors to substitute the feudal laws of inheritance for the law of Tanistry in his grants of peerages to the native chiefs. Quarrels had arisen from this cause in Thomond, Clanricarde, and the north, and had been suppressed. The feuds in Tyrone broke out afresh on the death of Con O'Neil, the new Earl of Tyrone. Henry seems to have been deceived by Con's representations as to his legitimate heir, and regranted his surrendered lands, and conferred his peerage, in remainder to Mathew and his heirs male; who, though the elder son, was base-born. Rumor, indeed, averred—and this was the material point according to Irish law—that he was not Con O'Neil's offspring at all, but was the son of a smith. Mathew, in the course of the struggle which was carried on in Con's lifetime, had been killed by some of Shane's men; and upon Con's death, in 1559, the tribe elected Shane, a younger son, but one of whose paternity there was no question, to be " The O'Neil," and contemptuously put aside the pretensions of Mathew's son, the new Baron of Dungannon.

Shane was a man of strong will and fierce passions, but able withal, and fully capable of meeting Elizabeth's tortuous ways with corresponding cunning. His ambition prompted him to gather to himself the whole power of the north, and to try to render himself independent of the English government. He stood forth as the champion of the old order of things; as the despiser of the new decorations, which had been so eagerly sought by his fellow-chieftains; and sneered bitterly at McCarthy More when the queen made him Earl of Clancarty.

The assumption by Shane of the title of The O'Neil was a direct challenge to the English government; and Sir Henry

Sidney, who was interim deputy in Sussex's absence, marched to Dundalk, to protect the borders of the Pale. At a meeting which then took place, Shane put his case so forcibly that Sidney agreed to lay the matter before the queen, and in the meantime to abstain from active measures.

Shane's claims seem to have made some impression on Elizabeth; but he was too dangerous a person to be left in full control of Ulster, and the English government determined to be rid of him either by fair means or foul. On Sussex's return an attempt was made to detach O'Reilly, the chieftain of Brefny, from his allegiance to Shane by creating him Baron of Cavan, and to enlist O'Donnel by promising him the projected earldom of Tyrconnel. For some years the Scots of Argyleshire had been migrating to the northeast coast of Antrim, and had materially strengthened Shane's hands by entering his service as mercenaries. It was determined to approach McDonnell, their captain, and so complete the combination against O'Neil. Shane, however, was too quick for Sussex. He burst into Brefny and overawed O'Reilly, compelling him to give hostages for his good behavior; he dashed into Tyrconnel and seized the persons of Calvagh O'Donnel and his wife, a daughter of the Lord of the Isles; and, turning on Sussex, who had seized and fortified Armagh, drove him and his army headlong before him, and marched within twenty miles of Dublin. Such was the terror inspired by Shane's name after this victory that Sussex was unable to bring his beaten army to face him in the field; he accordingly, with the queen's entire approval, had the baseness to endeavor to compass Shane's death by assassination, and suborned one Nele Gray, with a promise of a grant of land of the value of a hundred marks, to murder him. But the plot failed, and Nele Gray lost his reward.

Shane now retreated before Sussex's reinforcements, and consented to treat with his cousin of Kildare. The result of the negotiation was that Shane agreed to present himself in person to the queen and state his case to her. Having obtained a safe-conduct, he at once proceeded to the English court, where he and his body-guard of gallowglasses created considerable excitement. The thews and sinews of the stalwart Irishman seem to have attracted the eye of the susceptible Elizabeth; and, though advantage was taken of the cunningly worded safe-conduct, which guaranteed his return but omitted to fix a date for it, to keep him at the English court till he agreed to make his submission, her partiality for him induced her to respect his safety, and to permit him, after a three months' sojourn, to return to his country, with all the expenses of his visit paid. According to the terms of the submission, the queen allowed him to continue "Captain of Tyrone," and promised to withdraw her troops from Armagh, but refused to commit herself further on the question of his claim to the earldom; Shane, on the other hand, promised to reduce the Scots of Antrim, and to set O'Donnel at liberty. O'Donnel was accordingly released; but O'Donnel's wife, who was Shane's own stepmother by marriage—for Shane had been married to O'Donnel's daughter—continued to live with him as his mistress.

For over two years Shane and the government did not interfere with each other, further than that the sanctimonious Sussex made another attempt on his life by procuring an Englishman of the name of Smythe to send him a present of poisoned wine, which nearly caused his death; and in September, 1563, Elizabeth, with her hands full on the Continent and the Scottish border, her treasury empty, and her ill-paid and mutinous troops only fit to be disbanded, was glad to come to a settlement with him at any price, and entered into a formal treaty of peace, in which she conceded all the jurisdiction which his father, Con O'Neil, had enjoyed. Shane, though he knew that the English government was not to be trusted, seems fairly to have kept his side of the bargain. He effectually crushed the Scottish settlers, whom he surprised and cruelly massacred; he kept within his own borders, and did not interfere with the English; and he governed Ulster with a sort of rough justice, encouraging "all kinds of husbandry and the growing of wheat," and enforcing order in his own way. He did not attempt to disguise his feelings of hostility towards the English; there was a sort of armed neutrality between them; they would have taken every opportunity to ruin him, and he would have joined any league, either in or out of Ireland, to drive them out of the country. His position was that of an independent native prince. His case was that "his ancestors were kings of Ulster, and Ulster was his; with the sword he had won it, and with the sword he would keep it." He and the English government had gauged each other's capacity for mischief, and were content to watch each other for the present.

Early in 1566, Sir Henry Sidney returned to Ireland as lord deputy, with the express purpose of crushing the Irish chieftain. Shane held his vassal chiefs in a state of bondage; he had even ventured to domineer over his neighbors in Connaught, and, on a pretended claim for tribute, took from them a prey of four thousand cattle. He boasted that he could bring into the field a force of five thousand men of all arms. He entered into correspondence with Charles IX. and the Cardinal Lorraine, begging for a contingent of five or six thousand French soldiers; and allied himself with Argyle and the western islanders. Sidney set himself to work at the old game of gradually detaching his allies, and succeeded in inducing Hugh O'Donnel, the brother of Calvagh, to fall in with his plans. He managed to send round some men by sea and to throw them into Derry, and so to make a diversion from the north; while he took the field himself and marched across the border. Shane, who had been harrying the English Pale, but had been checked by the fortress of Dundalk and had made an unsuccessful attempt on Derry, found his flank threatened by O'Donnel; he turned upon him with the bulk of his force, and, crossing the Swilly at low water near Letterkenny, endeavored to carry by storm O'Donnel's intrenched position. O'Donnel made a stout resistance, and the attack failed; Shane's troops, beaten and broken, were driven back upon the river, where the rising tide cut off his retreat. Here near three thousand of his troops were either butchered by the men of Donegal, or drowned in the waves; and Shane himself barely escaped by a ford higher up the river into Tyrone.

He was now desperate: his army was gone; the chiefs were revolting; the hope of foreign aid had come to nothing; and, in despair, he determined to throw himself upon the generosity of the Scottish settlers of Antrim. This determination was fatal. The Scots were burning with revenge for his treacherous slaughter of their people a twelvemonth since; and, as soon as he arrived among them with the widow of O'Donnel and a few followers, they hewed him in pieces, and, having cut off his head, despatched it to the lord deputy at Drogheda, who sent it to rot upon a spearhead on the walls of Dublin Castle.

The English government was now relieved from the pressing danger which was always threatening from the north — not, indeed, by the valor of its own army, but by the remorseless vengeance of two injured Celtic chieftains. An act of attainder was passed on O'Neil,* and the country of Tyrone was declared forfeit. The vassal chiefs of Shane became vassals of the crown. Turlough Luinagh † O'Neil, who by the law of Tanistry had been elected by the tribesmen upon Shane's death, was permitted to occupy the position of chief of his own tribe, and became "The O'Neil." Elizabeth apparently thought it wiser not to force upon them the unpopular claims of the representative of the Baron of Dungannon.

---

* 11 Eliz. session 3, c. 1.
† So called because he was fostered by O'Luinagh of Tyrone.

CHAPTER VIII.

THE PLANTATION SPIRIT ABROAD. A.D. 1569–1576.

AFTER the death of Shane there was a short interval of quiet and recovery, which was occupied by Sidney in the holding of a Parliament for the purpose of filling the empty treasury by imposing a new duty on wines.* This measure was sturdily opposed by the gentry of the Pale, a class who were daily growing in wealth and influence; and there was also a furious controversy concerning the legality of the constitution of the Parliament itself, it being alleged that, with the view of packing the Commons, members had been returned by towns which were not incorporated, and that many sheriffs and mayors had returned themselves. Indeed, so unsatisfactory did the executive find both this Parliament and that summoned in the second year of the queen, that no other was assembled for fourteen years.

Though systematically plundered by the crown for the support of the army, and impoverished by the depreciated condition of the currency, the English Pale, which was now an extending instead of a contracting area, was gradually growing in prosperity. There was a steady rise in the value of its produce; the land was well tilled, and full of cattle; the cities and towns were populous; the houses well built, and furnished " with plate, furniture, and apparel;" the youth were sent abroad for education to Louvain, Dôle, and Rome, and to study law at the Inns of Court in London. The condition of the walled towns, both those on the coast and those in the interior, which were almost exclusively inhabited by people of unmixed English blood, was a great contrast to that of the open country: a brisk traffic was carried on between the citizens and the coun-

* 11 Eliz. session 4, c. 1.

try-folk, and the seaboard cities were the emporia of an increasing trade with other countries, more especially Spain. There had been a considerable addition made to the "shireland."* Anally, by the submission of O'Farrel, had been converted into the County of Longford; the County of Connaught had been subdivided into the counties of Mayo and Galway; and Roscommon had had Sligo and Leitrim carved out of it. Thomond had been denominated County Clare, and transferred from the province of Munster to that of Connaught. The territory of Desmond, however, was in a wretched condition. The hereditary quarrels between the Earls of Desmond and Ormonde had turned the country into a wilderness; and Sir Henry Sidney, in the description he gives of it, says that " he never saw a more waste and desolate land—no, not in the confines of other countries where actual war hath continually been kept by the greatest princes of Christendom."

Elizabeth's great difficulty was shortness of money. She grudged every shilling which was expended in the government of Ireland, and was constantly requiring schemes from her deputies for the making of the Irish government self-supporting. As the result of these searchings of heart, it was determined that trial should be made of Sussex's plan of governing the provinces by presidents, who should keep order each in his own government by maintaining a small standing army principally composed of native contingents, and should relieve the Dublin exchequer of all military charges by quartering the troops upon the people. This was, in effect, reviving for the benefit of the crown the old practice of coyne and livery, which had been condemned and prohibited over and over again when practised by the Irish nobles, and was universally acknowledged to have been the curse of the country. The first experiment was made in Connaught by the appointment of Sir Edward Fitton, a judge of the Queen's Bench in Dublin, to the office of president, with a commission to execute martial law. The immediate consequence of this supersession of the ordinary law of the land was a rising of various members of the O'Brien and

---

* 11 Eliz. session 3, c. 9.

Bourke families, which he vainly endeavored to put down by a succession of acts of violence; and when he had been all but driven out of the country, the government was compelled to recall him.

But the scheme which found most favor in the eyes of the queen and in the eyes of her iron deputy, Sir Henry Sidney, was the old one of planting the country with English settlers. England was full of men who aspired to be soldiers of fortune; the discovery of the New World had made them drunk with the spirit of adventure; they looked upon Ireland, as indeed at that time did even the majority of sober Englishmen, as a country ripe for colonization, inhabited by a race who deserved no better treatment than the wild beasts, and whose fat lands were the proper birthright of enterprising but impecunious younger sons. Cecil had a plan for drafting one able-bodied emigrant from every two parishes in England; and for meeting the expense of sending them over to Ireland, and supporting them for one year in their new domicile, by a rate to be levied on the counties from which they had been taken. In 1570, Shane O'Neil's territory being held to have escheated, a grant was made to one Thomas Chaterton and his heirs of a portion of the County of Armagh, and in the same year a grant of the district of Ardes and Clanaboy, in County Down, was made to the illegitimate son of Sir Thomas Smith, the queen's secretary of state, for the founding of an English Protestant colony; but the attempt of both the one and the other was a miserable failure, and the too adventurous colonists were all massacred by a tribe of the O'Neils.

A more determined effort was made in A.D. 1573 by Walter Devereux, Earl of Essex, to whom Elizabeth made a grant of half the County of Antrim, and the barony of Farney in Monaghan. She advanced a sum of £10,000 for the fitting-out of the expedition upon a mortgage of the earl's English estates, and gave him the title of President of Ulster. The district so allotted was principally occupied by the immigrant Argyleshire Scots, who had for many years been a thorn in the side of the government. These were to be exterminated, and part of the land leased to the English settlers and part to Irish natives.

Essex seems to have started with the idea that he was going to fulfil the functions of a patriarch of old, and, after expelling the heathen, to govern his people with paternal solicitude. The sequel was hardly according to his expectations. He was, of course, perpetually harassed by both the O'Neils and the Scots, and both he and his followers retaliated by committing a series of frightful atrocities. He induced Con O'Donnel to attend a conference, and then arrested him and sent him prisoner to Dublin Castle; he lured Sir Brian O'Neil of Clanaboy into the castle of Belfast—then, after a merry-making, treacherously seized upon him, his wife, his brother, and his retainers, and put them all to the sword, "men, women, youths, and maidens," two hundred in number; he attacked Rathlin Island, the stronghold, where the Scots had left their wives and their children, their sick and aged, and, after receiving the surrender of its scanty garrison, massacred them to a man, and hunted out and slew every living soul, man, woman, and child, who had taken refuge in the caves and fastnesses of the island—in all some 650 persons. Then, ruined in fortune and broken in health, after two years of fruitless endeavor, he abandoned his settlement and returned to Dublin to die, leaving his slumbering rights in Monaghan to be asserted by his heirs, when the English interest should be strong enough to push on to the line of the Blackwater.

But the most serious effort made towards a plantation, and the one attended by the most serious consequences, was the proposal made to colonize Munster by a number of gentlemen from the west of England. This was a most systematic scheme, and of a truly gigantic character. There were some twenty-seven volunteers—Sir Humfrey Gilbert, Sir Wareham St. Leger, Sir Peter Carew, Sir Richard Grenville, Courtenay, Chichester, and others—who offered to relieve the queen of all expense and trouble in Southern Ireland, in return for permission to confiscate the counties of Cork, Limerick, and Kerry. The leading spirit in this enterprise was an adventurer of ancient blood but broken fortune, Sir Peter Carew, who laid claim to vast estates in Carlow and Cork, the lands granted to Fitzstephen in the days of Henry II., which had passed by marriage to Carew's ancestors, but which had been deserted by them two hundred years since, had been reoccupied by the Cavenaghs and the Earl of Desmond, and had passed into the hands of third parties.

The claim of the Carews to Fitzstephen's lands had been inquired into and disposed of in the reign of Edward III., when it had been found that Fitzstephen, having been himself a bastard, and his daughter, through whom the Carews claimed, having been illegitimate, had died without heirs. Carew, nevertheless, at once set to work to bring actions of ejectment against the present owners. His claim was scouted by the courts of law, but was arbitrarily upheld by the deputy and the privy council; and so, taking the bull by the horns, he forcibly expelled many of the occupiers in Carlow, and retook possession.

There were many other estates which had, in a similar way, been lost to their Anglo-Norman owners in consequence of their deserting the country, the claims to which were doubly statute-barred by the several acts which had been passed depriving absentees of their properties; and these stale claims were bought up as speculations by the enterprising undertakers above referred to. St. Leger and Grenville took possession of a number of farms belonging to Desmond and McCarthy More, but were promptly expelled by the owners. Sir Peter Carew surrounded himself with a gang of ruffians, established himself at Leighlin, and seized some lands belonging to Ormonde's brother, Sir Edward Butler. The Butlers fell upon him, and tried to drive him out by force, cruelly wreaking their vengeance on some miserable Irish who had joined themselves to him; and Carew retaliated by attacking Sir Edward's house, and massacring every human being he found there, down to a child three years old.

The story of Carew's atrocities spread like wildfire. A suspicion of the secret plans for confiscation ran through the south. A league for self-defence was formed between the Geraldines, the McCarthys, and Ormonde's brothers, which was countenanced by Thomond, Clanricarde, and Turlough Luinagh. The Archbishop of Cashel was sent to beg for help from Philip II. and the Pope, and the standard of revolt was actually raised by Sir James Fitzmaurice Fitzgerald, a cousin of the Earl of Desmond. The earl and his brother, Sir John, had shortly before been seized by Sir Henry Sidney and forwarded to London, where they were lodged in the Tower, in order to compel them to accept an adverse decision on their quarrel with Ormonde, whose steady loyalty to the Tudor family was to be rewarded by a correspondingly steady support. The government, afraid that even Ormonde might grow disaffected if the confiscation conspiracy were authenticated, hastened to disavow all such intentions, loaded him with favors, and persuaded him to detach his brothers from the rebel cause. Sidney then collected a force and marched into Waterford, Tipperary, and Limerick, burning villages, blowing up castles, and hanging their garrisons. He overawed Connaught by occupying Galway and Roscommon; and he established Humfrey Gilbert at Kilmallock to strike terror into the people, which he effectually did by the indiscriminate slaughter of all who came in his way, irrespective of age or sex. Ormonde succeeded in pacifying his brothers, who made their submission and were forgiven, and James Fitzmaurice retired with his followers to lead an outlaw's life in the Kerry mountains.

By these brutal measures the incipient insurrection was crushed out, and Sir John Perrot was appointed President of Munster, to hunt down the rebels and to catch Fitzmaurice. For two years did Sir James set him at defiance, taking up his quarters in the inaccessible vale of Aherlow, under the Galtee mountains. Perrot blew up his castles, captured his towns, and hanged his followers, and finally took Castlemaine after a two months' siege. Then, stinted by Elizabeth both of men and money, and almost as exhausted as Fitzmaurice, he opened negotiations with the rebels, and the Geraldine came in, made his submission, and was pardoned.

CHAPTER IX.
THE DESMOND REBELLION. A.D. 1573-1583.

The first Desmond rebellion had been strangled in its birth; but the English government had so exhausted itself in the effort that the plantation scheme was allowed to slumber for a more convenient season. The Geraldines, however, felt that they were marked for destruction, and that their ruin was only a question of time; and the more determined of them began to turn their eyes towards the foreign enemies of England, in the hopes of succor.

Ireland was now growing to be a factor in England's foreign policy which had to be taken into consideration. It had long become apparent that it was England's exposed quarter, and that the perennial disaffection existing in the island might at any moment be turned to account for her serious injury. Scotland, her hereditary enemy, and the close ally of France, was a standing menace from the north; and the intimate relation existing between Scotland and Ulster, together with the close geographical proximity of the Western Isles to the coasts of Antrim, disclosed a road by which invasion on the northern border could be made terribly effectual, were Ireland in the hands of a foreign enemy.

In the reign of Henry VIII., James, the fifteenth Earl of Desmond, had held a treasonable correspondence both with Francis I. and Charles V.; Lord Thomas Fitzgerald and Shane O'Neil had both tried hard to obtain help from over the sea; and now an active course of intrigue was being pursued by Sir James Fitzmaurice Fitzgerald with Philip of Spain and the Pope.

The rebellious gentlemen who had embarked in these crooked ways had always endeavored to give a religious coloring to their actions; they had professed to be champions of the old faith against an heretical tyrant. But though this may have persuaded the Pope and others that the Irish nation was writhing under persecution on account of its belief, it had no great bearing on any of these risings as far as the people were concerned, who had not as yet had any practical experience of Protestant intolerance, the Act of Uniformity having hitherto of necessity remained to a great extent a dead letter.

The English government, however, was gradually growing to associate popery with rebellion. It saw Spanish gold and Spanish soldiers asked for in the name of popery; it saw the men who rejected its authority allying themselves with Roman Catholic princes who were at enmity with England; it found that those ecclesiastics who refused to conform took refuge at Rome, while Roman nuncios slid into the country, and Roman bishops were appointed by the Pope. More than all, the papal bull of excommunication launched against the queen, which professed to absolve her subjects from their allegiance, drove the government into taking active repressive measures against the Roman Catholics, and forced the Roman Catholics themselves into the false position of being traitors either to their sovereign or to their spiritual head. In this way the Oath of Supremacy became a test of loyalty; and the nationalist and anti-English feeling was identified with an adherence to the Roman communion.

This growing tendency was seized on by the Geraldines, who eagerly sought to connect Protestantism with the policy of confiscation; to teach the doctrine that national safety was only to be secured by the upholding of the ancient faith; and that the English invaders could be best confounded by an alliance with such good friends as the Spaniards.

The government had released Sir John of Desmond; and his brother the earl, who was detained in Dublin Castle, had effected his escape and reached his own territory, where he was received with the utmost enthusiasm by all the Southern Irish. Fitzwilliam, the lord deputy, had thought it most prudent to leave him in peace; but had sent Sir William Drury, Perrot's successor, to hold his courts in Desmond and supersede the earl's palatinate jurisdiction.

In the meantime, Sir James Fitzmaurice Fitzgerald, after a fruitless application to the court of France, repaired to Spain to form designs for the invasion of Ireland. Philip, though smarting at the countenance given by Elizabeth to the revolted Dutch provinces, was not at that moment prepared absolutely to break with England, and politely referred him to the Pope. Gregory XIII. entered warmly into the scheme, and scraped together a few ships and some eight hundred ragamuffins. These he placed under the command of a rascally English adventurer named Stukely, who had for several years lived upon his wits and the credulity of the King of Spain. Stukely was to land on the Munster coast; and Fitzmaurice was to join him with Dr. Nicholas Sanders, an exiled English priest whom the Pope had constituted his legate; and an Irish priest named Allen, who was to bring a consecrated banner, and a sheaf of indulgences granting the same privileges to all who fought against the English as to those who fought against the Turks. Stukely, however, carried the whole expedition off on a buccaneering expedition against the King of Morocco, and was never heard of again; while Fitzmaurice and his two clerical conspirators, with a few friars and a handful of Spaniards, landed at St. Mary Wick, or Smerwick, and threw up a small fortification.

The moment was well chosen. The whole country was ripe for rebellion. The north was ready to rise at the first success gained by the men of Munster; Connaught, which had been dragooned by Fitton's successor, Sir Nicholas Malby, and where a rising of the Bourkes had only just been crushed with the most sickening brutality, was barely held down by the garrison at Athlone. The native Irish had learned neither to trust the English word, nor to look for mercy, by the example set by Francis Cosbie and the planters in King's and Queen's counties, who had recently exterminated the remnants of the O'Moores and O'Kellys by a ruthless massacre in the rath at Mullaghmast. Rory O'Moore, the famous outlaw, was the terror of the County of Kildare. The towns of Munster were smarting under the infliction of Sir William Drury's bloody assize. Even the English Pale was disaffected, by reason of Sidney's recent endeavor to levy an illegal cess, and the queen's arbitrary imprisonment of those who had ventured to petition against it.

On the arrival of Fitzmaurice, Sir John of Desmond and his brother Sir James promptly joined the insurgents at Smerwick, the former committing himself beyond recall to the rebel side by the murder of two English officers and their servants at Tralee. The earl himself vacillated. He was not the man to lead a successful rising, and, though his sympathies were all with the insurgents, he could not make up his mind to throw in his lot with them openly. But the Desmond tribesmen flew to arms all over Limerick and Kerry; and three thousand tenants of the Geraldines rose in open rebellion.

At that time the whole of the southern portion of the County of Limerick was one vast forest, called the Great Wood of Kilmore, which afforded splendid cover for the insurgents. Here the raw native levies were quickly knocked into shape by the drilling of the Spanish soldiers from Smerwick, the cattle were driven for shelter, and supplies of all kinds collected. Fitzmaurice, with a small troop of horse, started off to cross the Shannon and to raise Connaught; but he was overtaken at the river Muckern, near Barrington's Bridge, by his cousin Sir William Burke of Clanwilliam and McBrien of Ara, who had remained loyal to the English, and there lost his life in a scuffle.

The death of Fitzmaurice was a great blow to the rebellion. The command devolved on Sir John of Desmond; and Sir William Drury took the field against him with a small force. For several weeks Drury carried on an unsuccessful campaign, and was finally forced to retire into Kilmallock. Broken in health, he gave up the command, and was succeeded by Malby, who, having been recruited with six hundred men from England, came upon the Geraldine brothers at Monaster, and, after a stubborn fight, put them to the rout; Sir John barely escaping with his life, and Dr. Allen, the Jesuit, being left dead on the field.

The vacillating Desmond was now declared a traitor by the government unless he came in within twenty days: and at length, convinced that there was no mercy for him, he openly joined the insurgents. Malby, crippled for want of men, thought it prudent to retire to his command at Athlone; and Munster was left at Desmond's mercy. He overran the whole country, captured and sacked Youghall, and threatened the city of Cork. Fresh supplies were coming from abroad, and some Spanish adventurers were mustering at Corunna.

Elizabeth sent over Ormonde to take the field against his hereditary enemy, and to co-operate with the new lord deputy, Sir William Pelham; and a systematic effort was made to crush the rebellion. Pelham and Ormonde advanced in two columns, the one from Dublin, the other from Kilkenny; while the fleet, under Sir William Winter, sailed round to support them on the coast of Kerry. The path of the two forces was marked by pitiless destruction of life and property: crops and cabins were burned, and every living being, the sick, the aged, the women, the infants, were all ruthlessly slaughtered. A junction was effected at Tralee, and they turned northward to destroy Desmond's castles in Limerick. Carrigafoyle, which was held by the Spanish and Italian band, was breached with cannon from the fleet, and the whole garrison put to the sword; castle after castle was captured, and Desmond and his countess, with Dr. Sanders, were hunted out of Castle-island. The two English commanders then continued their raid to the extremities of Kerry, plundering, burning, and murdering as far as Dingle and Valentia; they then brought their forces back to Askeaton and Cork. Resistance there had been none. Their small but disciplined forces, well armed with firelocks, had marched from one end of Munster to the other. The rebels, half-naked and armed with spears and knives, had been unable to meet them in the field; and when resistance had been attempted, it was behind stone walls. The ferocity of the English commanders had cowed the people into sullen quiet; and Desmond, his brothers, and the legate were reduced to the state of hunted fugitives, and had taken refuge in the mountains. Ormonde, in a state paper enumerating his services, is said to have put to death "88 captains and leaders, with 1547 notorious traitors and malefactors, and above 4000 others." Pelham would only accord a pardon at the price of the betrayal of other rebels.

The reduction of Munster was only just accomplished in time. A month later and the long-looked-for Spanish contingent arrived: four Spanish vessels eluded the vigilance of the English fleet, and landed eight hundred Italians and Spaniards in the fatal bay of Smerwick, who occupied the dismantled fort; at the same time, the smouldering disloyalty of the Pale broke out into open rebellion. The Desmond faction plucked up a little heart, and England again had her hands full. The lords of the Pale, who had resisted Sidney's illegal cess, had sullenly watched the progress of the rising of the southern Fitzgeralds; they waited for a sign from the head of the other great Fitzgerald family, but, like his cousin of Desmond, Kildare vacillated, and let the golden moment pass. Now that it was too late, an isolated attempt was made; but, hesitating as it was, it was a serious trouble to the English government. James Eustace, Lord Baltinglass, had been one of the petitioners in the matter of the cess, and had suffered imprisonment for his presumption. He was an ardent Roman Catholic, and had been much moved by Dr. Sanders's circular letters; he was intimately connected by marriage with the O'Byrnes of the Wicklow highlands, and he and they, with many refugees from Queen's County, hoping to form the nucleus of a more general rising, broke out into open revolt, and were joined by Sir John of Desmond and a band of Munster men from the fastness of Aherlow.

Lord Gray de Wilton had just arrived in Dublin as deputy, and hastily marched out to suppress the rising. The rebels were swarming in the valley of Glenmalure, and Gray recklessly sent his men into the narrow gorge, believing he was strong enough to hunt them out. When the troops were well in the difficult ground, a well-directed fire was poured in upon them from the safe cover of rocks and brushwood; flight was impossible, and they were all shot down, the ferocious Sir Peter Carew and Colonel Cosbie of Mullaghmast infamy being among the slain. Lord Gray made no attempt to revenge his defeat; he left the Pale at the mercy of the insurgents, who harried the country to the walls of Dublin, and, accompanied by Ormonde and a band of English adventurers, among whom were Sir Walter Raleigh and Edmund Spenser, proceeded by forced marches to Smerwick; the fleet came round to support him by sea, and a siege was commenced. After three days the garrison offered to capitulate on terms, but an unconditional surrender was demanded. Next morning the eight hundred Spaniards and Italians came out with trailing colors and laid down their arms; one and all were either shot or hanged by Captain Raleigh and his men, except the officers, who were reserved for a ransom.

Munster had been so effectually dragooned by Pelham and Ormonde in the early summer that not a man had stirred, and Gray swiftly returned to Dublin. There he arrested Kildare and Lord Delvin on suspicion, and flung them into prison; he turned savagely on the Wicklow insurgents, and, taught by his experience at Glenmalure, organized a number of small bands to hunt them from the mountains. Two of the Eustaces and Gerald O'Toole he caught and beheaded; but Baltinglass escaped to the Continent. A reign of terror then began at Dublin. A conspiracy to seize the castle and liberate the imprisoned peers was discovered, and martial law was proclaimed: the smaller men were hanged in batches, and nineteen of the best blood of the Pale were brought to trial for treason. Short work was made by pliant juries, and the whole of them were convicted and hanged; while Kildare was removed to England, and subsequently died in the Tower.

Nothing was now left to be done but to hunt down The Desmond, and those of his adherents who still clung to him. Ormonde was placed in supreme command in Munster; Captain Raleigh was in command at Cork; Captain Loach at Kilmallock; and Captain Achin at Adare. The sword and the gallows were the instruments for pacifying the country. Achin seized the castle of David Purcell, at Kildimo, and slew 150 women and children; Ormonde caught and hanged Lady Fitzgerald of Imokelly, and reports in his despatches the execution of 134 persons, and that the pardoned chiefs were bringing in the heads of other rebels by the sackful. So merrily went the reign of blood. Desmond, on the other hand, inflicted much damage on Ormonde's own country by occasional predatory raids; but his men were growing fewer and fewer in number. The people would not betray him; but they dared not assist him. His two brothers, John and James, had both been captured and put to death; and Dr. Sanders had died of exposure in the winter. Hunted from valley to valley, with a price upon his head, he was at length driven into the Slievemish mountains, beyond Tralee, where a party of English soldiers surprised him in the early morning in a cabin in which he was harboring, and slew him and cut off his head.

CHAPTER X.

THE PLANTATION OF MUNSTER. A.D. 1586.

THE last remnant of the Desmond rebellion had now flickered out. It had been crushed down by a system of ferocity as appalling as that with which Alva had been scourging Philip of Spain's subjects in the Netherlands. The results were apparent in the conversion of a fertile province into a desolate waste. "Whoever did travel," says Holinshed, "from one end of Munster to the other would not meet any man, woman, or child, saving in towns or cities; and would not see any beast." The harvests had been burned year after year, and famine cleared the land of those who escaped the sword. Here is the testimony of Edmund Spenser the poet, who shared in the campaign and participated in the spoil: "For notwithstanding that Munster was a most rich and plentiful country, full of corn and cattle, yet after one year and one half, they were brought to such wretchedness as that any stony heart would rue the same; out of every corner of the woods and glens they came, creeping forth upon their hands, for their legs could not bear them. They looked like anatomies of death; they spoke like ghosts crying out of the graves. They did eat the dead carrions, where they did find them, *yea, and one another soon after*, in as much as the very carcases they spared not to scrape out of their graves; and if they found a plot of watercresses or shamrocks, there they thronged as to a feast for the time, yet not able to continue there with-all; that in short space there were none almost left; and a most populous and plentiful country left void of man and beast." And the evidence of Sir William Pelham himself as to the mode of conducting the war: "Touching my manner of proceeding, it is thus: I give the rebels no breath to relieve themselves; but by one of your* garrisons or the other they be continually hunted. 1 keep them from their

---

* He was writing to the queen.

harvest, and have taken great preys of cattle from them, by which it seemeth the poor people that lived only upon labor, and fed by their milch cows, are so distressed as they follow their goods and offer themselves with their wives and children, rather to be slain by the army than to suffer the famine that now beginneth to pinch them."

This clearance was the necessary preliminary to the new plantation. By Desmond's treason his vast estates, which included those of some hundred and forty of his adherents who had taken up arms in his cause, were forfeited to the crown, to the extent of 574,628 Irish acres of good and profitable land, besides seigniorial rights over the four counties of Cork, Kerry, Limerick, and Waterford. The escheated lands of the Eustaces in Kildare and Dublin numbered 7800 acres. Sir John Perrot, who had had some experience in Munster, succeeded Lord Gray as deputy; and to him the government intrusted the conduct of the colonization scheme.

His first step was to summon a Parliament for the passing of acts of attainder against Desmond and Baltinglass and other rebels. This was the first Parliament which had met since Sidney's mutilated but unmanageable assembly in 1569. It was attended by a strong muster of peers of both races, twenty bishops and four archbishops, and representatives from all the then existing shires and some thirty boroughs. Many of the counties sent up Irish chiefs as knights of the shire, who were persuaded to adopt the English dress for the occasion. Two acts of attainder were passed,* specifically mentioning 140 knights and gentlemen of both English and Irish blood, under which the whole of their real and personal estate vested in the crown.

The plan for the colonization of the confiscated land was to divide it up into large tracts or seigniories of from 4000 to 12,000 acres, to be held in fee of the crown at a quit-rent of threepence per acre in Limerick and Kerry, and twopence per acre in Cork and Waterford. No rent was to be payable till A.D. 1590, and for three years after that only half-rent; for ten years the "undertakers" were to export their produce duty-free. Younger sons and brothers were invited to come over

---

* 28 Eliz. cc. 7, 9.

from England to take up the land; and large tracts were given to those who had been engaged in the war. The conditions of the grants were: that no native Irish should be taken as tenants; that the owner of every three hundred acres should provide one horseman and one infantry soldier; that farmers, hop-planters, gardeners, wheelwrights, smiths, masons, carpenters, thatchers, tilers, tailors, shoemakers, and butchers should be procured from England by the undertakers, and settled on the land; that each grantee of 12,000 acres should plant on portions of his estate eighty-six different families, of which twenty were to be freeholders, forty copyholders, and the rest small tenants of the laboring class, and should retain 1600 acres for his own demesne lands. Every precaution was taken to keep the colonists from amalgamating with the remnant of the native population, who were to be cleared out of the plains into the upland country. The colony was to be planted on the profitable land only.

The scheme being fairly launched, the distribution followed. About half the escheated land was restored to some of the old owners who had sufficient interest to secure pardons, as in the case of the White Knight, Patrick Condon, and some of the Geraldines. Of the other half, grants were made to about forty Englishmen, some receiving more than one seigniory, like Sir Walter Raleigh, who obtained 42,000 acres in Cork and Waterford. The rent of the whole reserved to the crown amounted to about £23,000 a year. Those who received some of the largest grants were Arthur Robins, who obtained 18,000 acres in County Cork; Sir William Herbert and Sir George Bouchier, who received 13,000 acres in Kerry and Limerick; Fane Beecher, Hugh Worth, Arthur Hyde, and Henry Billingsley, who each received 12,000 acres in Cork and Limerick; Sir William Courtenay, Sir Edward Fitton, and Sir Christopher Hatton, who obtained 10,500 acres in Limerick and Waterford. Among others, Ormonde got 3000 acres in Tipperary, and Sir Wareham St. Leger and Edmund Spenser 6000 acres and 3000 acres respectively in County Cork.*

---

* For a list of the undertakers of Munster, see Appendix II.

The land accordingly passed into the hands of new landlords; but the scheme of colonization was a failure. The farmers, the artisans, and the laborers did not come over in sufficient numbers; many of those who came returned to England on finding themselves harassed and spoiled by the dispossessed native Irish, who formed secret societies for the destruction of the settlers, and were known by the name of "Robin Hoods." The new demesne lords, in violation of their covenants, were fain to take on the natives as tenants at will, in order that the lands might be cultivated; the result was a change of ownership of the freehold, but not a change of the population. The Irish gentry had been rooted out, but what was left of the Irish peasantry remained on the soil. The intruded English were a mere handful of strangers among a hostile people, and the native Irish were exasperated without being exterminated. The only result of the ten years' desolation was the enriching of a few adventurers and a knot of Elizabeth's courtiers.

CHAPTER XI.
SOWING THE WIND. A.D. 1584–1595.

AFTER the suppression of the rebellion in Munster there was an interval of comparative peace in Ireland, which might have been prolonged until the tendency towards improvement which was growing in the country had borne satisfactory fruit, had not the blind folly of the English government precipitated a fresh quarrel.

The south had been "pacified" by fire and sword; so had Connaught, by the merciless sternness of the president, Sir Richard Bingham. There had been no concerted rising in Connaught; the great Earls of Thomond and Clanricarde had been steadily loyal to the crown; but there had been much smouldering disaffection among the cadets of the house of Bourke, which from time to time burst out into open insurrection, and which had equally from time to time been suppressed by massacre.

The lord deputy, Sir John Perrot, had succeeded in inducing the land-owners of Connaught to agree to pay the crown a fixed land-tax, in lieu of the irregular cess which was exacted for the support of the army; sheriffs were appointed to each county; and the west, like the south, was beginning to settle down.

In Ulster the chiefs were loyal, and both trusted and respected Perrot, who, though sternly severe with those whom he considered traitors, was animated by a strong spirit of justice. He even persuaded them, as he had persuaded the lords of Connaught, to agree to the payment of an annual tax for the support of 1100 men in Ulster; and he projected the division of the northern province into the counties of Armagh, Monaghan, Tyrone, Coleraine (Derry), Donegal, Cavan, and Fermanagh, in addition to the old ones of Antrim and Down. But this division existed on paper only for the present; the chiefs having the greatest dread and jealousy of the intrusion of the English sheriff, which was the first consequence of a country being made into "shire-land."

Sir John Perrot had many enemies. He was a man of hasty temper, who quarrelled with his subordinates. He had sent a challenge to Bingham, who detested him for endeavoring to curb his severities in Connaught; he had knocked down Sir Henry Bagnal at the council board, who differed in opinion with him upon matters of state; he made an enemy of Adam Loftus, the archbishop, by proposing to endow a university in Dublin out of the revenues of the Cathedral of St. Patrick, which had fallen to Loftus and his kinsmen as their share in the spoil of the monasteries. These and others were ever ready to whisper slanders of the lord deputy to the queen. It was always the fate of Irish deputies to have the ground cut from under them by the intrigues of the Irish council; but Elizabeth knew this, and paid no attention to the libels on Perrot, until it was told to her that he had refused to punish O'Rourke of Brefny, who, it was said, had dragged an effigy of her majesty at the tail of a horse. This absurd suggestion of indifference to her personal dignity roused her suspicious nature; and Perrot was recalled to eat his heart out and die in the Tower.

Perrot was succeeded by Sir William Fitzwilliam, who had filled the same position sixteen years previously, during an interval in Sidney's viceroyalty. Perrot's policy of conciliation was thrown to the winds, and every opportunity was recklessly taken by the incompetent new viceroy to exasperate the natives. Fitzwilliam was hasty and injudicious; he was also a victim to the vice of avarice, and the first thing he did was to start on a wild-goose chase in search of gold, which report said had been secreted by the survivors of the Spanish Armada, many ships from which had been cast away on the north and west and southern coasts of the island. As the gold was not forthcoming, he seized the persons of Sir Owen McToole and Sir John O'Dogherty, two of the most loyal subjects in Ulster, upon the pretence that they had concealed the much-coveted treasure, and, having incarcerated them in Dublin Castle, demanded a large sum for their enlargement.

This arbitrary proceeding created great irritation and apprehension among the native chiefs; but a still more gross piece of iniquity was to follow. Rossa McMahon, chieftain of Monaghan, had surrendered his territory to the crown and received a re-grant of it to himself and the heirs male of his body, and in default of such heirs to his brother Hugh. Rossa died without issue, and Hugh claimed the inheritance. Fitzwilliam demanded a large bribe of six hundred cows before seizin should be given him. Hugh came to Dublin, and complied with the deputy's requirements, and the latter set out with him to Monaghan to formally put him in possession. Fitzwilliam then trumped up against him a tale that he had two years previously recovered by force of arms some rent which was due to him in the barony of Farney, which constituted the offence of treason in "shire-land" according to English law, but was not an offence in Monaghan, which was not in the English jurisdiction. Hugh was promptly tried by court-martial and executed. The Church lands in his territory were given to Sir Henry Bagnal, Captain Willis, Captain Henslowe, and certain Dublin lawyers, the crown reserving thereout a quit-rent of £70. The residue, except the large tract already granted to the Essexes, was given to seven of the McMahon family, who were made to pay a round sum to the deputy, and an annual quit-rent of £259 to the queen.

There was yet another outrage, which had happened at a rather earlier date, for which Sir John Perrot was responsible, and which had a still greater influence on the temper of the native population. Sir Hugh O'Donnel, the Lord of Tyrconnel, had refused to receive a sheriff into his country, and, in order to get hostages for his good behavior, the lord deputy conceived and executed the following treacherous trick. He sent a vessel with a cargo of Spanish wine and a crew of fifty armed men round by sea to Lough Swilly. On its arrival Hugh Roe, or Red Hugh, O'Donnel's son, was induced to come on board to partake of the captain's hospitality; and when he was half drunk his arms were removed, and he was clapped under hatches. The cable was cut, the vessel put to sea, and young Red Hugh was lodged in Dublin Castle.

There were many more complaints from Ulster of the tyranny and injustice of the agents of the government. Fermanagh was raided on the one side by the Binghams, and on the other by Henslowe, the new seneschal of Monaghan, who drove McGuire's cattle, killed the women and children, and exacted illegal ransoms. Edmund McGuire's head was cut off and insolently kicked about as a football by the soldiers. Sheriffs were forced on the chieftains, contrary to agreement, and in spite of bribes paid for exemption. No notice of the chieftains' remonstrances was taken by the government, and the complaints were carefully not reported to the queen.

For six years was Fitzwilliam in office, and on his supersession by Sir William Russell, in A.D. 1594, the new lord deputy found Ireland again in a state of ferment. All the northern tribes were discontented. O'Rourke and McGuire were in open rebellion. Red Hugh had broken out of Dublin Castle—not without the connivance, as some say, of the venal lord deputy—and, after many hair-breadth escapes, had reached Donegal in safety, where his old father resigned the chieftainship in his favor, and he was enthusiastically elected Lord of Tyrconnel. Connaught was growing exasperated by the intolerable oppressions of Sir Richard Bingham. Even the Earl of Tyrone, who had hitherto been regarded as most loyal to the crown, was suspected of wavering in his allegiance.

Hugh O'Neil, the son of Mathew, the first Baron of Dungannon, was one of the most prominent of the Ulster nobility. He was a man of great ability and tenacity of purpose. He had been educated at the English court, and was cultivated in all the accomplishments of the best society of the day. He had had a commission in the English army, and had fought at Smerwick under Gray against the Spaniards. From his knowledge and experience in England he had been able to gauge the resources of the government, and had accordingly adhered to the policy of his father and grandfather, that of loyal obedience to the crown. He was in high favor with both the queen and the deputy; and had been confirmed not only in his hereditary title of Earl of Tyrone, but in the possession of the Tyrone territory, which had been surrendered by and regranted to his grandfather. A compromise had been effected with Turlough Luinagh, "The O'Neil," who was now growing an old man, and who was to be allowed to retain the more northern portion of the disputed territory, and his overlordship over the two chiefs who still owned allegiance to him as titular Prince of Ulster.

Tyrone had married a daughter of Sir Hugh O'Donnel, and the treacherous capture of his brother-in-law, Red Hugh, was felt by him to be a serious grievance. His sympathies were also roused by the wrongs which his brother chieftains in Ulster were compelled to endure; but he knew the strength of England if she chose to put it forth. He knew that without help from Spain a rising would be madness; and he also knew that Spain was a broken reed to lean upon. Whether, then, from prudence only, or whether from a sincere desire to be at peace with the government, he threw his influence upon the side of order. He assisted the deputy to put down the rising in Fermanagh; and strove to hold down Red Hugh, who was burning with an implacable but natural hatred against the authors of his capture and his two years' imprisonment. Another circumstance which at this time influenced Tyrone was that his wife had died, and he had formed a romantic attachment to the beautiful sister of Sir Henry Bagnal, the lord marshal. Bagnal forbade the match, and Tyrone eloped with the lady and married her in Dublin. His interests were in this way still further bound up with the maintenance of order; and he consented to Tyrone and Armagh being made shire-land, to receive a sheriff, and to build a county jail.

But, on the other hand, Tyrone's marriage had converted Sir Henry Bagnal into an implacable enemy. The lord marshal was determined to ruin the earl, if possible; he never ceased trumping up accusations of treason to the council and the queen, and basely intercepted the answers which Tyrone made to the charges brought against him. Sir William Russell had, at Bagnal's instigation, proposed to arrest him while he was on a visit to Dublin under a safe-conduct, but the rest of the council overruled him. Elizabeth's suspicions in time became aroused, and, though she was heartily sick of Irish wars, she thought it prudent to reinforce the army in Ireland, which had been weakened by drafts for the Low Countries, with a force of three thousand men, under Sir John Norris, the brother of Sir Thomas, the President of Munster.

Tyrone was now beginning to see that there were two divergent courses open to him: he must either abide by the government which distrusted him, and was swayed by Bagnal, who had vowed his destruction; or he must throw in his lot with the northern chieftains, who would welcome him as a mighty acquisition to their cause. He was rapidly drifting in the latter direction. He knew that if he was to hope for success there must be union among the Irish, and that a determined effort must be made to obtain the *bona fide* assistance of Spain. O'Donnel, since his escape, had been at open war with the government, and had repeatedly endeavored to induce his brother-in-law to join him. His counsels at length prevailed; and these two now set themselves to work to form an extensive confederation against England.

Once chosen, Tyrone pursued his course with set purpose. An agreement of the two great northern clans of O'Donnel and O'Neil was in itself a formidable coalition. It became far more serious when, with calculating deliberation, the other leading chiefs of the north, whose independence it had been the policy of the government to foster, gave in their adherence to the scheme. McGuire of Fermanagh, McMahon of Monaghan, O'Rourke of Brefny, McGuiness of Down, and the Scots of Clanaboy, all joined the league. They enlisted Theobald and Ulick Bourke, O'Dowd and O'Connor of Sligo, with the O'Kellys and McDermots in Connaught, and some degenerate English in Meath, led by one Captain Tyrrel and some of the Nugents. They were joined by O'Byrne of Glenmalure, and two bastard Geraldines of the Kildare house in Leinster, with some of the O'Tooles and Kavenaghs, and fragments of the decimated tribes of Leix and Offaly. A solemn engagement was entered into between all the confederates to stand by each other, and to make no submission and accept no terms which did not include them all. An appeal was distinctly made to Roman Catholics as Roman Catholics to treat the question as a religious one, and to join the movement in the defence of their faith. Tyrone and O'Donnel wrote joint letters to Philip, to Don Carlos, and to Don Juan del Aguila, pressing them to send them troops "to restore the faith of the Church, and to secure to the king a Catholic kingdom." The old chief Turlough Luinagh most opportunely died, and Tyrone promptly adopted the title of "The O'Neil."

CHAPTER XII.

THE WAR WITH TYRONE. A.D. 1595–1603.

THE league of the north was not a cut-and-dried plot, but a thing of gradual growth. First the Ulster chiefs had combined; then Connaught was raised; then the discontented in the Pale and Leinster were infected; and, finally, the restless spirits of Munster who survived the Desmond insurrection were induced by Tyrone, after his first success, to try one more throw for the independence of their country.

The boundary of Tyrone was the river Blackwater; and the rebel earl commenced hostilities by seizing the English fort which commanded the passage of the river; while O'Donnel proceeded to overrun Connaught. The government sent Norris to Newry to face Tyrone; Bingham was compelled to act on the defensive in the west; and a successful raid by the lord deputy into Leinster resulted in the capture and death of O'Byrne.

After a good deal of desultory fighting on the frontier in Monaghan and Armagh, in which the English had by no means the best of it, efforts were made at negotiation; and Elizabeth, despairing of an end of Irish troubles, was willing to patch up a peace on almost any decent terms. Tyrone, who was anxiously looking for help from Spain, did his best to spin out the correspondence. The demands of the confederates were the withdrawal of all garrisons from territory under Irish jurisdiction, and liberty of conscience. These terms the government could not agree to; and on the arrival of three Spanish frigates, with arms and ammunition, in Donegal Bay, hostilities were recommenced. Sir William Russell had been succeeded by Lord Burgh; and the latter, after successfully recovering the fort on the Blackwater, was so severely pressed by the Irish that he was compelled to retire to Newry, where he died of his wounds. Archbishop Loftus, and Gardner, the lord chancellor, were then appointed lords justices by the council; Ormonde was despatched to overawe Leinster; and Sir Henry Bagnal was appointed to command the army of the north.

In August, 1598, Bagnal started from Newry with four thousand men, with the intention of relieving the garrison which Lord Burgh had thrown into the Blackwater fort, and which Tyrone was besieging. After leaving Armagh, Bagnal found the Irish army strongly posted on the river Callan. He attacked, and an obstinate battle was fought, which ended in the complete overthrow of the English, Sir Henry Bagnal himself being among the slain. Nearly half the English force was annihilated; their guns, colors, and baggage fell into the hands of the enemy; and a disorderly crowd of fugitives took refuge in Dundalk.

This signal defeat came like a thunderbolt upon the English government. The Blackwater fort at once surrendered; so did the garrisons of Monaghan and Armagh. All Ulster, save Carrickfergus, was in the hands of the insurgents, and nothing lay between them and the walls of Dublin except the forts of Dundalk and Drogheda. In Connaught the revolt was general; the whole of Leinster was in rebellion; and Ormonde himself was cooped up in Kilkenny. Tyrrel, who in " Tyrrel's Pass" had just cut off a thousand men despatched under Lord Trimleston to reinforce the army of the north, was master of Meath. He and Sir Piers Lacy and O'Moore of Leix had ravaged Ormonde's palatinate of Tipperary, and, having occupied Kilmallock, had forced Sir Thomas Norris, the President of Munster, to take refuge in the city of Cork. The planters of Munster were driven out of their farms. The castles of Desmond were reoccupied by Fitzmaurice of Lixnaw. The White Knight and the Knight of Glyn, with other survivors of the Geraldines, the Roches, the O'Donoghues, the McCarthys, joined the insurgents. A nephew of the late Earl Gerald, the Sugan Earl, or Earl of Straw, as he was called, assumed the title of "The Desmond," and agreed to hold his recovered country of "The O'Neil." All Ireland was in the hands of the rebels (with the exception of Dublin and a few garrison towns), who rioted in all the enormities of revenge, lust, and rapine, in every quarter of the kingdom.

This third native war was the most terrible crisis in Ireland that Elizabeth had had to meet. Not only was there, almost for the first time in Irish history, a united effort being made on the part of the native population to expel the English, and to re-establish the ancient laws and the ancient faith, but the relative strength of the two parties was comparatively altered. The English forces were depleted by desertion; their officers drew pay for the nominal strength, and pocketed the overplus. The troops themselves, ill paid and ill fed, were utterly demoralized and undisciplined. They were raw levies; many of them were boys of inferior physique to the Irish kerns. They were a greater source of fear to the peaceable inhabitants than to the enemy; and had long been the scourge of the country-people, on whom they billeted themselves indiscriminately. The Irish, on the contrary, could now put a formidable army in the field. They had taken a lesson from their masters; instead of being, as formerly, a horde of half-armed savages, they were drilled and disciplined. They were commanded by men who had served with the queen's colors; and Elizabeth herself complains that one third of her forces had been recruited from natives who had served in the ranks and then deserted to the enemy with their arms. Nor were they less completely supplied with arms and ammunition. A large quantity was imported from Spain, and the English trader was then, as in more modern times, not so scrupulous as to how he turned a dishonest penny. The ill-paid English soldiers sold their weapons and their powder cheap to the Dublin dealers, who retailed both the one and the other at exorbitant prices to the Irish enemy.

The old queen, on finding herself face to face with this new danger, betook herself sternly to the crushing of it. In the spring of 1599, she sent over 20,000 infantry and 1300 horse, the largest army she had ever despatched to Ireland, and put it under the command of her favorite, Lord Essex, who had recently won golden opinions by his daring surprise of Cadiz, where he burned the town and sixty Spanish galleons in the harbor. The necessity for prompt measures was urgent, for it was estimated that in Meath and the four provinces the Irish had over 18,000 men under arms.

The plan of the campaign, which had been settled at the council-board in England, was to send round the fleet to Ballyshannon and Lough Foyle, and so occupy strong positions in the rear of the enemy; while Essex, with the bulk of his army, was to invade Tyrone from the bases of Newry and Dundalk. On arriving at Dublin, Essex seems to have been persuaded by the Irish council, many of whom had a considerable stake in the new plantations in Munster, to defer the campaign in the north and to strike at the rebellion in the south. Accordingly, after reinforcing the four Ulster garrisons, and Naas and Wicklow, he proceeded with 7000 men, accompanied by Ormonde, along the old highway through Kilkenny and Tipperary, and captured the castle of Cahir. From here he advanced to Limerick, where he was joined by Sir Conyers Clifford, the President of Connaught, and the Earls of Thomond and Clanricarde, who of all the Irish alone remained faithful to the crown. He succeeded in relieving Askeaton, and turned homeward by way of Fermoy, Lismore, and Kildare. The Irish were far too cautious to be drawn into an encounter in the field; but during the whole of his expedition harassed him by repeated attacks more or less serious, in which he lost not only rank and file, but many veteran officers. In the meantime, Sir Conyers Clifford had left him and returned to Connaught; and, in an attempt to relieve Coloony Castle, was cut off with half his men by O'Donnel in the Curlew mountains.

Elizabeth, who had made great sacrifices to pour what she had believed to be an overwhelming force into Ireland, was furious at the smallness of the results. She taunted Essex with incapacity, and upbraided him for not attacking the heart of the rebellion in Ulster. But, angry as she was, when he admitted that, what with garrisoning the fortresses and his losses from disease and in the field, his effective forces were reduced to some 8000 men, she sent him a reinforcement of 2000 more.

In August, Essex marched from Newry in the direction of

Carrickfergus. Tyrone, anxious to gain time, asked for a parley. A conference was held at a ford in the Lagan between the two earls. What passed at the interview will never be known; but Essex agreed to an armistice, in order to lay the grievances of the Irish before the queen. It was whispered that, in view of the speedy death of the old queen and the possible accession of the King of the Scots, a traitorous correspondence was held between Essex and Tyrone, in which it was suggested that, if Tyrone would assist Essex to secure the English crown, Ireland should be left to the O'Neils. However this may have been, another indignant letter from Elizabeth, warning Essex that "to trust this traitor upon oath is to trust a devil upon his religion," determined him to return to England to explain and defend his conduct. At first he determined to take with him a picked body of troops, and to march on London; but he abandoned this idea to throw himself at his sovereign's feet, and left Ireland in September never to return.

The queen appointed Charles Blount Lord Mountjoy to be lord deputy in the room of Essex. Mountjoy at once set to work to reform the abuses of the army upon a rigid and almost a Puritan scheme. Not only was the punishment of death to be inflicted on any person guilty of such offences as stealing of stores, duelling, sleeping on duty, falling out of the ranks, or exceeding furlough, "except he can prove he was stayed by the hand of God," but also on those who "spoke against the Holy and Blessed Trinity," or contravened the articles of the Christian faith. Impiety, blasphemy, and unlawful oaths were punished by fine and imprisonment, and so was a wilful absence from morning and evening prayers.

As soon as he had succeeded in recasting the army, Mountjoy proceeded to increase the garrisons in all parts of the country, and to maintain the chain of forts upon the northern frontier. Sir Henry Dockra was sent round to Lough Foyle with 4000 men, where he occupied and fortified Derry; and Sir Arthur Chichester and Sir Samuel Bagnal were instructed to lay waste systematically all the country within reach of their respective commands at Carrickfergus and Newry.

An attempt had been made to intercept Tyrone at Mullingar, on his way back to the north from Cork and Tipperary, where he had been receiving the homage of the Southern Irish; but he succeeded in giving the deputy the slip, and hastened back to defend the line of the Blackwater. The watchful Mountjoy now gave him enough to do in his own territory to keep him from assisting the other rebels; and in the meantime the tide began to turn against the insurgents in other parts of Ireland. Leix was overrun, and O'Moore was shot. All the standing corn in the country, to the value, it was said, of over £1000, which had been grown by the returned Irish after the expulsion of the planters, was cut down and destroyed. Sir George Carew, the new President of Munster and brother to Sir Peter, had broken up the league in that province, and was hunting the Sugan Earl from place to place, and capturing and garrisoning his strongholds. As Mountjoy showed himself to be strong and capable, so many of the native chiefs began to change sides. Mountjoy and Carew accepted their submission, and put a price of £1000 on the heads of Tyrone and the Sugan Earl. Shortly afterwards the latter was handed over to the President of Munster by the White Knight, who made his peace with the government, and pocketed the promised reward. But no bribe could prevail on the Irish to betray "The O'Neil," in such reverence were his name and office held. As events were marching, there was every sign of the great confederacy going to pieces, when suddenly a Spanish fleet of fifty sail, with 3000 men on board, commanded by Don Juan del Aguila, appeared in the harbor of Kinsale.

The Spaniards landed and occupied the town, and their fleet sailed away. To isolate and, if possible, to reduce them before they could effect a junction with the Irish chieftains was Mountjoy's prompt decision. He and Carew brought up every available man, even withdrawing the garrison from Armagh, to shut them into the town on the land side, while some English ships of war blockaded the harbor. A close siege was commenced. O'Donnel and Tyrone, with all the forces at their command, each hurried from the north to relieve their Spanish allies. An attempt made by Carew to cut off Tyrrel and

O'Donnel in Tipperary before Tyrone came up was defeated by O'Donnel's vigilance; and the Irish, eluding him by forced marches, pushed on by a circuitous route to the south coast of County Cork. Here six more Spanish vessels were sighted off Cape Clear. The Irish of the rocky promontories of Southern Cork and Kerry, who had hitherto looked on in sullen silence, rose to a man, and O'Sullivan of Beare and O'Driscol of Castlehaven received Spanish garrisons into the castles of Dunboy and Baltimore.

Tyrone effected a junction with O'Donnel, and took up a threatening position to the north of the English army, which was closing its lines round Kinsale. For fourteen days the armies sat watching one another. Straitened for want of food and forage, and suffering bitterly from exposure, the English intrenched themselves, and from time to time repulsed the sallies from the town. Their position was growing extremely critical: they had in their turn become besieged; and though their communications by sea were open, the return of the Spanish fleet might at any moment make their surrender a mere question of time. So confident of success were Tyrone and the Spaniards that they "were in contention whose prisoner the deputy should be and whose the president." On December 24th, Tyrone, persuaded against his better judgment, endeavored to surprise the English lines. Information of his designs had been carried by a deserter to Carew, and the English were under arms ready to receive him. After a sharp conflict the Irish gave way. The panic spread to the main body; the flying natives streamed through the camp; the rout became general, and the whole Irish army fled in hopeless confusion towards Bandon.

This unexpected deliverance of Mountjoy's force was the turning-point of the war. All hope of relieving Kinsale was abandoned, and Tyrone led back his broken regiments to defend the borders of his own country. O'Donnel, in despair, fled to Spain to beg for further help, where he shortly afterwards was poisoned by an emissary from England. Del Aguila and the Spaniards surrendered Kinsale on honorable terms, and returned to Spain, whither they were accompanied by crowds of Irish refugees; and Carew was left to reduce the rock fortress of Dunboy, which was desperately held by O'Sullivan Beare.

The rebellion in Munster was now stamped out with awful ferocity. No quarter was given on either side. The returning planters and Carew's flying columns laid waste the whole country, " not leaving behind man or beast, corn or cattle." In the north, the lord deputy was gradually hemming in Tyrone. A secure hold was taken of his country by the fortifying of the two positions of Mountjoy and Charlemont on the southeast, and Derry, Donegal, and Lifford on the northwest. His friends deserted him right and left, and made their submission to the government, which the lord deputy would only accept upon their "doing some signal service on their own people," that is, the betrayal of their friends.

Elizabeth was now slowly sinking into the grave, and to terminate the war before the chance arose of a disputed succession was all-important. There was great apprehension of a fresh descent on the Irish coast by a Spanish fleet, which would be removed were hostilities to cease. Tyrone, though not yet a hunted fugitive, saw that all hope of final success was gone. His territory was so wasted that the people were dying of starvation by hundreds; the country was strewed with unburied carcasses; while an active and determined enemy was gradually drawing the net more tightly round him. Under these circumstances, he came in person under a safe-conduct to Mellifont, and terms were come to: honorable, indeed, to Tyrone, and sufficiently satisfactory to the crown. The earl made his submission. He surrendered his estates, and renounced forever all claims to the title of "O'Neil," or suzerainty over his neighbors. He abjured alliances with all foreign powers, especially Spain; and promised to introduce English laws and customs into Tyrone. On the other hand, he was to receive a full pardon and a regrant of his title and lands by letters-patent, and a general amnesty was given to his followers, and the full possession of their estates. At the moment when Tyrone was on his knees before the deputy at Mellifont, Elizabeth had already breathed her last.

CHAPTER XIII.

THE INTRODUCTION OF ENGLISH IDEAS. A.D. 1603–1606.

MOUNTJOY and Carew had now stamped out every spark of rebellion in every part of Ireland. The power of the Irish was completely broken by the process of starvation. The system pursued both in the south and in the north of destroying the crops removed the whole source of sustenance on which the mass of the people depended. To add to the loss of the food at hand, Elizabeth's practice of debasing the coin had doubled and trebled the price of every purchasable article, and a fatal pestilence had followed upon the famine. The people in Ulster died of hunger by thousands. Moryson, who was Mountjoy's secretary, and afterwards President of Ulster, tells awful stories of how the carcasses of people lay in ditches, their dead mouths green with the docks and nettles on which they had endeavored to support life. How young children were trapped and eaten by the starving women who were hiding in the woods on the Newry; and how he and Sir Arthur Chichester witnessed the horrible spectacle of three young children devouring the entrails of their dead mother.

The subjugation was ruthlessly accomplished; but we must remember that the nature of the country was such that it could not well be subdued by the recognized methods of warfare pursued against more civilized countries. There was no central government in Ireland with whom the lord deputy could treat. There was no capital city or fortress, no arsenal or camp, the capture of which would paralyze all after-efforts at resistance. The whole island was, to a great extent, impassable to an army. There were a few main roads radiating from Dublin; the great highway to Galway; the high-road to Carrickfergus along the coast; the high-road, also along the coast, to Wexford; and the great road by the way of Naas over Leighlin Bridge to Kilkenny, and thence, breaking through the hills at Cahir, to the city of Cork, a branch from which led round by Limerick to the fortress of Athlone. Along these main lines of communication the deputies had hitherto always proceeded in all their raids or "hostings," marching from block-house to block-house, and from one walled town to another, along the line, and laying waste the enemy's land as they went. The country lying between and beyond these main arteries was either mountainous or boggy or densely wooded, with patches of cultivated and pasture land interspersed among it. Into these impenetrable fastnesses the natives, on the approach of the royal forces, invariably retired, and it was hopeless and highly dangerous to follow them. To send an invading army against such an enemy in such a country was like striking a feather-bed—no resistance was made, and no result was produced. Mountjoy and Carew came at the end of a long line of soldiers who had broken their hearts in the endeavor to subdue the Irish with insufficient forces. They now had the men at their command, and were determined to do their business thoroughly. They did so in the only way in which they could hope to succeed—namely, planting garrisons at intervals in the disaffected country, keeping up the lines of communication effectually between them and the old fortified positions, scouring the intervening country with small parties of horse and foot, burning the huts, driving the cattle, and utterly laying waste every patch of cultivation.

The great mass of the Irish were still in, or rather had sunk back into, a semi-barbarous condition. The incessant fighting among themselves and the Norman settlers, and afterwards the desolating wars of Elizabeth's reign, had effectually checked their progress towards civilization. Their only wealth was cattle. There was very little actual money in use, and fines and cesses were paid and taken in kind. The Anglo-Irish lords and the Irish chieftains were many of them fairly educated, though we find a large proportion of the latter executed their indentures of submission by subscribing their mark. They lived in moated stone castles, some of which had lead roofs; and their dress was a shirt dyed with saffron, a short jacket with wide sleeves, and over all a cloak of fur. The class below, or the gentry, lived a good deal rougher life, especially those of Ulster, where some, indeed, occupied clay houses with raftered roofs, but more lived in rude cabins, built for safety on small islands in the midst of large pools of water. Chimneys were unknown, the smoke from the fire in the centre coming out at a hole in the roof. Furniture and bedding they had none, a heap of straw or rushes doing duty for the latter. Their usual food was oat-cake, strong cheese and butter, and milk; the better sort indulging in joints, fowls, rabbits, and bacon. Their ordinary clothing was made of homespun wool and flax, but their fighting attire was a quilted leathern jacket, with long hose and leathern boots. The poor churls were in a miserable condition; they lived where they could and how they could; they commonly went stark-naked, even the women. They slept in the same hovel and on the same litter as their beasts; they lived, when they could get it, on the flesh of swine and horses which had died of disease; more often on milk and curds. Nothing would induce them to kill a cow for food, unless it was old and gave no milk.

The chief, nearly the only, industry was cattle-growing; large herds were still pastured on the common lands of the tribe, flocks of sheep still throve on the uplands, and droves of hogs were still turned out to grub in the woods. A considerable amount of grain, chiefly oats and barley, was grown, partly for food, partly for the production of "usquebaugh," or whiskey, and partly for exportation; the ploughing being accomplished with the help of five or six horses abreast, which were fastened to the plough by their tails. The towns, especially the towns on the sea-coast, approximated far more to the towns in England. They were well walled and fortified, and the houses were substantial, and built with regularity. The citizens lived and dressed like English people, and carried on a considerable export trade in corn, flax, wool, hides, lead, and timber. The fisheries, both sea and fresh-water, which were extremely abundant, appear to have been generally neglected.

Into this battered, ruined, famine-wasted, plague-stricken inheritance came James VI. of Scotland in 1603. He had coquieted considerably with the Roman Catholic party both at home and abroad prior to the queen's decease, and this had raised hopes in the Romanists of Ireland that the old forms of religion would be restored. In this they were grievously disappointed. The citizens of the corporate towns of the south, who were rejoicing "that Jezebel was dead," and had rather prematurely taken steps to reintroduce the mass, were roughly brought to their senses; and a royal proclamation was issued to the effect that no tolerance to the Roman Catholic religion would be given; that all Jesuits and Romish priests should quit the country; and that the penal clauses of the Act of Uniformity, which Elizabeth had allowed to remain a dead letter, would be strictly enforced.

This course was adopted, partly under pressure from the growing Puritan party in England, and partly in deference to the opinion of the Irish council, who were gradually developing the theory that the Popish priests were at the bottom of all Irish disaffection. There is no doubt that at this time great numbers of English, Irish, and Spanish Jesuits had openly swarmed over into Ireland from the Continent, as they had, at the risk of their lives, secretly invaded England from Douay and St. Omer. They had taken a most active part in the recent wars, many of them even fighting desperately in the field. The Pope, too, had organized a complete Roman Catholic hierarchy; regularly appointing, as vacancies fell, archbishops and suffragans to all the Irish sees. Still, though many Jesuits and friars had been hanged, there had been as yet no general persecution of the laity. Numbers of Irish Roman Catholics had fought in Mountjoy's army; and all the English Pale, though Roman Catholics to a man, were strictly loyal.

Mountjoy, rewarded with the earldom of Devonshire, had returned to England. He had been succeeded by Sir Arthur Chichester. Sir Arthur was a man of strong Puritan tendencies, and determined to act rigorously on the proclamation. Accordingly, sixteen of the aldermen and chief citizens of Dublin were ordered to attend divine service in Christchurch; and on their not appearing were heavily fined, and flung into prison, by order of the Castle Chamber. Great indignation was felt throughout the Pale. The Roman Catholic peers and gentry petitioned the king; but the instigators of this movement were imprisoned, and Sir Patrick Barnewell sent to England and confined in the Tower. The taking of the Oath of Supremacy was enforced on all persons called to fill any office, civil or military; which practically excluded all Roman Catholics from the magistracy, the privy council, the bench, the bar, and the army. The penalty of twelve pence for not attending church on every Sunday and holyday was sternly exacted by the lord deputy in Meath and Westmeath, in King's and Queen's counties, and by the presidential courts in the towns of Munster and Connaught. And Sir John Davis, the attorney-general, the leading spirit in the council, flattered himself that a great reformation was being effected "through the civil magistrate."

In England legislation had formed habits which had resulted in a general change of faith. The Irish government fondly imagined that they could effect the same thing in Ireland. Elizabeth, for the purpose of educating young men for the ministry, had founded Trinity College, Dublin, and endowed it with the lands of the Monastery of All-hallows. King James greatly increased its endowments. He very wisely had the Bible and the Liturgy translated into Irish, and copies of the same were supplied to the parish churches. But, unfortunately, the parish clergy were Englishmen, "like the priests of Jeroboam, taken from the basest of the people," who knew no Irish, and consequently could not make use of the books, and their flocks profited nothing. Sir John Davis complains of the character of the clergy, and thus sums up the case: "The churches are ruined and fallen down. There is no divine service, no christening of children, no receiving of the sacrament, no Christian meeting or assembly—no, not once a year; in a word, no more demonstration of religion than amongst Tartars and cannibals." And yet the government wondered that the people clung to the friars upon the hill-side.

King James, as soon as he had leisure to turn to Ireland, determined to enforce order over the whole island. The old Brehon law was to be utterly abolished, and the means of appealing to English law brought within the reach of every one. Ulster was first of all to be settled, and provision made for the security of the inferior members of the sept. After obtaining a regrant of their territory from Henry VIII., the chieftains had continued to oppress the other members of the tribe with their customary exactions ; and James's professed object was to protect this class. Accordingly, when Tyrone and the other chiefs of Ulster renewed their submission to James and received their letters-patent, he compelled them to accept as defined freehold estates their own demesne lands only, and to give up all claim to the rest of the tribal land, otherwise occupied, only reserving to them a fixed rent-charge out of these lands, for which their irregular "cosherings" were commuted. The sub-chiefs were confirmed in the land occupied by them, which was defined in the same manner, and accepted as an estate in fee subject to the payment of the rent-charge; and in this way it was hoped that a regular system of landholding, according to the English tenure, would be developed out of the old tribal system.

This scheme, however, only provided for the more powerful members of the tribes, and took no account of the inferior members, each of whom, in his degree, had an undeniable, if somewhat indefinite, interest in the tribal land. Sir John Davis, who carried out the plan, seems to have thought he had gone quite far enough in erecting the sub-chiefs into freeholders; his real object being not so much to protect their interests as to weaken the power of the chieftains. It never occurred to him that the humblest member of the tribe should, if strict justice were done, have received his allotment out of the common territory; and the result of his settlement, accordingly, was that the tribal land was cut up into a number of large freehold estates, which were given to the most important personages among the native Irish, and the bulk of the people were reduced to the condition of tenants at will.

In order to carry out this great revolution in land-tenure, royal commissions were issued to survey the country and to inquire into titles. Provision was made that two judges should go circuit twice a year to try offences against the law, and claims to property, by the help of juries, in supersession of the Brehon's arbitrations. All the shires were formally recognized, and sheriffs and coroners appointed to each. A decision of the Queen's Bench in Dublin in an ejectment suit decided that the law of Tanistry and gavelkind was nothing but "a lewd and damnable custom;" and that land was descendible only according to the limitations of English law.*

The immediate result of this was that the northern chiefs found themselves plunged in litigation. Tyrone had a lawsuit with O'Kane in respect of his seigniorial rights over O'Kane's territory; and, on the case being tried by the council, it was conveniently discovered that neither party had any right to the subject-matter in dispute, but that it had been vested in the crown since 1570! The Bishop of Derry had a claim against O'Kane with regard to certain Church land, upon which the bishop charged him with having made encroachments. And so the actions multiplied and the lawyers throve.

Tyrone had been over to the English court; had been graciously received by the king; and had returned to Ireland with the intention of settling down as a loyal subject. Rory O'Donnel, Red Hugh's younger brother, had also made his peace with the crown. He had been created Earl of Tyrconnel, and received a grant of the County of Donegal, his brother the O'Donnel's country.

Though shorn of a great deal of their influence, these great chieftains might still be dangerous; and the government accordingly watched them narrowly for any opportunity to destroy them. Sir John Davis had instituted a galling system of espionage over Ulster, so that Tyrone complained that " he could not even drink a full carouse of sack, but the State was within a few hours advertised thereof." Insulted by the king's officers, harassed by litigation, and worried by spies, he appears to have dropped some incautious words to Lord Delvin, and the latter seems to have held some secret conversation with Tyrconnel at Maynooth Castle, when on a visit to the Earl of Kildare. There is no reason to suppose that this vague talk

---

* McBrien v. O'Callaghan, Davy's Reps., pp. 28, 49.

was in any way serious; but, whatever it was, Lord Howth, who was admitted by the government to be unworthy of credit, managed to obtain an inkling of it, developed it into a cut-and-dried plot to seize the Castle and murder the deputy, and embodied it in a letter, which he purposely dropped at the door of the council-chamber.

Tyrone, who was shortly to appear in London on the hearing of the appeal in the suit with O'Kane, received information that it was the intention of the government to arrest him on his arrival in England; and he and Tyrconnel determined, in a panic, to fly to the Continent. They hastened with their families on board a vessel lying in Lough Swilly, and eventually reached Rome, where Tyrconnel died the following year, and Tyrone, broken and blind, lingered eight years longer. Lord Delvin was formally arrested, and made a comprehensive confession. He was shortly afterwards created Earl of Westmeath; and Lord Howth was rewarded by the command of a troop of horse.

A few months after the flight of the earls, O'Dogherty of Inishowen and some of the O'Donnels broke out into a futile revolt in the extreme north of the island. They were promptly crushed, and a hunted remnant of their following ruthlessly exterminated in their last refuge, Torry Island. In the meantime, O'Kane had been put on his trial for treason, a charge for which there does not seem to have been a shadow of foundation. But as a Donegal jury had recently acquitted Sir Neal O'Donnel, it was considered unsafe to try to obtain a legal conviction in Ulster, and he was forwarded to the Tower, where he afterwards died. So, one by one, the heads of the Ulster poppies were falling.

CHAPTER XIV.

THE PLANTATION OF ULSTER. A.D. 1611.

NOTHING could have been more opportune for James's schemes for "pacifying" Ulster than the flight of the earls. The door was at once thrown open for a wide and wholesale plantation of all the north. By the "treason" of the chiefs, six counties were held, by a stretch even of English law, to be escheated to the crown. The whole map of Ulster was a clean chart, for the king to draw upon as he pleased. The opportunity, most gratifying to the pedantic vanity of James, was given to constitute a new social and political system. The old order of things was to be clean wiped out, and a new creation was to come into existence, "as if his majesty were to begin a new plantation in some part of America."

According to English law, all that would have fallen to the crown were the freehold lands of the persons attainted. But though it suited the government in 1604 to cut down the rights of the chieftains to their demesnes, to exalt the lesser chiefs into freeholders, and to hold out fixity of tenure as the great benefit to be obtained by the introduction of English law and the creation of shire-ground, in 1610 the theory was that the fee of the chieftains extended to the whole soil of Ulster, and that the newly created freeholders were no better than tenants at will.

The greatest care was taken to make the new plantation a success. Three royal commissions were at work in 1608, 1609, and 1610. Long and anxiously were the scheme and its details discussed by the king and Sir Arthur Chichester with Sir John Davis and the other commissioners. The plantation in Munster had been an acknowledged failure, by reason of the enormous size of the grants made to the undertakers. The grantees, who were too big to settle and farm personally, drew the rents, and took no trouble to plant English farmers on the land, but suffered the Irish to continue in occupation. The plantations of Leix and Offaly had been equally a failure, because the English planters and the old Irish had been allowed to live as neighbors in unrestricted intercourse.

These errors were to be avoided in Ulster. The tracts granted were to be of a manageable extent; the natives were to have locations of their own, to which they were to be removed; the new settlers drawn from England and Scotland were to be massed and grouped together, so as to be a strength and protection to each other; and the "swordsmen," the turbulent gentry whose occupation was gone with the war, and who were an idle and dangerous class, were to be shipped to Sweden and induced to enlist under Gustavus Adolphus, or to be transplanted into convenient places in Kerry, Tipperary, and Roscommon. The escheated lands, both temporal and Church lands, which were all brought into "hotch-pot," were to be divided into lots of 2000, 1500, and 1000 acres each, and to be granted, at a reserved quit-rent of $1\frac{1}{4}d.$, $2d.$, and $2\frac{1}{4}d.$ per acre, in fee partly to English and Scotch undertakers, partly to English "servitors" —that is, those who had held civil or military appointments during the war—and partly to the native Irish. Reservations were made for the crown, for the bishoprics, for the building of free schools, and the erection of forts and corporate towns. The country was mapped out into parishes; and portions of glebe were allotted in each for the support of the parochial clergy. Every undertaker of the larger lots was bound in a bond of £400 within four years to build a castle or mansion-house and a bawn, and within five years to plant on his estate four fee-farmers each on 120 acres, six leaseholders each on 100 acres, and eight families of skilled workmen and laborers. Every undertaker of the smaller lots was under similar and proportionate obligations. No land was to be sublet for less than twenty-one years, nor was it to be alienated for five years to come to any one but the tenants themselves. All tenants were to build houses and keep good store of arms. The houses were to be built in groups so as to form towns and villages, and not to be isolated and scattered. All the grantees and their tenants were to take the Oath of Supremacy. None of the undertakers were to be permitted to take the natives as tenants. Only the servitors and the Church were permitted, in their own discretion, to let a farm to an Irishman. The corporation of London and the twelve city guilds agreed to take up the whole county of Coleraine, upon the terms that they would maintain the forts of Culmore, Coleraine, and Derry. In aid of their undertaking, the king created the order of baronets who bear on their coat the bloody hand of Ulster with which the shield of the O'Neils was charged, and each recipient of the patent was bound to pay into the exchequer three years' pay of a soldier for service in Ulster.

As a most necessary preliminary, an accurate survey of the whole of the confiscated country was made, the surveyors taking their measurements under the protection of mounted troopers; and the commissioners, supported by the military, collecting evidence, by the help of grand-juries in each county, of what land was temporal and what was ecclesiastical property. A proclamation was then issued, stating what land was assigned to the undertakers, to the servitors, and to the natives respectively. The natives fetched down Dublin lawyers to argue that they had estates of inheritance which would not be forfeited on the attainder of their demesne lords, and to plead the king's public proclamation, given five years before on the flight of the earls, that all the inhabitants should be secured in their possessions, and that he had specially taken them under his protection. It need hardly be said that that legal sycophant Sir John Davis was equal to the occasion, and that his sophistries and ingenious quibbles soon put the presuming Dublin lawyers to silence.

Slowly and sullenly the Irish gentry removed themselves and their belongings into the contracted locations to which they had been appointed, away from the "fat lands" to the "lean lands," from the rich pasture to the barren moor. Slowly and sullenly the mass of the people followed them, thrust out of their homes, to find new refuges wherein to lay their heads: some among the servitors; some in the "lean lands;" some transplanted in gangs, at the command of the government, into waste land, which no one wanted, in Munster and in Connaught. Exiled to make room for the planters, evicted, though promised security, they wandered forth, bearing in their hearts a store of bitter hatred for the invaders who had broken faith with them; and yearning for the vengeance which they were to snatch in 1641.

The whole of the six counties which were confiscated contained about 2,836,837 Irish, or, according to modern surveys in English measure, 3,785,057 acres. Of this four fifths were barren or "lean" land, and 511,465 Irish acres were valuable or "fat" land. The bulk of the Irish were cleared from the fat land into the lean land; and the 511,465 acres were partly reserved for public purposes, and partly divided among 50 English and 59 Scotch undertakers, 60 servitors, 286 natives "of good merit," and the London companies. The 286 natives obtained only about one tenth of the whole. The following table will show the way in which the land was apportioned:

	Acres.
* English undertakers, 50 in number	81,500
* Scotch undertakers, 59 in number	81,000
* Servitors, 60 in number	49,914
Meritorious natives, 286 in number	52,279
London guilds	61,437
Trinity College, Dublin	9,600
Bishops, and deans and chapters	77,666
Glebes for parochial clergy	19,268
Free schools	2,700
Corporate towns and forts	47,101
Several persons as abbey lands	21,552
Restored to certain individual Irishmen	7,448
Total	511,465

The object of James was to introduce a thoroughly Protestant and anti-Irish element, which should dominate the Roman Catholics and natives. The success of the plantation became apparent in a few years, when commissioners were sent down to inspect the progress which was being made. The English

---

* For a list of the undertakers and servitors, see Appendix III.

and Scotch gentry who had taken up the land were *bonâ fide* occupying it with their wives and families. The Londoners had fortified Derry—London Derry, as thenceforward it was called—with ramparts twelve feet thick, drawbridges, and battlemented gates. Fair castles, handsome mansions, and substantial farm-buildings were springing up in every part of the country; "fulling-mills" and "corn-mills" were utilizing the ample water-power; windmills were spinning on the rising ground; limekilns were smoking, in preparation for more extensive building operations. There were smiling gardens and orchards and fields in "good tillage after the English manner." Market towns and villages were rising, with paved streets and well-built houses and churches; schools and bridges were in course of construction.

Nevertheless, the complete scheme was never carried out in its entirety; nor was it possible that it should be so. If all the natives had been removed to a man, the planters would have had no laborers. Though numbers of Scotch and English hands were introduced, the full complement was far from made up, and the temptation was considerable to keep on the Irish, who were ready at hand, and willing, to become hewers of wood and drawers of water. The necessity of this was admitted by the government; and the king's warrants for the removal of the natives were from time to time suspended to meet the difficulty. The consequence was that, contrary to the terms of the planters' grants, many Irish were taken as tenants; the planters even offering to pay double quit-rent to the crown if permitted to employ native labor; and the natives outbidding the strangers by promises to pay higher rent to the land-owners. The planters in many cases violated their agreements with the crown in another way. They refused or neglected to give definite leases of twenty-one years to their English and Scotch tenants; and many of these, who had been induced on promise of a lease to take farms and expend money thereon, retired in disgust into England, and sold their interest in the holdings, and the value of the capital they had sunk in the land, to the natives, who were only too ready to get back on to the soil at any price and at any risk. These practices were winked at by the planters, who were glad to get less independent tenants, until the custom of selling and buying the tenant right became established in Ulster as a recognized portion of the unwritten law of the province.

CHAPTER XV.
THE MUZZLING OF THE PARLIAMENT. A.D. 1613.

THE momentous revolution in Ulster had been accomplished through the instrumentality of royal proclamations and royal warrants, following upon verdicts of "guilty" wrung from the juries before which the earls had, in their absence, been indicted. It was now thought desirable to put the seal of legality upon what had occurred by summoning a Parliament and passing an act of attainder against them.

Great wrestlings of spirit did the king and the deputy and Sir George Carew endure in respect of the composition of this Parliament. The spirit of religious intolerance was now fully awake. Every Irish interest was identified with Popery; every English interest with Protestantism. The government had determined to convert Ireland to the Reformed faith by the terrors of the law. And in order to have a Parliament which would work, it was necessary, in their eyes, that there should be a competent Protestant majority. Seeing that the freeholders of the greater part of Ireland and almost all the burgesses were of the Roman Catholic persuasion, it was a moral certainty that at a free election only a very small number of Protestants would be returned. How to avoid this difficulty was the task which fell to Carew and Sir John Davis; and after weighing the reports of the provincial presidents, and balancing the *pros* and *cons*, they calculated that by incorporating the infant towns which were projected and partly built in Ulster, and certain judiciously selected garrison towns elsewhere, to the number of forty, these, with the representatives of the newly planted counties, would be sufficient to swamp the "recusants" of the other three quarters of the kingdom. They felt safe with respect to the peers, for they reckoned that " of the forty-four spiritual and temporal we may assure ourselves of the nineteen bishops; of the temporal lords, three are under age and five are Protestants, and so we shall sway the Upper House by seven voices." It was the Commons who were the stumbling-block. There were thirty-three counties in all, Wicklow having been recently carved out of the county of Dublin, and that portion of the present county of Tipperary in which Holy Cross is situated being reckoned as a separate shire by the name of "the Crosse."

Moryson, the President of Munster, reported that there might be as many as ten Protestant knights of the shire returned for his presidency, the only freeholders in the greater part of the province being of the recent plantation in Desmond; but that Tipperary and Crosse would return recusants. Of burgesses for Limerick, Waterford, and Cork, he says there is "no hope of any Protestant." For Kinsale, Kilmallock, Clonmel, Cashel, Fethard, "no hope of any conformable;" and for the rest of the ancient corporations but three Protestants would be chosen. By the creation, however, of eight new boroughs, sixteen supporters of the government would be secured; so that, on the whole, he concludes, "if it be so, the Protestants will exceed them six voices."

Sir Oliver St. John, the President of Connaught, reported that "he could not assure himself of the five counties of more than two Protestants;" and of the ancient boroughs of Galway and Athenry, "no hope of any Protestant." The new borough of Athlone, however, a garrison town, he says will send two Protestants; and of the "boroughs to be newly erected" he believed all would send Protestants except Loughreagh, which "peradventure would send Papists;" but that it might be as well, nevertheless, to incorporate it, "as it would gratify the opinion of partiality (*sic*) in erecting the new boroughs." So that, on the whole, he hopes "the government of Connaught will send to the Parliament twenty-two Protestants for fourteen Papists."

It was hoped that, in view of the recent plantation in Leinster,* several of the county members in that province would be Protestant. But, out of the five shires of the Pale, only one Protestant was expected from Westmeath and one from the county of Dublin. Of the burgesses from the thirty ancient bor-

---

* See next chapter.

oughs in Leinster and the Pale but seven Protestants could be reckoned on. In Ulster, on the other hand, all the counties, being recently planted with English Puritans and Scotch Presbyterians, would return Protestants *en bloc;* and as twenty-five corporate towns were to be erected there, each returning two members, the general conclusion on the whole calculation was that the government would have a working majority of about eight-and-twenty.

Upon the news getting abroad that a Parliament was about to be called, and that the king was going to incorporate the Ulster block-house forts, there was a very general belief that the object of the government was to pass a stringent penal statute against the Roman Catholics. And so strong was the fear that the Parliament would be made the instrument of James's arbitrary designs that the gentry actually forwarded a petition to the king not to summon it, a petition which James treated with silent contempt.

On the issuing of the writs, a vigorous contest took place over the whole kingdom. It was the desperate struggle of a nation against the riveting upon them of the shackles of the law by the introduction of the thin end of the "Protestant ascendency." The Roman Catholics strained every nerve to carry the elections; and their energy was rewarded in the counties by the rejection of the government candidates and the return of recusant Dublin lawyers. The measures of the government had, however, been sufficient to secure their majority; and the new house consisted of 226 members, of whom 125 were Protestants and 101 were Roman Catholics, the government having a majority of 24.

On the assembling of this Parliament, the first business was to choose a speaker. The recusants, however, objected to this being done, until the validity of the return of certain members for boroughs which had been created since the issue of the writs had been determined. The government candidate for the speakership was the subtle courtier Sir John Davis, and the recusants put forward Sir John Everard. On a motion that the election of the speaker should precede all other business, the house divided, and the supporters of the government went into the division lobby to be counted. Thereupon the recusant party refused to go into the other lobby, but shouted, "An Everard! an Everard!" and seated their candidate in the chair. The others, on being counted, numbered 127, a clear majority of the whole house, and rushed back into the chamber. Upon finding Everard installed in the chair, they indignantly demanded his withdrawal, and on his refusing proceeded, amid a scene of indescribable confusion, to seat Sir John Davis in his lap. Everard was then forcibly dragged from the chair, and the recusant party thereupon left the house in a body.

After this indecent scene, there was nothing to be done but to suspend the sittings of the house, and to refer the whole case to the king and accept his decision. Accordingly, delegates from each party went over to England, and laid their respective views before his majesty. James found the case of the recusants upon the question of the invalid elections too strong to be ignored; and after rating them well in a long, rambling oration, as incoherent as it was flippant, he cancelled thirteen of the returns, and confirmed the election of Sir John Davis to the speakership.

Parliament was assembled for business, and proceeded to pass an act of attainder* upon O'Neil, O'Donnel, O'Dogherty, and thirty gentlemen of Ulster, by which the forfeiture of their estates was confirmed. All Ireland was now subject to the king. The king's writ ran in every part of the island; the king's courts went their complete circuits. Each shire had its sheriff; and the old Irish law had been everywhere superseded. It remained only to recognize all the inhabitants as the king's subjects, and formally admit the native Irish to the protection of the English law, in the eye of which until now they had been no more than outlaws. Accordingly, an act was passed repealing the old statutes which prohibited commerce, intermarriage, and fosterage between the two races, and extending the privileges and perils of the English system of jurisprudence to all the king's subjects alike.† Notwithstanding all his manœuvring, James considered he had got a stubborn Parliament. But, stubborn though it may have been, it was loyal enough to grant him a substantial subsidy.

---

* 11, 12 Jac. I. c. 4.   † Ib. c. 5.

CHAPTER XVI.
THE PLANTATION OF LEINSTER.   A.D. 1612–1625.

JAMES was so pleased with the success of his plantation in Ulster that he determined to apply the process of planting to the rest of Ireland. There had been no rising, no attempt at disturbance, so that the old excuse for confiscation was not available; it was necessary to invent a system of plundering by process of law to provide the wherewithal for the vain monarch to reconstruct the map of Ireland. "A commission to inquire into defective titles" was sent down into those parts of the country with which it was determined to deal, to collect evidence as to the number and condition of the inhabitants and their lords, what rents were paid, and what and how estates were held; *and to inquire into the title which the crown had to any part thereof.*

The countries which were still principally inhabited by the native Irish were, first, the mountainous strip which runs from Dublin towards Wexford Haven, sloping to the sea upon the east, and comprising the counties of Wicklow and Wexford; secondly, the broad belt of low country, then largely consisting of bog and forest, which skirts the great chain of lakes and rivers lying between Sligo on the north and Lough Derg on the south, and comprises the counties of Leitrim and Longford, and the western portions of Westmeath, King's County, and Queen's County. These tracts were still occupied, the one by the tribes of McMurrough, O'Toole, and O'Byrne, and the other by those of O'Rourke, O'Farrel, O'Melaghlin, O'Molloy, O'Doyne, and McGilapatrick.

It was gravely said that whereas these countries had been originally granted to English colonists in the days of the Plantagenets by the crown, which had no right to make the grant, and these colonists had, in the evil days of the Anglo-

Norman settlement, been driven from their land by the lawful native owners, and had retired into England; and, further, that by various statutes concerning absentees the deserted lands had reverted to the king—the native tribes now in occupation had no prescriptive right by virtue of three hundred years' possession of what was, after all, their own property, and that the whole of the land was vested in James. Leitrim and Longford had been surrendered by the O'Rourke and O'Farrel of that day to Elizabeth, and subsequent acts of rebellion were sufficient to show the king's title in these cases, while Art McMurrough's indenture with Richard II., in A.D. 1394, was raked up to do duty for a title to Wexford.

To give an appearance of legality to these iniquitous proceedings, juries were empanelled, and forced to give verdicts in favor of the crown; witnesses were compelled to give satisfactory evidence; and both jurors and witnesses, if they had the boldness to withstand the pressure of the crown lawyers, were hauled before the Castle Chamber, imprisoned, pilloried, and branded.

Even the Anglo-Irish did not escape the inquisitorial scrutiny. Wherever land could be proved forfeit, so it went, by every low trick and legal artifice that could be practised. It became a regular trade to pick holes in people's titles; every trifling flaw that could be hit upon was carefully noted. The old pipe rolls in Dublin were scanned, and the patent rolls in the Tower of London were searched, to discover ancient rents reserved and unpaid; discrepancies between the patents passed in Ireland and the king's warrant transmitted from England; prior grants or invalid grants; even clerical errors, trivial informalities, and inaccurate terms. One of the principal motives for these proceedings was the replenishing of the royal exchequer. If a flaw could be found in a man's title, he could be frightened into accepting a fresh patent upon the terms of his paying a round sum by way of a composition. If he refused, the land could be granted to some one else at an annual quit-rent, the enterprising " projector " or " discoverer " sharing the plunder with the king. And so the game sped merrily.

Sixty-six thousand eight hundred acres were in this way

declared to be vested in the king in Wexford alone, and in the midland counties no less than 385,000. The ancient proprietors were required to sign submissions and surrenders of their land; and then, after setting apart a sufficient and convenient portion for glebes, schools, forts, and corporate towns, and a fourth part of the whole for English undertakers, the residue was regranted to "the more deserving" of them to hold of the king at certain fixed rents. Small proprietors were especially discouraged, no one being allowed to hold less than a hundred acres "as not good for themselves." The plausible argument was advanced that the natives would be pleased with the change because they obtained a definite estate of inheritance in place of an uncertain estate for life, and that this advantage was a fair equivalent for the loss of more than one fourth of their gross amount of territory. Whether this were so it is unprofitable to inquire, because the natives, in fact, owing to the dishonesty and greediness of the commissioners and surveyors, never obtained anything like the proportion of land which they were promised.

In Longford, which contained 50,000 acres, they obtained less than one third, twenty-five of the O'Farrel family being absolutely deprived of every rood. A large tract was reserved to satisfy a claim of £200 a year made by the heirs of Sir Nicholas Malby, and another of "120 beeves" made by Sir Francis Shane of Granard Castle. Twelve hundred acres were given to undertakers, of whom half were servitors with allotments of 300, 400, and 600 acres each.

In Leitrim, where 201 proprietors executed surrenders, they obtained by regrant half, in Queen's County about two thirds, the remnant of the tribe of the O'Moores being transplanted bodily into Kerry.

In Wexford there were in all 31* undertakers, to whom 33,000 acres were set out. Only 57 natives received any land at all, and to these 57 were allotted 24,615 acres. Three hundred and ninety others who claimed a right to freeholds had no land assigned to them; and they and "the residue of the

---

* For a list of the undertakers of Wexford, see Appendix IV.

inhabitants, estimated to be 14,500 men, women, and children," had the choice of either being evicted "at the will of the patentees," or being permitted "to dwell in that country as their tenants." It was then discovered that half the county had been fraudulently given to the undertakers under the name of a quarter, and it was only after much petitioning and agitation that the land was resurveyed, and a provision made for 80 more native freeholders.

In most cases the discrimination of the surveyor was sufficient to set out the good land to the undertakers and the unprofitable land to the old possessors.

There was, not unnaturally, the strongest opposition to the new plantation. The discontent was deep and widespread; but a rising was seen to be hopeless, and no attempt at resistance was made. Many of the old proprietors who were removed from their lands betook themselves to the woods and an outlaw's life. Agrarian outrages began to occur, " when the nights grew darker and the winter came on." The Lord Deputy St. John, the successor of Chichester, endeavored to hunt down the expelled land-owners, and boasts of having exterminated three hundred of them in three years; though he adds, " When one sort is cut off, others arise in their places, for the countries are so full of the younger sons of gentlemen who have no means of living, and will not work, that when they are sought to be punished for disorders they commit in their idleness, they go to the woods to maintain themselves by the spoil of their quiet neighbors."

In the meantime Sir Richard Boyle, the lord chancellor, who had got possession of Sir Walter Raleigh's extensive grants of land in Munster, had been making a most methodical plantation on his own account at Tallow. It was an armed colony of 522 men—" horsemen," " pikemen," and " shot-furnished;" every one was a sound Protestant; villages were planned, and schools and churches built for their accommodation. The company of East India merchants also planted three colonies near Dundaniel, on the coast of County Cork, where they started iron-works, and constructed a dock, and built " offices, houses, smiths' forges, and other storehouses." So plentiful and so fine was the timber, growing even to the water's edge, that the ship-building trade grew apace. "Two ships of 400 and 500 tons apiece" were launched in the spring of 1613.

Wicklow had yet to be dealt with, the ancient territory of the O'Byrnes. The commissioners reported that at the death of Pheagh McHugh O'Byrne in the rebellion in 1577, his country escheated to the crown, but that Elizabeth had directed a regrant by letters-patent to his son Phelim; that James had given a like direction, which had never been carried out; and they recommended that surrenders should be taken and fresh grants made in the usual way to the O'Byrnes, "at the highest rents procurable." This plan was projected, and a rent of £150 reserved. Provision was made for a plantation, and Phelim O'Byrne was to receive letters-patent confirming him in his estates.

A conspiracy was, however, set on foot by Sir Richard Graham (an officer in the army), Sir James FitzPiers Fitzgerald, Sir William Parsons (the surveyor-general), Sir Henry Belling, and Lord Esmond (one of the new undertakers in Wexford*), to obtain a conveyance of O'Byrne's land to themselves. They accordingly trumped up a charge against him and his five sons of corresponding with an outlawed gentleman of the family of Kavenagh. They lodged an information against them, on the testimony of one Thomas Archer, which they wrung from him by torture on a hot gridiron, and that of three vagrant Irishmen who owed O'Byrne a grudge for his having issued his warrant against them as a justice of the peace. Two of the young O'Byrnes were thereupon confined in Dublin Castle, and Phelim and all the five were prosecuted at the Carlow assizes for treason. The grand-jury threw out the bill, for which they were heavily fined by the Castle Chamber, and a fresh indictment was preferred at the Wicklow assizes. The grand-jury was this time carefully packed with neighboring undertakers to secure the finding of a true bill, and notorious convicted thieves whom Phelim had convicted at petty sessions were called as

---

* The Commissioners of Plantations in Wexford were Sir Laurence Esmond, Sir Edward Fisher, Sir William Parsons, and Nicholas Kenny.

witnesses, and pardoned on giving evidence of the prisoners' guilt. The scandal was so abominable and glaring that Sir Francis Annesley and some other gentlemen took up the case and obtained a royal commission to inquire into the matter, which resulted in the O'Byrnes being set at liberty. Their estates, however, covering half the County of Wicklow, of which during the prosecution Parsons and Esmond had been put in possession by the sheriff of Wicklow, were not restored to them, and the plot in that respect was eminently successful.

Success had attended James's plans in Ulster and Leinster, with the additional advantage of filling the empty coffers of the state. Not only had the revenue been swelled by the chief rents reserved from grants to the new freeholders, and from the fines levied on the occasion of the surrenders and regrants, but the immediate result of the improved condition of agriculture, consequent upon the introduction of thrifty English and Scotch farmers, and the progress exhibited by the natives who were not dispossessed, was to increase the annual receipts from the customs duties from £50 to between £9000 and £10,000. Notwithstanding these advantageous circumstances, however, the want of economy was such in the military and civil expenditure, and the waste and jobbery so great in the way of conferring pensions and sinecures on the Castle clique, that there was an annual deficit in the accounts of over £16,000.

A project was set on foot by the commissioners whom the king sent over to examine into the state of the revenue, for the replenishing of the royal exchequer by attacking the property of the Irish corporate towns. Many of them had received grants of land conditionally upon their efficiently maintaining their bridges, walls, and fortifications; and wherever breaches of these conditions could be discovered, it was proposed that the king should resume the corporation lands, and raise the sum of £50,000 by fines on regrant. This scheme, however, was considered too hazardous to be carried out, and was laid aside.

Connaught showed the best prospect of supplying the deficiencies. It was the only province which had not been planted. The lords and gentlemen of Connaught and County Clare had been persuaded by Sir John Perrot in Elizabeth's reign to compound for the queen's exactions in kind by an annual cess for the support of the army. They had simultaneously surrendered their estates to the crown and received regrants of the same. They had, however, in most cases, owing to the disturbed condition of the times, neglected to have their surrenders enrolled and to take out their letters-patent. Accordingly, in 1616, fresh surrenders were made to James; new patents were made out by him, and received the impress of the great seal. Owing, however, to the neglect of the clerks in Chancery, neither were the surrenders nor the grants enrolled on this occasion, although the grantees had actually paid fees in respect of the enrolment to the amount of £3000.

Here was an opportunity not to be lost. The titles were one and all declared defective, and the lands held to be vested in the crown. A plan was announced for a new plantation after the fashion of those recently conducted in Leinster, and a promising harvest anticipated. Great was the alarm which spread through the western province. The injustice of the proceeding was bitterly felt. But, as it was well known that money was what the king stood most in need of, it was determined to bribe him into relinquishing his design. An offer was made to double the amount of the annual tax, and to pay the king in cash an equivalent for the share which would have fallen to him if the plantation had been carried out on the lines of the previous ones; and this equivalent was estimated at £10,000, a sum equal to £100,000 at the present day.

The proposal was received by his majesty with considerable satisfaction. The plan for the plantation was suspended; but before the compromise could be effected the king died; and the squeezing of Connaught was reserved for his still more unscrupulous successor.

The general result of the plantation policy was to flood Ireland with a host of needy Englishmen and Scotchmen, who looked upon the country as a grand field for enterprising persons with slender means. The colonists in Ulster were in a great measure the scum of both nations, debtors, bankrupts, and fugitives from justice. Shoals of land-jobbers and land-speculators came over to obtain a share in the general division. The hangers-on of the Castle, the conforming lawyers, the poor relations of the Council of State, became large landowners and country gentlemen, and were put into the commission of the peace. Every act of spoliation was carried out under the protection of the law; every legal form and every legal step was strictly adhered to with a surprising ingenuity which makes the account of the most unfair and arbitrary acts read like a narrative of strict but inevitable justice.

To hold a large landed estate was in those days, as it is now, to secure power, influence, and rank; the penniless adventurer, having become possessed of acres, frequently by means which would not bear the light of day, was promptly made a county magistrate, and often elevated to the peerage. Half the peerage of Ireland at the time of the Union was composed of persons whose ancestors had come to Ireland as fortune-hunters after the Elizabethan wars. Being a freeholder, the *novus homo* was one of the few who were qualified to act as justice of the peace, to vote for a member of Parliament, to fill the office of sheriff. He became a small despot in his own part of the country, having very considerable control over the liberties of his neighbors. The institution of a local magistracy, which answered well enough in England, where there was a certain amount of public opinion, was a local tyranny in Ireland, where the large land-owner had it all his own way, where there was no public opinion except that of the other local landowners, and where no notice would be taken by the Castle of any complaints, if such complaints ever succeeded in arriving there.

Of the new nobility which sprang up at this time and swamped the old nobility of the Pale, the most remarkable was Richard Boyle, "the great Earl of Cork." He was the son of a Herefordshire squire, a man of very considerable ability, but utterly unscrupulous. Having found it advisable to absent himself from England by reason, as his enemies say, of his "forgeries, rasings, and perjuries," or because, as he himself puts it, "it pleased Divine Providence to lead him into Ireland," he arrived in Dublin in 1588, with little else in the world but two suits of clothes, a diamond ring, a gold bracelet, and £27 3s. in money. He managed to wriggle himself into the office of deputy escheator of the lands of Munster, under cover of which, by a series of frauds, he became possessed of a considerable extent of the forfeited Irish estates. He was twice indicted for felony, and committed to prison in Dublin six times in five years; but, by his adroitness and the skilful use of bribes, succeeded in cheating justice, and becoming secretary to Sir George Carew. "God having blest him with a reasonable estate," as he piously says in his memoir, his new patron, the President of Munster, made his fortune for him. He advised and assisted him to advance money to the amount of some £1500 to Sir Walter Raleigh on the security of his vast grant of land in Cork and Waterford. The mortgage was foreclosed, and Raleigh's widow and children afterwards complained, in a fruitless petition to the crown, that the estates had been "juggled away." Carew introduced him to Sir Geoffrey Fenton, the queen's surveyor-general, whose daughter he married; and he knighted him on the day of his wedding. Protected by Carew, Essex, and Cecil, with all of whom he was careful to ingratiate himself, he escaped the reward of his misdeeds, and was successively created Baron Youghal, Viscount Dungarvan, Earl of Cork, and a privy-councillor.

William Parsons was another upstart whose career resembled that of Boyle. An Englishman of low birth, and with no education beyond that of reading and writing, he had gone over to Ireland with £40 in his pocket to seek his fortune. Having got into the service of one Kenny, the escheator-general, and saved some money by a combination of hard work and sharp practice, he married a niece of Sir Geoffrey Fenton, the surveyor-general, and in A.D. 1602 succeeded to that office, and became a commissioner of the escheated lands in Ulster. Taking advantage of his position, he took care not to be left out in the allotment of lands, obtaining 1890 acres in Tyrone and 2000 acres in Fermanagh alone. By these means and others still more scandalous, as in the case of the estates of the O'Byrnes of Wicklow, he secured over 8000 acres and amassed an immense fortune. Having secured the patronage of Buckingham, he set at defiance all accusations made against his proceedings, and, in company with the Earl of Cork, was one of the most influential members of the privy council. He was the ancestor of the earls of Rosse of the first creation.

Many of the *novi homines* of this date were army men, who obtained large tracts of land as undertakers or as rewards for services. Of these the most conspicuous were Sir Richard Wingfield, who was rewarded with the Powerscourt estates of the O'Byrnes, and other grants under the Ulster and Wexford plantations; Sir Charles Coote, who secured large estates in Leitrim, Sligo, Roscommon, and Queen's County; Sir Toby Caulfield, who had served under Mountjoy, and who obtained lands in Tyrone and Armagh, and was created Viscount Caulfield; and Sir Arthur Chichester, the lord deputy, and the superintendent of the Ulster plantation, who took advantage of his position to secure the whole territory of Innishowen in Donegal, besides lands in Tyrone, and became Baron of Belfast.

Another class of persons who made their fortunes at this time were clergymen. A newly ordained youth, like Adam Loftus or Dr. Jones, would come over as chaplain to the lord deputy, and quickly be pushed into a deanery, a few big livings, or a bishopric, and, living comfortably at Dublin, draw his large income, which he invested in land. Others leased out the Church lands, and took large fines for renewals, or secured long leases of Church lands to themselves at low rents. More than one ample estate was put together in this fashion, and more than one family founded which will be found in the Peerage of Ireland.

It was at this time and in this way that the new English interest became developed. The new adventurers hung together and intermarried with each other. They did not exhibit the tendency to amalgamate with the people whom they found in Ireland to nearly the same extent as those who had gone before them. They were essentially strangers in the land, who felt that they had gone in for a good speculation, and who would have to do their uttermost to maintain their position.

At the same time, they knew that they must have England at their back, and so they studiously cultivated the English government, and supplanted the old Anglo-Irish families in the favor and good-will of the deputies. They were the embryo of the "Protestant ascendency" of the eighteenth century.

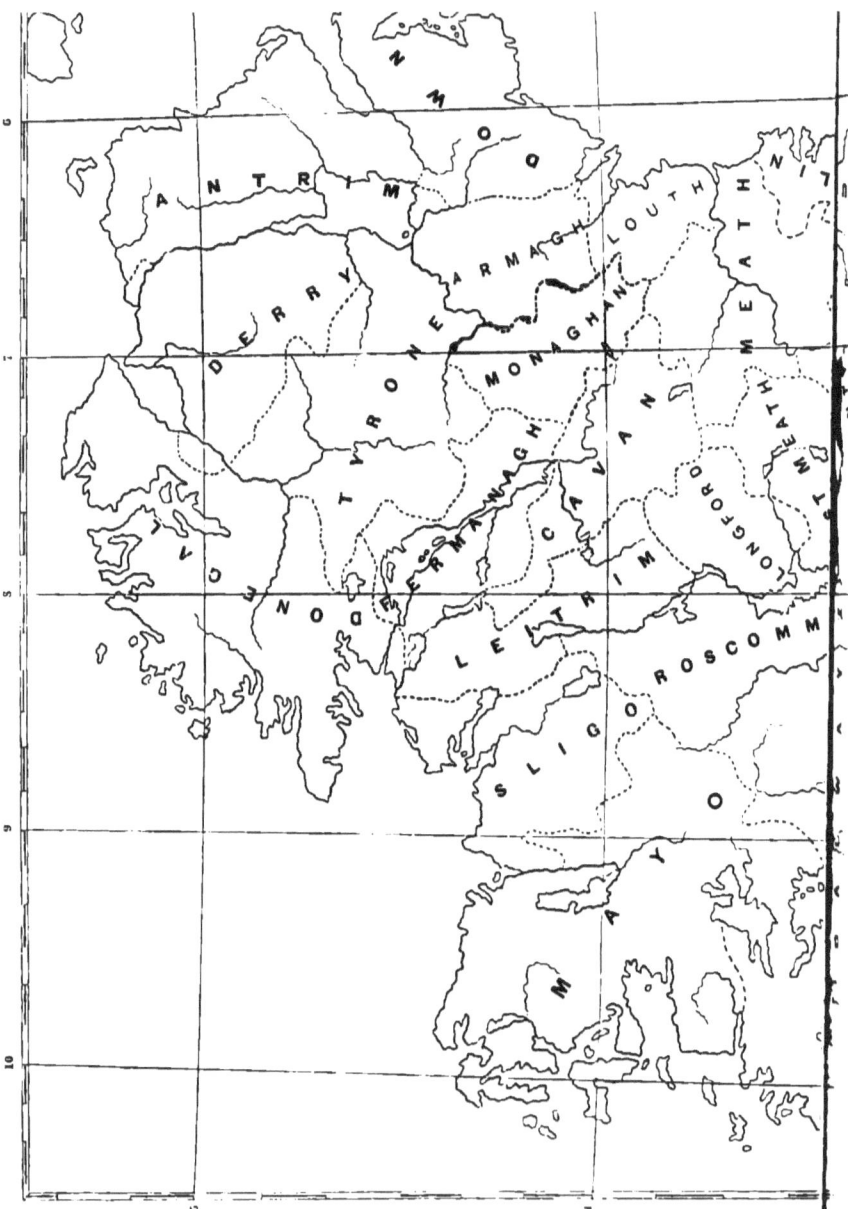

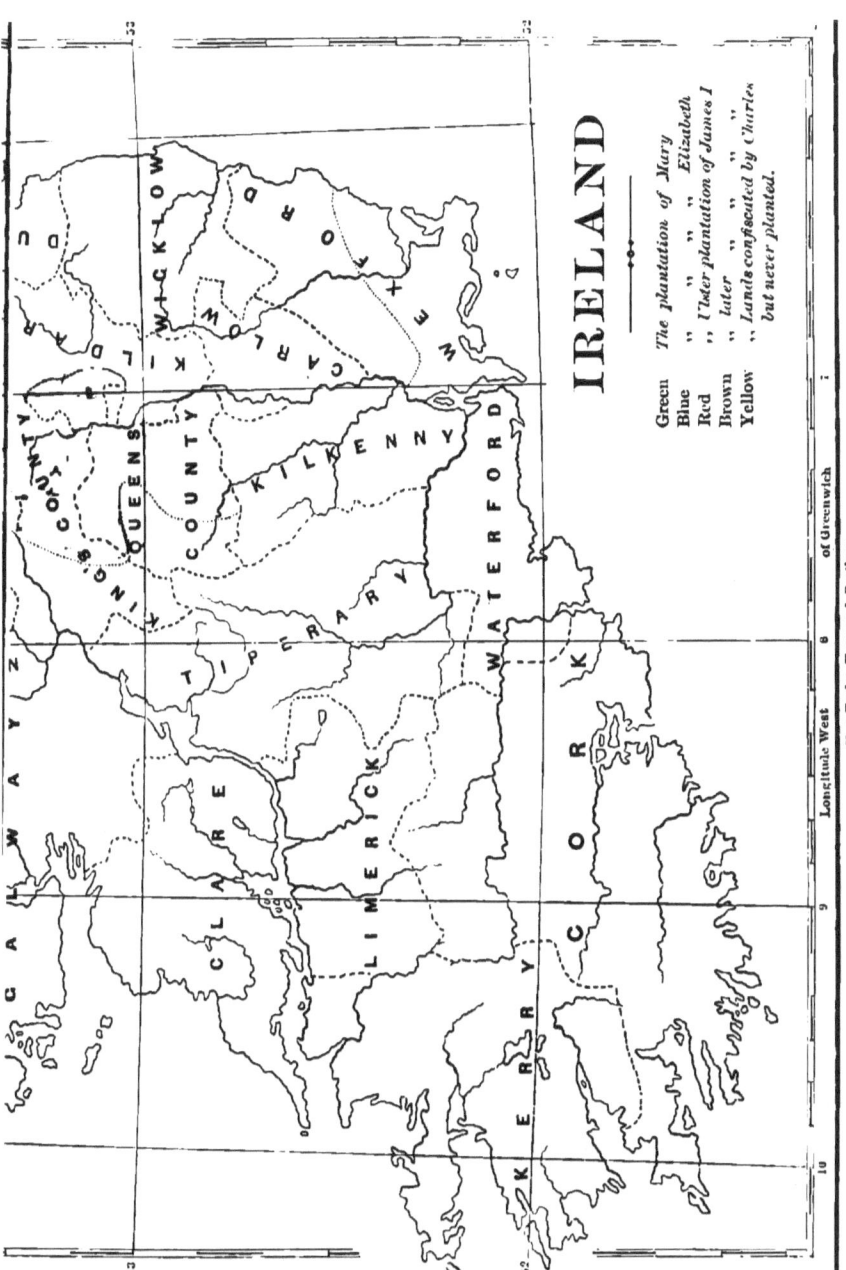

Book IV.
THE SECOND CONQUEST

CHAPTER I.
SOWING THE WIND AGAIN. A.D. 1620–1629.

THE new men, such as Boyle, Parsons, and Loftus, into whose hands the reins of power had now fallen, were all of strong Protestant tendencies. The policy which excluded the Roman Catholics from every office of state, of necessity placed the government in the hands of the extreme men of the contrary way of thinking. Accordingly, we find a regular harassing of the Roman Catholics by the Castle authorities, the Oath of Supremacy being constantly required, and the Act of Uniformity steadily enforced, to the exclusion from public offices and professions, and the systematic impoverishment, of those who refused the one or disobeyed the other. The bishops, with Usher at their head, were one and all of the extreme ultra-Protestant school. Usher introduced the Nine Articles of Lambeth concerning predestination, grace, and justifying faith, with one or two of his own composition identifying the Pope with Antichrist, all of which were accepted by Convocation. Many of the Presbyterian clergy, who had come over with the Scotch colony, were inducted into Ulster livings; while "to grant the Papists toleration" was denounced from all the pulpits as "a grievous sin."

James, on the other hand, who had his eye on the subsidies, was anxious, in the later years of his reign, to hold out to the recusants the prospect of toleration in return for a liberal vote of money. He discouraged the persecution of the recusants, and, in deference to their complaints, replaced the Puritan deputy, Sir Oliver St. John, by Lord Falkland, a man of much less pronounced views. On the accession of Charles, who was believed to have strong leanings towards the Roman Catholics, the hopes of the latter rose, and some attempt was made to restore the Romish worship in a few of the churches. Even a

Roman Catholic seminary was opened, and a body of Carmelite friars ventured to establish themselves in Dublin. The result was a furious outcry on the part of the clergy and the Protestant faction. The Popish College was seized, and handed over to the University of Dublin, and the friars were driven from their monastery by a file of musketeers. So was the see-saw kept up between toleration and persecution, the crown ever ready to take advantage of the latter in a profitable bargain wherein the former was to be bought and sold.

Charles, on coming to the throne, found himself mightily hampered with his father's debts. James's extravagance and bad management had left the treasury empty, and the country was embroiled in a disastrous war for the restoration of his son-in-law to the Palatinate. Money was to be raised at all events; and the king was prepared to promise anything for a good round sum in hard cash. He was perfectly willing to be bribed by the recusants into granting them liberty of conscience, or to close with the offer of the Connaught land-owners and confirm their titles for a consideration. But the Protestant party, though small, was powerful. Concession, therefore, to the recusants was dangerous, and to enroll the Connaught grants was to kill the goose with the golden eggs. The easiest way out of the difficulty was to promise everything, secure the money, and then shuffle out of the performance; and such a scheme especially commended itself to a mind like that of Charles.

A deputation from the principal nobility and gentry of Ireland waited on the king, and offered a voluntary contribution of £120,000, to be paid in three years, in return for the concession of civil and religious liberty. The concessions to be made were reduced into writing, and were comprised in fifty-one articles; they were denominated "Graces," and were in the nature of a "petition of right." The substance of them was that the king's title to land should not be set up where the owner had had sixty years' possession. The surrenders in Connaught were to be enrolled without payment of further fees. The Connaught landlords were to be confirmed in their estates by statute, and a Parliament for effecting that object was shortly to be summoned. All undertakers were to be allowed an extension of time for the fulfilment of their covenant. The extortion practised by the Court of Wards was to be restrained, as also was the oppressive levying of the king's taxes by means of the soldiery. The jurisdiction of the Court of the Castle Chamber—the Irish Star-chamber—in private causes was to be restricted; and the testimony of convicted and condemned felons was to be refused where the liberty of the subject was concerned. Recusants were to be allowed to practise in the courts of law, and sue the livery of their lands out of the Court of Wards, an oath of civil allegiance being substituted for the Oath of Supremacy, while the clergy were to be prohibited from committing the "contumacious" to their own private prisons. Such was the very reasonable charter of liberty asked for by the leading men of Ireland, which, it is hardly too much to say, if Charles had honestly conceded it, would have reduced the rebellion of 1641 to a local rising without a prospect of success.

The king gave his word, and consented to the granting of the "Graces" with alacrity. Formal instructions as to their substance were transmitted to the lord deputy; great satisfaction prevailed; and the first subsidy of £40,000 was cheerfully paid. Falkland at once issued writs for the summoning of a Parliament, which was to give the royal promise the force of law, and convert what was mere waste paper into a binding instrument. And here the duplicity of the king declared itself. Care was taken *not* to obtain the king's license under the great seal for the holding of the Parliament, and that no heads of the bills to be introduced were previously sent over to the English privy council, in conformity with the provisions of Poynings's Act. It was suddenly discovered, when it was conveniently too late, that, in consequence of the omission of these formalities, the issuing of the writs was illegal and void. No fresh writs were forthcoming, and the promised Parliament for confirming the "Graces" was relegated to the limbo of violated pledges.

CHAPTER II.

THE WENTWORTH SCOURGE. A.D. 1632–1641.

FALKLAND was driven to resign by the Irish council, who persecuted him on account of his leniency towards the Roman Catholics, and the government was left temporarily in the hands of lords justices, Lord Cork and Lord Loftus.* Charles had a pet scheme for governing the three kingdoms by means of a favorite minister in each, reserving a general control over the whole to himself. Laud was to answer for England, the Marquis of Hamilton for Scotland; and the man of all others for Ireland was Lord Wentworth, who, as president of the north, had screwed up the revenue of his province from £2000 to £10,000 a year. Accordingly, in the spring of 1632, Wentworth was appointed lord deputy, and took up his residence in Dublin in the July of the following year.

Sir Thomas Wentworth was a Yorkshire baronet of ancient lineage. Shortly after attaining his majority he became his own master, and the possessor of what was then the princely income of £5000 a year, by the death of his father. His ambition prompted him to take part in the stirring public life of the day; all his associations and predilections attached him to the royalist party; and he came into Parliament as representative of his native county, with Calvert, the king's secretary of state, as his colleague. At first he took no part in debate, and gave a silent support to the government; but having incurred the enmity of the Duke of Buckingham, and hoping to increase his importance by showing an independent spirit, he began to form an alliance with the opposition. This drew down upon him the vengeance of the court, and he was successively pricked

---

* Adam Loftus, nephew of the Earl of Sussex's chaplain, was Lord Chancellor of Ireland in 1619, and created Viscount Loftus of Ely in 1622.

for sheriff, deprived of the office of *custos rotulorum* of his county, and sent to the Marshalsea for refusing to pay a forced "benevolence" to the crown. His advances spurned by the government, and his indignation boiling over at his six weeks' imprisonment, he flung himself into the arms of the patriots, and made common cause with the leaders of the popular party. All through the stormy session of 1628 he denounced the arbitrary government of the king, and stood shoulder to shoulder with Eliot and Pym in support of the Petition of Right. His violence and desertion of the royal cause had their reward. On the prorogation of Parliament, Charles opened communications with him. His liberal friends, being of no further use to him, were cast aside, and he returned to his allegiance to the king. Then came the reward—a peerage, and the presidency of the north. Charles had won a devoted servant, Lord Wentworth a career for his ambition.

Such had, shortly, been the previous history of the new lord deputy. In his presidential court at York he had given the reins to his imperious will. A fine field for despotic rule lay open in Ireland. With Laud to support him at the council-board in England, he prepared to carry out his policy of "Thorough," both in Church and State, and to make the sister isle an example for the rest of the kingdom to follow.

Wentworth had a supreme contempt for the sordid oligarchy in whose hands he found vested the government of Ireland. He believed in paternal government, and honestly wished to rule the Irish people with justice and moderation, so long as the king's interests were not interfered with. His hand was heavy on the jobbers of the Castle, the mushroom nobility of the plantations, and the great land-owners of the west, because both the one and the other resisted his plans for draining their pockets into the king's treasury. But to the mass of the people he endeavored to secure a just administration of the law; to the recusants he desired to be tolerant, holding that "our own Church should be first reformed." He secured the shipping trade by sweeping the swarms of Algerine pirates from the sea; and though he ruthlessly crushed the woollen trade, for fear it should compete with that of England, he had the wit to see that the soil was suitable for the growth of flax; and, having imported Flemish weavers and erected mills, laid the foundation of the Irish linen-manufacture. His main objects were to make Charles "the most absolute prince in Christendom," and that, too, in the person of the king's deputy; to raise a large revenue to relieve the king's necessities in England, and so render him independent of English parliaments; to discipline and reform the Irish army, which might perhaps become an important factor in any dispute between the king and his English or Scotch subjects; and to drive the Low Church Irish clergy into the High Church ceremonial and doctrine of Archbishop Laud.

His first step on arriving in Dublin was to summon a Parliament. Charles was horrified at the suggestion. He had had experience of "that hydra," and had found it "as well cunning as malicious." But Wentworth knew what he was about, and saw that an Irish Parliament clenched in the vice of Poynings's Act could be used as a tool without risk of its becoming dangerous.

He had got the Irish council well in hand, having snubbed them into sullen obedience at his first interview. On their showing signs of independence at the drawing-up of the heads of bills for transmission to London, he had rated them soundly and awed them into silence. The time-honored claim of the lords of the Pale to be consulted on the projected measures was contemptuously set aside, and the only thing remaining to be done was to manipulate the elections. So dexterously was the packing of the Parliament managed that the Protestants and Roman Catholics nearly balanced each other; and a picked handful of military men were returned who could be depended on to turn the scale as the lord deputy desired.

Wentworth was careful to open Parliament with a ceremony and magnificence the like of which had never before been seen in Dublin. Upon the assembling of the houses, he harangued them in a loud, bold voice, demanding subsidies of £100,000 to clear off the debts of the crown, and £20,000 to meet the annual deficit in the revenue. He announced that there would be two sessions, "one for the crown," in which the subsidies were to be voted, "and one for them," in which the "Graces" should be considered; and he wound up his initiatory lecture by advising them "to take heed of private meetings and consults in their chambers of design, and privily beforehand to contrive how to discourse and carry the public affairs when they came into the houses," for the king "expected not to find them muttering and mutinying in corners."

Browbeaten and dismayed, the Commons did their part at once, and voted six subsidies of £45,000 each, amounting in all to £270,000.* The Lords, less submissive, complained loudly of the public grievances; and drew up several bills to be transmitted to England. But Wentworth cut them short by telling them that this was in contravention of Poynings's Act, and their powers were limited to petitioning the crown. The second session, "their session," was held in the following October. Wentworth, having got his subsidies, had no intention of confirming the "Graces." He had purged the privy council of his most obstinate opponents; and to that subservient body he now dictated a petition to the crown that a number of the "Graces" might be annulled, as being inconsistent with the king's interest. Upon the strength of this, he coolly announced to the Parliament that the "Graces" would not be confirmed; and, having discreetly set the Protestants and recusants by the ears, with the help of the former got a division in his favor; and so the session ended.

Having filled the treasury, and relieved his mind with a series of gleeful despatches to Laud, he turned upon the Church. The latter was in pitiful need of reconstruction. Its condition had gone from bad to worse. The buildings were in ruins; the parish clergy either non-resident or in a state of beggary. The glebe-lands and tithes had been recklessly alienated by greedy and fraudulent incumbents; and none but the most ignorant and profligate persons could be induced to take the livings, which had been plundered of their endowments. In the diocese of Ferns and Leighlin, the livings were farmed out to the patron at £2, £3, and £4 per annum for long periods. In

---

* 10 Car. I., session 1, cc. 1, 2.

Connaught a vicar's stipend was seldom greater than 40s. a year. Even the revenues of the bishoprics had been shamefully reduced, either by absolute grants, or long leases of the Church lands made by unscrupulous Churchmen to their relations and friends; some having fallen as low as £50 per annum.

The lord deputy went to work with a will.* All the impropriations which were vested in the crown were conveyed to the clergy. A commission was issued for the repair of churches; and suits were promptly instituted in the Castle Chamber to recover Church property which had been appropriated by the laity. The Earl of Cork was compelled to disgorge tithes and lands belonging to the College of Youghal and the see of Waterford to the value of £2000 a year. The Bishop of Killala, who had made a fraudulent compromise in relation to certain Church lands, was summoned to the presence-chamber. where Wentworth roughly told him "that he deserved to have his rochet pulled over his ears;" and, as he chuckles to Laud, "so warmed his old sides as he made him break the agreement and crave pardon."

But Wentworth and the Archbishop of Canterbury were not content with restoring the Church temporalities, they aspired to a "uniformity of religion." In their eyes the Presbyterian of Ulster was as hateful as the Popish recusant, and the Calvinistic character of the bishops and clergy of the Irish establishment more shameful than either. The Court of High Commission was established in Dublin, and set to work to expel the Presbyterian ministers from the plantations. Bramhall, a vehement High Churchman, whom Wentworth had brought over with him, was made Bishop of Derry. Convocation was summoned and soundly rated, and required to repudiate the articles of Lambeth and adopt those of the English Church. When the unwilling Usher submitted to the lord deputy a draft of the canon to be propounded, Wentworth boldly drew up one of his own, which he forced the Convocation to accept. Laud's plan of shifting the communion-table from the body

---

* See 10 Car. I., session 3, c. 1; 10, 11 Car. I. cc. 2, 3.

to the east end of the church was carried out where possible, and a more elaborate ceremonial introduced; while Wentworth's old enemy, the Earl of Cork, was, to his intense indignation, compelled to remove a mighty family monument which he had erected on the site of the old high altar in St. Patrick's Cathedral.

Wentworth, having dragooned both the Parliament and the Church, now proceeded to replenish the treasury still further by attacking the Connaught landlords. The threat of a plantation in Connaught had hitherto been a most useful lever for the extortion of money. The crown had obtained subsidy after subsidy by alternately brandishing the rod of confiscation, or dangling the bait of a confirmation of titles, over their devoted heads. Wentworth felt that the game was nearly played out, and that the time had come to see what could be made of killing the goose which had laid so many golden eggs. He began by unearthing the original grants of Henry III. to Richard De Burgh, and traced the devolution of the province, through the earls of Ulster and March, to its vesting in the crown in the person of Edward IV. He exhumed the surrender of O'Connor to King John, the regrant, and the subsequently alleged forfeiture. The ingenuity of the court lawyers sufficed to pick holes in the letters-patent of Elizabeth and James, and the inevitable conclusion was of course arrived at, that the whole of Connaught was the property of Charles.

Forthwith he went with the Commissioners of Plantation into Roscommon, Mayo, and Sligo. The juries, carefully composed of "persons of such means as might answer the king a round fine in the Castle Chamber in case they should prevaricate," were terrified and bribed into finding verdicts for the king; and, having carried his point in the north and east of the province, he turned to deal with Galway, where some show of resistance was expected. Here the population was almost wholly recusant, and devoted to the Earl of Clanricarde; the greater portion of the freeholders were either Bourkes or allied to Bourkes by marriage. Wentworth cared not. He held his court in the earl's own castle at Portumna. He silenced the recusant lawyers by imposing the Oath of Supremacy as a condition precedent to their being allowed to plead, and fined the sheriff £1000, and imprisoned him also, for empanelling an obstinate jury. But coercion was met with stubborn resistance, and the juries found verdicts for the land-owners. Wentworth, furious at the resistance to his will, dragged the jurors before the Castle Chamber, where they were cross-questioned and fined £4000 apiece, and sentenced to imprisonment until the fines were paid and they should retract their decision. The wretched sheriff died in prison; the old Earl of Clanricarde sank into the grave from mortification; and, sooner or later, overmatched in the struggle, the land-owners gave way and submitted.

But Wentworth, though he had a plantation in view, was principally concerned to extort money, and the land itself to no great extent passed into other hands. The landlords were allowed to compound by the payment of fines and fixed quit-rents, and in some cases by the surrender of a portion of their estates, especially where provision was required for the Church. The principal business of the commission for defective titles, after the king's "just and honorable title" had been found, was to receive these compositions; and the Chief-justice of the Common Pleas and the Lord Chief Baron, who presided over the inquisitions, were stimulated to "intend it with a care and diligence such as if it were their own private," by the receipt of a commission of 4s. in the pound on the first year's rent extracted from the confiscated estates.

If Wentworth's hand was heavy on the great landholders of the west, it was none the less so on the more modern English nobility. Lord Wilmot, an officer of Mountjoy's army, who had become a landed proprietor, a peer, and Governor of Connaught, was forced to account for lands he was said to have usurped from the crown; Sir Piers Crosby was dismissed from the council for opposing in Parliament one of the government bills; Loftus was deprived of his office, and imprisoned, for refusing to obey an order of the privy council for the payment of his daughter's marriage portion; and Lord Mountnorris, for some incautious words let fall at the lord chancellor's table, was court-martialled and actually sentenced to be shot.

But a storm was brewing in England and Scotland, which

was destined to ruin both the lord deputy and his master. For ten years Charles had been trying the experiment of governing without a Parliament, and had endeavored to keep his treasury full by means of monopolies, forced loans, and the illegal levying of customs dues. The country was on fire at the gathering of ship-money, which had been declared a legal impost by a corrupt bench of judges. Laud had made himself hateful in England by his rigorous Church policy. The fined, pilloried, and mutilated Puritans cried aloud for justice; and the Scotch, on whom he had recklessly ventured to force a new liturgy, had signed the Covenant, and were in open rebellion.

Charles, in despair, sent over for Wentworth, who came and formed a secret junto with Laud and Hamilton. An immediate blow at the Scotch was at once decided on. The fortresses of the south were to be held with Irish garrisons; the treasury was to be filled by the long-delayed Parliament; a voluntary loan was to be started, with Wentworth's name at the head for £20,000. Wentworth himself was to return to Ireland as lord-lieutenant and Earl of Strafford—a title twice before solicited by him in vain. Irish subsidies were to be obtained, and the Irish army, under the command of the young Earl of Ormonde, held in readiness for active service. Strafford's energy had raised the Irish revenue to an excess over expenditure of £60,000 a year. His measures of army reform had produced a well-paid, well-armed, well-provided force of 8000 foot and 1000 horse, which were assembled at Carrickfergus and awaiting transport. An obedient Parliament promptly voted four subsidies;* and Strafford, tortured with gout, hurried over again to England to take command of a broken, disaffected army, and to find the treaty of Ripon signed with the Scots behind his back.

The end was now at hand. It was too late to bring over the Irish army. Charles had upset all the calculated plans of the busy-brained earl, and had cut the ground from under his feet. The Long Parliament had assembled—a very different body from that expected by the king and his ministers. The sup-

---

* Irish Stats., 15 Car. I. c. 13.

pressed mutterings of three kingdoms against the well-hated viceroy were rising into an overwhelming storm. The Irish Commons, released from his dreaded presence, impeached four of the privy council who were his creatures. The victims of his tyranny, Connaught landlords, Castle officials, Presbyterian pastors, swarmed over to England to accuse him. All England and Ireland watched with breathless interest the trial of the man who, in the words of the impeachment, " had endeavored to subvert the fundamental laws of the realm, and to introduce arbitrary and tyrannical government;" and rejoiced when his selfish, thankless master, whom he had devotedly served, as he had himself so often boasted, " at the peril of his head," signed the bill of his attainder* and sent him to the scaffold.

---

* English Stats., 16 Car. I. c. 1.

CHAPTER III.

PROVINCIAL INSURRECTIONS IN 1641.

UPON the death of Strafford, the king, in deference to the views of the English Parliament, appointed Sir William Parsons and Sir John Borlase, an old soldier, to hold the office of lords justices. The island, to all appearances, was in a state of complete tranquillity; and though there were rumors of disaffection in the air, and some significant warnings were given, the lords justices paid them no attention.

But, notwithstanding this apparent quiet, the minds of the native Irish were greatly stirred by many things. There was a bitter feeling of suppressed hatred throughout the country. The wholesale confiscations were neither forgotten nor forgiven, and the smouldering fire of discontent had only been prevented from bursting forth by the terror of Strafford's government. The religion of the people was proscribed by law; and, though its free exercise was to a great extent winked at, and practically, with the exception of an occasional outburst of intolerance, there was little or no persecution, the law might be put actively in force at any moment; and, rightly or wrongly, a very general belief had got abroad that the English Puritans had determined to stamp out Popery in Ireland. The ruthless proscriptions of Elizabeth had done their work; and a host of Irish had been driven over the sea with a fierce hatred of England in their hearts, to become hardy and experienced soldiers in the service of Spain, and to foster in exile the hope of revenge upon their great enemy; while at home Strafford's disbanded army, which was almost wholly composed of Irish Roman Catholics, was ready and waiting to be re-enlisted by the first popular leader who should concert a rising. The recent successful appeal to arms by the Scotch in the cause of religious liberty had been duly noted; as also had the increasing state of tension in the relations of the king and the English Parliament. What the Scotch had done, the Irish might fairly expect to do; and, as usual, the embarrassment of the English government was the opportunity of the Irish. They overlooked the fact that the rebellion of the Scotch was successful because the English Commons sympathized with them both in their purpose and their faith; that the struggle was between the king and two nations; whereas an Irish rebellion meant a national and religious war in which the Irish would be confronted with the old antagonism of race, and the united bigotry of Scotch Presbyterian and English Puritan.

At this time an Irish gentleman of great address and ability, named Roger (or Rory) O'Moore, was earnestly canvassing the possibility of making a stand against the English government. Rory O'Moore was the representative of the ancient house of the O'Moores of Leix, which had been well-nigh exterminated by the plantation of Queen's County. He had passed some years on the Continent, where he had been very intimate with the titular young Earl of Tyrone, Hugh's only surviving son. He had secretly enlisted Lord McGuire, Baron of Enniskillen, who had been restored to a portion of the McGuire estates in Fermanagh; Sir Phelim O'Neil of Kinnard, the representative of a collateral branch of the O'Neil family; and Richard Plunket, a gentleman of the Pale. They were soon joined by several gentlemen of the ancient septs of the north—McMahon, McGennis, O'Reilly; and also by Hugh O'Byrne of Wicklow, and Sir James Dillon. Hopes were entertained of seducing the Roman Catholic lords of the Pale, and Lord Mayo, the head of the Northern Bourkes. The conspiracy was quickly matured and the closest secrecy maintained.

The plan of action decided on was, by a *coup de main*, to seize Dublin Castle, which was weakly guarded with barely fifty men, but which contained a great store of powder, a large stand of arms, and thirty-five guns. Simultaneously the forts and garrison towns in the north were to be surprised, and the gentry made prisoners in their country-houses, as hostages for the persons of the insurgent leaders in case of defeat. The whole enterprise was to be carried out with as little bloodshed as possible, and the Scottish settlers were to be treated as kinsmen and allies and not to be interfered with. The expressed object of the movement was to compel the king to re-establish the Roman Catholic religion, to repeal Poynings's Act, and to restore the confiscated estates. And though some of the leaders were for breaking away from England altogether, the more moderate appear, at any rate at this time, to have had no intention of renouncing their allegiance to the king.

The whole of the available troops in the country numbered but 2000 men; and these were scattered in companies of fifty in the different forts and towns. Sir William Parsons had ample warning both from the local magistrates and from England that mischief was brewing; but, having already largely profited by the confiscation of estates, he appears to have been criminally careless, if not actually desirous of a rising as affording a pretext for fresh forfeitures. No precautions were taken to concentrate the troops, or to put the provinces in a posture of defence; and it was not till they were told, on the very eve of the outbreak, of the plot to seize the Castle that the lords justices took any active measures. They then closed the gates of the city and arrested McMahon and Lord McGuire. These arrests were made at daybreak on the 23d of October, 1641, the morning fixed for the attack; and, upon finding the plot was discovered, O'Moore, O'Byrne, and Plunket escaped with their adherents.

But, though the attempt on the Castle had failed, a simultaneous rising in Ulster was carried out with astonishing precision. The ancient Irish tribes which had been evicted, transplanted, and dispersed seemed to start out of the ground in all their old individuality. There were the O'Reillys, the O'Hanlons, the McGennises, the O'Quins. There were the McGuires, the O'Farrels, the McMahons, the O'Kanes; each with their representative chief, and intent on their old domains; and of course an O'Neil at the head of the insurrection. The fort of Charlemont, the most important position in the new plantation, was treacherously seized by Sir Phelim O'Neil, who had asked himself to dinner with old Lord Caulfield, the governor. Dungannon and Mountjoy, which completed the chain of forts dominating Tyrone, were surprised the same night; and the gates of Newry, with its small store of arms and ammunition, were opened to Sir Con McGennis. Every town in Ulster and in the County of Longford fell into the hands of the insurgents, with hardly an exception. Only Derry, Coleraine, and Enniskillen on the one side, and Lisburn, Lurgan, Belfast, and Carrickfergus on the other, closed their gates in time, and were defended by the English settlers and a handful of troops. The country-houses and farms of the planters were seized and plundered by the Irish; their occupants being driven forth to find refuge in the forest and in the few towns which held out. Men, women, and children were stripped naked and sent to find their way across country to Dublin. Hundreds died of exposure to the bitter weather, and fell exhausted by the way; hundreds only escaped to Dublin and Carrickfergus to die.

As yet, however, the gentlemen who had organized the rising managed to keep their followers fairly under control; personal outrages were the exception; and the terms on which the defenders of castles and country-houses surrendered were honorably respected. Where moderate men were in command, murder was promptly checked. Indeed, in Cavan, where the two O'Reillys, one the sheriff and the other the member for the county, were the leaders, the revolution was almost bloodless. But it was far otherwise in Armagh, and the neighboring portions of Tyrone and Down, where Sir Phelim O'Neil had his headquarters.

This dissolute ruffian, who had been bred up in England in the Protestant faith, and had reverted to the ancient creed, had prior to the rebellion wasted the paternal acres by extravagance and debauchery, and had eagerly joined in Rory O'Moore's conspiracy in the hopes of recovering the vast domains of the O'Neils. The rising in the north had been intrusted to his organization, and he found himself in a few days' time at the head of a rabble of some 30,000 men, armed principally with knives and pitchforks. With these disorderly forces, which he designated "the Catholic Army," he attempted to storm the castle of Augher and the towns of Enniskillen and Lisburn. Furious at being repulsed, and maddened with drink, he determined to wreak his vengeance on the defenceless Protestants within his reach. He caused Mr. Blaney, the member for Monaghan, to be hanged; and old Lord Caulfield, his prisoner, to be shot. He ordered all the Scotch and English to be killed in three adjacent parishes after the defeat at Augher; and, on hearing that Newry had been recovered by Lord Conway, he burned the town and cathedral of Armagh, and murdered some hundreds of the inhabitants, although they had surrendered on the promise of their lives. He hounded on the Irish to massacre the planters and their families. These wretched people were swept out of their villages, and driven by hundreds into the Bann and the Blackwater, and flung over the bridge at Portadown. The houses in which women and children had taken refuge were set on fire and the inmates burned. Men were hanged and butchered with knives. Women were systematically ripped up, especially the pregnant ones, though they appear generally to have been spared the last wrongs of dishonor. Rory McGuire in Fermanagh seems to have caught the infection from O'Neil and rivalled him in his crimes, stripping, killing, and ripping in the same indiscriminate fashion. In recounting the ferocity of the Irish insurgents, it should not, however, be forgotten that there were frequent cases of English and Scotch Protestants being protected by their Irish neighbors, and owing life and safety to their unselfish generosity. Some of the Irish priests and Jesuits were especially conspicuous for these acts of Christian mercy, hiding the terrified suppliants under the altar-cloths, and striving to stop the bloodshed at the risk of their own lives.

There has been great difference of opinion as to the number of persons who suffered death at this period of the outbreak. It is next to impossible to make even an approximate estimate; no doubt the numbers were greatly exaggerated both at the time and since, both unintentionally and for political purposes. When we consider the number of the original undertakers, and the number of tenants they covenanted to plant on their estates; and that as a rule they never fulfilled their covenants to the extent of one half, but that the greater portion of the English lived in the walled towns—allowance also being made for the numbers which escaped into the fortified cities and to Dublin during the week's respite which occurred between the original outbreak and the commencement of the slaughter, and the comparatively limited area over which the massacre extended—we shall most likely be nearest the mark if we accept the figures of Dr. Warner, a Protestant writer who made an especially careful investigation of the evidence, which give between four and five thousand as murdered in cold blood, and eight thousand as victims to exposure and ill-usage.

All this while a parallel but wholly independent movement had been going on among the old Anglo-Irish families. They hated the new English interest as cordially as the king detested the sturdy patriots who were resisting his arbitrary conduct in England. They were to a man Roman Catholic. The men of the new English interest were Protestant to the backbone. Community of interest drew the old Anglo-Irish and Charles together, just as community of interest was arraying the Puritan Dublin oligarchy on the side of the English Parliament. The clamor of the latter had compelled Charles unwillingly to disband the Irish army which Strafford had labored to construct; but he still hoped that Ormonde and Antrim would be able to reassemble it, and that he would find it possible to rely on the old Anglo-Irish nobility for the subjugation of his troublesome subjects at home. The foolhardy Antrim was ready to raise the whole Pale in defence of the king, and to drive the lords justices into the sea. Ormonde was more cautious, and, while Charles was nominally in accord with his government at Dublin, took his orders from them. The rising of the native Irish upset Charles's plans and forced his hand. "The fools," says Antrim, "well liking the business, would not expect our manner for ordering the work, but fell upon it without us, and so spoiled it." The native Irish cared nothing for Charles, and only desired national independence. The old Anglo-Irish wished only for liberty of worship, and freedom from the greedy usurpations of the new English interest. Charles vainly hoped to make use of both these divergent bodies for his own purposes. He spread the discord instead of allaying it. He converted a provincial rising into a national rebellion against England. All through the complicated events of the ensuing ten years we find four distinct parties, generally pulling in different directions; four antagonistic forces which nothing could reconcile. There was the old Irish party, whose aim soon resolved itself into separation from England; the old Anglo-Irish party, whose object was civil and religious liberty, and no separation; the Puritan party, which became complicated with the Presbyterian interest of the Scotch in Ulster, and was strongly anti-Irish in every sense; and there was the Royalist party, personified by Ormonde, which trimmed between the three others, and had as its ulterior aim the crushing of the third by means of the other two.

After the first shock of the revolt, the English began to steady themselves and to hold their own. The king managed to send over 1500 Scots to Carrickfergus, whose first performance was to sally forth and slaughter some thirty Irish families in the peninsula of Island Magee. The refugees in the towns were drilled and armed, and the offensive cautiously assumed. O'Neil, finding Carrickfergus too strong for him, drew his men south, and besieged Drogheda, which was gallantly defended by Sir Henry Tichborne. The lords justices in the meantime had summoned Ormonde to the capital and appointed him lieutenant-general of the army. Ormonde, if he had been allowed to have his own way, especially when some reinforcements arrived from England, would soon have crushed the rising while it was confined to the north. But for this the lords justices had no mind, and he was confined to making raids within thirty miles of Dublin.

The lords justices, owing to the strife of parties in England, were in a very peculiar and delicate position. Rory O'Moore had issued a subtle and ingenious manifesto, saying that he and his friends had been compelled to take up arms to secure the rights which they believed the king would willingly grant them, were he not restrained from doing so by the Puritans in England; and that they held the forts and towns which they had captured till the king should be in a position to guarantee them civil and religious liberty.

In England the king and the Parliament were bracing themselves for the death-struggle which was to end on the scaffold at Whitehall. They both well knew what use might be made of an Irish army. The king was consequently ready to make any terms with the Ulster insurgents in order to release the Irish troops, and possibly obtain material assistance from the insurgents themselves. The Parliament dreaded nothing so much as a termination of the revolt, fearing that the king would obtain the sinews of war to an unlimited extent from Ireland, and knowing that when they had settled matters with Charles they could at any moment turn and repress the rebellion.

The lords justices were in strong sympathy with the English Parliament, and determined to play into their hands; and, at the same time, knowing that they were secure in Dublin, or, at the worst, could retire in safety into England, were willing to see the area of the revolt extended as much as possible, as upon its final, inevitable suppression the spoil would be all the greater. In England the accounts of the massacre were magnified, and published, in order to justify severe measures with the Roman Catholics. The ignorant people were persuaded by the ranting preachers that the wild Irish were upon them, and were in hourly fear that the Ulster fury would begin at Bradford and Halifax! Parliament voted large sums of money and bodies of troops for Irish service; and passed a significant act which, after reciting that "divers worthy and well-affected persons perceived that many millions of the rebels' lands which go under the name of profitable lands would be confiscated," gave powers to open subscription lists for the raising of a war fund upon the security of two and a half millions of Irish acres, which it was reckoned would become forfeit and open to a vast new plantation.* But neither the troops nor the money reached their destination, and the Irish rebellion was a convenient excuse both to Parliament and the king for the levy-

---

* English Stats., 16 Car. I. c. 33.

ing of soldiers, who were to be employed on more urgent occasions nearer home. The lords justices accordingly contented themselves with holding Dublin, and sending foraging parties "to kill, burn, and destroy," within easy reach of the walls, regardless of whether the sufferers were in rebellion or not.

The first indication of the spread of the revolt was a rising of the O'Byrnes and O'Tooles in the half-planted districts of Wicklow. This isolated movement was easily suppressed, Sir Charles Coote being despatched against them with a small force from Dublin. He recovered Wicklow Castle and drove the rebels out of the town, and then proceeded to vie with the perpetrators of the Ulster massacres by cruelties as wholesale and indiscriminate, and the wanton slaughter of men, women, and children. "Nits will be lice," was his brutal answer when remonstrated with for impaling the babies at the breast.

Connaught had hitherto been kept tranquil by the efforts of Lord Clanricarde, Lord Dillon, and Lord Mayo, who loyally supported Lord Ranelagh, the president. Munster, though agitated, and exasperated by the injudicious severities of Sir Wareham St. Leger, the president of that province, was still quiescent. The lords of the Pale, the old Anglo-Norman families, on the first outbreak in Ulster had unanimously expressed their loyalty to the government, and had at the commencement of the revolt implored Parsons to summon the Parliament to announce the confirmation of the "Graces," to which the king had now agreed, and distribute arms and ammunition for the protection of the Pale. The lords justices, who suspected them of disaffection to themselves, and were only too anxious to drive them into revolt, imprisoned their spokesman, Lord Dunsany, prorogued the Parliament after two days' sitting, suppressed the Graces, and even recalled the arms which they had at first sparingly given out. They even went so far as to refuse to permit any of the Pale families to enter Dublin for refuge. The Pale lords thought they had a golden opportunity; they believed that, if they threatened revolt, Charles would be compelled to grant all their demands. They also believed that the king would not be sorry to be forced into countenancing their action against the government, and that he might be driven to buy their support at the price of large concessions. Finding themselves, therefore, flouted by the lords justices, whose helpless inactivity they despised, and with some reason believing their line of conduct not otherwise than agreeable to the king, at the same time unarmed and defenceless in case of an onslaught by the rebels, they listened to the specious overtures of Rory O'Moore. Seven peers and one thousand of the leading gentry met the rebel leaders on the hill of Crofty; and by the middle of December all the Pale was in revolt.

The defection of the Pale turned the local rising in Ulster into a national rebellion. Leinster rose, and Lord Mountgarret occupied Kilkenny and the city of Waterford. Munster followed under the leadership of Lord Muskerry, the Barrys, and every branch of the house of Butler; Ormonde, who had been brought up in England as a Protestant, being the only one who remained loyal. Clare was overrun by the O'Briens, in spite of the Earl of Thomond, who held by the government; and Connaught, deserting the traditional leadership of Clanricarde, joined the insurgent banner at the call of Lord Mayo. In those parts of the three provinces thus tardily joining the confederates, where the remnants of the old evicted Irish tribes were waiting for their revenge upon the planters, isolated acts of cruelty were perpetrated upon the helpless English families with the same horrid incidents as those committed in the north. These were, however, the work of a few ungovernable ruffians, and were promptly checked by the leaders of the rebellion, who did their utmost to provide for the safe convoying of the expelled people to places of safety, and honorably kept the terms of surrender entered into with the scattered parties of besieged residents.

By the end of the year all Ireland was in the hands of the rebels, with the exception of Dublin and Drogheda and some of the fortified seaports, as Cork, Limerick, and Galway in the south and west, and Enniskillen, Derry, and Carrickfergus in Ulster. One or two garrisoned towns, such as Athlone and Kildare, were held for the king; and a few country gentlemen's castles were defended gallantly against overwhelming odds.

CHAPTER IV.

THE CONSOLIDATION OF THE REVOLT. A.D. 1642, 1643.

NOTWITHSTANDING the universal character which the rebellion had now assumed, the lords justices still procrastinated. The minds of the new English interest were less bent upon the speedy crushing-out of disaffection than on paving the way to a grand division of the spoil which they foresaw would be at the disposal of the government. They were busy enough in Dublin in the preparation of charges against the owners of estates who were playing with the fire of treason. No less than four thousand indictments were laid in three days, in the most business-like fashion, and the rack was freely used to extract satisfactory evidence from the witnesses; Mr. Barnewall of Kilbrue, an old gentleman of sixty-six years, being among those who were put to the torture.

In the south, the ever-rapacious Earl of Cork, now sinking into his grave, who had fortified his castle of Lismore, and organized his tenantry under his three sons—Lord Dungarvan, Lord Kinalmeaky, and Lord Broghill—for the defence of his territory, forwarded to the speaker of the Long Parliament eleven hundred indictments against the land-owners of South Munster, with an urgent request that they might be returned to him at once with authority to proceed against the accused as outlaws. He did not live to reap the profits of this wholesale work, though the infamous Broghill, worthy son of such a sire, made his fortune and secured an earldom by judicious fishing in the troubled waters of the day.

Even when Sir Phelim O'Neil had raised the siege of Drogheda, in despair of ever taking it, and Ormonde, who had now a strong force at his command, implored leave to follow and annihilate his retreating forces, the lords justices peremptorily refused permission.

The rising in Ulster had now to a great extent burned itself out. The Irish had no arms or ammunition; while the Scots, reinforced by the troops under Munroe and Chichester, were taking the offensive everywhere. Sir Phelim was utterly incompetent to command an army; and, one by one, Newry, Down, Armagh, and Dungannon were abandoned by him, while Sir William Cole at Enniskillen was threatening to take him in flank. His troops deserted him in great numbers; and so hopeless seemed the cause in Ulster that a wholesale emigration into Argyleshire was contemplated by the disheartened native Irish. At this juncture arrived in Donegal Bay Colonel Owen O'Neil with a single ship and a store of ammunition, and one hundred Irish officers who had received a military education, in camp and in the field, in foreign service. Owen O'Neil, or Owen Roe (Red Owen) as he was more commonly called, was a nephew of the late Earl of Tyrone. He had, like many other Irish exiles, entered the Spanish service, and had served with distinction in Flanders. He had the reputation of being an excellent soldier, and had engaged to come to the assistance of O'Moore and his confederates when the original rising was planned. He set to work at once, on his arrival, to organize the undisciplined Irish levies into regular regiments. He was unanimously chosen by the Irish chiefs to take the supreme command in Ulster, and to supersede Sir Phelim. He severely condemned the cruelties which had been committed, and even burned the houses of those who had had the largest share in them, as a warning to others for the future. The effect of his presence was magical. The desponding Irish recovered heart; the Scots and the English volunteers again resumed the defensive; and Munroe, whether through apathy or under instructions from the lords justices, retired into his quarters at Carrickfergus.

Simultaneously with the coming of Owen Roe, the southern rebellion was strengthened by the arrival at Wexford of Colonel Preston, brother of Lord Gormanston, one of the lords of the Pale, with five hundred exiled officers, and a store of ammunition and some field and siege artillery. There was no concert between these two auxiliaries. Each of the two parties, the old Irish and the Anglo-Irish, had looked for help to their outlawed friends on the Continent; and the answer came to each independently. Though recognizing the action of each other, the two parties had hitherto proceeded, to a great extent, on parallel lines. The next step was to effect a union between them.

This object was effected by the Roman Catholic clergy, who met at Kilkenny and made arrangements for the summoning of a national convention. The insurgents in the different provinces were all acting without any system or order: the convention was to unite them and to constitute a kind of provisional government.

Accordingly, in October, 1642, there assembled at Kilkenny fourteen of the Roman Catholic peers, the Roman Catholic bishops and clergy, and 226 Roman Catholic deputies from the counties and principal towns. They sat in one chamber, but as two houses; the inferior clergy sitting in convocation in a separate assembly. The government was to consist of a supreme council, of which Lord Mountgarret was president.* It was composed of twenty-four members elected by the general assembly; six from each province. In it were vested the fullest executive powers; and it had also a judicial side, constituting a final court of appeal in all civil and criminal matters. A council of twelve was to sit in each county to serve as magistrates and judges in civil suits, with an appeal to a provincial council which was to consist of two deputies for each county. Colonel Owen O'Neil was then appointed to command the forces in Ulster, Gerald Barry in Munster, Colonel Preston in Leinster, and Sir John Bourke in Connaught. A seal was ordered to be cut, a printing-press was set up for issuing proclamations, and a mint established for the coining of money.

It is remarkable that the old Irish element was by no means

---

* The original members were: *from Leinster*, the R. C. Archbishop of Dublin, Lord Gormanston, Lord Mountgarret, Nicholas Plunket, Richard Belling, and James Cusack; *from Ulster*, the R. C. Archbishop of Armagh, the Bishop of Down, Philip O'Reilly, Colonel McMahon, Heber McGennis, and Turlough O'Neil; *from Munster*, Lord Roche, Sir Daniel O'Brien, Edmond Fitzmaurice, Dr. Feunell, Robert Lambert, and George Comyn; *from Connaught*, the R. C. Archbishop of Tuam, Lord Mayo, the Bishop of Clonfert, Sir Lucas Dillon, Geoffrey Brown, and Patrick Darcy.

predominant in the new government. The Anglo-Irish party took command of the ship, and some of the earlier instigators of the rebellion, such as Rory O'Moore and Sir Phelim O'Neil, retired from the movement altogether. But the political platform which was adopted was substantially the same as O'Moore's. The commission from Charles, which Sir Phelim had forged, and adorned with an impress of the great seal picked off a patent he had found at Charlemont fort, was wisely ignored. The old Irish and the new Irish were to be treated as one people. The war was professedly directed against the Protestants, who were comprehensively denounced as "Puritans." The Roman Catholic religion was to be re-established in all its pristine glory; and unswerving loyalty to the king was ostentatiously proclaimed.

Meanwhile the civil war had broken out in England, and Charles was eagerly calculating on the assistance of Ormonde and the Irish army. The lords justices were nominally still acknowledging the king's authority, while in fact they were intriguing with the Parliament, and had appointed Reynolds and Godwin, two agents whom the Parliament had sent over to Dublin, to act as members of the privy council. Terms with the rebels meant the release of the king's Irish troops for service in England, and this was to be prevented at all hazards. Ormonde, an ardent Royalist and a devoted adherent of Charles, but at the same time a stanch Protestant, was watching for an opportunity to come to what he considered honorable terms with the rebels. The executive and the commander-in-chief were apparently ignoring the fact of the rupture in England, and at the same time were doing their best to hamper each other in their dealings with the insurrection, in order to influence its event to the advantage of their respective parties.

Hostilities had hitherto been carried on intermittently. There had been a good deal of desultory fighting, with considerable loss of life. Little quarter had been given on either side, and both parties had been guilty of cruel reprisals. The balance of success, which had hitherto been pretty evenly distributed, was now decidedly inclining towards the Irish. In the north, Munroe and Owen O'Neil were cautiously watching one another. In Leinster, Ormonde would have cut off Preston after an engagement at Ross had not the lords justices purposely detained his transport. In Connaught the important towns of Limerick and Galway were surrendered to the insurgents; while in Munster, St. Leger, cooped up in Cork, had died, and been succeeded by Inchiquin, who was with difficulty keeping the enemy at arm's-length. The royal army was in a miserable condition. Half-starved, clothed in rags, and with its pay hopelessly in arrear, its complaints against the misconduct of the government were loud and deep, and the ill-victualled garrisons of the beleaguered towns were approaching a state of starvation.

At length the king determined to strike a blow at the Dublin oligarchy. He created Ormonde a marquis; removed Parsons from office, and replaced him by Sir Henry Tichborne, a determined Royalist and the gallant defender of Drogheda. At the same time, he directed the late lord justice and the rest of his gang—Temple, Meredith, and Loftus, members of the privy council—to be prosecuted for high-treason, a step which drove Reynolds and Godwin in hurried flight to England. The field was now clear for negotiation with the rebels; and a meeting having been held between Ormonde and their commissioners at Castle Martyn, a cessation from hostilities for one year was agreed upon, on September 15, 1643, each party consenting to occupy the respective positions they then held, and the confederates undertaking to give Charles a free contribution of £30,000, and provide a contingent of troops for the king's service in Scotland.

CHAPTER V.

PLOTS AND COUNTERPLOTS. A.D. 1643-1649.

THE news of an accommodation with the Irish insurgents was received in England with the greatest indignation. The people, who had been terribly excited by the reports of the massacres, and who looked upon the whole body of the Irish Roman Catholics as the instigators or accomplices of the murderers, loudly demanded revenge, and denounced the notion of peace until the insurrection had been stamped out in blood. Still stronger grew their anger when two thousand men from Ormonde's Leinster forces were landed in North Wales, and occupied Chester, and when a small force from the Irish rebel army passed over into Scotland to join Montrose. But the good fortune which had attended the king in the first twelve months of the war had now begun to desert him. Gloucester, reduced to its last barrel of powder, had been relieved by Essex; and the Irish contingent was cut to pieces at Nantwich by Fairfax. A still more powerful combination began to threaten, in the taking of the Solemn League and Covenant by the English peers and commons in St. Margaret's Church at Westminster; while the very fact of the king's overtures to the Irish so disgusted his English friends, that many of them threw up their commissions, left his service, and went over to the Parliament.

In Ireland, Munroe and his Scots refused to recognize the armistice, and solemnly took the Covenant in the church at Carrickfergus. Inchiquin, disappointed at finding that the king had bestowed the presidency of Munster upon the Earl of Portland, openly declared for the Parliament, and expelled all the Roman Catholic population from Cork, Youghal, and Kinsale. Lord Esmond, in the fort of Duncannon, which commanded Waterford harbor, followed his example.

More and more the king began to look to his rebellious Irish subjects to crush his rebellious English subjects, and became more and more anxious to patch up a peace with the former on any terms. Ormonde was accordingly advanced to the dignity of lord-lieutenant, and given full power to offer the confederates the most advantageous terms. The principal demands of the rebel executive were—a free Irish Parliament, untrammelled with Poynings's Act; the free exercise of their religion, unfettered by any penal statutes; and a general act of oblivion, and the reversal of all indictments and attainders. Some months were fruitlessly occupied with delegations from the rebels, and counter-delegations from the Protestant faction in Dublin, to the king at Oxford; and by that time Cromwell's Ironsides had destroyed Rupert's army at Marston Moor, and Cromwell, had he had his way, would have made Newbury a no less crushing defeat. The king, who never meant to keep inconvenient promises, was perfectly ready to concede everything in return for the despatch of reinforcements, and simply instructed Ormonde to make the best bargain he could. Ormonde, however, saw that such concessions would be simply fatal to the royal cause, as it would not only drive every Protestant in Ireland, including the soldiers of his own army, into the arms of the Puritans, but would make it next to impossible for the king to come to any terms with the Parliament, with whom he was at that very time negotiating at Uxbridge. The marquis accordingly concealed the extent of his instructions, and would only promise that the penal laws should not be put in force, and that, without repealing Poynings's Act, the king would grant a variety of fresh Graces. For months the negotiations dragged along; the Irish, who were fully aware of the king's necessities, and were expecting great things from their agents at the courts of France, Spain, and Rome, being in no hurry to conclude a treaty.

Charles, in the spring of 1645, impatient of Ormonde's wariness, despatched Edward Somerset, Earl of Glamorgan, to agree to the terms of the confederate council behind his back. The overthrow at Naseby, in June, crushed out the king's hopes in England, and the ransacking of his captured cabinet disclosed the fulness of Ormonde's instructions. The demands of the rebels now rose to include the public exercise of their religion, with the use of all the churches not then actually enjoyed by the Protestants, and a readjustment by an Irish Parliament of all the plantation lands. Glamorgan agreed to everything unreservedly, only making it a condition that these concessions should be embodied in a secret treaty, which was not at present to be disclosed, and that a formal treaty, upon the basis of Ormonde's propositions, should be executed for immediate publication. The consideration for the king's concession was an army of ten thousand men, to serve the king in England, Wales, or Scotland, and a grant of two thirds of the revenues of the clergy for three years. With this secret treaty in their pocket, the confederate commissioners came to terms with Ormonde, agreeing with him to waive the religious question for the present and refer it to the king's future arbitrament, without prejudice to any Graces which the king might subsequently accord to them. The Irish appear to have had as little intention of despatching the soldiers as Charles had of ratifying the secret treaty when he was no longer necessitous.

During these months of protracted negotiation, the Scots in the north, and Inchiquin in the south, ignored the cessation, and from time to time indulged in hostilities with the Irish. As the English Parliament became aware of Charles's practices with the rebels, they began to pay more attention to the wants of their party in Ireland. Money and stores were sent over, and Sir Charles Coote, worthy son to him of Wicklow notoriety who had been shot in a skirmish in 1642, made a dash upon Sligo and captured the town. The Roman Catholic archbishop of Tuam, a warlike prelate, raised the Connaught Irish in an attempt to recover it. The storming party was beaten off, and the archbishop left dead on the field. On his person was found a copy of Glamorgan's secret treaty, which was at once sent to London and published, and thence transmitted to Dublin. The revelation of the king's duplicity was perceived by Ormonde to be fatal; and, as a desperate effort to save Charles's credit, he recalled Glamorgan from Kilkenny, and flung him into prison on a charge of treason in exceeding his instructions.

Charles, prompted by Lord Digby, his confidential minister in Dublin, boldly denied his authority to Glamorgan, and declared his "amazement that any man's folly and presumption should carry him to such a degree of abusing our trust." Glamorgan himself joined in the farce by stating that what he had done was not binding on his majesty, but that he had acted out of excess of zeal in the king's service. Upon the angry demands of the confederates that he should be set at liberty, he was released on bail, and returned to Kilkenny and resumed the negotiations as if nothing had happened.

There had now appeared upon the scene a man who was to sow discord among the confederates. Rinucini, Archbishop of Fermo, had been despatched to Ireland by Pope Innocent X. as his nuncio, and had landed in October, 1645. He cared nothing for Charles, and had but one thing at heart—the re-establishment of the Roman Catholic religion in Ireland in all its original grandeur. On his arrival at Kilkenny, the seat of the rebel government, he at once threw all his energies into the opposing of anything like a peace with the king, except on the basis of the complete reinstatement of his Church. There were, and always had been, two parties among the confederates, corresponding to the two separate races of which they were composed—the extreme party, mainly composed of the old Irish and the clergy, who aimed at nothing less than national independence, and a total extinction of the Protestant interest; and a moderate party, consisting of the Anglo-Irish peers and gentry, who were anxious to be reconciled to the king, provided they could secure sufficient guarantees for certain civil reforms and the complete toleration of the Roman faith. The lay element had already shown considerable jealousy of the clerical influence in the council; and when the nuncio, appealing to every feeling of bigotry and national vanity, had raised up a violent opposition to the peace party, the council became split by a fierce schism into the party of the nuncio and the party of Ormonde. The moderates, however, for the time prevailed; a new general assembly had been convened on the 6th of March, and the long-delayed treaty was eventually signed on the 28th; the only provision as to the religious question being an exemption for Roman Catholics from the Oath of Supremacy.

The peace came too late, so far as the king was concerned. Chester, the last place of importance which was held for him, had been surrendered; and he was himself a prisoner in the hands of the Scots, writing under compulsion to Ormonde to break off all negotiations with the Papists, and secretly begging him through Digby to conclude the treaty at once. The Irish had overplayed their game. Their safety depended on the triumph of the king; and by standing out for higher terms they had lost the chance, if there ever was one, of saving him.

In Ireland the conclusion of the peace was the signal for disturbance. The party of the Parliament were all astir, denouncing the adhesion of Charles to the Roman Catholics. The Irish were furious at what they considered the betrayal of their faith by the confederate council. The men of Ulster were dismayed at the want of a provision to restore them to the plantation lands. At this moment Owen O'Neil met Munroe and his Scots at Benburb, and inflicted upon him a crushing defeat, which placed the northern province at his mercy. The nuncio flew from town to town denouncing the treaty, and preaching a renewed resistance. At Waterford and Clonmel the heralds sent to proclaim the peace were driven out by the people. At Limerick the mayor was beaten for attempting to publish it. Rinucini, to whose schemes Glamorgan had irrevocably committed himself, collected a party of ecclesiastics at Waterford, where he thundered his excommunications against the Irish commissioners, and launched an interdict against all places in which the treaty had been recognized. Preston, who commanded the rebel army in Leinster, held aloof at Birr, undecided which side to take; while Owen O'Neil with ten thousand victorious troops hurried south to support the nuncio.

The council at Kilkenny were in helpless amazement at the turn which events were taking. Mountgarret and Muskerry sent to Ormonde to suppress the commotion. Ormonde arrived with two thousand men, but was forced to retreat to Dublin on the approach of O'Neil from the north. The nuncio, supported by O'Neil, made a public entry into Kilkenny. He drove the supreme council from the council-chamber and flung them into prison. A new council was established with Rinucini as president; a plot was hatched for Charles to escape to Ireland, and throw himself into the arms of the Ultramontanes; and the joint armies of O'Neil and Preston, who now thought it prudent to throw in his lot with the extreme party, marched to within six miles of Dublin and threatened to lay siege to the city.

Ormonde was now in desperate case. The city walls were crumbling with age; he had no provisions and but little ammunition; the king had been surrendered by the Scots; the royal cause was hopeless; the channel was swarming with Parliamentary cruisers; and, preferring to submit rather to the English than the Irish, he besought the Parliament for help, and offered to surrender Dublin into their hands. Even at this, the eleventh, hour a wearisome intrigue was set on foot. Preston and O'Neil, always jealous of each other, quarrelled outright; and, on a false alarm that a Parliamentary force had landed at Dublin, the siege was raised. O'Neil and the nuncio retired to Kilkenny, and Preston remained to tamper with Ormonde. This condition of things, however, soon came to an end. Rinucini threatened Preston's army with excommunication, and he hurried back to headquarters. Ormonde, on July 28, 1647, put an end to his anomalous position by handing over the capital to the agents of the Parliament, and, relinquishing his government, joined Queen Henrietta and other Royalist refugees who were safe in exile at Versailles.

Rinucini's *coup d'état* made him for the time triumphant. But the moderates were only crushed for the moment. On the unavoidable meeting of the general assembly, the imprisoned members of the council were released; and the strife between the two parties grew more bitter than ever, so that even swords were drawn in the council-chamber. The force of events soon turned the scale in favor of the moderates. The Parliamentary troops, now that the king's cause was effaced, began to show signs of life. Colonel Michael Jones marched from Dublin, now the headquarters of the Parliamentary party, to the relief of Trim, which was invested by Preston. The two armies met on Dungan hill, and Preston was defeated, with a loss of five thousand men and all his guns and baggage. In the south, Lord Inchiquin had taken Cahir and pushed his way to Cashel, which he took and burned, shooting down numbers of the wretched inhabitants and some twenty priests who had crowded for safety into the cathedral; and when Lord Taaffe with the Munster army fell upon him at Knocknanoss, near Mallow, the confederate forces were completely broken, and their camp and artillery captured.

And now the shifting scene displays the tables more completely turned than ever. Inchiquin, who considered himself slighted by the Parliament, made overtures to Preston. Ormonde was sounded in Paris, and a coalition was formed against the Parliament, between the moderate section of the confederates and the loyal Protestants of Munster. The nuncio, breathing forth excommunication and interdict, fled to O'Neil's camp at Maryborough. Preston and Inchiquin joined forces, and marched against O'Neil, and so the flame of a second civil war burst forth in the ranks of the insurgents themselves. Jones, who suspected his own soldiers of a sneaking loyalty to Charles, was delighted to see the confederates divided; and so bitter was the hatred between the Ultramontanes and the moderates that O'Neil and the nuncio actually made terms with Jones against their common enemies at Kilkenny. Ormonde now came over from France, and was warmly received by the moderate confederates. Rupert, who had escaped with sixteen frigates from the English fleet, appeared in Kinsale harbor; and the shattered remnants of the Royalists in England flocked across the Channel for a last rally round the royal standard. In England, Cromwell and Fairfax had crushed the Royalist rising in Essex and South Wales, and had chased the Scottish army from Preston and Wigan across the border. The king, who had still hoped to win by setting the Presbyterians against the Independents, and, breaking his word with both, had fallen between the two stools. Rumors of his approaching trial stimulated the supreme council to come to terms, and a new treaty was made between them and Ormonde in the king's name, upon the basis of a free Parliament and a complete repeal of the penal laws.

Hardly had the peace been signed, when news was brought of the king's execution; and Ormonde promptly proclaimed the Prince of Wales at Cork and Youghal.

A still further complication of parties now occurred. The nuncio, seeing that the king's death was uniting all parties under the leadership of Ormonde, fled from the country in despair. Inchiquin and Ormonde, Castlehaven and Clanricarde, with all the moderate rebels, became the great rallying-point of the Royalists. Prince Charles was lingering at the Hague, undecided whether to swallow the Covenant, in spite of what he was pleased to call his conscience, and to head the Presbyterians in Edinburgh, or to pass over to Ireland and throw in his lot with the Roman Catholics. Upon the final rupture between the Presbyterians and the Independents, the Scots in Ulster, who since the battle of Benburb had kept within their quarters, declared for Charles, and joined themselves to Ormonde. They were on the one hand pressing the siege of Derry, which Coote held for the Parliament, and on the other were confronting O'Neil and his Ulster Irish, who was covering Dundalk, where Monk, his new ally, had been sent by Colonel Jones from Dublin.

The first blow was struck by Inchiquin, who captured Drogheda, and cut off some supplies which had been sent by Jones to O'Neil. Monk's garrison mutinied, and Dundalk was surrendered, and Newry, Carlingford, and all the garrisons in Ulster, with the sole exception of Derry, fell into Inchiquin's hands. At the same time Ormonde, with Lord Dillon of Costello, commenced the siege of Dublin.

The Parliament was now thoroughly aroused to the necessity of taking Ireland seriously in hand, and in March, 1649, Cromwell was appointed lord-lieutenant, and commander-in-chief of the English forces there. The Royalists believed that he would land in Munster, and detached Inchiquin to oppose him. Reinforcements were pouring over from England into Dublin; and Ormonde, hoping to capture the city and cut off the Parliament from their only footing in the island, sent Purcell and 1500 men to effect a night surprise. But Ormonde's calculations miscarried, and Jones, sallying forth to meet him with a strong force, drove in Purcell upon the camp at Rathmines. The battle became general. The Irish were not expecting an attack. Four thousand men were slain in action or cut down in flight; two thousand laid down their arms; and Ormonde withdrew the remains of his shattered army to Kilkenny. The blow so crippled the Royalists that they were at once thrown on the defensive; and though strengthened by the tardy adhesion of O'Neil, whom the strait-laced Parliament had cast off in indignant horror at the bare idea of an alliance with the Roman Catholics, Ormonde had barely time to throw Sir Arthur Ashton with a garrison of 3000 picked men into Drogheda, when Cromwell landed at Dublin with 8000 foot, 4000 horse, a formidable train of artillery, and a military chest containing £20,000.

CHAPTER VI.

THE SUBJUGATION. A.D. 1649-1652.

CROMWELL was at the head of the flower of the English Republican army, which, under his wondrous leadership, had marched from victory to victory—an army composed of sober fanatics, who fought for a principle, who were at once a warlike machine and an intelligent political organization. With the horrors of the Ulster murders, now eight years old, still fresh in their memories in all the fulness of highly colored exaggeration, and hot against the Royalists with indignation fiercely fanned up by the late king's persistent duplicity, the soldiers came as on a crusade of vengeance upon "the bloody Papists" and the "malignant" Ormondists. Liberty of conscience was the bone of contention between the Independents and the Presbyterians; that is, liberty of conscience to all the sects as opposed to the domineering intolerance of the Established Presbyterate. Toleration even to the Roman Catholics was their watchword in England. What said Cromwell in Ireland? "I meddle with no man's conscience. But if by liberty of conscience you mean a liberty to exercise the mass, I judge it best to use plain dealing with you, and to let you know, where the Parliament of England has power, *that* will not be allowed."

And now the eight years' war of rebellion was about to be crushed out. The Irish were to be ground to powder; a terrible vengeance was to be exacted "to prevent the effusion of blood for the future." The first blow was struck at Drogheda, which Ormonde believed to be impregnable. One day's fierce bombardment and a practicable breach was made: the storm was ordered and the English were driven off. On the second attempt "God was pleased so to animate them that they drove the enemy from their intrenchments," and the town was won.

Sir Arthur Ashton and all his officers were hacked to pieces on the Millmount by Cromwell's orders. By his express command no quarter was given to any that were found in arms. The whole garrison, with the exception of thirty men, were put to the sword, and "all the friars were knocked on the head but two." How far there was a general massacre of the citizens we can never know. It has been affirmed and denied by the enemies and the admirers of Cromwell. If the plain tale told by Captain Thomas Wood, who was present at the storm, as related in the diary of his brother, Anthony Wood, the Oxford historiographer, be no invention, the wholesale butchery of the children and "the flower and choicest of the women and ladies," who had taken refuge in St. Peter's Church and the vaults beneath, goes far to support the charges of the former. Be it how it may, "it is good," as Cromwell piously observes, "that God above have all the glory."

Having avenged the Ulster massacre by the indiscriminate slaughter of Ormonde's soldiers who had had nothing to do with it, Cromwell marched on Wexford by way of the seacoast. Here another "marvellous great mercy" was prepared for him—while in treaty for the surrender of the city, the castle was betrayed by Captain Stafford. The troops rushed in and turned the guns upon the town. A desperate stand was made by the Irish round the market-cross. As at Drogheda, no quarter was given; the troopers "put all to the sword that came in their way." Two boat-loads of the citizens, who were trying to escape across the river, were sunk, "whereby were drowned near 300." Of the garrison there fell "not many less than 2000," and the town was given over to the pillage of the soldiers, so that "of the former inhabitants scarce one in twenty could challenge any property in their houses."

These two fearful examples of ferocity struck terror into the hearts of the Irish. Town upon town surrendered upon Cromwell's summons. His stern discipline in his army, and his scrupulous honesty in paying for all he took, gave confidence to the country-people, who readily brought in supplies. The Irish army fell back from the Slaney to the Barrow, and from the Barrow to the Nore, and were straining every nerve to cover the city of Kilkenny. Cromwell, " after seeking God for direction," surprised Carrick-on-Suir, and so laid open the road to Dungarvan and the south on the one hand, and the city of Waterford on the other. The fleet which had been fitted out by the energy of the council of state had chased Rupert and his revolted ships from Kinsale, and blockaded all the Irish ports. While Lord Broghill, who but a few weeks back had been meditating going over to the Royalist party, was now making use of all the Boyle interest in South Munster in favor of the Parliament, and had persuaded Cork and Youghal to receive a Republican garrison. Cromwell's grasp was tightening all round the south of the island. In the meantime Venables had been despatched into Ulster to co-operate with Coote, who was advancing from Derry. Carlingford, Newry, Lisburn, and Belfast surrendered without a blow. Coleraine was betrayed to Coote, who put all the garrison to death; and the two forces, having formed a junction, proceeded to besiege Carrickfergus, which capitulated in December.

Cromwell's available forces were now considerably reduced in number by the garrisons he was obliged to leave in the towns which had been recovered, and the remainder were sickening under the effects of the humid climate to which they were unaccustomed. He accordingly went into winter-quarters for a few weeks, at Youghal and Dungarvan. Having rested his men and received reinforcements, he proceeded to advance by two roads on Kilkenny, the headquarters of the Royalist government. Ireton and Reynolds moved from Carrick to Callan; while the lord general, pushing forward from Youghal to Mallow, turned to the east under the Galtee mountains, crossed the Suir, and occupied Fethard, Cahir, and Cashel. In the meantime Hewson, advancing from Dublin, had recovered the County of Kildare, and secured the passage of the Barrow by the capture of Leighlin Bridge; and in March the united Parliamentary army was concentrated round Kilkenny.

All this time the Royalists were quarrelling bitterly among themselves. The greatest distrust of Ormonde and Inchiquin prevailed among the citizens of the towns, insomuch that many of them absolutely refused to admit either them or their soldiers within their walls. The smouldering hatred of the ecclesiastical faction had broken out afresh, and Ormonde was thwarted by the clergy at every turn. Owen O'Neil had died shortly after becoming reconciled to the Royalist party, and the command of the six thousand Northern Irish who composed his army had devolved on his cousin, Hugh O'Neil. Two thousand of these, under Hugh's command, had been thrown into Clonmel, and the rest were at Waterford and Kilkenny.

On Cromwell's approach, Ormonde hurried into County Clare to organize a relieving force, and left Sir Edward Butler in command of the town. It was bravely held by the plague-stricken garrison for eight days, and then surrendered, and Cromwell then turned to reduce Clonmel, which, with the exception of Waterford, was the only town of importance now held by the Irish in the south.

Here he met with a stubborn resistance. When his guns had made a sufficient breach, an assault was ordered, and, after four hours' desperate fighting, the besiegers were driven back with terrible slaughter. In the night the garrison quietly evacuated the town and fell back on Waterford, and Cromwell next morning, in ignorance of their departure, received the capitulation of the citizens.

The backbone of the Irish war was now broken. All Ulster, except the fort of Charlemont, had been reduced by Coote. Broghill had overrun the counties of Cork, Limerick, and Kerry. Every place of any strength in Leinster and Munster, but isolated Waterford and the city of Limerick, was in the hands of Cromwell; and the distracted Irish were driven to make their last stand behind the Shannon.

Cromwell had done his work. His lieutenants could well accomplish the remainder of the task. His own presence was urgently needed across the water; and on May 29, 1650, leaving Ireton in command as lord deputy, he hurried back to lead his Ironsides to victory at Dunbar.

After Cromwell's departure, the war dragged on for another two years before the Irish were finally beaten to the earth. But after the fall of Kilkenny and Clonmel it was merely a question of time; and the work of subjugation, if it proceeded

more slowly, was done thoroughly. In June the remnant of
Owen O'Neil's army chose as its general Heber McMahon, the
Roman Catholic bishop of Clogher. This militant priest, having rashly posted off to recover Ulster, was met by Coote near
Letterkenny, who annihilated his army and took him prisoner,
and hanged him next day. Charlemont soon after fell. Waterford, after a gallant resistance by Preston, was surrendered to
Ireton, the garrison marching out with all the honors of war.
The rest of the year was occupied in securing the positions recovered, and in hunting down the "tories," or bodies of *franctireurs*, who attempted to maintain a guerilla warfare from the
vantage-ground of the impenetrable forests and morasses.

In the camp of the Royalists confusion was worse confounded.
So unpopular was Ormonde that both Limerick and Galway
refused to receive him. The fanatical Irish clergy hated him
for being a Protestant, and attributed the successes of the Republican troops, not without some justice, to his incompetence.
At length, when Prince Charles signed the Covenanters' declaration against Popery, acknowledging the sin of his father in
marrying his "idolatrous mother," and denouncing the peace
concluded with the "bloody Irish rebels," the uncompromising priesthood got the upper-hand and drove the marquis into
exile.

The old Irish party, who had thus again sprung to the front,
in desperation invited the Duke of Lorraine to come to their
assistance and assume the sovereignty of Ireland, when they
were roughly shaken out of their chimerical plans by the enemy
at their doors. Ireton and Coote, after resting in winter-quarters, commenced an early spring campaign. Limerick was the
principal object of attack; but the city could not be effectually
invested from the Munster side. The line of the Shannon was
held by the remains of Ormonde's army and a few raw levies.
Castlehaven, whom Ormonde had left in command, was watching the passes of the river below Lough Derg; while Clanricarde, to whom the marquis had committed the office of lord
deputy, was guarding the river between Loughrea and Portumna. Coote, with two thousand horse and two thousand infantry, made as though he would attack Sligo, and drew off

Clanricarde to its relief; then turning to the left, and forcing the passes of the Curlieu mountains, he burst into Roscommon and appeared before Athlone. Athlone fell before Clanricarde could relieve it; and, the line of the Shannon being lost, the earl, summoning Castlehaven to his assistance, fell back to cover Galway. Ireton overpowered the weakened guard of the ford at O'Brien's Bridge, and the ford at Killaloe was betrayed; Castlehaven's forces melted away, and Ireton sat down before Limerick.

The end was now at hand. Limerick capitulated after a resolute defence by Hugh O'Neil; and Galway shortly followed, upon articles securing to the inhabitants their houses and estates. A few isolated castles were taken in detail; and Clanricarde, after a feeble attempt to hold out in Donegal, accepted the conditions of the Republic.

CHAPTER VII.
"THE CURSE O' CRUMMELL." A.D. 1652–1656.

THE second conquest of Ireland was complete, and the doom of the Irish was sealed. The soil of the whole island was held to be forfeit. Three fourths of the whole population were to be expelled, and the vacant lands repeopled with new English planters. The accumulated arrears of the pay of Cromwell's soldiers had been secured to them by debentures, which were to be satisfied out of a proportionate part of the confiscated Irish land. The "adventurers," who in 1642 had filled the subscription lists for the Irish war-loans, were the inequitable mortgagees of 2,500,000 of Irish acres, and were clamoring to be put in possession of the foreclosed provinces. "Justice" upon the murderers of 1641 was demanded by the popular scream in England; and the shambles of the courts-martial, in the name of justice, were to help to clear the country for the new plantation.

On Ireton's death, Fleetwood was appointed lord deputy, and with him were associated in the civil government four commissioners—Ludlow, who commanded the army, Corbet, Jones, and Weaver. Courts-martial were held at Dublin, Athlone, and Kilkenny for the trial of those who had been concerned in the massacre. Men and women were shot or hanged on the most shadowy evidence. Lord Mayo and Colonel Bagnal were convicted and shot in Connaught; in Leinster Lord Muskerry was honorably acquitted. Sir Phelim O'Neil was dragged out of the retirement he had sought on his supersession by Owen Roe, and tried at Dublin and hanged. He was the only man convicted in Ulster; and in all Ireland the whole number against whom the commissioners were able to prove any complicity with massacre did not exceed two hundred.

In August, 1652, the Parliament passed an ordinance "for

the settling of Ireland," * which in effect was a proscription of the whole nation. "Mercy and pardon both as to life and estate" were to be extended to all "husbandmen, ploughmen, laborers, and artificers;" for the new land-owners would require hewers of wood and drawers of water. And also to those who since 1641 had manifested "a constant good affection to the interests of the Commonwealth of England"—a very small company, as it turned out, seeing that one who paid even a forced contribution to a confederate or royal officer was held to have shown no *constant* good affection. The Presbyterian land-owners of Down and Antrim were involved in the same condemnation as the Irish. For had they not latterly shown Royalist proclivities, and broken away from the Independents? They were to lose their estates, and be transplanted to allotments in Leinster. The rest of the Irish people—peers, gentles, and commons, land-owners and burgesses, were to be driven from their homes in Ulster, Leinster, and Munster, and banished into Connaught and Clare, where the desolated lands of the people of the west were to be parcelled out and allotted to them for their bare sustenance and habitation. Death was to be the penalty if they had not transplanted by May 1, 1654. Death was to be the penalty if they returned without a license. Here they were to be hemmed in, as in a penal settlement, with the ocean on the one hand and the Shannon on the other, forbidden to enter a walled town under the death penalty, with a fringe of disbanded soldiers planted in a belt one mile wide all round the sea-coast and along the line of the river, to keep them from approaching the border-line.

But transplantation was the mildest penalty to which the Irish were subjected. Death, and forfeiture of all property, were decreed for all who within twenty-eight days did not lay down their arms; to all who, since the assembling of the Kilkenny Convention, "had contrived, advised, counselled, promoted, acted, prosecuted, or abetted" the same by "bearing arms, or contributing men, arms, horse, plate, money, victual, or other furniture or habiliments of war;" to all Jesuits and Roman Catholic

---

* Ordinance, Aug. 1652, c. 13.

priests, and all persons who had "anyways contrived, advised, counselled, promoted, continued, countenanced, aided, assisted, or abetted the rebellion;" and finally to Ormonde, Castlehaven, Clanricarde, and twenty other peers, one bishop, and eighty knights and gentlemen, all especially mentioned by name.

The first step towards the accomplishment of this comprehensive scheme was the removal of the disbanded soldiers of the Irish army. The bulk of the proscribed officers and leaders of the confederates had already elected to suffer voluntary banishment, and had sought safety on the Continent. The rank and file who had laid down their arms upon articles, or had dispersed to their homes, were pressed to enlist on foreign service. Whole regiments of them were eagerly recruited by the agents of the kings of Spain and Poland and the Prince of Condé. As many as 34,000 were in this way hurried into exile. There remained behind, of necessity, great numbers of widows and orphans and deserted wives and families; and these the government proceeded to ship wholesale to the West Indies—the boys for slaves, the women and girls for mistresses to the English sugar-planters. The merchants of Bristol—slave-dealers in the days of Strongbow—sent over their agents to hunt down and ensnare the wretched people for consignment to Barbadoes. Orders were given them on the governors of jails and work-houses for boys "who were of an age to labor," and women "who were marriageable and not past breeding." Delicate ladies were kidnapped, as well as the peasant-women, and forced on board the slave-ships. Between six and seven thousand were transported, before the capture by the unscrupulous dealers of some of the wives and daughters of the English themselves forced the government to prohibit the seizure of any person without a warrant.

And now commenced the great transplantation of the inhabitants of the three easterly provinces across the Shannon. The order was proclaimed by beat of drum in the middle of harvest. Every owner of land, with their wives, their children, their tenants, their servants, and their cattle, must pass the river by the following May, on pain of death. The flight was to be in the winter. The men were to go first, and prepare rough huts for the temporary harboring of their families till their final allotment was made out. A court of claims was set up at Athlone to superintend the migration. Each proprietor, before leaving, was bound to give in to the revenue officer of his district written particulars of all that he was intending to take with him, with full descriptions of each person who was to accompany him. A certificate was given him in return, which entitled him, on presentation at Athlone, to a few acres on which to sojourn during the inquiry into his claims. The court was then to receive evidence of the extent of land he had held in his old home, and of the degree of "good affection" or disaffection which he had exhibited during the war; in proportion to which he was to receive an allotment in a Connaught barony, the occupation of which he would have to dispute with the old proprietor in possession.

And now rose up all over Ireland a great cry for a little longer time. Even the Republican officers represented that the people should be encouraged to sow the new year's crop, lest a famine should arise in the land. Petitions for dispensations were poured in to the commissioners; and a short respite had to be given to the aged ladies, the sick, and the infirm. Slowly the beggared nobility and gentry set out on their sorrowful pilgrimage. The Anglo-Irish, who in Henry's II.'s reign had dispossessed the native Irish, were driven forth from the estates they had held for five hundred years. The season was wet, the roads were well-nigh impassable, and the squalid multitude, as they straggled into the west, found that the barren land to which they had been sent was all too small for the promised accommodation. When the exiles reached Connaught, they were pillaged by the officers employed to set out their allotments, who had to be bribed, either with money or a portion of the land awarded, before they would stir in the business. These worthies—the Kings, the Binghams, the Coles, the St. Georges, the Ormsbys, the Gores, the Lloyds—having cheated the transplanters of a portion of their lots, bought up the remnant for a few shillings the acre, to the extent of eighty thousand Irish acres.

But the exodus did not proceed speedily enough. The adventurers were loudly demanding their new estates. The government was anxious to disband its troops upon the confiscated territory. And so the tardy emigrants were distrained on, arrested, and imprisoned, and some even were hanged *pour encourager les autres*. The walled towns, which were exclusively inhabited by people of English blood, were cleared like the country. The Cork and Waterford merchants went into exile, and carried their enterprise to Ostend, to Rochelle, to Cadiz, and even to Mexico. The flourishing trade of the ancient chartered towns was a thing of the past. The wealthy burgesses of Kilkenny and Tipperary were alike expelled with Walter Cheevers of Monkstown, or Lord Roche of Fermoy. And Galway, whose quays had lately been laden with cargoes from French and Spanish merchant-vessels, was knocked down to the citizens of Liverpool and Gloucester in discharge of their advances to the Parliamentary army.

The three provinces being in a fair way to be cleared of the old proprietors, the new plantation was taken in hand. Commissioners were sent into every county to obtain statistics of the nature, extent, and value of the lands; so that the sums secured to the batches of planters might be proportionately allocated to the different districts. An elaborate survey of the whole island with the exception of Connaught, for which Strafford's survey was held sufficient, was made by Dr. Petty, physician to the forces, for the price of £30,000—a sum which he never received in cash, but for which he obtained an equivalent in the shape of large allotments of the confiscated estates. By the Act of Parliament "for the new planting of Ireland,"* the government had reserved to itself all the towns, all the Church lands and tithes, and the four counties of Dublin, Kildare, Carlow, and Cork. The sum advanced by the "adventurers" amounted to £360,000, which was to be charged upon the County of Louth, and upon the halves of ten counties: Waterford, Limerick, and Tipperary, in Munster; Meath, Westmeath, King's and Queen's counties, in Leinster; and Antrim, Down, and Armagh, in Ulster. The arrears of the

---

* 1653, c. 12.

soldiers came to £1,550,000 to be charged upon the other halves of the same counties, and also upon the counties of Derry, Tyrone, Fermanagh, Cavan, Monaghan, Wexford, Kilkenny, and Kerry. The County of Sligo and part of Mayo and Leitrim were subsequently taken from the transplanted Irish to satisfy arrears due to part of the English army which had fought in England during the civil wars. And the counties of Donegal, Longford, and Wicklow, and half the County of Leitrim, were appropriated to the garrisons of the Munster cities which had revolted from Inchiquin to Lord Broghill in 1649.

Each soldier had received a bond or debenture which acknowledged the amount of his arrears, and his claim to an allotment; and lists were made of these claims in each regiment, and the land was plotted out by the surveyor-general in proportionate tracts. Each regiment then drew lots for its location among the baronies at their disposal, and each man in the same way received by lot his particular parcel. Company by company, and troop by troop, they were marched on to the ground, disbanded, and put into possession. It was not till the end of 1656 that the disbanding was complete; and in the interval the traffic among the debentures had been briskly carried on. Money was advanced on them. The common soldiers gambled for them, or sold them for a little ready cash. The officers largely bought up the claims of the men in their company; and so considerable was the dealing that a crowd of debenture-brokers sprang into existence, who sold and bought on commission at the current market price. Large estates were put together by the purchase of these claims to allotments; and no little chicanery was practised by those who superintended the distribution of the allotments, for the advantage of themselves and of their friends.

Dr. Petty tells us that the whole area of Ireland contained 10,500,000 Irish acres, of which 3,000,000, consisting of water and waste, were contemptuously left to the native Irish; that of the remaining 7,500,000 acres, 300,000 held by the Church in A.D. 1641 were reserved by the government; and that the Protestant planters of James and Elizabeth held 2,000,000, and the remaining 5,200,000 belonged to the Roman Catholics and "delinquent" Protestants. He calculates that these 5,200,000 Irish acres were confiscated by the Republican government. According to English measurements, more accurate surveys give us 20,806,260 *statute* acres as the total area of the island, while that of Clare and Connaught is 5,223,773; and these figures give us 15,582,487 English acres as the total area of the three confiscated provinces.

The English government had a grim excuse for repeopling Ireland. The desolation of the island was complete: one third of the people had perished or been driven into exile; famine and plague had finished the work of the sword; the fields lay uncultivated; and the miserable remnants of the flying population were driven to live on carrion and human corpses. The wolves so increased in numbers, even round the city of Dublin itself, that the counties were taxed for their extermination, and rewards were paid of £5 for the head of a full-grown wolf and £2 for that of a cub. But though the object and intention of the government was to make an effectual plantation over three quarters of the island, and though the land itself changed hands, as in Elizabeth's and James's time so was it now found impossible to expel a nation root and branch. In spite of all that persecution could do, the old proprietors still clung, in numbers of cases, to their old country, and wandered about their old domains as vagrants, or were admitted by the new owners as tenants-at-will. The younger and more active fled into the forests and bogs, and swelled the ranks of the Tories. There they lived a lawless life of brigandage, robbing and murdering the settlers and destroying their property. Stern measures were adopted to put them down. They were stalked by regular parties of armed men, smoked out of their caves, and killed without mercy. A price was set upon their heads, as upon those of the wolves; but the wild country was too difficult of access for the government to succeed in exterminating them. As the Tories and the wolves were killed down, so were the priests. Proscribed, hunted, and transported as soon as caught, they still hung about the country in all sorts of disguises and in all kinds of hiding-places, performing the offices of their religion in secret, and at the peril of their lives, to their scattered coreligionists.

The plantation failed, like the earlier ones, by the planters being absorbed by the Irish. Notwithstanding the most stringent regulations to the contrary, the soldiers intermarried with the young Irish girls. The natives were taken as servants by English masters. The old process was begun over again which had been at work in the days of the Plantagenets; the settlers succumbed to the old influences. Forty years after the settlement had been accomplished, numbers of the children of Cromwell's soldiers were unable to speak a word of English. Dr. Petty's great estates, which he had obtained by the purchase of debentures and by way of compensation for his labors in the Down survey, passed, by the marriage of his daughter with the Earl of Kerry, to one of the oldest Anglo-Irish families of the Norman colony.

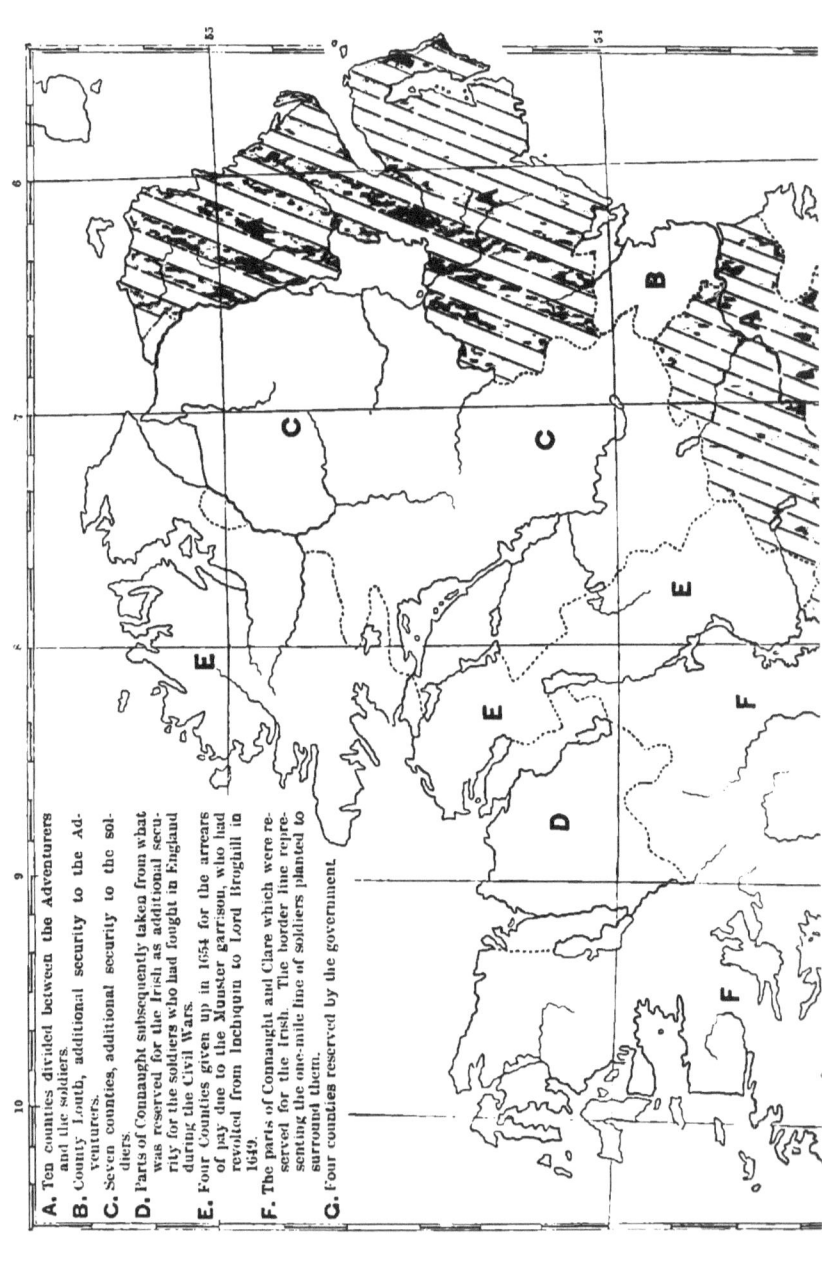

A. Ten counties divided between the Adventurers and the soldiers.
B. County Louth, additional security to the Adventurers.
C. Seven counties, additional security to the soldiers.
D. Parts of Connaught subsequently taken from what was reserved for the Irish as additional security for the soldiers who had fought in England during the Civil Wars.
E. Four Counties given up in 1654 for the arrears of pay due to the Munster garrison, who had revolted from Inchiquin to Lord Broghill in 1649.
F. The parts of Connaught and Clare which were reserved for the Irish. The border line representing the one-mile line of soldiers planted to surround them.
G. Four counties reserved by the government

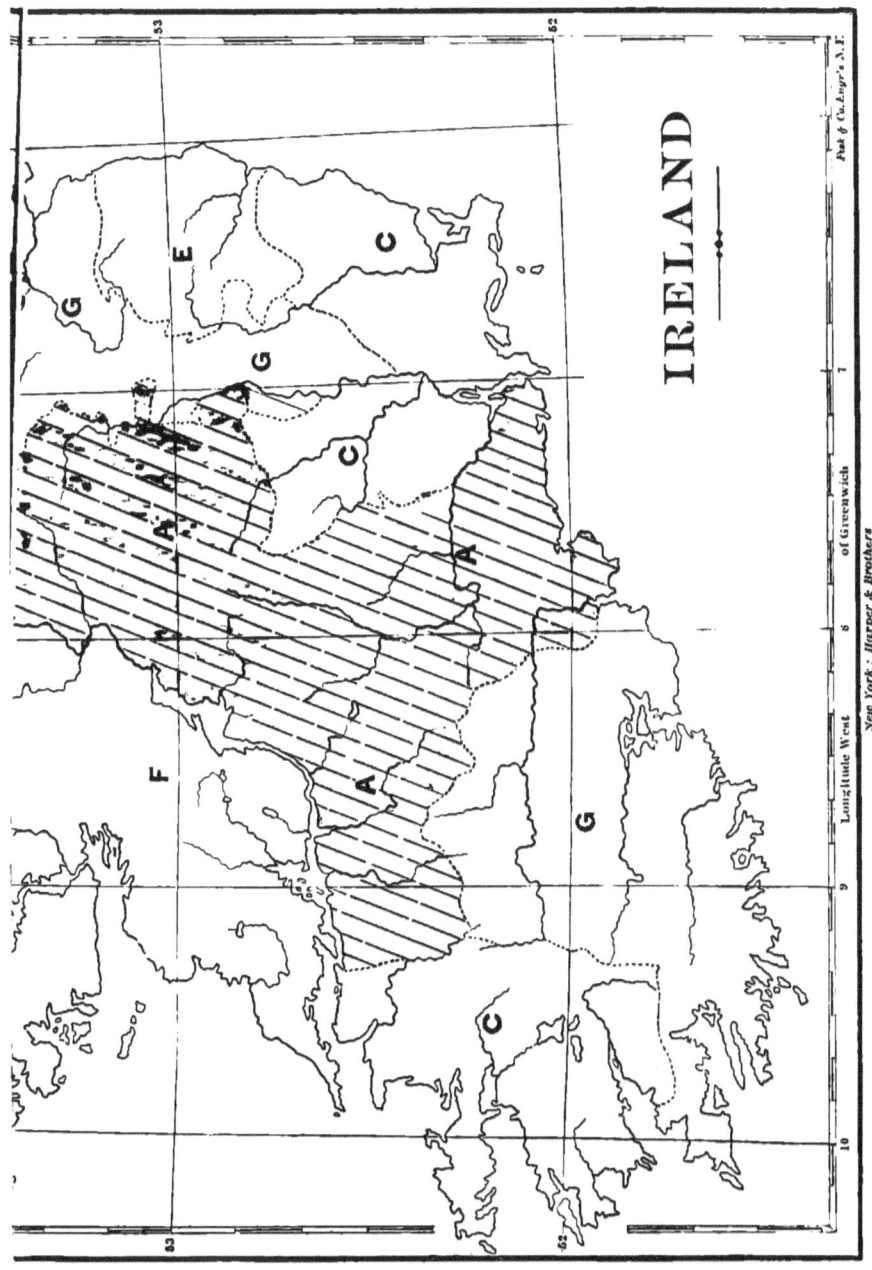

Book V.

THE THIRD CONQUEST

CHAPTER I.
RESTORATION COMPROMISES. A.D. 1656–1666.

WHILE the redistribution of the land in Ireland was proceeding, events were marching rapidly in England. The Royalists had received their *quietus* at Worcester; and Cromwell and the army were masters of the situation. The residue of the Long Parliament had been driven from the House by a company of musketeers. The "Barebones" convention had been a fiasco. Two Houses of Commons, elected upon the basis of an extended franchise and a redistribution of seats, in which for the first time sat thirty members from Ireland, had been summarily dissolved; and Cromwell had finally established a military despotism upon the ruins of the outraged Commonwealth.

The proclamation of the Protectorate was favorably received in Ireland, except by a few sound Republicans like Ludlow, who sullenly resigned office. Soon Henry Cromwell was sent over as lord-lieutenant; and his mild and steady government went far to conciliate all parties, and to promote order in the country. The energy of the settlers soon began to bear fruit. The traces of the ten years' war disappeared, and the fertile country began to show a smiling face. New buildings rose on the newly made estates, new plantations sprang up, new roads were engineered; and the exported farm produce began to compete with that of England in the English markets.

And now the great Protector's course was run, and he had been quietly succeeded by his son Richard. The members for Ireland appeared again in Richard's Parliament; and upon its swift dissolution followed the fall of Richard, and the recall and the expulsion of the Rump by the army. All were now looking to a restoration of the monarchy, as the only escape from the despotism of a military faction. The Presbyterians, steady Royalists since the king's death, were holding up their heads, and the army of Scotland was marching on London, to the dismay of Lambert and Fleetwood and the army of England.

In Ireland, when it became apparent which way the tide was setting, the new landholders perceived that to secure their allotments they must make their peace with the king. Broghill and Coote, the presidents of Munster and Connaught, who had both secured enormous estates under the new settlement, though hitherto ardent anti-Royalists and sample Cromwellians, had already been intriguing with Charles, and inviting him to land at Cork. They surprised Dublin Castle, and sent prisoners to England Sir Hardress Waller and three commissioners of the Parliament; and, having secured the principal garrisons in the island, raised the cry for a free Parliament. The army, in which their influence was unbounded, was secured by providing for the payment of its arrears, and for its future maintenance. The Scotch Presbyterians of the north were only too ready to welcome a restored king who had subscribed the Covenant; and, on the Declaration of Breda being transmitted to Ireland, Charles was proclaimed in all the principal cities.

The restoration of the monarchy excited lively hopes in the minds of the dispossessed Irish. They thought that as the king "had come to his own again," so should they. Some of them accordingly endeavored to retake possession of their old estates by force, which rash proceeding gave the new English the opportunity of raising a false alarm of a fresh Irish insurrection, and so to impress the king with the belief that the safety of the kingdom depended on the maintenance of the Protestant interest. The king's first act was to restore the Established Church to its former position, and to reward with peerages the turncoats who had intrigued for his return. Monk was created Earl of Albemarle, Coote was made Earl of Montrath, and Broghill Earl of Orrery; and these two last, with Sir Maurice Eustace, the lord chancellor, were intrusted with the government of the kingdom as lords justices.

Then came the great question of the land. The Royalists were loud in their demands for a general restoration of their estates. On the other hand, the soldiers and adventurers were in possession, the latter by virtue of an act of Parliament * assented to by the late king; and Charles II. had been reinstated at the instance of these very men and their leaders, whom it would be exceedingly dangerous to disturb. There was still some of the reserved land undistributed, and the estates allotted to certain of the "regicides" were resumed by the crown; and so, on Coote's and Broghill's recommendations, the king published a declaration for the settlement of Ireland, which professed to be an arrangement by which all parties were to be satisfied. This scheme was based upon the plan that the existing new owners should be undisturbed; with the exception that the Church lands were to be disgorged, and that certain select adherents of the king like Ormonde, and the dispossessed Protestants and Roman Catholics who should prove themselves innocent of any complicity in the original rebellion, were to be at once restored to their estates; in which case the new men now in possession were to be "reprised" by the grant of lands equivalent in value out of the unallotted lands. In order that the number of innocents should be reduced as low as possible, the mere fact that a man had lived quietly on his estate while the country round was in the hands of the insurgents, or of his having in any way corresponded with them while he was living in the English quarters, was declared to be a bar to his restoration as an innocent; much more was the joining of the confederacy before 1649, or the adhering to the party of the nuncio, or the negotiating with any foreign prince. Officers who had served the king before the peace of 1649 were to receive allotments from the lands still undistributed in Wicklow, Longford, Leitrim, and Donegal, as far as they would go: while of the insurgents who had submitted to Ormonde's terms in 1649, those who had accepted from the Parliament a portion of land in Connaught or Clare were to stay there, having put themselves in this position by their own act; those who had left the country and served his majesty abroad were to be restored to their estates, provided the present occupiers should be first reprised.

---

* 16 Car. I. c. 32.

The successful working of this arrangement depended upon the existence of a sufficiency of the reserved and undistributed land wherewith to "reprise" the adventurers and soldiers who were to be removed. Of this there was not nearly enough for the purpose, and it was, besides, considerably reduced by the prodigal grants made out of it by the king to Ormonde and other special favorites. He gave 120,000 acres in Tipperary, the estates of the regicides, to his brother the Duke of York, and 20,000 acres to the Church over and above the 300,000 it possessed before A.D. 1641. The cities and towns, though they had also been reserved by the late government, were not available for the purposes of reprisal, as not only had many of them been colonized by Cromwellians, but Charles—who knew the value of having them filled with his own adherents—specially reserved the right "to restore them to such of the corporations as should be found fit for that our grace and favor;" which meant that he should plant them with Royalists, and appoint Royalists to be mayors and aldermen.

On the 8th of May, 1661, the Irish Parliament met to confirm the king's "declaration," in Chichester House,* a building on College Green, erected by Sir Arthur Chichester, and accepted by the government in discharge of a debt of £10,000 from his estate. As the greater part of the freeholders of the counties and the burgesses of the towns consisted of the new settlers, the Commons were very largely composed of men of the "new interest." Only one Roman Catholic was returned. The bill, drawn as it was by men of the "new interest," and substantially confirming the "new interest" in its new possessions, soon passed the Lower House in all its stages. The House of Lords, in which numbers of the old Anglo-Irish sat, gave it a very different reception. For many of the old peers it meant ruin to themselves and their friends. For the Orrerys, the Montraths, the Albemarles, the Massarenes, it was the title to their newly acquired estates. Every effort was made by the

---

* Chichester House was pulled down in 1728, and in the following year the first stone of the Parliament-house was laid on its site by Archbishop Boulter. It was completed in 1739.

old peers, led by the Earl of Kildare, to increase the amount of the reprisal ground at the expense of the new interest. It was discovered that the commissioners had made clandestine grants of the reprisal ground to their own friends, and loud complaints were raised against "the doubling ordinance" passed by the English Parliament during the civil wars, which entitled each adventurer who, in addition to his first venture, advanced one fourth more to receive lands to the value of double the original loan. At length the bill passed the Upper House, and having been transmitted to England for the king's approval, the struggle was transferred to Whitehall, where Richard Talbot, a violent Roman Catholic, was the not over-judicious champion of the old Irish cause. For six months the agents of the two Irish parties contested every point, till Charles, sick and tired of the prolonged wrangle, disallowed the doubling ordinance, and approved the bill.*

Ormonde now went to Ireland as lord-lieutenant with the title of duke, and was presented by the Irish Parliament with £30,000.† A court of claims was, on February 13th, 1663, set up in Dublin, in which the dispossessed land-owners proceeded to press for their rights. It sat for three months, during which time 158 judgments of innocent were given and only nineteen of guilty. The "new interest" took alarm at these results, for the innocent were entitled to immediate restitution of their lands, and there was great fear that the supply of reprisal ground for those who were to be supplanted would fall short. The Protestants believed that they were going to be sacrificed to the Roman Catholics. A great agitation was raised. A few of the "new interest," including some members of Parliament, engaged in a plot which had been hatched by Blood (afterwards of regalia celebrity) and the more desperate of the Presbyterians, who were suffering from the persecution of the reinstated Episcopal Church, to seize the Castle and restore the Republic. The plot was betrayed and stifled; but the government became alarmed. The time by which the decrees in the Court of Claims were to be obtained was limited

---

* Act of Settlement, 14, 15 Car. II. c. 2.   † 14, 15 Car. II. c. 16.

to one year from the date of its first sitting, at the expiration of which time it was closed; so that, out of some four thousand claims ready for hearing, but eight hundred only were disposed of. A "bill of explanation" was introduced for the protection of the "new interest," and another interminable wrangle was maintained in London. At length, from sheer weariness a compromise was come to, by which the adventurers and soldiers agreed to give up one third of their land for the satisfaction of the Royalist claims, and the "'49 officers" to accept ten shillings in the pound for their arrears. The House of Commons was purged of certain members who had been concerned in Blood's conspiracy, and their places filled with supporters of the government. The explanatory act* was passed, and five commissioners appointed to carry out its provisions.

The outcome of the confiscation and subsequent settlement was that, whereas before the rebellion the Irish Roman Catholics held two thirds of the profitable land of Ireland, in 1672 they held but one third. The king seized the occasion to secure to the crown a considerable revenue by reserving a quit-rent of from 1d. to 3d. per acre from both the restored and the confirmed proprietors. Ormonde got back all his estates and something considerable in addition, in all 130,000 acres. Lord Clanricarde, Lord Inchiquin, Lord Roscommon, Lord Antrim, Lord Westmeath, Lord Castlehaven, and many others who had managed to secure friends at court, were also capriciously selected for restoration to their lands. Numbers who claimed, with quite as much justice as many who were restored, to be "innocent" and "loyal," like the Barrons of Burnchurch, were left in their poverty without a shadow of compensation, and retired to the Continent, railing bitterly against the king's ingratitude; while the timeserving new men, the Cootes, the Clotworthys, the Hills, the Fortescues, the Taylors, who had now got the country in their grasp, secured every acre they had acquired without any deduction. Dr. Petty calculates that the Roman Catholics recovered of their forfeited property

---

* 17, 18 Car. II. c. 2.

about 2,340,000 Irish acres; while of the 7,500,000 acres of good land, which he estimated the island to contain, the Protestants held 5,220,000. The net result of this attempt on the part of the Irish to emancipate themselves from the rule of the English oligarchy was that they lost just one half of the lands they before had held, and had seated the English oligarchy still more firmly on their shoulders.

CHAPTER II.

TOLERANCE AND INTOLERANCE.   A.D. 1660–1687.

THE clergy of the Established Church had come back in triumph. The twelve vacant bishoprics had been filled up, and the new prelates consecrated in St. Patrick's Cathedral with great pomp and solemnity. The Church had suffered considerably under the Commonwealth. In England the bishops had been driven from their sees and from the House of Lords, and their lands had been sold. The parish clergy had been ejected from their benefices, and compelled to give place to those who were willing to take the Covenant. In Ireland the Church had been completely overwhelmed by the storm of civil war; and Bishop Bramhall, "the Irish Laud," as Cromwell called him, had been scheduled with Castlehaven and Inchiquin as incapable of pardon either of life or estate. And now the Church had got the upper-hand, and it signalized its return to place and power by an outburst of bigoted intolerance. It was not the party of Usher, but the party of Laud, which found itself master of the situation. Bramhall had come back as Archbishop of Armagh, and John Leslie to Raphoe; Henry Leslie was appointed to the see of Meath, and Jeremy Taylor to Down and Connor. A drove of shepherds to look after a few score sheep! Of the 1,100,000 souls which constituted the whole population of the island, 800,000 were Roman Catholics, 100,000 were Presbyterians, 100,000 were Independents, Anabaptists, and Quakers, and but 100,000 were Protestants of the Establishment. To provide for the spiritual comfort of this 100,000, there was an establishment of four archbishops and eighteen bishops. Many of the parish clergy held mere sinecures; most of them were pluralists. With no congregations, in many cases, to look after, they lived away in Dublin or in England, and left an ill-paid curate to perform a service where a few stray persons should be gathered together. There were some who drew from their united livings as much as £1000 a year without performing any duty whatever.

The Presbyterians of Ulster were a flourishing body. The Scottish army which had come over to Carrickfergus with Munroe had formed a second Scotch colony in Antrim and Down. The army chaplains had gathered congregations round them, and had swelled the number of ministers established under the Presbytery. They had been threatened with transplantation by Cromwell; and they looked at least for toleration from a king who had himself taken the Covenant. There was nothing the bishops hated so much as the Covenant, the solemn obligation which pledged the subscriber to exterminate not only Popery, but prelacy; and now their day had come to enjoy the privilege of persecution. While in England the Episcopal clergy had in their turn ejected the Presbyterians from their livings, and the Conventicle Act and the Five Mile Act, in violation of the Declaration of Breda, were driving the Nonconformists from the towns and crowding them into the jails, a corresponding retribution was exacted by the Church from the Nonconforming bodies in Ireland. A new Act of Uniformity* was passed, which compelled all persons holding any preferment to be lawfully ordained, to use the liturgy—now recast and made still less acceptable by the Caroline bishops—and to subscribe to a declaration that it was unlawful "on any pretence whatever to take arms against the king," and that the Covenant was an unlawful oath. The Roman Catholics were left to themselves—so far as the Church was concerned, they could do as they pleased: the State would be sure to look after them. But the Presbyterians who would not conform to the act were breakers of the law. All "unlawful assemblies" had been forbidden by royal proclamation; and so their kirk sessions were proscribed. The Presbyterian ministers were brought before the magistrates and fined. They were summoned to appear before the bishop, their livings were declared vacant, and orthodox clergy were sent down to fill

---

* 17, 18 Car. II. c. 5.

their places. Jeremy Taylor himself declared vacant thirty-six churches in one visitation. Out of sixty-eight ministers in Ulster, but seven submitted to be ordained; the remainder were expelled. Not only were they summarily deprived of their homes and means of living, but were forbidden to preach or exercise the ministry in public. Guiltless of and abhorring conspiracy, they were held by the government to be implicated in Blood's plot. Some were summoned to Dublin and thrown into prison; some were arrested and sent to Carrickfergus and Carlingford; others were dragged before the ecclesiastical courts and excommunicated. With no pretence of trial, they were banished from the kingdom, and took refuge with their kinsmen in Scotland. Then followed the flight of their congregations: men sold their property and left the country where there was no liberty of worship; some went to Scotland; more went to America, and found a refuge among the Puritan colonists of New England.

Charles, who in exile had secretly changed his religion for that of the Church of Rome, was determined to obtain toleration for the Roman Catholics; and published a declaration of indulgence for their benefit, though nominally to relieve the Nonconformists. He instructed Ormonde to deal leniently with the Irish Roman Catholics, and to wink at all their proceedings. The beaten party accordingly began to show signs of life. The priests came out of their hiding-places and crept back into their parishes. The exiled friars straggled back from the Continent; even a few religious houses sprang up, and some Jesuit schools were opened.

The Protestants soon took alarm, and rumors of plots and massacres and French invasions filled the air. The outlawed Tories still continued to make their depredations, to burn the isolated farm-houses, and to murder the farmers. The farmers began to form themselves into local regiments of militia, in fear of another rising. Ormonde, who was too able and honest a man for Charles and the Cabal ministry, was superseded by Lord Robarts; and Lord Robarts by Lord Berkeley, a creature of the duke of Buckingham. The persecution of the Nonconformists was renewed, and indulgence to the Roman

Catholics increased. Peter Talbot, brother of Richard the vehement advocate of Irish claims at Whitehall, was Roman Catholic Archbishop of Dublin. Berkeley allowed him to appear before the council in his archiepiscopal robes, and sent him the Castle plate and hangings for use at a grand celebration of high-mass. Recusants were put into the commission of the peace, and licenses were granted for their admission into corporations. After a bitter struggle, some Roman Catholic aldermen and common-councilmen were forced upon the city of Dublin; and Richard Talbot got up a petition to the king to reopen the recent settlement of the land question. An angry remonstrance from the English House of Commons crushed this attempt in the bud; and Berkeley was recalled; and so matters smouldered on for another five years: the Roman Catholics enjoying a degree of toleration which they had not experienced for half a century; the Protestants watching them with intense suspicion, and vainly pressing the government to put the law in force.

Charles and his brother, with Clifford, Arundel, and Arlington, had entered into a deep-laid plot with Louis XIV. Their aim was to re-establish arbitrary government and the Romish religion in England, and to overrun and partition the United Provinces. Louis was to contribute six thousand French soldiers and £200,000 per annum to Charles to carry out the first branch of the design, and Charles was to lend Louis the English fleet to help to execute the latter. Though the infamous treaty of Dover had not seen the light of day, suspicions of the king's treachery were abroad. The dread of Popery and of a second Stuart tyranny was working up the people of England to a pitch of unreasonable frenzy. The Test Act, forced on the government by indignant public opinion, had disclosed the startling facts that the Duke of York, the lord high admiral, was a Papist in disguise; that so also was Clifford, the lord high treasurer; and so were many others, both in the army and civil service. The king was in the pay of Louis, the great persecutor of Protestants; and Danby was suspected of being the unwilling agent of his master's venality. For a people frantic with suspicion, well founded against the king and his co-conspirators, some tangible evidence of a Popish plot was all that was required to set the country in a blaze. This was afforded by the foul false-witness of Titus Oates and his co-perjurers, and the mysterious murder of Sir Edmondbury Godfrey. Common-sense at once vanished, and stern measures with the luckless Roman Catholics were fiercely demanded.

Part of the lying tale was that the plot extended to Ireland, and that a French invasion was in preparation. And though there was no shadow of a foundation for the charge, and Ormonde, whom the king had again made lord-lieutenant, himself had no belief in it, so loud and violent was the popular clamor that extraordinary measures of severity were adopted. All Roman Catholics were ordered to surrender their arms within twenty days. All Romish ecclesiastics were ordered to quit the kingdom by the expiration of two months' time. Rewards were offered for priests and Jesuits who remained after that date. All Romish convents, schools, and seminaries were dissolved. The markets were ordered to be held outside the principal towns; and Roman Catholics were prohibited from attending a public meeting, or residing within a garrison town. All garrisons were confined to barracks. Rewards were given for the discovery of any soldier who attended mass; and the Roman Catholic inhabitants of Galway, Limerick, Clonmel, Kilkenny, and Drogheda were ordered to withdraw without the walls.

Archbishop Talbot, who was actually on his death-bed, was accused of being concerned in the plot, and imprisoned in Dublin Castle, where he lingered on till his decease. Old Lord Mountgarret, bedridden and over eighty, was dragged from his bed, and thrown into jail. London was crowded with Irish informers, men of the worst possible character, cattle-lifters, jail-birds, and apostate friars. Dr. Plunket, the Roman Catholic Archbishop of Armagh, a man held in the greatest respect by Protestants and Roman Catholics alike, was dragged over to London, and charged by two priests, whose profligacy he had censured, with having obtained the primacy from the Pope on condition that he would raise 70,000 Roman Catholic soldiers in Ireland, and with having organized the descent of 40,000 French troops in

Carlingford Bay. The absurd charge was credited, a conviction was obtained, and the innocent old man was hanged and quartered at Tyburn. All reason was at an end; victims were demanded, and when no evidence could be obtained of a Popish plot at all, perjury supplied the deficiency.

Fanaticism at length had had its fling. Charles, foreseeing the reaction which would set in, and not venturing to oppose the popular madness, allowed the fit of fury to spend its force; and when the storm had subsided, Shaftesbury fell, Monmouth was banished, and Charles and the Duke of York calmly reverted to their old policy.

The Duke of York had all along looked to Ireland and his coreligionists there both as a fulcrum for the arbitrary projects of his brother and himself, and also as a refuge in case of failure. Charles and he had formed the design of remodelling the army to the exclusion of Protestants; but before the plan could be developed Charles died, and James found himself in a position to carry out a new policy of "Thorough." Ormonde was recalled, and the government was intrusted to two lords justices— Archbishop Boyle, a High Churchman, who favored the recusants, and Sir Arthur Forbes, Lord Granard, a Presbyterian; the latter appointment being made to soothe the apprehensions of the Protestants till matters were in train.

When the new king had established himself firmly on the throne, and suppressed the rebellions of Argyle and Monmouth, Ireland was taken in hand. The lords justices gave way to James's brother-in-law, Lord Clarendon, who was to be used as a dummy, while the real power was put into the hands of Richard Talbot, the fanatical Roman Catholic who was the chief leader of the Irish party, and now sent over to command the army with the title of Earl of Tyrconnel.

Nothing could exceed the bitterness and suspicion which divided the Protestants from the Roman Catholics. The former were extremely uneasy at the turn events were taking, and were overwhelmed with a dread that their ascendency would no longer be upheld by the government. The latter were exultant at the prospect of getting the upper-hand, and with the hope of at last breaking off their necks the galling yoke they had borne so long, and of recovering the estates which had been taken from them. James's schemes were rapidly advancing. Regiment after regiment was disbanded, and reconstructed of Roman Catholic recruits; Protestant officers were cashiered, and replaced with Roman Catholics. The militia were dissolved on the pretence that they had sympathized with Monmouth, and their arms were transported to Chester. Roman Catholic sheriffs and justices of the peace were appointed. Even the judges of the superior courts were changed; and men were shamefully raised to the bench and sworn in as privy-councillors, whose only qualification was an unscrupulous devotion to the Roman Catholic cause. An agitation was then set on foot to repeal the Act of Settlement. A petition to that effect was forwarded to the king. It was hinted that the Cromwellians had best surrender another third of their estates. Suits of ejectment were brought by the old proprietors in the court of the new chief baron, who had boasted " that he would drive a coach and horses through the Act of Settlement." The English settlers' case was accordingly refused a hearing; and decrees of restoration were made with startling rapidity. Deliberate attacks were made by the government upon the charters of every city and borough in the island. Judgment was given against the city of Dublin on a writ of *quo warranto*, and every other corporation shortly suffered the same fate. These bodies were then reconstructed by the wholesale introduction of Roman Catholics. Only in some of the greater cities, where the English interest was dominant, was it provided that one third of the members should consist of Protestants.

Everything was now ripe for the appointment of a Roman Catholic viceroy. Accordingly Clarendon was removed, and Tyrconnel put in his place with the title of lord deputy.

CHAPTER III.

THE SECESSION. A.D. 1687-1689.

THE appointment to the post of viceroy of a man so violent and so bigoted as Tyrconnel produced a sudden panic among the Protestants. A hurried exodus at once took place. Fifteen hundred persons left Dublin on the departure of Clarendon; and Protestants from all parts of Ireland flocked to the seaports, and fled across the Channel to England and the Isle of Man, even in open boats. A rumor ran through the island that, on December 9th, there was to be a universal massacre of Protestants; and those who did not emigrate drew together into the country-houses, and remained upon their guard with loopholed walls and barricaded windows. An attempt was made by the government to throw Roman Catholic garrisons into Derry and Enniskillen, with the result that the Protestant inhabitants treated their reconstructed town-councils with contempt, closed the gates of those cities, and prepared to stand a siege.

At a crisis such as this the Prince of Orange landed in England, and James precipitately absconded into France. Tyrconnel was astounded at the flight of the king, and for a time was doubtful whether to fly himself or to make terms with William. The latter was not, however, as yet in a position to employ coercion in Ireland; and Tyrconnel plucked up courage, and proceeded to stir the Irish into action on behalf of the house of Stuart. The priests, most of whom were scions of the old dispossessed Irish families, exhorted their flocks to be ready for a rising. The army, consisting of forty-eight regiments, was filled with eager recruits. Bodies of irregular troops, or "rapparees," as they were called, were collected, till near upon 100,000 men were under arms. The Protestants were disarmed. They were ordered to bring in their weapons by a certain day to the parish churches; and such as retained their arms had their houses pillaged by the soldiery. The whole country was given up to plunder. The regular troops were quartered on the farmers. The rapparees took up their quarters in the mountainous parts of Leitrim, in the Galtees, and in the Wicklow hills. The houses of Protestants were robbed, their horses requisitioned, and their sheep and cattle driven off, from rich and poor alike. Some were hidden in the mountains, others were cooked and eaten on the spot; vast numbers were killed out of pure mischief, and left to fester where they fell. In six weeks' time some fifty thousand oxen and from three to four hundred thousand sheep were butchered in this fashion. The scattered Protestants in the south and west were helpless and made no resistance. The important towns were soon in the hands of the government, and the isolated country-houses which the owners had fortified were surrendered at discretion or deserted. Those who were able travelled into the north, where the English interest was forming a combination for self-defence under Lord Mount-Alexander, Lord Blaney, and Sir Arthur Rawdon, to find that William and Mary had been proclaimed king and queen in Derry and Enniskillen.

Tyrconnel determined to reduce the Protestants of the north before they had time to organize themselves; and despatched Richard Hamilton, a volunteer envoy from William who had broken his word and betrayed his trust, with a strong force into Ulster. As the Irish advanced the Protestants retreated from town to town, breaking down the bridges, and burning every house, behind them. Hopeless of making a stand at Coleraine and Omagh, they retreated behind Lough Foyle, and thirty thousand persons sought refuge behind the walls of Derry; while the inhabitants of Cavan and the neighboring country turned to bay in Ballyshannon, Enniskillen, and the castle of Crom.

Meanwhile the Irish, who used to look for foreign aid from Spain, were now looking towards France. Spain was sinking gradually into the position of a second-rate power, and France was the most powerful state in Europe. Louis XIV., the persecutor of the Huguenots, was looked upon as the great champion of the Church by the Roman Catholics; and the old Irish party were only too willing to accept the protection of a sovereign who had done his best to humiliate England, and to overwhelm the country of the man who was now England's king, and who was expected to prove another Cromwell. Negotiations accordingly took place between Tyrconnel and Louis; and James, who had been received with great respect and hospitality at the French court, petitioned urgently for the assistance of a French army. Soldiers Louis was not prepared to provide, but he was liberal enough with other sinews of war. He assembled at Brest a fleet of fourteen ships of war, six frigates, and three fire-ships. Arms and ammunition for ten thousand men were put on board. One hundred French officers and twelve hundred Irish refugees filled the transports, and a sum was placed at James's disposal of £112,000 in gold. The ex-king of England was accompanied by a few English Tories — Lords Powis, Seaforth, Dover, and Melfort, Bishop Cartwright, and his own bastard the Duke of Berwick. Among the French officers were De Rosen, Maumont, Pusignan, and Boisseleau; among the Irish refugees we find the names of Sarsfield, John and Anthony Hamilton, and Simon and Henry Luttrell. The Comte d'Avaux was attached to the expedition by Louis as confidential minister.

James landed at Kinsale, March 12th, 1689, and proceeded thence to Cork and Dublin, where he was received with triumph. After a hasty visit to Derry, where the siege was assuming the form of a blockade, he proceeded to summon a Parliament, which met on the 7th of May. Most of the sixty-nine Protestant peers and the twenty-two bishops had fled to England. Only seven of the former and five of the latter remained. Of the eighteen Roman Catholic peers only nine took their seats, and of these two were minors. To swell the number of the Upper House, James made six fresh creations: Fitton, the lord chancellor, was made Lord Gosworth; Nugent, the chief-justice, Lord Riverston; Colonel Justin McCarthy, brother of Lord Clancarthy, was made Viscount Mountcashel; Sir Valentine Brown, Viscount Kenmare; John Bourke, Lord

Bophin; and Walter Cheevers, Viscount Mountleinster; while he reversed the outlawries of fifteen of the old peers who had taken part in the rebellion, so that, including four of the bishops who attended, the Upper House mustered forty-one. The House of Commons, of course, consisted almost entirely of Roman Catholics, only six Protestants being returned, and of these two were for the University. The Protestant freeholders in the counties had either left the country or were besieged in Ulster; and the late reconstruction of the corporations rendered the return of a Protestant for a borough impossible, so that the Roman Catholics had it all their own way at the elections. Two hundred and thirty-two members were returned, and of those one hundred and sixty-five were of Anglo-Irish and sixty-seven of ancient Irish extraction—almost all descendants of the land-owners who had been displaced by the Cromwellians.

The first care of the Parliament was to secure its own independence in the event of a restoration of the king to the English throne. It was declared that no English statute should bind Ireland, and that writs of error and appeals to England should be unlawful. It followed of necessity, from James's position in Ireland, that Poynings's Act was repealed. A bill was passed, of great moderation considering the state of the law during the Protestant ascendency, to establish liberty of conscience and freedom of worship. There was an act to "protect" the trade of Ireland; and the payment of tithe was adjusted by giving to the Roman Catholic clergy the tithe payable by the Roman Catholic land-owners. The burning question, however, was of course that of the forfeitures. It was close upon forty years since the estates of the Irish and Anglo-Irish nobility and gentry had been torn from them and given to the "new interest." It was but twenty-five years since that the unsatisfactory compromises of the Restoration had set a seal on the confiscations of 1652. In the meantime the dispossessed land-owners had never lost sight of the one object of recovering their ancient properties. Though out of possession, they had continued to devise and settle the lands, and to charge them with jointures and provisions for younger children, as though their rights were still existing and tangible; and they lost no opportunity of petitioning and agitating for a revision of the Act of Settlement. Now their day had come. They took little heed of the fact that much money had been sunk in the land in improvements, which had greatly raised its value, nor that numbers of the present owners had purchased for valuable consideration of the Cromwellians. These men, they said, had bought with a knowledge of what the vendor's title was—which was true enough; and so the knights and gentlemen in the Lower House, and the restored lords of the Pale in the Upper, hastened to pass an act to enable themselves to resume the estates of their ancestors, and considered that they had more than met the justice of the case by inserting a clause which provided that purchasers for valuable consideration should be compensated out of the lands of those who were attainted of treason to King James. The act was as defensible as the act which deprived them of their land, and at any rate as much an act of justice, or as little one of injustice, as the handing-back in England of the estates of the Church and cavaliers after the Restoration. The next step was one of vindictiveness, an act of attainder launched against their political adversaries. As in the acts of proscription passed by Elizabeth, James, and the Commonwealth, a long list of persons was made out who had either thrown in their lot with the Prince of Orange, or had fled from the country, or were in correspondence with his adherents. Two thousand four hundred and forty-five names in all appear in the act; among them those of two archbishops and seven bishops, the Duke of Ormonde, and sixty-three temporal peers, eighty-three clergymen, and 2289 ladies, knights, gentlemen, yeomen, and tradesmen. Many of these were inserted haphazard, or from personal spite, or for the sake of their estates, which as a consequence became forfeited to James, and were greedily desired for distribution; while, in addition to the exclusion of the absentees from pardon and the sequestration of their lands, the whole of their personalty was vested in "his majesty." So well had the lesson of confiscation been learned by experience.

To meet current expenditure, the Irish Parliament granted

James a tax of £20 a month on all real estate ; but as this did not nearly meet his requirements, and as nothing came in from the customs and excise, by reason of the complete collapse of trade, he took the fatal course of issuing base money. Having seized some authorized coining-machines in Dublin, he set up a mint, and gathered all the refuse metal he was able to collect; from every pound of which he produced, and compulsorily circulated as legal tender, coins amounting to the *nominal* value of £5 and of the *actual* value of 4*d*. This meant ruin to the country, but especially to the Protestants, who were now compelled to receive these counters in exchange for their goods, and were forced to accept the same rubbish in payment of all debts due to them on mortgage, bonds, or bills.

In the meantime, the English in Ulster were fighting for their lives with unexampled doggedness. The famished garrison of Derry, after enduring a siege of 105 days, had at length been relieved by the tardy arrival of three provision-ships under Kirke's convoy ; and De Rosen and the Irish army had raised the siege in despair. The gallant Enniskilleners, upon whom three bodies of troops were converging under the Duke of Berwick, Colonel Patrick Sarsfield, and Colonel Justin McCarthy, after checking the former two, boldly attacked the last with inferior numbers, and utterly overthrew him at Newtown-Butler, with a loss of two thousand men, to whom no quarter was given. Sarsfield was driven back on Athlone, and Sligo occupied by Kirke. The whole Irish army of the north, abandoning its stores, was in full retreat upon the Blackwater; and in two months' time the veteran Duke of Schomberg had landed with one thousand men at Bangor, in the County of Down.

The half-hearted James was in despair at this succession of disasters. The cold-blooded Frenchman D'Avaux urged him to a general massacre of the Protestants in the three southern provinces; but the suggestion was indignantly repelled. That which had filled James with despair roused the Irish to renewed activity, and very shortly the decimated regiments from Ulster were filled with eager recruits, and increased enthusiasm was kindled throughout the Irish quarters. The Irish infantry soldiers were individually brave, but they were ill-armed and ill-trained. Few of their officers had had any military experience, or had the knowledge to enable them to drill the raw material into shape. Still, now that the danger became pressing, great efforts were made, both by Dé Rosen and the French officers, and by the Irish themselves, to procure a better organization and to complete the transport. James did his best to prevent all robbing and plundering, by stringent orders and summary executions; and, according to Dr. Gorges, Schomberg's secretary, the behavior of the Irish army was very different from that of William, which rioted and lived at free quarters on its friends.

Schomberg, to whom Carrickfergus capitulated after a few days' siege, took his way to Lisburn, Berwick retreating before him and burning the towns of Carlingford and Newry. But Schomberg's army was hardly more efficient than that of James, and was considerably inferior in numbers. His Dutch and French refugee regiments were seasoned men, but his English troops were raw recruits, hurriedly enlisted in England, and ignorant even of how to let off their muskets. Worse still, through the frauds of the army contractors, the stores were uneatable, the tents were rotten, and the supply both of clothing and of horses was deficient. On reaching Dundalk, he formed an intrenched camp, not daring to attack the enemy, who greatly outnumbered him, and who were encamped on the neighboring heights some few miles off; and he determined to await reinforcements from England before he risked a battle. For two months the wary old general kept his men in their quarters, striving to infuse skill and discipline into his recruits. Exposure to the wet climate, and poor living, brought on fever and dysentery, which thinned his numbers terribly; and at length the Irish army, in despair of drawing him into an engagement, broke up its camp and went into winter-quarters; and Schomberg drew the remnants of his army off to Lisburn, and went into winter-quarters also.

CHAPTER IV.

THE RECONQUEST. A.D. 1690-1691.

IN the spring De Rosen and D'Avaux, disgusted with James's imbecility, obtained their recall to France; and shortly afterwards Louis despatched to Ireland a reinforcement of five thousand French troops, under the Count de Lauzun; but, in return, there were drafted off, for service on the Dutch frontier, an equal number of Irish soldiers, under the command of Colonel Justin McCarthy. Schomberg's army was getting over its demoralization, reinforcements were streaming over from England; and the important fortress of Charlemont, after a determined defence, surrendered to the English.

At length, in June, William landed at Carrickfergus, and took the supreme command. His strict discipline and unselfish example soon restored order and enthusiasm to his troops; and, supported by his ships, which moved in parallel course along the coast, he marched southward and occupied the northern bank of the Boyne, where he was confronted by James's army upon the opposite side of the river. James's army was the smaller of the two. He had thirty thousand men, including six regiments of French infantry, and but twelve field guns. William had forty pieces of heavy artillery and four mortars. His army, which decided the fate of Ireland and the Stuarts, consisted of about thirty-six thousand men. Its composition was of a very motley character: about half was composed of English soldiers; the other half of foreign mercenaries—Danes, Swedes, Dutch, Swiss, Finns, Brandenburgers, French Huguenots—the Protestant churches of Northern Europe come to meet the Roman Catholics in an Irish Armageddon.

After the battle, in which they lost but fifteen hundred men, the broken Irish army retired through the pass of Duleek, its retreat covered by the French contingent, and then fell back in good order upon the capital. But the pusillanimous James, who had had the courage in earlier days to gloat over the bruised and crushed Covenanters in the "boots" at Edinburgh, when the members of his council rushed from the room, took care never to expose his precious skin in the battle, and fled early in the afternoon to Dublin. Nor did his flight stop here. Having hurriedly called together the members of the Dublin corporation, and ungenerously laid the blame on the courage of the Irish troops, he posted off through Wicklow to Waterford, and never rested till he was safe at Brest. "Change kings," said Patrick Sarsfield later on when all was lost, "and we will fight you again." Could it have been so, the history of the world might have been startlingly different.

Dublin was evacuated and occupied by the English. William issued a proclamation offering pardon and protection to the laborers, farmers, artisans, and common soldiers who should return home and lay down their arms; but the Roman Catholic gentry were excepted with a view to future confiscation, and a commission was appointed to seize all forfeited estates. The upper classes, excluded from mercy, had no way open to them but to prolong the war; and the peasantry were driven into the same course by the open violation of William's orders of protection by the English and foreign soldiery. And so the Irish, deserted by their king, but encouraged by news of the French victory at Beachy Head, determined to make another effort for national independence.

The main body under Tyrconnel and Lauzun fell back upon the Shannon. A strong garrison under the command of Colonel Grace was thrown into Athlone. Cork and Kinsale were well prepared for defence, and the bulk of the army entered Limerick, where they were shortly joined by the garrisons of Waterford and Kilkenny, and other towns in Leinster, which had either retired, or marched out, on terms at the approach of William. The latter, disturbed at the gloomy despatches from England, was on the point of hurrying back to London, but on the receipt of better news, and having secured the harbors of Wexford and Waterford, he moved through Tipperary to invest Limerick. There he was joined by Douglas, whom he had despatched through Meath against Athlone, and who had found the Irish there so strongly posted that he did not venture to attack. Lauzun, who was sick of the hardships of Irish campaigning, declared Limerick absolutely untenable. He was supported by Tyrconnel, now broken with age and disaster; but Colonel Sarsfield was of a different opinion, and insisted that Limerick should be defended. Tyrconnnel and Lauzun, with the French regiments, accordingly retired to Galway; and the Irish troops, thirty thousand in number, remained, under Boisseleau and Sarsfield, to wipe out the memory of the Boyne.

William had with him only field guns, but a heavy siege-train was shortly expected from Dublin. Sarsfield determined to make a daring attempt to intercept it. Taking with him five hundred horse, he crossed the river at Killaloe, under cover of the night, slipped by hill-tracks through the Kieper mountains, and surprised the convoy in easy security but seven miles from the English camp. A detachment sent by William to meet them only arrived in time to find the guns burst with their own powder, and Sarsfield's troopers disappearing in the darkness. This success greatly emboldened the besieged, and William had to wait till he could bring up two guns from Waterford. At length the siege commenced. The antiquated fortifications of Limerick were breached, and an assault was ordered. The struggle was long and fierce. The Irish fought with awful desperation, even the women flinging stones and broken bottles in the hottest of the fight. The storming party, who had made their way into the town, were driven back to the ditch; a mine exploded and destroyed a whole battalion of Germans, and after four hours' fighting the retreat was sounded. Next day, his powder exhausted and the pestilential rainy season setting in, William raised the siege and withdrew to Clonmel.

It was now mid-autumn, and his presence was much needed in England. Accordingly, leaving the command in the hands of Ginkel, and having appointed Lord Sydney, Sir Charles Porter, and Mr. Coningsby lords justices, he sailed from Waterford to Bristol. Active campaigning was at an end for this year, when an unexpected blow was struck with unexpected success. By a dashing naval expedition of five weeks' duration, and with the support of some regiments under the Duke of Würtemberg, detached from Ginkel at Clonmel, Marlborough succeeded in reducing Cork, where five thousand men became prisoners of war. Kinsale followed in quick succession, the garrison, twelve thousand strong, being permitted to march out and retire to Limerick.

And now the opposing armies desisted from further operations till the spring. Half the island was held for King William and half for King James. Ulster, most of Leinster, and half of Munster were in the hands of the former; while Connaught, and Kerry, Clare, and Limerick counties, and a portion of the midlands, were occupied by the Irish. The Protestants began to return from England, under the protection of the new government. The corporations were restored to their old condition. The offices of sheriff, lord-lieutenant, and deputy-lieutenant, and the commission of the peace, were all refilled with returning Protestants. The judges went circuit, and severe orders were issued to control the actions and domiciles of those Roman Catholics who remained within reach of the law. With the return of the English, trade began to revive; and the customs showed a considerable increase. But this was chiefly in and near the towns; the state of the country was miserable in the extreme. William's foreign mercenaries, with their pay in arrear, lived at free quarters on the farmers and peasantry, and laughed at the royal orders for protection. The Irish country-people fled with their cattle from the English into the Irish districts. All the long winter through, bands of Irish *franc-tireurs*, formerly called Tories, now called rapparees, from the Irish name of the short pike with which they were armed, raided into the English quarters, and burned and robbed the restored English homesteads. Nothing could exceed the boldness and cunning with which they eluded the English patrols, and spread terror almost to the walls of Dublin.

In Limerick the leaders of the Irish were divided by unworthy jealousies. Lauzun and his French soldiers had sailed for France, much to the relief of the Irish, who found them anxious only to promote the advantage of Louis by making a diversion in Ireland, and callous to the interests of either James or the Irish. Tyrconnel had been to France, and had returned with a small supply of money and clothing; and was presently followed by the French general St. Ruth, who held James's commission to take the chief command. St. Ruth was able, but cruel and haughty. He treated the Irish with contempt. He quarrelled with Tyrconnel, and he quarrelled with Sarsfield; but, at the same time, by strenuous exertions he succeeded in restoring order to the half-mutinous Irish soldiery. Nor did he begin his task a moment too soon, for by early spring Ginkel was marshalling his army at Mullingar, and, having obtained a formidable siege-train, was marching upon Athlone. Ere the new campaign began, William, not only anxious in his own interest to close the war, but by nature tolerant, and "touched," as Sir Charles Wogan says, "by the fate of a gallant nation that had made itself the victim of French promises," offered the Irish Roman Catholics the free exercise of their religion, half the churches in the kingdom, and the moiety of their ancient possessions. But the Irish were still sanguine; they knew how critical William's position was, and how great were the risks he ran in Flanders when half his available forces were locked up in Ireland; and no response was made.

Athlone, the ancient fortress built by King John upon the Shannon to overawe the septs of Connaught, like many other towns in Ireland consisted of an English quarter and an Irish quarter. The former, on the Leinster shore, was of no great strength. The Irish town lay on the Connaught side; and the deep and rapid river was spanned by a single bridge. Ginkel advanced and commenced the siege. The Irish soon evacuated the English town, and retired into the Irish town, breaking the bridge behind them. Ginkel, who was strong in artillery, pounded the devoted city for several weeks; silenced the few brass cannon in the town; and breached the walls in several places. But the strong stream of the Shannon effectually prevented an assault, and his attempts to repair the bridge were gallantly defeated by the Irish. St. Ruth, with the whole Irish army, had come to support the garrison, and lay encamped a mile or two off upon the Connaught side, too contemptuous, though warned by Sarsfield, of the possibility of the English forcing the passage of the river. There was a dangerous ford some way below the bridge, and by this Ginkel determined to make an attempt to cross. Under cover of the darkness the forlorn hope plunged into the water, and struggled to the other side. A short fight at the breach, and Ginkel's men had entered the town, seized the broken end of the bridge, and held it till it was hastily repaired. Their comrades poured across, and Athlone was taken.

St. Ruth, thunderstruck at what had happened, drew off his army and took up a strong position behind the Suck. Ginkel, after putting Athlone into a state of defence, advanced to Ballinasloe. He found the Irish strongly posted on rising ground, surrounded by a quaking morass, and their right resting on the ruined castle of Aughrim.

Late in the afternoon of July 12th, he determined to attack. From five o'clock till nine a desperate battle was fought. At one moment the English centre, staggered by the stout resistance, gave way and fled; and St. Ruth believed the day to be his. But a regiment of English cavalry under Mackay, and one of French Huguenots under Ruvigny, managed to struggle over a narrow causeway in the bog, and turned his right flank; and as he rode down to fling his cavalry upon them, a cannon-ball took off his head, and the Irish were without a commander. The Irish now fought each for himself, and without method or plan. The English centre was rallied by Talmash. The Irish were driven up the hill into the camp, and, being unable to hold it, fled headlong, some taking the way to Galway and some to the city of Limerick. And now began a scene of frightful butchery. The English and Danish cavalry pursued and cut down the fugitives; no quarter was given, and the flying Irish were hewn to pieces indiscriminately. Seven thousand were slaughtered, and only four hundred were taken prisoners. An eye-witness from the top of the hill of Kilkommeden next day saw the country, for miles in the line of flight, white with the naked bodies of the slain.

CHAPTER V.

THE BROKEN TREATY. A.D. 1691–1700.

THE last line of defence had now been broken through, and a pitched battle fought, which made it impossible for the Irish again to meet Ginkel in the field. Their only hope was to maintain themselves in the city of Limerick until the rainy season brought them the terrible ally of pestilence, which had before stood them in good stead at Dundalk, and at the siege of Limerick in the previous year. Ginkel had occupied Loughrea and Athenry, and advanced to the city of Galway, which was held by Lord Dillon, and, after a short siege, had received its surrender on favorable terms to the inhabitants, its garrison marching out with all the honors of war, and retiring on Limerick.

Limerick was now the last refuge of the Irish. It was crowded with the broken remnants of the Irish army. Tyrconnel lay dying in the castle, and Sarsfield was in command, with high hopes of repeating the successful defence of the previous autumn. Ginkel invested the town on August 25th, and opened fire upon it with fifty guns. The English fleet sailed up the Shannon to cut off all hope of French succors. September came, and with it the news that Kilmallock had been abandoned and Sligo had surrendered. Still the town held out; and Ginkel, with private instructions from William to finish the war on the best terms he could, was growing anxious at the duration of the siege. On September 22d an attack was made from the Clare side of the river. There was desperate fighting on the Thomond bridge. The Irish were driven across, and the defenders of the island portion of the town, fearful lest the English should enter pell-mell with the fugitives, drew up the drawbridge, and their comrades were either cut to pieces or flung into the water.

This was the last fighting of the war; and an armistice was agreed upon for three days. The Irish were willing to surrender if they could get favorable terms. Ginkel, who knew the risks of prolonging the war into the autumn, and how welcome to William would be the release of a portion of the army of Ireland for service on the Continent, was equally willing to grant them. Military articles were agreed upon, permitting all officers and soldiers, "and also those called rapparees or volunteers," in the Irish quarters to embark, with their "families, household stuffs, plate and jewels," for any place beyond sea; passports, convoys, and transport being provided for them.

The civil "articles of Limerick" were drawn up, and were signed by Sarsfield and by the lords justices on October 3d; and, among other things, provided as follows: (i.) "That the Roman Catholics of Ireland shall enjoy such privileges in the exercise of their religion as are consistent with the laws of Ireland, or as they did enjoy in the reign of King Charles II.; and their majesties, as soon as their affairs will permit them to summon a Parliament in this kingdom, will endeavor to procure the said Roman Catholics such *further* security in that particular as may preserve them from any disturbance upon the account of their said religion;" and that (ii.) "all the inhabitants or residents of Limerick, or of any other garrison now in the possession of the Irish, and all the officers and soldiers now in arms under any commission of King James," either in the English quarters or in the counties of Limerick, Clare, Kerry, Cork, and Mayo (Galway had been dealt with on much the same terms in the treaty signed on the capitulation of that city), "and all such as were under their protection in the said counties," should possess and enjoy the estates they held, enjoyed, or were rightfully or lawfully entitled to in the reign of Charles II., and all their goods and chattels. Provision was also made that they should be permitted to follow, without restriction, the same trades and professions which they had followed in the same reign; and that they should all have the benefit of a general pardon, the only thing demanded on the other hand being the taking of the bare oath of allegiance. This treaty was subsequently confirmed by William by letters-patent. The unscrupulous Irish Parliament of 1697, consisting wholly of the new English Protestant interest, passed an act* which professed to confirm it, but in fact so mutilated it as to cut out all parts which were vital to the interests of the Roman Catholics, and left an empty husk which afforded them no protection. The first article, providing for freedom of worship, was simply ignored. The clause for securing the Irish their estates was pruned of the words "and all such as were under their protection in the said counties," which had been inserted in the draft of the treaty, but had been accidentally omitted in the document itself, and which had been reinstated with this specific explanation in the king's letters-patent. The clause providing for the free exercise by Roman Catholics of their professions was also carefully omitted. The rest of the treaty, which was comparatively valueless and consisted of various minor details, was solemnly ratified by statute. The perjured Roman senate, when their army had surrendered at the Caudine Pass, could hardly have surpassed the Irish government in flagrant breach of faith.

A few days after the signing of the treaty, a French fleet, under Chateau Renard, consisting of 18 men-of-war and 20 transports, with 3000 soldiers, 10,000 stand of arms, and stores and ammunition, appeared in the mouth of the Shannon, proving De Ginkel's anxiety to complete the capitulation at any cost was well founded. Its only duty now was to sail back to Brest with as many of the soldiers of the Irish army as it could accommodate. De Ginkel was anxious to enlist the Irish troops in the service of William, but they preferred voluntary exile, and the prospect of being a thorn in England's side when in the service of England's enemies. Some three thousand accepted De Ginkel's offers. The rest, in all about twenty thousand men and officers, were shipped for France—some on board the French squadron; some, under Sarsfield, sailing from Cork; and the rest in English ships provided by the government for that purpose.

On their arrival in France they were incorporated with the

---

*9 Will. III. c 2.

five thousand men who had, under General Justin McCarthy, been exchanged for the French contingent under Lauzun, and were formed into the "Irish Brigade." The first body under McCarthy had consisted of three regiments—Mountcashel's, commanded by McCarthy, whom James had created Lord Mountcashel; Clare's regiment, commanded by the Honorable Colonel Daniel O'Brien, son of Lord Clare; and Dillon's regiment, commanded by the Honorable Arthur Dillon. To these three were added ten infantry regiments, and two regiments of horse commanded by Colonel Dominic Sheldon and Lord Galmoy. These regiments, recruited from time to time from Ireland, were some of the best troops in the French army. They bore the brunt of the battle in many campaigns, under Catinat in Savoy, at Blenheim, and at Ramillies; and helped to deal many a heavy blow at the prestige of England, as at Landen, Almanza, and Fontenoy. Precluded from all hope of distinction in their own country, the Irish Roman Catholics took service abroad, and rose to the highest positions in the civil, military, and diplomatic services at Paris, Rome, Vienna, and Madrid. So steadily was the recruiting for the brigade carried on, that it has been computed that between the years 1691 and 1745 no less than 450,000 Irishmen died in the service of France.

By the departure of these voluntary exiles, Ireland lost the best of her children. Almost the whole of the Roman Catholic nobility and gentry were to be found among the officers of the Irish army; and the rank and file was largely made up of the younger sons, brothers, and tenantry of the officers. There were outlawed altogether 3921 persons. More forfeitures of course followed, and the treaty of Limerick was treated as waste paper. Forfeiture of estates was the penalty for treason: here it was the penalty for being worsted in a stand-up fight. There could, strictly speaking, be no treason, as the Irish had adhered to the king *de jure*, and had never owned allegiance to the king *de facto* against whom they had fought. Rebellion there was none. There was a war of nationalities, and the Irish were beaten. The victorious English simply seized the land as spoils of war; and the wretched remnant of that which had been left to the Roman Catholic proprietors by the Acts of Settlement and Explanation was vested in the crown to the extent of 1,060,792 Irish acres.

William was kindly disposed towards the beaten nation; he was anxious to treat the Irish with all moderation and clemency. He accordingly restored to the old land-owners over a fourth of the confiscated land, either under the treaties of Limerick and Galway or by royal favor, or by the granting of pardons. But, at the same time, he did not fail to reward his own supporters, especially his Dutch friends, by vast grants of territory out of the estates of those Irish proprietors who were beyond sea. As many as seventy-six grants were made by him in this way, some of a most immoderate character. To Sidney, Lord Romney, he gave 49,517 acres; to Keppel, the Earl of Albemarle, 108,633 acres; to William Bentinck, eldest son of the Duke of Portland, 135,820 acres; to Ginkel, whom he made Earl of Athlone, 26,480 acres; to Ruvigny, created Earl of Galway, 36,148 acres; and 95,649 acres of the estates which James had absorbed at the Restoration he gave to the Countess of Orkney, who had formerly been his mistress. This last, however, was not a portion of the newly forfeited land, but, strictly speaking, was crown property. Eight years after the war was concluded, when Irish proprietors had been reinstated by decrees of "not guilty," and when the grants made by William had many of them been sold to third parties, the English House of Commons, in ill-humor with the king, and staggered with the magnitude of the country's pecuniary liabilities, turned their eyes to the Irish forfeitures for the partial liquidation of the six millions which the Irish war had cost. A commission of inquiry was issued, which made a report very hostile to the king; and then, amid bitter heart-burnings, the Commons, by sending the "resumption bill" up to the House of Lords tacked to a money bill, reconfiscated all the forfeited land, and made it over to thirteen trustees to be sold to the highest bidder "for the benefit of the state." *

From 1700 to 1703 a court sat at Chichester House to hear

---

* English Statutes, 11 and 12 Will. III., c. 2.

claims on the estates, and auction sales were held from time to time until the whole was disposed of. A considerable portion, consisting, among others, of the lands of Lord Clancarty, Sir Patrick Trant, James Fitzmaurice, Thomas and Nicholas Skiddy, was bought by the "Hollowblade Company" as a speculation for resale. Other portions were knocked down to Dublin merchants and English capitalists. Where the estates were entailed, and the tenant for life only had suffered outlawry, the deferred rights of those in the entail were sustained before the court. And, later on, some of the old stock had sufficient interest to obtain the reversal of their outlawries as a matter of grace by special act of Parliament. An Irish act* passed in the second year of Queen Anne empowered the government to let on lease to Protestants the "coarse," "barren," and "surplus" lands which were "a receptacle for thieves, robbers, and Tories, to the great detriment of the country." Of this there seems to have been a very considerable quantity; and it is to be observed that in all calculations of the quantity of land confiscated, made by Sir John Davis, Sir William Petty, and the commissioners appointed to inquire into the state of the Irish forfeitures in 1698, account is only taken of the "profitable land," and not of the waste, and the area is reckoned in *Irish* acres, which are to English acres in the proportion of thirteen to eight.†

So wholesale and complete had been the transfer of the land from the Roman Catholic proprietors to the Protestants that at the beginning of the eighteenth century, when the era of summary confiscation by forfeiture may be said to close, the former were the owners of less than one seventh of the whole area of Ireland.

---

* 2 Anne, c. 8.

† An English acre contains 4840 square yards; an Irish acre, 7840 square yards.

CHAPTER VI.

THE OUTLAWRY OF THE ROMAN CATHOLICS. A.D. 1692-1727.

THE state of the country at the conclusion of the war was indescribably wretched. It had been desolated from end to end by the opposing armies. The wretched farmers who remained had been ruined by requisitions, both from the Irish troops and the foreign mercenaries. In many parts it had been impossible to sow grain; in most the herds had been destroyed: so that the absence of the crops and the loss of the cattle brought the people to the verge of famine. In the towns the small traders had lost heavily by the issue of James's base coin, and the complete interruption of all commercial dealing. The seaports were harried by privateers, which sailed under letters of marque from James. And, though the country was utterly reduced and nominally quiet, the English inhabitants found their ricks burned, their cattle houghed, and their houses broken into by gangs of men with blackened faces, who beat and otherwise maltreated them. In 1711 the outlaws in Galway and Mayo issued proclamations signed "Ever Joyce," and robbed, burned, and mutilated, till they were the terror of the country-side. Stringent acts were passed, which were perpetually being renewed and made more severe, for the "better suppression of Tories and rapparees,"[*] under which rewards were given for the bringing-in of the outlaws dead or alive; pardon was given to any Tory who slew two others, and compensation was given to those who had suffered from the crimes of the Tories, and was levied on the barony wherein the offence had been committed. Where the Tories were suspected of being Roman Catholics, the fine was levied on the Roman Catholic inhabitants; where they were suspected of being Protes-

---

[*] 7 Will. III. c. 21; 9 Will. III. c. 9; 2 Anne, c. 13; 6 Anne, c. 11.

tants, on the Protestants. As might have been expected, fraudulent claims were not infrequently made, sham attacks and larcenies being manufactured as a speculation, and compensation demanded and obtained where no loss had been incurred at all.

The government was now absolutely in the hands of the Protestant minority. The English Parliament had passed an act* abrogating the Oath of Supremacy in Ireland, and requiring members of both Houses to take the oaths of Allegiance and Abjuration of Popery, and to subscribe to the declaration against transubstantiation, thereby practically excluding Roman Catholics from a seat in either of the Irish Houses. The Irish Parliament, bound hand and foot as it was by Poynings's Act to the Parliament of England, and a mere court for the registration of the decrees of an English cabinet, in so far as it represented anything represented the Protestant English colony in Ireland. The English colony were the owners of nearly all the soil of the island; monopolized every office of trust and emolument, the commission of the peace, the seats in the town-councils. It had fastened its grip firmly on Ireland; and lest at any time the Roman Catholic majority should again lift itself up, the English colony and the English government, which had suffered so much in maintaining its ascendency, were determined, as far as acts of Parliament could avail, that the land of Ireland should never again pass into Roman Catholic hands, and that every effort should be made to stamp out the Roman Catholic religion altogether. With this intent, a series of acts were passed during the reign of William and Anne, by the Irish Parliament, which were of a character quite unparalleled, and were in flagrant violation of the treaty of Limerick.

By the English act above referred to, the Irish Parliament was ignored, and the Parliament at Westminster imposed, under a penalty of £500, the two oaths of Allegiance and Abjuration, and the making of the declaration against transubstantiation, upon every Irish archbishop and bishop; every

---

* English Statutes, 3 Will. and Mary, c. 2.

member of both Houses of Parliament; every person holding office ecclesiastical, civil, or military; every governor, head, and fellow of the university; every master of a hospital or school; every barrister-at-law, clerk in chancery, and attorney; and every professor of law or physic or any other science.

The Irish Parliament was then permitted to complete the code.

THE FIRST OF THE PENAL STATUTES passed by the Irish Houses was aimed at the education of the Roman Catholics, and their connection with the Continental seminaries.*

It provided that every one who sent a child abroad, or went abroad himself, to be trained in the Roman Catholic religion should be liable to the forfeiture of all his real and personal estate; and should be disabled from acting as a guardian, executor, or administrator, from filling any office, or from taking the benefit of any legacy or deed of gift.

That any one suspected of contravening this act should be liable to be brought before a magistrate and bound over in recognizances of not less than £200 not to quit the kingdom, and to appear at quarter sessions and take his trial for this offence.

That any common informer could set the law in motion and recover half the forfeiture, the other moiety going to the crown; the burden of proof of innocence being cast on the accused.

No Papist was to keep a school or teach scholars in a private house under a penalty of £20, or three months' imprisonment; and it was further provided that two old acts,† one of Henry VIII. and the other of Elizabeth, for the erection of free schools in every parish, which had become a dead letter, should be put into execution. These latter provisions remained as much a dead letter as the acts of Henry and Elizabeth.

THE NEXT STATUTE had for its object the disarming of the Roman Catholic population.‡ It provided that before March 1, 1696, all Papists should deliver up to the justices of the

---

* 7 Will. III. c. 4. † 28 Hen. VIII. c. 15; 12 Eliz. c. 1.
‡ 7 Will. III. c. 5.

peace in their neighborhood all arms, armor, and ammunition. The magistrates were empowered to break open and search for concealed arms; and any person suspected of such concealment might be brought before the justices on the information of any common informer, and examined on oath. A Papist was forbidden to keep a horse of greater value than £5; and power was given to any Protestant to obtain a search-warrant from a magistrate, with power to break open doors and to search for and secure any such horses. The informer might then, upon tendering the owner the sum of five guineas, take possession of any such horse for his own property.

Where persons refused or neglected to conform to the act, the penalty was for the first offence, in the case of a peer, £100; of a commoner, £30. All persons who committed a second offence were to be held guilty of *præmunire*, an offence for which the penalty is imprisonment for life and forfeiture of all goods.

The only exception was in favor of those noblemen and gentlemen who had the benefit of the treaty of Limerick; and they were permitted to keep one sword, one case of pistols, and one gun "for fowling." Makers of fire-arms were prohibited from taking a Roman Catholic apprentice under a penalty of £20, both upon the apprentice and the master. And any apprentice professing Protestantism, whose belief was suspected, might be tendered the Oath of Allegiance as a test.

THEN FOLLOWED AN ACT which was intended to have the effect of expelling all Roman Catholic ecclesiastics from Ireland who were in correspondence with Rome; and to prevent their return, or the entry of any fresh ones, into the kingdom. The existing parish clergy were not interfered with, but a subsequent act put them under a strict system of registration.

The first provided* that all bishops, Jesuits, monks, friars, and "regular" clergy should depart out of the kingdom by May 1, 1698, or suffer imprisonment until they could be transported to the Continent.

Any who should venture to return were held to be guilty of

---

* 9 Will. III. c. 1.

high-treason, the punishment for which was hanging, drawing, and quartering. Those who came into the kingdom for the first time were to be liable to twelve months' imprisonment, and to be transported to the Continent; and on their return would be equally guilty of high-treason.

Any person knowingly relieving any of the aforesaid clergy were to be liable for the first offence to a penalty of £20, for the second to a penalty of £40, and for the third to the forfeiture of his lands.

This statute was re-enacted by 2 Anne, c. 3.

The act for the registration of the resident Popish clergy * enacted that all Popish priests then in the kingdom should be registered, and give security for their good behavior, under penalties similar to those just mentioned to which the " regulars " were subjected; while the apostatizing of the Roman Catholic clergy was invited by the grant of a pension of £20 per annum (raised by 8 Anne, c. 3, to £30) to any priest who should turn Protestant; such payment to be a charge on the county rate.

It was further provided that no one should bury in the precincts of any suppressed abbey, monastery, or convent, under a penalty of £10; that no chapel should have either bells or a steeple. Magistrates were enjoined to suppress all friaries, and to apprehend all unregistered priests; and in order to guard the guardians it was enacted that a magistrate who neglected his duty should be liable to a fine of £100, and be disabled from serving as a justice of the peace for life.

THE SOCIAL RELATIONS were then attacked, and a blow aimed at what in earlier times had done more than anything to assimilate the new English to the older inhabitants.

To accomplish this an act † was passed to prevent the marriage of Protestants with Roman Catholics, and provided that any Protestant woman having an interest in land who should marry any person without a certificate from a minister or a justice of the peace that the husband was a known Protestant should forfeit her estates to the next Protestant heir; such woman and her husband should be incapable of being an ex-

---

* 2 Anne, c. 7.   † 9 Will. III. c. 3.

ecutor, administrator, or guardian to a Protestant, and the right of guardianship should pass to the next Protestant of kin.

Any person giving them in marriage should be liable to a year's imprisonment and the penalty of £20.

Any Protestant man who married any woman without the above-mentioned certificate was *ipso facto* to be deemed a Papist, and be subject to all the disabilities of a Papist. He was to be disabled from being an executor, administrator, or guardian, from sitting in Parliament or holding any office, unless the wife should be converted within twelve months, and should receive a certificate of conversion from a Protestant bishop.

THE PROFESSION OF THE LAW, which had always teemed with recusants, was, notwithstanding the proviso of the treaty of Limerick, to be thoroughly purged.

A special act* was passed to disqualify Roman Catholics from practising as solicitors without taking the oaths, under a penalty of £100, to be recovered by any common informer.

Solicitors who had not taken the oaths were disabled from acting as executors or administrators, or from taking the benefit of any legacy or devise; and no solicitor was to be permitted to practise who did not educate his children in the Protestant faith.

So systematically was this statute evaded, and the oaths swallowed, that a supplemental act† was passed in the sixth year of Queen Anne, which raised the penalty to £200, and provided that any person might tender a solicitor the oaths, and, on his refusing to take them, should thereupon be entitled to recover the penalty and record the solicitor as convict.

Another section prohibited any Papist from serving on a grand jury, and forbade an attorney to take a Roman Catholic clerk.

A yet more stringent act was passed in the seventh year of George II.,‡ which prohibited any one from practising as a solicitor who had not been a Protestant since the age of fourteen, or been five years articled to some clerk in Chancery in England or in Ireland.

---

* 10 Will. III. c. 13.   † 6 Anne, c. 6.   ‡ 7 Geo. II. c. 5.

At the commencement of Queen Anne's reign it was found that, like every other severe and unjust law, the penal acts were largely evaded; and the "Protestant ascendency" believed that the mischief which they sought to counteract could be overcome by fiercer statutes. Accordingly, in grossest breach of the Limerick treaty, the savage acts of the second and eighth years of Anne were passed, which were so carefully drawn as to leave no possible loophole for escape, if they could have been drastically administered. The object of these statutes, besides the strengthening of those already in force, was to insure the withdrawal from the hands of the Roman Catholics of the fragments of the land to which they still clung; and to make it impossible in the future that they should ever acquire a title to a single acre. To secure this end, these statutes made inevitable the gradual cutting-up and dispersion of the estates of Roman Catholics; deprived them of the power of settling their land, or disposing of it by will; even broke up in some cases settlements already made; and provided a ready machinery by which unscrupulous children and unfaithful wives, by the simple process of apostatizing, and even the lowest common informer, could tear to pieces, or transfer to themselves, both the income and the property of every unfortunate landowner who adhered to the religion of his fathers.

The first act provided as follows:* Any person who perverted a Protestant should be guilty of *præmunire*. Any person who sent an infant beyond sea without a license should be liable to the penalties of 7 Will. III. c. 4.

The court might order the maintenance and education of a conforming child by his Popish parent, and appoint a Protestant guardian. No Papist was to be a guardian, under a penalty of £500.

Where a Roman Catholic father held his land in fee, his eldest son, by simply turning Protestant, *ipso facto* acquired an interest in the estate as tenant in tail, and converted the father's interest into a mere life-tenancy. If the sons of a Papist were also Papists, the estates were to descend in equal

---

* 2 Anne, c. 6.

shares among them all. But if the eldest son were a Protestant, he should inherit the whole.

Every Papist was to be disabled from purchasing land, or holding any mortgage on land; and even from taking a lease of more than thirty-one years; nor could he hold such a lease, unless a rent was paid by him of at least two thirds of the full annual value.

No Papist after February 1, 1703, unless he should conform within six months, should be capable of taking any estate by descent, devise, gift, remainder, or trust. But such estate should during his life, or till his apostasy, pass at once to the next Protestant heir. Advowsons belonging to Papists vested in the crown until the owners should conform.

It was also provided that no Papist should vote at an election without taking the oaths.

No person should hold office, civil or military, without taking the oaths and subscribing to the declaration against transubstantiation, and receiving the sacrament on Sunday in church.

No Papist was in future to take up his residence in Galway or Limerick, and those now inhabiting were to give security for their good behavior.

All pilgrimages to St. Patrick's Purgatory or to holy wells were to be deemed to be riots and unlawful assemblies. The penalty for being present was 10s.; and, if the fine was not paid, the culprit might be publicly whipped at the cart's-tail. Further, magistrates were ordered to destroy all crosses, pictures, and inscriptions which they should find anywhere set up.

This searching statute was still evaded by the ingenuity of the legal profession, by the devotion of friends, and the straining of the conscience by a pretended conforming. Accordingly the statute-book was again amended; and a further appeal made to the self-interest both of the family circle and the outside public to ruin the Roman Catholic owners of land.

By THE SECOND ACT* all fines levied, and all recoveries suffered, to bar a Protestant were made void, unless the sale or

---

* 8 Anne, c. 3.

mortgage affected thereby should be a *bona fide* transaction in favor of a Protestant for valuable consideration.

It was made lawful for any common informer to prefer a bill in chancery to compel any person to discover any secret trusts which had been created in favor of Papists. Any issues of fact were to be tried by a jury of known Protestants, and upon a decree in his favor he was at once to be entitled to the lands affected by the trust.

No Papist was thenceforth to be capable of taking an annuity chargeable on land. And no convert was to be deemed a Protestant unless within six months he should receive the sacrament, and take the oaths and subscribe the declaration. The wife of a Papist was encouraged to apostatize by being permitted, upon her conversion, to obtain a jointure charged on her recusant husband's estates and on one third of his real and personal chattels. Apostatizing children were empowered to bring their Popish parent into Chancery in order to obtain an allowance. The father was to be examined on oath as to his means, and ordered to pay the charges and to make an allowance to the child of not more than one third of his whole income. Nor was the father safe after one decree. The same process could be repeated by any other child, or by the same child if the parent had not made a full discovery or his property had been subsequently augmented.

The impossibility of stamping out a religion by act of Parliament had been effectually demonstrated, but this ferocious statute goes on to enact the most stringent endeavors in that behalf, and endeavors at any rate to secure the helplessness of ignorance for the Roman Catholics, if their conversion could not be achieved.

A Papist schoolmaster was to be liable to the same penalties as a Papist "regular," and no person was to be qualified to be a schoolmaster unless he should take the oaths at the assizes or sessions.

Rewards were announced for the discovery and convicting of Romish functionaries according to the following scale: For an archbishop or bishop, £50; for a friar, Jesuit, or an unregistered priest, £20; for a schoolmaster, £10. The amount to be levied on the Popish population like the fines for damage done by the Tories.

No Popish priest was to officiate in any parish but the one for which he was registered; he was to be compelled to take the Oath of Abjuration at the time of his registration; and any two magistrates were empowered to summon any Papist before them to give evidence on oath as to when, where, and by whom he had heard mass celebrated, and who was present; refusal to answer was punishable by £20 fine or twelve months' imprisonment.

Two magistrates were also empowered to summon any man over sixteen to appear and take the oaths. If he should refuse, he was liable to a fine of 40s., or three months' imprisonment; on further refusal, to a fine of £10, or six months' imprisonment, and, in addition, to find security for his appearance at quarter sessions. On a third refusal he was to be held guilty of *præmunire*.

By another section no Papist trader was allowed to take more than two apprentices, except in the favored linen trade.

THE CROWNING STATUTE OF THE PENAL CODE was an act passed in the first year of George II., by which every Roman Catholic was absolutely disfranchised, and deprived of his vote both at parliamentary and municipal elections.*

Such was the substance of the penal code, as unjust as it was inefficacious. Appealing as it did to everything that was base in human nature, and proscribing all progress and improvement, no system could have been invented which would more certainly corrupt and demoralize the nation on whom it was brought to bear. If it did not achieve the results which its authors intended, it at any rate secured the ruin of the bulk of the old Irish gentry.

---

* 1 Geo. II. c. 9, s. 7.

Book VI.

THE FOURTH CONQUEST

CHAPTER I.
THE SHACKLING OF THE ENGLISH COLONY.   A.D. 1700–1719.

DISFRANCHISED, disinherited, disabled from exercising the most ordinary civil functions, the Roman Catholics, the bulk of the Irish nation, endured all the social and moral disadvantages, all the contempt, all the bitter sense of injustice, of a subject race. With no room for honorable ambition, no scope for enterprise, they were condemned to the swinish existence for which the evil of the day is sufficient, and which takes no thought for the morrow. They were so broken and crushed that neither in 1715, nor when George II.'s throne was more seriously threatened in 1745, did a single Irish Roman Catholic venture to raise a finger in the cause of the Pretender, though "Prince Charles's" army was crowded with Irish officers, who had followed him over from the Continent, no less than thirty-three surrendering at Inverness to the Duke of Cumberland. On the contrary, the Roman Catholics were rather looking to the government for protection against the Protestant colony, and their clergy were working hand in hand with the Castle to detect anything like disaffection.

Ireland was not for the Irish, but for the Protestant English colony, or the Protestant garrison, as they called themselves. Taxes were laid upon, and collected from, the whole island, and laws were passed by the Protestant Parliament elected by the Protestant minority only. The political history of Ireland during the eighteenth century is the history of the Protestant colony. All the jealousy, the bitterness, the heart-burnings, the Whig and Tory quarrelling, the rising spirit of independence, the patriotism, as it was called, exhibited in the Parliament of Ireland were the jealousy, the bitterness, the heart-burning, the quarrelling, the independence, the patriotism, of the English colony. The Irish nation lay all the while in sullen stupor, only roused now and again, and here and there, into ineffectual resistance.

Even the Protestant colony was not allowed to govern itself its own way. The English government, sick to death of Irish wars, embraced the selfish, hopeless, fatal policy of keeping Ireland poor in order to keep her from being troublesome; and its plan was to maintain a tight hold on her by means of Poynings's Act, and all its anachronistic machinery; and to render the Irish Parliament a pliant tool in its hands by a frightful system of corruption, which converted the Irish revenues into one vast fund of secret-service money.

When Anne came to the throne, the country had fairly settled down after the last war of independence; trade was beginning to revive; but the jealousy exhibited by England led the English in Ireland to look to a more close connection with the mother-country, as the only way to secure prosperity. They were strongly in favor of the abolition of the Dublin Parliament, and of a legislative union with England. In 1703 the Irish Parliament went so far as to petition the queen for a union between the two countries. But the English government determinedly rejected the proposal. The English colony was accordingly thrown back upon itself, with the certain consequence that in time it would coalesce with the subject Irish. A contemporary writer says that "there was scarcely an Englishman who had been seven years in the country, and meant to remain there, who did not become averse to England and grow something of an Irishman." But as yet they felt the injustice of being ranked with "a disloyal and turbulent people who could only be rendered harmless so long as they were disabled by poverty;" and were inclined to exhibit a spirit the reverse of subservient.

There was a strong party in the Parliament, who, so long as it existed as a separate body, opposed all attempts to invade its independence. Mr. Molyneux, one of the members for Dublin University, published a book called "The Case of Ireland being Bound by Acts of Parliament in England Stated," which was savagely condemned by the Parliament of England, and ordered to be burned by the common hangman; but the opposition soon died out under the judicious manipulation of the Castle; and from time to time English statutes were passed binding Ireland, without remonstrance or protest. Even the judicial functions of the Irish peers were denied, and a quarrel arose between the English and Irish Houses of Lords on the question of jurisdiction. The Irish peers having reversed a judgment of the Irish Court of Exchequer Chamber, a counter-appeal was taken to the English House, which affirmed the judgment; and the dispute was eventually put an end to by the English Parliament passing an act "for the better securing the dependency of Ireland upon the crown of Great Britain," which not only formally deprived the Irish House of Lords of any appellate jurisdiction whatsoever, but also went on to declare that "the English Parliament had, hath, and of right ought to have full power and authority to make laws and statutes of sufficient force and validity to bind the people and kingdom of Ireland." *

The sixth of George I. was the last rivet which fixed the chain upon the Irish legislature. Poynings's Act,† which was an Irish act, said that no bills should be passed by the Irish Houses which had not been approved in England and transmitted thence *before the opening of Parliament.* The Act of Philip and Mary,‡ also an Irish act, which "explained" the Act of Poynings, was passed to enable the Irish Houses to pass all bills which should *at any time during the session* be certified to the king by the viceroy and privy council as expedient for the kingdom, and be returned under the great seal of England. Under these statutes the practice which grew up was as follows: A member of either House might bring in "heads of a bill," which, if agreed to by both chambers, were carried to the viceroy. He referred them to the Irish privy council, who made such alterations as they desired, and certified them to the king under the great seal of Ireland. The English privy council referred the document to the English attorney-general, who altered it as he thought advisable; and the approval of the English privy council being then obtained, it was returned to

---

* English Statutes, 6 Geo. I. c. 5.   † 10 Hen. VII. c. 4.
‡ 3 and 4 Philip and Mary, c. 4.

Ireland under the great seal of England. The Irish Houses could thereupon either accept it or reject it *in toto*, but had no power of alteration. The bill, which was liable both to summary rejection and unlimited alteration by either the English or the Irish privy council, having then a second time passed the House from which it had emanated, received the royal assent and became law.

CHAPTER II.

THE STATUTORY DESTRUCTION OF IRISH TRADE.

A.D. 1692–1727.

THE infatuation of England in respect to the economic laws by which Ireland was to be hindered from growing wealthy was the more extraordinary inasmuch as the mischief was inflicted, not so much upon the beaten-down native population as upon the thriving English citizens in the towns and seaports, who were intended to be the mainstay of the English ascendency. The English commercial world had always been absurdly jealous of the least prospect of Irish prosperity. Strafford had done his best to ruin the rising woollen manufactures in order to protect English clothiers. Cromwell had indeed conferred the same commercial privileges on Ireland as were enjoyed by England; but in 1663 the English landed interest became alarmed lest the rents of their grazing land should fall by reason of the imported Irish cattle diminishing the growth of English beasts; for Ireland was always a great pasture country, and cattle her chief source of wealth. A hasty bill* was passed by the unreasoning Royalist Houses absolutely prohibiting the importation of Irish cattle, sheep, swine, salt meat, or bacon; and declaring such importation to be a "common nuisance:" and so violent was their ignorant ill-temper that a contribution of Irish cattle generously offered by the Irish gentry, for the relief of the citizens of London who had been ruined by the great fire, was ungraciously denounced as an attempt to undersell the English growers.

In the year 1663, Ireland was carefully omitted from the "Act for the encouragement of trade,"† which amended the Navigation Act of 1660, the consequence of which was that

---

* English Statutes, 18 Car. II. c. 2.   † Ib. 15 Car. II. c. 7.

all the carrying trade in Irish-built ships with any part of his majesty's dominions was forbidden, under the penalty of forfeiture of ship and cargo. And in 1696 all direct import trade with the British colonies was absolutely prohibited, and all colonial produce was first obliged to pass through and pay duty in England.*

Now that, on the return of peace to the distracted island, trade had rapidly revived, and the Irish, unable by reason of the English laws to make a profit out of the growing of cattle, had turned their pasture into sheepwalks, it was found that the woollen manufactures were showing signs of increased vitality, and the English traders fell into a selfish panic, lest Irish competition should reduce their gains, and clamored for legislative protection. The ruin of the Irish woollen trade, almost wholly, be it remembered, in the hands of the Protestant English colony, was decreed, and remorselessly effected. The servile Irish legislature was compelled to pass an act,† "in grateful acknowledgment of his majesty's royal care, favor, and protection," putting a prohibitive export duty on all broadcloths, kerseys, serges, and flannels; while the English Parliament passed an act‡ prohibiting the export of either Irish wool or woollen goods to any port in the world except to Milford, Chester, Liverpool, and certain ports in the Bristol Channel, under a penalty of £500, and the forfeiture of both ship and cargo; and forbade its shipment from any Irish port except Cork, Drogheda, Dublin, Kinsale, Waterford, and Youghal.

English and Irish wool was the best in the world. England was by English law the only market for Irish wool, and she could take it at her own price, otherwise Ireland had no purchaser. The English manufacturer therefore had a monopoly of the best wool at a low price. But what put money into the pockets of the English traders was the ruin of the Irish manufacturer and the Irish grower; and the hands who had been employed in the manufacture of woollen stuffs were thrown out of employment, and streamed away to America and

---

* English Statutes, 7 & 8 Will. III. c. 22.   † 10 Will. III. c. 5.
‡ English Statutes, 10 & 11 Will. III. c. 10.

the Continent, never to return. Wool was a drug in the legitimate market. And woollen goods had no market at all but the home market; of the briskness of which we may judge, when we find an act* passed in 1733 "to encourage the home consumption of wool," obliging every corpse to be buried in a woollen shroud, under a penalty of £5, to be recovered from the executors. Thrown back on the growth of the raw material, which, as there was but one customer legally available, was now smuggled largely to Continental buyers, the whole island had rapidly been converted into pasture. Not only was there a large contraband trade in wool, but there was also a large business done in salted meat. As the trade in salt meat increased, so again did the demand for pasture; and the quantity of cultivable land grew narrower and narrower. Farm after farm was laid down in grass, and tenant after tenant evicted to make way for the grazier. An estate which had supported twenty or thirty farmers with their laborers came to be easily managed by one or two herdsmen. Depopulation was the result. The stream of emigration increased, and so did the shoals of beggars who wandered about the country.

An attempt was made in 1716 to encourage agriculture, and the Irish Parliament sent over heads of a bill to authorize the breaking-up of five out of every hundred acres held by tenants who were (and this was the case in the majority of holdings) forbidden by their leases from so doing, and giving a small bounty on the export of corn. But even at this innocent proposition the interests of England took alarm—not in horror at the introduction of a false economic nostrum, but for fear the Irish should undersell the English farmer, and notwithstanding the fact that for years the large proportion of grain consumed in Ireland was imported from England. Ireland's commercial interests, or what were believed to be her interests, were sacrificed to those of England; and the attempted legislation came to nothing. It was only after a potato famine eight years later, in which thousands of the peasantry in Ulster died of starvation, that tardy permission was given

---

* 7 Geo. II. c. 13.

to cancel these severe clauses in leases, and a small portion of the land suffered to be given up to tillage.*

The inevitable consequence of putting prohibitive duties on the great staple of Irish trade was a wholesale system of smuggling. Fleece wool in Ireland cost 5*d*. a pound, and combed wool 1*s*. In France the prices were respectively 2*s*. 6*d*. and 4*s*. 6*d*. a pound. French and Spanish wool, if mixed with a portion of Irish wool, would produce as good cloth as the best that could be made in England; and one sack of Irish wool would work up three sacks of French wool. The coast of Ireland, honeycombed with bays and fiords, gave the most convenient shelter to the fast-sailing French vessels. The revenue officers were helpless in a country where the whole population sympathized with and profited by the contraband trade, and pocketed a handsome price for their inactivity. The government cruisers were overmatched by the smugglers' sloops, and, as they received no encouragement from the authorities, never left their stations at the important harbors. Wool was stored in caves at the mouth of every little river in Cork and Kerry, shipped on board the French vessels, and swiftly borne to Brest and Rochelles. Cargoes of brandy, claret, and silk came over in payment on the return journey, with an occasional Irish exile to recruit "wild geese" for the Brigade or the Pretender. The government was powerless to watch such a hopeless and extensive coast-line; and equally so to put the law in force upon the land side. For the whole country-side, squires, magistrates, clergy, were in league with the smugglers, on whom depended for an outlet the whole financial well-being of the landed interest. When the judges came circuit, the grand jury threw out the bills, or the petty jury acquitted the prisoners. One common bond of sympathy, resistance to a code of unjust laws, was cementing together in the southwest Protestants and Roman Catholics, Irish and English; as a common religion had united the Celts and the Anglo-Normans in the days of the Desmonds.

---

* The Tillage Act, 1 Geo. II. c. 10.

CHAPTER III.

PROTESTANT ASCENDENCY AND ITS WORKS. A.D. 1702–1756.

NOT by all the penal laws against Roman Catholic priests could it be hoped, by the most fanatical disciple of brute force, that the old faith could be ever supplanted by the new, so long as the condition of the English Church in Ireland continued to be nothing else but a scandal. While there were no less than three thousand registered Roman Catholic priests, there were for all the parishes in the island but six hundred resident Protestant incumbents; and of these six hundred the large majority were wretchedly poor, their incomes being but about £100 per annum, notwithstanding the fact that they were all pluralists, some holding as many as twelve or thirteen benefices. Numbers of parishes had no church at all, or only a battered ruin, in which no service was ever performed. Few had schools, and the few Protestant families who were to be found in the south and west were left to shift for themselves, and in course of time fell away.

The bishops, on the other hand, had absorbed all the Church revenues, and were very wealthy. The land belonging to Irish sees was estimated at 623,598 Irish acres, or 998,000 English acres—about one nineteenth of the entire soil of the island. All of them of the extreme Laudian type, they had through good and evil times preached the doctrine of passive obedience; and, though from their experiences under James they had had reason to modify these ideas, they still continued Jacobites at heart, and were ever the rallying-point of disaffection to the house of Hanover. Their political influence was very considerable. As members of the Upper House, which the absentee system had largely depleted of its lay element, they were an important and an impracticable faction, which the government was constantly compelled to humor. Ecclesiastical influences had always been remarkably felt in the Dublin privy council, the primate for the time being filling the office of a lord justice in the absence of the lord deputy or lord lieutenant.

In proportion to the smallness of the influence of the Church upon the mass of the people was the jealousy shown by the bench of bishops towards the Presbyterians. The bitterness and injustice with which the latter had been attacked in the reign of Charles II. were redoubled in the reign of Anne. A clause * had been slipped into the penal statute of the second of Anne by the English privy council, as a sop to the bishops to secure their adherence to the bill, imposing the test on Nonconformists as well as on Roman Catholics. The taking of the sacrament according to the rites of the Episcopal Church was made a condition precedent to their holding any office, civil or military, above the rank of constable, and by this means every Dissenter was subjected to the same disabilities as a Roman Catholic. Armed with a new Test Act, the bishops hastened to extirpate schism. Nonconformists were cleared out of Derry and Belfast, and dismissed from the commission of the peace in Ulster. They were prohibited from opening a school. Their marriages were attacked, and declared void; and men were prosecuted in the consistory courts as fornicators for living with their own wives. Even the Regium Donum, an annual subvention granted to the Presbyterian clergy by King William as an acknowledgment of their loyalty and determination in 1688, was suspended.

All efforts by the government to repeal the test clause, or even to pass a Toleration Act to secure to them the use of their chapels, were rejected through the violence of the bishops in the Upper House; and it was not till after the exposure of Jacobite rascality on the death of the queen, and the fall of Bolingbroke and the Tory party, and after the Irish bench had been leavened by the appointment of pliant men from England, that a meagre Toleration Act took its place upon the statute-book.† Even this did not stem the stream of emigration to New England, and a steady drain went on of the best

---

* Section 15. † 6 Geo. II. c. 5.

blood of the north to join their Puritan kinsmen in a land where liberty of conscience was respected. Nor was the condition of the parish clergy improved. The only sign of activity was an effort made by the Protestant laity in 1733, under the auspices of Archbishop Boulter, to found industrial schools under a royal charter in different parts of the country, where the children of the poorest Roman Catholics were taught, fed, and clothed, and apprenticed to a trade.

The Irish Parliament was torn by factions, and it was the pleasing task of the English government and the lord-lieutenant to play off one against the other, and to purchase the support of the most refractory by the gift of places and pensions in order to get the estimates passed, or to carry any government bill which was determined on. Appointments in the Church, the law, and the civil services were invariably filled up with Englishmen, unless it was necessary to buy off some determined member of the opposition.

The opposition originally consisted of disappointed Jacobites, who, with the support of the bitter pen of Swift, the disappointed Dean of St. Patrick's, applied their energies to the persecution of the Presbyterians and to proving themselves a thorn in the side of the government. They called themselves the "Patriotic" party, and were gradually joined by all those who were indignant and disgusted at the selfish policy of England. They were a small party, temporarily swelled from time to time by the vote of self-interested and factious politicians, which prior to 1753 could not count on more than twenty-eight steady votes against the government.

The bulk of the House was composed of the nominees of the great Protestant land-owners. Their influence in the counties, where the number of freehold voters was but limited, was overwhelming; while the boroughs, nearly all of which were erected on land owned by some great freeholder, and in which the franchise was usually limited to some half a score of aldermen and the mayor, or "sovereign," who composed the corporation and were the freeholder's creatures, were, to all intents and purposes, the private property of the "Patron." The consequence was that a very large proportion of the borough and county members sat by favor of a few magnates—peers and others—who could accordingly control the votes of their *clientèle* upon a division. The great object of the powerful and wealthy families of the Protestant ascendency was to get the command of as many seats as possible. The control of votes meant political influence and power, and grew into a most effectual engine for the extraction of lucrative posts from the government. A combination between two or three persons who could each direct the recording of some dozen or more votes in the Commons could hardly be otherwise than irresistible.

There was no limit to the existence of an Irish Parliament; it sat on year after year till the king chose to dissolve it, or a dissolution came in course of law by his death. A mere provincial assembly for the granting of supplies and the confirmation of government bills, it gradually lapsed into the practice of sitting but once in two years, and voting money bills for the two twelvemonths. The opposition could never turn the government out and come into office; for the government was the lords justices and the privy council and certain officers of state, and was an irresponsible and irremovable oligarchy. The crown officials were occasionally changed when there was need; and if the government was not supported by such a majority of the members of the House of Commons as to carry the estimates, it fell back on a prorogation, and intrigued with the waverers until it secured one.

The opposition did their best. They vehemently protested against the iniquitous commercial restrictions, and even endeavored to induce their fellow-countrymen to bind themselves to buy nothing but Irish goods, and "to burn everything which came from England except the coal." They were triumphant in 1725, mainly by the means of Swift's unscrupulous letters of "the Drapier," in raising such a storm that the government was compelled to withdraw the patent which had been granted to Wood for the issue of a debased copper coinage, the profits of which were to put £40,000 into the pockets of himself and the king's German mistress, the Duchess of Kendal. They inquired into the misappropriation and embezzlement of public money by public servants, whose crimes were winked at by the government in consideration of their support. They asked unpleasant questions about the disposition of the hereditary revenue of the crown, the rapid increase of the amount granted by way of pensions, and the application of the surplus revenue. Nor were they much beside the mark in so doing. Half the receipts of the Irish Exchequer consisted of hereditary revenue, derived from a perpetual grant of the excise and customs made at the Restoration,* from crown-lands, and quit-rents reserved to the crown. Vast sums of this money were wasted on royal mistresses, royal bastards, and the nominees of the king and his ministers. In 1723 the pension list amounted to £30,000. Ten years later it had risen to £69,000. The grievance was not a new one. One king after another had paid for his illicit pleasures through the Irish establishment. Catharine Sedley, James II.'s mistress, had enjoyed a pension of £5000 a year; and the Duke of St. Albans, Charles II.'s bastard, one of £800. The Duchess of Kendal had a pension of £3000 a year; and her daughter, Lady Walsingham, £1500. The Countess of Leinster, Sophia Kilmanseg, had laid her hands on a pension of £2000; Lady Darlington one of £1500, and her daughter, Lady Howe, the modest annuity of £500; while Madame de Walmoden enjoyed £3000 a year, standing in the names of Lord Cholmondeley and Sir Robert Walpole. Besides these horse-leeches, there was Lady Stanhope, who drew £2600 a year; Baron Bernstoff, who had £2500; and the Dowager Queen of Prussia, George II.'s sister, and many others who battened upon the Irish treasury in various amounts. It is not surprising that the national debt, which in A.D. 1715 was but £16,106, and arose from extraordinary precautionary expenditure during the Jacobite rising in Scotland of that year, in A.D. 1717 stood at £91,537, in A.D. 1725 was nearly doubled, and in A.D. 1733 amounted to £371,312.

The lord-lieutenant spent half his time in England, and the government was in the hands of the lords justices—those gov-

---

* 14 & 15 Car. II. c. 9.

ernors who, according to constitutional usage, were elected by the privy council when the king's representative was not in the country, and who usually were the primate, the lord-chancellor, and the speaker of the House of Commons. Archbishop Boulter, who became a lord justice in 1726, was the virtual ruler of Ireland for eighteen years, and the reins of government passed from him to Archbishop Hoadly, and afterwards to the unscrupulous and ambitious Archbishop Stone. The spirit of corruption, which had eaten the heart out of English political morality, was fast destroying all ideas of honor and honesty among the public men of Ireland. The Patriots had discovered that the road to advancement and wealth was opened by agitation. Noisy attacks on the English system, all the more easy to assail by reason of its injustice and its imbecility, were bought off with pensions and places of emolument. The mouths of the exposers of English iniquity were stopped with colonelcies of regiments, peerages, and office; and the country was further plundered to provide the hush-money.

During the last years of the reign of George II. matters were coming to a crisis. The government was entirely in the hands of one of the lords justices, the arch-corrupter Primate Stone, through whose hands the stream of patronage flowed. Henry Boyle, the speaker, was also a lord justice, but had none of the patronage, and was determined to secure it by ruining the primate. He accordingly joined himself to the Patriot party, and figured as their leader. The Patriot party had been growing stronger and stronger. One of their most sturdy warriors was Dr. Lucas, who had incurred the enmity of the Castle by attacking the interference of the British legislature in Irish affairs. He had been prosecuted in 1749 by the government, and had fled to England. Then, when the storm had blown over, he had returned and been elected to serve in Parliament by the city of Dublin. The Patriots had also been joined by the Earl of Kildare, who went the length of personally presenting an address to the king, setting forth a series of complaints against the corruption of the government, which were especially levelled at Stone. The most eventful struggle had been fought over the exposure of the peculations of Nevill, the surveyor-general, a creature of the Duke of Dorset, the viceroy, and of his worthless son and chief secretary, Lord George Sackville. Victory had remained with the Patriots, and Nevill had been driven from the House of Commons. Another contest with the Court party had been fought over the right, claimed by the crown, to dispose of the surplus revenue. And, when neither party would give way, the Commons evaded the difficulty by carrying out a number of public works, roads, canals, and bridges, so that no surplus remained to fight over.

It happened that Lord Bessborough was the happy possessor of some fourteen seats, which gave him a considerable influence with the Lower House. The primate, hoping to strengthen himself, formed an alliance with him. The bargain was that the noble earl should in return for his support have a share in the patronage, and that Boyle should be ousted from the speakership in favor of Lord Bessborough's son, Mr. Ponsonby. Boyle, however, refused to be elbowed out. He could on his part command no less than sixteen votes in the House, and was supported by the Patriot party, who believed him to be disinterested and honest. At length, in 1755, the English ministry, disturbed by these cabals and intrigues and by the discontents exhibited at the disregard of Kildare's memorial, recalled the Duke of Dorset, and despatched Lord Hartington in his room, who was an intimate friend of Kildare. Immediately upon the arrival of the new viceroy, Lord Bessborough deserted the primate, and made overtures to Boyle and Kildare. And this new triumvirate, being strong enough in its tail of clients in the Commons to bring the whole business of the session to a standstill by factiously supporting the opposition, were able to make their terms with Lord Hartington, and grasp the whole power and patronage of the country. The primate was accordingly struck off the list of the privy council; Anthony Malone, an energetic Patriot, became chancellor of the exchequer; Stannard, another Patriot, succeeded Malone as prime-sergeant; Ponsonby was gratified with the speakership; and Boyle went to the Upper House, and received a pension of £2000 a year and the earldom of Shannon.

The so-called "Patriot" leaders had carried the day and

gorged themselves with the spoil. The remnant of the betrayed party closed their broken ranks, and prepared themselves for more trenchant measures of reform. They formed the nucleus of a national party, whose object was to emancipate the Irish legislature from the servitude imposed by the sister island. By the steady insistence of the national claims they created and moulded a strong public opinion outside the walls of Parliament. The doctrines of Molyneux, the advocacy of Swift, the agitation of Lucas, had initiated a line of policy which, under the guidance of pure and single-minded men, was soon to become an irresistible national impulse.

CHAPTER IV.
THE RESULTS OF BONDAGE. A.D. 1760–1768.

SEVENTY years had now passed since the surrender of Limerick, and George III. had succeeded to the throne. During these seventy years the Roman Catholics had shown no sign of resistance. There had been a rising in Scotland in 1715, on behalf of the Pretender, which was absolutely unfelt in Ireland. Thirty years later a more serious rising had occurred in the same country and in the same cause. The English government had sent over Lord Chesterfield to Ireland as lord-lieutenant, to encourage the loyalty of the Roman Catholics by granting them some indulgences in relation to the exercise of public worship; and so quiet was the country that, notwithstanding the alarm of the Protestant garrison, he was able to despatch four battalions of English troops to the assistance of the Duke of Cumberland.

In 1760, during the Seven Years' War, an abortive attempt was made by the French to land at Carrickfergus; but no sign was given by the Roman Catholics in their favor, or any attempt made to co-operate. On the accession of the new king a loyal address was presented to him by the Roman Catholics of Ireland, which was graciously received; and a half-shame-faced feeling was beginning to grow in men's hearts, both in England and in Ireland, that the penal laws were an abuse of power. The Roman Catholics themselves began to pluck up heart. Anonymous works were published by Dr. Curry and Mr. Wyse putting forward the Roman Catholic case, and showing what a picture of cruelty and injustice the history of Ireland exhibited. A few of their leading men, chiefly among the merchant class, even ventured to form a "Catholic Committee" in Dublin, to watch over and help on the interests of the Roman Catholic community. But even in this feeble effort disunion seems to have prevailed; and after five or six years the movement sank to sleep.

Half a century's experience of the penal laws had left its mark on the Roman Catholic population. The poorer classes were more attached to the persecuted religion than ever, and at the same time were sunk in hopeless ignorance. All education emanating from Roman Catholic sources was forbidden by law; none was provided from any other source; and but for the persevering energy of the registered priests, who, despite the penal code, in the wilder country ventured to open schools and in the less remote districts taught the ragged children the elements of education in the fields and by the roadside, every spark of religion and knowledge would have died out from end to end of the island. The patient persistence of the Roman clergy was very remarkable. The intention of the penal laws was that, no fresh clergy being permitted to enter Ireland and the ordaining powers being banished, the then existing registered clergy should gradually die out, and so the race of priests become extinct.

To enforce the statutes, however, strictly was in fact impossible. The good feeling inherent in a large proportion of the Protestants, who had the administering of the law, revolted from the idea of putting it strictly in force. The government, who grew to look upon the Roman Catholics as a useful counterpoise to the Jacobite tendencies of many of the Ascendency, winked at breaches of the law; and the succession of priests, who for the most part received their orders from the Continent, was steadily kept up, though, according to the strict interpretation of the law, after the clergy originally registered had died out, every priest in Ireland was liable to be hanged, drawn, and quartered. Besides living under the ban of outlawry, the Roman Catholic clergy were wretchedly poor. They were supported by the voluntary contributions of their poverty-stricken parishioners. Each person gave what he could, some a few shillings, more but a few pence, and those who could not spare money gave in kind. Small collections were made in the chapels on Sundays: the sum total of which at the end of the year was considered handsome if it amounted to a pound. The whole income of a parish priest did not come to more than thirty or forty pounds, and part of this would go to pay a curate. Still the devoted band worked steadily on, a startling contrast to the clergy of the Establishment, doing their utmost to improve the condition and to raise the moral tone of those around them, and only rewarded by the loyal affection of the flocks which they served so well.

On the whole, the earth-tillers deteriorated less than the gentry. The latter were more directly affected by the degrading influence of the penal code. Their self-interest was appealed to; their truth and honesty were undermined; and the door was closed to every ennobling impulse. There was no way out of obscurity for ambition, no scope for energy and enterprise, except at the price of the surrender of what they had been taught was necessary to their salvation. Sham conversions were therefore common. By the year 1738 as many as a thousand Roman Catholic families of rank had nominally joined the Established Church; and no scruple was felt in taking the oaths, when perjury could be atoned for, as it constantly was, by a small penance which purchased absolution from the priest.

Numbers of the gentry, thrown back on a vegetable existence in the country, lapsed into low and unworthy habits, and spent their lives in drinking and wagering, with no idea above a horse-race or the wiping-out of imaginary insults with a rapier or pistols. Others, finding themselves the victims of the law, took refuge in acts of open lawlessness, and revenged themselves upon the English strangers by acts of shocking violence. It was a terribly common crime for these reckless men to cheat the statutes relating to marriage which deprived their class of the land, by seizing and carrying off into the mountains wealthy Protestant widows and heiresses, and ruthlessly violating them, in order that to hide their shame the miserable women might consent to marriage, upon the ready production of some disreputable priest who was willing to lend himself to the vile plot. Not only did the Roman Catholics become degraded, but many of the English Protestants who lived among them, either through example, intermarriage, or compulsion, became in time assimilated to their neighbors.

The great curse of absenteeism, which had from the earliest times undermined the prosperity of Ireland, grew to its most monstrous proportions. It was calculated that as much as one third of the whole rental of Ireland was annually drained away to England for the support of absentee landlords. A proposal was made to tax the income of those who lived abroad, but their influence was strong enough in England to secure the rejection of the bill. The great land-owners lived away in Bath and London, with no other thought for their Irish properties than the extraction of so much rent. Whole territories were leased out in large tracts to "middlemen," who let the land again at exorbitant rents to others, who sublet again; and this process was repeated till the estate was sometimes underlet and underlet six deep. Or the property was managed by stewards and agents, whose orders were to remit the revenues and to spend not a penny in improvements of any description. The country-houses fell out of repair; the woods were recklessly cut to increase the revenue; whatever fencing or reclamation was done was done by the tenant, and done with as little show as possible, lest the keen eye of the agent should note it, and raise the rent accordingly. The tenant received no encouragement to make the most out of the land. His position was too insecure. Swift's opinion as to what was wanted in 1729 was "good, firm penal clauses for improvements, with a tolerably easy rent, and a reasonable period of time."

It was in 1761 that public attention first became directed towards the state of the peasantry. The condition of the earth-tillers had rapidly been growing worse and worse. In the old days before the plantations they had been little better than serfs, so autocratic had the clan chiefs and the Anglo-Norman lords become; but the tie of family and old association was strong, and one faith was common to both; so that the earth-tiller followed his master to danger and death with infrangible fidelity. Even in the case of the earlier planters common interests had established a friendly feeling between the new land-owner and the old tenant. But the later confiscations, especially those after the war of 1791, created a gulf between the old tenant and the still newer land-owner which was never bridged over. There was no bond of sympathy between them. Of different faith and different habits, the newest race of landlords were essentially land-speculators, who bought the land as an investment, determined to make every possible shilling out of their purchase. They cared not to live in a barbarous island among strangers: all they wanted was their rents; and the tenantry and peasantry never saw their faces from year's end to year's end. The landlords, who were extending grass-lands wholesale, managed to get pasture-land exempted from the payment of tithe, so that this hated tribute to an alien Church fell wholly on the growers of grain and roots. The wretched tenants-at-will were transferred to the tender mercies of the "middlemen," who raised their rents to swell their own profits, and allowed them as some set-off the run of the open waste. The grazing fever set in, the land fell out of cultivation, so that, according to Swift, "even ale and potatoes were imported from England as well as corn." The rate of wages fell to nothing; the small farmers and laborers were cleared out of the country, and huddled into the towns. The agents then enclosed large tracts of what had hitherto been common bog and moor, and the wretched peasants who now counted among their number the descendant of many an old proprietor, who had squatted on what was once his own demesne, and who carefully devised by his will to his sons and grandsons the ancestral acres of which he was no longer the possessor, were driven from the bit of rough pasture on which they had been accustomed to turn out a pig or a cow.

Rack-rented by the remorseless middlemen, squeezed out of the narrowing cultivable lands and hunted from the common, they at length took the law into their own hands, and thought, in their ignorance, that justice could be achieved by means of a secret society. In the dark nights of the winter of 1761 and the spring of 1762, mysterious parties of men with white shirts over their clothes sped over the counties of Cork, Limerick, Waterford, and Tipperary, pulling down the fences, levelling the banks, and digging up acres and acres of the pasture. As the terror grew which they inspired, they were not content with a war against grass-lands and enclosures, but proposed to remedy all the wrongs from which the tenant suffered. Threatening letters were sent, signed Captain Dwyer and Joanna Meskell, demanding a reduction of rents, the enforcement of the Tillage Acts, moderation in cattle-breeding, and relief against the action. of the tithe-proctors. Obnoxious persons were brutally ill-treated, tortured, and mutilated, and their cattle were houghed. Strong measures were taken by the government to suppress the disorder; but the law was powerless. When the judges came round on circuit, no juries would convict, and no evidence could be procured. The people, harassed by the Whiteboy oath on the one hand, and the judicial oath on the other, preferred to perjure themselves on the side of their friends. The military was called out, and patrolled the country. Bodies of volunteers were formed by the resident gentry. Many of the Whiteboys were killed in hot blood; others were court-martialled and hanged; some of their reputed leaders were tried and executed. But, though order was by these means in some sort restored, the Whiteboys continued to infest Munster for many years.

While the peasantry of the south were despairingly appealing to the law of force, the peasantry of the north and the working classes in the manufacturing towns had resorted to the same expedient. The public highways in Ireland were reparable by the householders. Every man was bound to give six days' labor in the year, and whoever had a horse was bound to give six days' use of the horse as well. There had long been complaint that the poor only had been compelled to work, and the rich were exempted even from giving payment in place of manual labor. Not only was the work enforced upon the highways, but also upon private roads, while the grand juries exacted the cess from the farmers only. In 1763 a general refusal to work was followed by a rising and a demand for a redress of all grievances against waywardens, tithe-proctors, and landlords. Green boughs of oak were worn in the hats of the rioters, who went by the name of "Oakboys."

These disturbances were hardly put down by the military when the troops were again called out to suppress the rising of the "Hearts-of-steel Boys," which was a comparatively local disturbance arising from the refusal of Lord Donegal, Mr. Upton, and other large absentee proprietors, to relet farms when the leases had expired except upon the terms of the payment of a somewhat decreased rent and a heavy fine. The farmers, though able and willing to pay the old rents, had not the capital to pay the fine, and were evicted in favor of wealthy undertakers, who, having paid the fine and taken the land as a speculation, doubled all the rents which had up to that time been reserved. The avarice of the landlords, who were only careful to raise large lump-sums of money to spend out of the country on their own indulgences, had driven the Protestant farmers into a league against "landlordism," with the result that they were compelled to throw up their farms. The farms were t~~~~y Roman Catholics, who were only too ready to get back upon the land at any price; and the sturdy yeoman, who had been cast upon the world, took refuge in the New England colonies.

Royal commissions were issued to inquire into the causes of the disturbances both of the Oakboys, the Hearts-of-steel Boys, and the Whiteboys; and the difference in the results which followed is a striking illustration of the way in which party feeling and class interests have always been the first consideration in Ireland. No help was forthcoming for the Steelboys, whose grievances were against their landlords. There was no hope for them but in emigration. Lord Donegal was, however, subsequently made a marquess, and Mr. Upton a viscount. In the case of the Protestant Oakboys, the old act relating to highways was repealed, and provision was made for the future repair of roads by a rate levied on rich and poor alike in every barony.* In the case of the Roman Catholic Whiteboys, whose grievances were also against the landlords, not only was no step taken to prevent excessive enclosures, or to strengthen and enforce the Tillage Acts, but a bill was passed which made it felony for more than six persons to assemble at night and to level fences and dig up pastures, and gave damages to the injured parties, to be assessed on the barony in which the offence had been committed.† The grievances of the peasantry and

---

* 5 Geo. III. c. 14.   † Ib. c. 8.

the farmers were refused a hearing, and the policy of coercion was carried out, with the natural result that the mischief of discontent was driven in upon the system to grow into disaffection and rebellion. The half-serious sneer of Lord Chesterfield was sadly too near the truth: that "if the military force had killed half as many landlords as it had Whiteboys, it would have contributed more effectually to restore quiet." "For," he adds, "the poor people in Ireland are worse used than negroes by their masters, and deputies of deputies of deputies."

CHAPTER V.

THE BEGINNING OF CORRUPTION. A.D. 1767–1775.

THE government had bought the venal portion of the Patriot party, but the residue, led by Lucas, and Pery (the member for Limerick), who had now found a powerful ally in young Henry Flood, continued their assaults on the pension list. The annual charge of this scandal in 1763 was no less than £72,000; while the private revenue of the crown, on which alone it could with decency be charged, was but £30,000. One of the latest jobs was a pension of £1000 a year in the name of George Charles to M. de Verois, the Sardinian ambassador, for having negotiated the peace of Paris. Besides this £72,000, the number of regiments had been raised from thirty-two to forty-two without adding to the number of men, with the sole object of increasing the court patronage by means of the *Gazette;* and this had entailed the expenditure of an additional £75,000 per annum in the pay of general officers alone.

The imports and exports were taxed as heavily as they would bear. The revenue was annually falling short of the expenditure. The national debt, after having been liquidated in 1754, had rapidly grown up again in consequence of the cost of the Seven Years' War, and, taking the annual deficits into account, was calculated in 1765 to amount to about £1,000,000.

After repeated motions relating to the pension list, which were defeated by considerable majorities, and after the rejection of a bill "to prevent the buying and selling of offices which concern the administration of justice, or of the collecting of his majesty's revenue," the Patriots felt that the self-interested court party were too strong for them on this point, and turned their attention to obtaining an instalment of parliamentary reform.

There was no limit to the existence of an Irish Parliament

but the demise of the crown or a dissolution. That which had been elected at the commencement of George II.'s reign expired only with his death, having sat for no less than thirty-three years. The duration of the English Parliament was limited by the Septennial Act; and the question which was now beginning to excite general interest, and which had drawn the pledges of a considerable proportion of the candidates at the last general election, was that of a Septennial Act for Ireland.

The government, now that it held in its pay the leaders of the Commons, whose united dependants could at any time insure a majority of the house, was beginning to find that the monopoly of votes which it had secured was anything but a satisfactory purchase. The rapacity of the placemen was insatiable; and, if they did not obtain all their desires, they did not scruple to revenge themselves by going into the opposition lobby. The wire-pullers of the privy council, the Boyle and Ponsonby oligarchy, who monopolized the office of lord justice, were in the habit of bargaining with each new lord-lieutenant as to the terms upon which they would "undertake" to "carry on the king's business;" for, as all the loaves and fishes, places, pensions, and preferments passed through their hands, they could command an enormous majority, and had it in their power to bring matters to a deadlock. If the lord-lieutenant was refractory, they joined with the opposition and withheld the supplies, with their band of mercenaries behind them. If the lord-lieutenant was compliant, the opposition were left in a minority, and the government measures carried.

Lord Chatham's government, hoping to break up the junto which had been unwittingly created, sent over Lord Townshend in 1767 as lord-lieutenant to reduce the Irish House of Commons to obedience. It was determined that thenceforward the lord-lieutenant should reside permanently in Ireland, the consequence of which necessarily was that all the patronage would be conferred directly from the viceroy in each case, instead of passing through the hands of the lords justices, who had absorbed it in his absence. To strengthen himself against the "undertakers," and to strike at their monopoly of the constituencies, he encouraged the Patriots to bring in a Septennial Bill. Three times under Lord Hertford's lieutenant-governorship had the Patriots, with the support of many members who dreaded the measure from the bottom of their hearts, but who reckoned on the British cabinet rejecting it, sent over the heads of a Septennial Bill to England; and it had never as yet come back to Dublin. Now, for a fourth time, a bill was transmitted in the usual way; and this time the English cabinet returned it, only changing the limit from seven to eight years. The government was extremely anxious to pass a bill for the increase of the army, nominally on the ground of the necessity for a larger force wherewith to suppress the Whiteboys, but really for the purpose of having the means wherewith to coerce the American colonies. The return of the bill was a bribe to purchase the neutrality of the opposition, and to hinder the aristocratic junto from putting pressure on the government. The sham Patriots, in the pay of the junto, were greatly disconcerted at the return of the bill, which reduced their occupancy of a seat from an indefinite period to one of eight years. They had voted for it under the belief that the cabinet would be certain to "cushion" it. The interference of the English privy council was a sore point, which had already wrecked a bill for making the appointment of the judges perpetual during good behavior, instead of depending on the caprice of the sovereign; and they still hoped that, as the limit had been so materially altered, the House of Commons might, after all, reject the measure. But the Irish people were too delighted to get the bill back at any price, either for Patriots to raise a point of privilege, or pseudo-patriots, who hated reform, to venture to reject it. The bill accordingly passed into law amid the greatest popular exultation and rejoicing, and the Parliament was dissolved.*

Popular as the passing of the Octennial Act made Townshend for the time, the struggle between him and the Commons was yet to come. The great Irish families, who held one sixth of the seats in their grasp, and who hired upwards of one third

---

* 7 Geo. II. c. 3.

more by the distribution of government favors, were furious at having their patronage taken from them. The Army Bill had been duly passed; the Patriots relapsed into opposition; the outmanœuvred aristocratic faction threw themselves again into their arms. The viceroy was again at fault, and, in order to overcome the coalition, was compelled to enter upon a course of wholesale bribery.

One of the great issues between the government and the Irish Parliament was the question of the right to initiate a money bill. The Commons contended that, Poynings's Law or no Poynings's Law, the representatives of the people could alone hold the purse-strings, and that the originating or alteration of a money bill by either the English or the Irish privy council was a gross breach of privilege and a violation of the Constitution. An attempt to dictate to the House the amount of the vote was made by Lord Sydney in 1692, which resulted in the rejection of one of the money bills, and the passing of the other with an accompanying resolution that it was not to form a precedent for the future. Prior to the first sitting of the first Octennial Parliament in 1769, Townshend had moved heaven and earth to influence the election. Sixteen months had been allowed to elapse between the dissolution of the old and the reassembling of the new Parliament, and large sums had in the meantime been expended to strengthen the Court influence. When Parliament met, a money bill originated by the privy council was introduced, and after a stormy debate was rejected on the second reading. In order, however, to show that their conduct was not factious, the Commons brought in a bill of their own and granted the supplies. Townshend accepted the supplies, and, chafing under his defeat, made an angry protest, which the Commons refused to record on their journals. Then, after some sharp skirmishes with the Patriots, he prorogued the Parliament—a course which elicited a storm of invective both from pamphlets and the press.

The conduct of the lord-lieutenant was called in question in the English Parliament and an attack was made on Lord North's government, which, however, was defeated. Emboldened by this success, and encouraged by the defection from the popular party of Pery, Tyrone, Loftus, and other Patriots, who now yielded to his allurements, and by the doubly securing with fresh pensions of such waiters on events as Hely Hutchinson and Tisdale, Townshend, after a lapse of eighteen months, again met Parliament. The first Lord Shannon was dead, but his son reigned in his room: the viceroy took the bold step of dismissing him, Ponsonby, and five others from the privy council and from their offices for breaking their compact to support the crown, and intimated to all other office-holders that they held their places only during good behavior. He had appointed four additional commissioners of inland revenue, all of whom had seats in the House of Commons. By free use of the old shameful process of pension-giving, to the amount of £25,000 a year, and the distribution of places and appointments in the church, the army, and the law; by the granting of seven new peerages, and by the skilful social bribery of banquets, fancy-balls, and masquerades at the Castle, he had now secured a working majority.

All went smoothly for a time, and the opposition was helpless, till at length the old bone of contention, the origin of the money bills, was too much even for his newly purchased allies; and, when supply was asked for in the obnoxious form, on the motion of Flood the bill was rejected without a division, and the necessary sum voted in a new bill originating in the Commons. Flood attacked the transparent job of the new commissionerships; the venal crew of placemen again deserted their patron, and the government was beaten by the casting-vote of Pery the new speaker, now doubly a deserter. Matters were going hard with the viceroy, notwithstanding all his labor. When in the midst of his difficulties, overtures came from Lord Shannon, whom he had so recently dismissed; and so, swallowing his pride, he surrendered to the inevitable, and, having made an alliance with the great wire-puller whose influence he had intended to break, he foiled the opposition, and carried on to the end of the session with flying colors. But Townshend was sick of Ireland. He had come over to purge the Augean stable, and he had rendered it ten times worse. He had started on a mission to break the oligarchy, and he had ended in hauling down his colors to the greatest malefactor of them all. In 1772 he resigned, and was succeeded by Lord Harcourt, who was accompanied by Colonel Blacquiere as chief secretary. Shannon made his bargains with the new viceroy, and the usual shower of peerages, pensions, and places followed. But the key-stone was put to the arch of corruption when Henry Flood, the steadfast, the unapproachable champion of the popular party, the rejector of money bills, the advocate of septennial bills, of free trade, and independence, agreed to support the king's government, and accepted a vice-treasurership, a sinecure of £3500 per annum.

CHAPTER VI.

THE REVOLT OF THE COLONY. A.D. 1775-1779.

ENGLAND had done her best to ruin her Protestant colony in Ireland. She had starved its manufactures, destroyed its trade, made a farce of its legislature, billeted all her disreputable dependants upon her revenues; and, in order to maintain her grasp, she had shamefully plundered it and spent the money in corrupting the guardians of its interests.

She had, besides the colony in Ireland, a colony planted on the eastern shores of the North American continent which had come into existence principally through the misconduct of the mother-country. New England was the outcome of the bigotry of the Established Church, and was peopled by Puritan and Quaker emigrants who had fled from persecution. The flow of emigration had been largely fed from Ulster. From the Restoration onward in an intermittent stream, thousands of Presbyterian families had been driven by the bishops from the Irish colony to the colony across the Atlantic, and more recently the numbers had been augmented by the farmers who had been evicted by their greedy absentee landlords. Notwithstanding by-gones, the North American colonists were loyal subjects of King George, and had rendered material assistance in the reduction of the neighboring French colony of the Canadas in the late war. That war had rolled up the English national debt to the figure of one hundred and fifty millions; and George Grenville and Charles Townshend had not unreasonably expected that the colonies, in whose defence a large part of the expenditure had been incurred, should contribute towards the payment of the interest. Had they asked them to make a grant for the purpose, they would have cheerfully complied; but the pride, prejudice, prestige, and what not, of Great Britain required the acknowledgment of the principle that the mother-country had the right to lay her taxes on her colonies, without consulting them or their representatives; and the quarrel thus begun in 1764 culminated in 1775 in an appeal to arms.

The English colony in Ireland were watching the issue with intense interest. Their position was in many respects similar to that of the Americans; only their case was far harder. Close under the elbow of England, their chances of successful resistance were slender, for England could pour in troops at a moment's notice, and blockade their harbors with her fleet. But as events moved on the scene began to shift. The Americans, beaten at first, as had been expected, carried on a Fabian war, and then the surrender of Burgoyne took place at Saratoga. France, who was burning to revenge herself for the loss of her colonies, came to the assistance of the revolted Americans, and declared war against England. Spain soon after joined the league, and every ship and man which England could spare was doubly wanted in this formidable struggle.

It never seems to have occurred to English statesmen that the English colony in Ireland could be dangerous. Up to the last moment their interests were sacrificed to those of the stronger island. Upon the pretence of overawing the Whiteboys, the army had been raised from twelve to fifteen thousand men; but the extra three thousand had never been employed in Ireland. The troops quartered there numbered on paper twelve thousand men, but of these over four thousand had been drafted off to America, and the actual strength of the depleted regiments which remained was but three thousand men in all. The army serving against the colonists was to be victualled from Ireland; and, in order that the government should be able to buy salted meat cheap, the Irish farmers were deliberately excluded from any other market by the laying of an embargo upon the export of provisions from all the Irish ports. The consequence of the embargo was that widespread ruin fell upon the farmers, and that the trade in cured beef was transferred to other countries. The American war had put a stop to the declining linen trade between Ireland and the colonies, and this brought disaster upon the operatives of the north. England had broken her engagements, even in respect to the linen trade. For, when she destroyed the manufacture of woollen cloth, she promised that the manufacture of hemp and flax should be encouraged and protected; and yet she had done her best to cripple it by giving bounties to her own linen-manufacturers and levying duties on imported Irish sail-cloth, which had simply had the effect of driving the trade elsewhere. The artisans in the towns and the laborers in the country were alike starving and supported on charity. Rents were unpaid, and land offered at fourteen years' purchase found no buyers. The revenue dwindled. The exchequer was empty. The projected loans were not responded to. The pension list, which exceeded the whole charge of the civil establishments, had doubled in twenty years, and now stood at £90,000. The coast was wholly unprotected. Paul Jones was swooping down upon the Irish harbors, pillaging, sinking, and cutting out vessels. The fortifications were crumbling to pieces. The Channel was swarming with swift French and American privateers, which captured merchantmen and plundered the mail vessels with impunity.

Amid all this misery and insolvency, the fortunes of the American rebels were eagerly watched; and freedom of trade, as the only remedy for the deplorable state into which Ireland had sunk, was beginning to take shape as a popular demand. At the general election in 1775, the government had striven hard to extend its influence. Five viscounts were advanced to earldoms, seven barons to viscounties, and no less than eighteen new barons were made in one day, who promised to support the government in the Upper House, and to secure pliant voters in the seats which they vacated. But the importunity of public opinion was becoming too strong to be resisted. The excitement of the people grew day by day more formidable. The cry out-of-doors was emphasized in Parliament by the purified Patriot party, now led, since Flood's defection, by the unsullied Henry Grattan.

The war was carried into England; and Lord Nugent and Edmund Burke, in the English House of Commons, moved that a committee of the whole House should consider the trade of Ireland. Five resolutions in favor of allowing certain relaxations were carried; but, when a bill was brought in to give them effect, so great was the clamor of Liverpool, Glasgow, Manchester, and Bristol, that nothing remained of it but the removal of the embargo, and permission to export to Africa and the West Indies all home products *except* wool, woollen and cotton goods, hats, glass, hops, gunpowder, and coals!* Lord North, however, was alarmed at the rising storm. He cast his eyes upon the Roman Catholics in hopes of finding a counterpoise to the mutinous Protestants, and endeavored to draw the people off the scent by promoting in the Irish Parliament some bills for Roman Catholic relief. In 1764, leave to bring in a bill to enable Roman Catholics to advance money on a mortgage of freeholds had been summarily rejected; and in 1771† the magnificent concession was made to them of permission to hold long leases of fifty acres of bog for reclamation, provided it was not within a mile of any city or town. And now, in 1778,‡ a more substantial act of justice was carried through: Roman Catholics, on taking the oath of allegiance, were to be allowed to hold a lease of 999 years. The lands which were still in their possession were made descendible, divisible, and alienable, like those of other subjects; and Protestant heirs were deprived of the privilege given them by the statute of Anne to plunder and defy their recusant fathers.

But Ireland had now many friends in the English Parliament who would not let the trade question rest; especially the Irish absentees, who, owing to the miserable state of the country, had received no rent for two years. In 1779, Lord Shelburne, in the Lords, moved an address to the king upon the state of Ireland. In the Commons various efforts were made to open to Ireland the colonial trade, and to enable her to export her manufactures. Lord Newhaven endeavored to obtain the repeal of a clause in the Navigation Act which prohibited the importation of sugar into Ireland unless it came first through England. Again the clamor of the English manufacturers prevailed. Every effort was made to rouse an anti-Irish feeling in the country. The table of the House was crowded with peti-

---

* English Statutes, 18 Geo. III. c. 55. † 11, 12 Geo. III. c. 21.
‡ 17, 18 Geo. III. c. 49.

tions; and Lord North, who at one time had looked with favor upon the proposed measure, set his face against it, and it was lost by sixty-four to fifty-eight.

Angry and desponding, the Irish now bound themselves to retaliate upon England by consuming no English goods which could be produced in Ireland; and so earnestly and faithfully was the resolution kept that the trade of the English merchants was materially diminished. How long England would have scouted the Irish claims it is impossible to surmise. But now that she was harassed with a ruinous war, and was unable to maintain her ascendency by force, and was even threatened herself with invasion, Ireland suddenly found herself in a position to assert herself. When the government had drained her of troops, and she was left defenceless and exposed to the attacks of Paul Jones and his friends, a proposal had been made to raise a national militia, Protestants only to be enrolled. An act was passed to empower the government to carry out the plan;* but the attempt came to nothing by reason of the bankrupt condition of the Irish treasury. The peers, the country gentlemen, and the trade-guilds in self-defence then set about raising bodies of volunteers for the protection of the coast. The call to arms was cheerfully responded to; corps after corps was raised; the local magnates vying with each other (often with a fatal recklessness of expense, which made itself felt afterwards), in the completeness and efficiency of the equipments. Forty-two thousand men were enrolled in a few months' time. The government began to look upon them with suspicion, but dared not refuse the application for a distribution of arms, and sixteen thousand stand were delivered to them from the government stores. The great questions which were stirring the hearts of every citizen were earnestly discussed by the volunteers. It soon became apparent that the arguments of men with arms in their hands have weight; and the movement which began in an effort to secure the country from foreign invasion, rapidly developed into an engine for the resisting of English usurpation.

---
* 17, 18 Geo. III. c. 13.

At the opening of Parliament on October 12, 1779, Grattan moved, as an amendment to the address, that "it was by *free export* and *import* only that the nation was to be saved from impending ruin." Hussey Burgh suggested that the words "an opening of the ports" should be substituted; when Flood, who for five years had sat tongue-tied on the government benches, and who had grown jealous of the position of champion of the rights of the nation which Grattan had achieved, broke away from the silken chains of court favor, and proposed that "free trade" should be the crucial words of the amendment. Grattan accepted the alteration, and the amendment was carried with but one dissentient voice. Next day, when the speaker and the whole House of Commons marched in procession to present the amended address at the Castle, the streets were lined with the Dublin volunteers, drawn up in arms under the command of the Duke of Leinster.

The popular excitement was now tremendous. The volunteers were reviewed on King William's birthday on College Green, and two field-pieces were drawn up in front of his statue, ticketed "free trade or this." The Dublin mob wrecked the house of the attorney-general Scott, one of Townshend's purchased Patriots, who was known to be hostile to the volunteer movement. The House of Commons itself was invaded, and the members made to swear to vote for "free trade" or "a short money bill." The speaker's carriage was stopped, and the same oath tendered to him. When the viceroy, on the 24th, asked for the usual vote of supplies for two years, the government was abandoned by its chief supporters. The House, amid the greatest excitement, voted a six months' money bill by 138 to 100. "Talk not to me of peace," shouted Hussey Burgh, when denouncing the restrictive English statutes: "it is smothered war. England has sown her laws like dragon's teeth, and they have sprung up in armed men."

Lord Buckinghamshire, who was now lord-lieutenant, wrote over to the ministry that the repeal of the trade restrictions must be immediate and complete. Lord Shelburne in the Lords, and Lord Upper Ossory, supported by Edmund Burke, in the Commons, moved a vote of censure on the government for not granting to Ireland what, now that it was too late, they had offered to America. Lord North yielded and brought in three bills of repeal, the substance of which was to allow Ireland the free export of her wool, woollens, wool flocks, and glass, and the free importation of foreign hops; to remove the prohibition against the carrying of gold and silver coin from England into Ireland, and to permit her to trade directly with the "Levant seas" and the English colonies upon the same terms as Great Britain. These bills * were rapidly passed through both Houses, and copies were forwarded to the viceroy. The concession was received by the Irish with the most extravagant gratitude. Dublin was illuminated, bonfires blazed, and the guns of both the garrison and the volunteers rivalled each other in firing *feux-de-joie.*

---

* English Statutes, 20 Geo. III. cc. 6, 10, 18.

CHAPTER VII.

THE CONCESSION OF HOME RULE.   A.D. 1780-1782.

Though many of the Patriot party were inclined to rest and be thankful, it was not long before Grattan began to follow up his victory. What one English Parliament had conceded another might take back again; it was necessary to go a step further to obtain security. The legislative independence of Ireland had been the great goal at which earnest Irishmen had aimed from the time of Molyneux onwards. The early questionings of Poynings's Law had been met by the declaratory act of George I.;* and, from the days of Lucas's arguments in the *Freeman's Journal*, the principal efforts of the opposition had been directed at some of the minor and more pressing evils. Now that the way was clear, and argument was backed up by upwards of one hundred thousand disciplined troops with two hundred pieces of cannon, the great issue again came to the front.

In April, 1780, Grattan moved that "the king with the consent of the Lords and Commons of Ireland are the only power competent to enact laws to bind Ireland," and that "Great Britain and Ireland are inseparably united under one sovereign." But both the government and the opposition were afraid of testing their strength, and the motion was eventually withdrawn. The House, in its first enthusiasm upon the repeal of the restrictive acts, granted the supplies for the next eighteen months, and authorized the lord-lieutenant to raise a loan of £260,000. Thereupon the English ministry, presuming on their majority in the Irish Commons, went out of their way to rouse their susceptibilities by deliberately altering, to a most material extent, two Irish bills which had been transmitted in

---

* English Statutes, 6 Geo. I. c. 5.

the usual way. They sought to make the triennial Mutiny Bill one of perpetual duration; and a clause was struck out of the Supply Bill which had been inserted in order to prevent the English sugar-manufacturers from underselling the Irish manufacturers, by giving the latter the same bounties as the former enjoyed at the expense of the taxpayer. The Mutiny Bill was extremely distasteful to the Irish. The Mayor of Clonmel refused to find billets for a party of troops passing through the town, though the inhabitants, to show there was no hostility to the soldiers personally, entertained them all as guests. Still the government was determined to force it on the country, contrary even to the opinion of the lord-lieutenant. The popular excitement grew apace: crowds of petitions were presented against the alterations in the bills; the merchants' volunteer corps held a threatening meeting at Dublin; and Fox attacked the government in the English House of Commons. But Lord North was obstinate. The Castle party in the Irish Commons was unbroken; and the bill passed by 114 to 62.* In October of the following year, when Lord Carlisle, the new viceroy, met Parliament, the condition of the national debt, swollen by the annual deficits, and now amounting to over two millions and a half, was exposed by Grattan; and the attack on Poynings's Act was renewed by Flood, who, after his desertion of the government on the free-trade question, had resigned his office and been dismissed from the privy council. The returned prodigal was, however, at first but coldly received. The Patriots refused to follow him, and the government majority stood steadily at two to one.

The volunteers had chosen Lord Charlemont to be their commander. Their *esprit de corps* had been kept up by frequent reviews in various parts of the country; and, feeling strongly that the corrupt House of Commons in no sense represented the opinion of the colony, determined to secure the full expression of the popular will. On February 15, 1782, at the instigation of Lord Charlemont, 242 delegates, representing 143 corps in Ulster, assembled in the church at

---

* 19, 20 Geo. III. c. 16.

Dungannon, and passed thirteen resolutions in favor of legislative independence; and no sooner were these doings known in the other provinces than similar meetings were held in every quarter of Ireland, which declared the adherence of the other volunteer regiments to the resolutions of Dungannon.

And now Lord North's administration had come to the end of its tether. Holland had joined the league against England. The disastrous news had arrived that Cornwallis and his army had been compelled to lay down their arms at Yorktown. Lord North, suffering defeat, or virtual defeat, in division after division, had no other course open to him but to resign. The king, in disgust at the failure of his most cherished designs, had half determined to retire to Hanover, but, unhappily, had thought better of it; and a Whig ministry had come in under Lord Rockingham, with Shelburne and Fox as secretaries of state.

The expectations of the Irish were high, for the late opposition had steadily supported their interests; nor were they disappointed. The Duke of Portland came over to supersede Lord Carlisle with a message of hope and promise. When he met Parliament, Grattan moved as an amendment to the address a declaration of rights and grievances, which was unanimously carried. On May 17, Shelburne in the Lords, and Fox in the Commons, moved resolutions for the repeal of the 6 Geo. I. No opposition was offered to the motion, and a bill embodying its substance was introduced and became law on June 21, 1782.*

The English Parliament had done all that it was in its power to do. Poynings's Act was an Irish act passed by the Irish Parliament, sitting at Drogheda. The repeal of this statute was the first act of the emancipated Houses.† Thenceforth, bills were brought in, read, committed, and passed by the Irish Parliament without the interference of the privy council, English or Irish, and then required only the assent of the king to become valid statutes. Other acts followed for which Ireland had waited in vain. A national bank was established.‡

---

* English Statutes, 22 Geo. III. c. 53.   † 21, 22 Geo. III. c. 47.
‡ Ib. c. 16.

The appointments of the judges were, as in England, to be during good behavior, instead of during the pleasure of the crown.* The Mutiny Act was again to be biennial.† The marriages of the Presbyterians were to be valid in the eye of the law,‡ and Ireland was to have the benefit of a Habeas Corpus Act,§ a statute which England had extracted from the crown one hundred years before.

The free concession made on the part of England was received with the warmest gratitude by the Irish. The Commons promptly voted £100,000 for the raising of twenty thousand seamen for the British navy, and then turned to pay a tribute of thanks to Grattan, whose unflagging courage, high endowments, and incorruptible honesty had so materially contributed to his country's emancipation. A proposal was made that the nation should grant him the sum of £100,000. He refused to receive it, but subsequently was persuaded to accept half the amount. He was the first of the Patriots who received his retainer from the people and not from the crown; and he was one of the few who never betrayed their client.

---

* 21, 22 Geo. III. c. 50. † Ib. c. 43. ‡ Ib. c. 25. ‖ Ib. c. 11.

CHAPTER VIII.

THE DEMAND FOR PARLIAMENTARY REFORM.   A.D. 1782–1784.

FLOOD, who had once been the foremost leader of the Patriot party, was now consumed by the most bitter animosity against the man who had taken the helm when he had deserted the ship. And this ungenerous jealousy drove him to take up a more advanced line than Grattan, in hopes of regaining his old popularity. What the country now wanted was repose. It had regained its constitution, and had shaken off the trammels which fettered its trade; and time was required to work off the evil effects of the old system, before the good results of the new order of things could be secured. Flood was heedless of this. He attempted to undermine Grattan's influence by getting up an agitation for "simple repeal;" the gist of which was an express renunciation by the British Parliament of the right to bind Ireland by statute. After being twice beaten on the question of simple repeal by heavy majorities, he made an attack on the government on the question of reducing the standing army. A collision took place between the rival orators, in which Flood received a terrible lesson from Grattan's scathing invective. He was unable in any of his efforts to obtain any substantial following in the House, and Lord Shelburne cut the ground from under him by passing " an Act of Renunciation,"* in the following year, "for the removing of doubts," which declared that "the right claimed by the people of Ireland to be bound only by laws enacted by his majesty and the Parliament of that kingdom, and to have all actions and suits at law and in equity instituted in that kingdom, decided in his majesty's courts therein finally, and without appeal from thence, shall be, and it is hereby declared to be,

---

* 23 Geo. III. c. 28 (English Statutes).

established and ascertained forever, and shall at no time hereafter be questioned or questionable."

Foiled on the question of simple repeal, Flood took up a different point, which had much more substance in it—the reform of the Irish House of Commons. As in England, so in Ireland, a large proportion of the constituencies were rotten boroughs. The House consisted of three hundred members. The thirty-two counties each returned two knights of the shire; seven cities each returned two citizens; Dublin University had two members; and one hundred and ten boroughs were represented by two hundred and twenty burgesses. The bulk of the boroughs had been fabricated by the house of Stuart. Forty had been called into existence by James I. for the express purpose of swamping the representatives of the counties by a pack of crown nominees. Thirty-four had, from time to time, been created by Charles I. and Charles II. with much the same object; two by James II., and two by Anne. The number of electors in each borough was absurdly small. In eighty-six of them the representatives were returned by the members of the corporations, consisting of some twelve persons, many of whom were non-resident. In fourteen of them the elective franchise was in the hands of the Protestant inhabitants at large, who were called "potwallopers." Five were "manor towns." One and all were under the complete control of the "patrons," that is to say, the owners of the soil on which the borough stood. Harristown and Bannow were absolutely uninhabited. Fifty out of the whole number of borough members, or one sixth of the whole House, were each returned by as few as ten electors; and two hundred borough members, or two thirds of the whole, enjoyed the privilege of being returned by the votes of fivescore and under. The borough-mongers had it all their own way. The seats were openly bought and sold; as much as £11,000 was given for Belturbet for one session. Accordingly, territorial interest and sale in the open market brought a large proportion of them into the hands of the big political families. No less than one hundred and sixteen seats were owned by as few as twenty-five proprietors; and it was this monopoly which had given to the old jobbing oligarchy such a commercial value for each successive viceroy. Lord Shannon was able to command no less than sixteen seats; Lord Bessborough and the Ponsonbys, fourteen; Lord Hillsborough, nine; the Duke of Leinster, seven; Lord Loftus, seven; Lord Granard, four; Lord Clifden, four. The Castle itself had appropriated twelve. One hundred and twenty-three members of the Lower House were the nominees of fifty-three of the Upper. The government reckoned on 186 votes, or a majority of thirty-six in the whole house. Eighty-six of these were given by men who held proprietary seats let to the government in consideration of titles, or places of emolument; forty-four by men who held office under government, and were liable to dismissal for an adverse vote; twelve by the government nominees; thirty-two more by men who lived on hope or promises; and twelve by men who supported the government on public grounds. Besides these, there was a party of twenty-nine waiters upon Providence. The regular opposition consisted of only eighty-two.

Reform was indeed terribly necessary. The subject was one which was rapidly coming to the front; and Flood saw and grasped the opportunity of again becoming the people's idol. Flood, who had been one of the last to put on a volunteer's uniform, was now doing his best to flatter that body of men, and to effect a breach between them and Grattan. Grattan, who fully approved of reform, was of opinion that the time had not come for raising the question, and therefore stood aside. A second meeting of delegates from the volunteers assembled at Dungannon, where resolutions were passed in favor of reform; and it was decided that a convention should be held in Dublin in the following November. The agitation was kept up in the press and on the drill-ground. Lord Charlemont was still in command; but a strange, wild, ill-balanced man, Hervey, Earl of Bristol, Bishop of Derry, began to take the lead, and to head the more unsettled spirits in the corps. There was something like division growing up in their ranks, and the point of departure was a religious one. Charlemont and Flood were stanch Protestants. The bishop and his party were inclined towards toleration of the Roman Catholics, and wished to include them in any scheme of reform. Grattan's resolutions at the first meeting at Dungannon had included one in favor of religious toleration. Though originally strictly confined to the Protestants, the ranks of the volunteers now numbered many Roman Catholics, and a feeling was beginning to grow up that religious differences should be sunk, and that all parties should combine for the common welfare.

On November 10, 1783, one hundred and sixty delegates from the volunteer associations assembled in the Rotunda at Dublin. They marched through the streets of Dublin to take their seats, with much demonstration of military display: all of them were in uniform; they were escorted by two or three mounted corps and by the Dublin Artillery; the streets were lined with volunteers, guns were fired, and bands were playing; and the bishop magnificently brought up the rear in a carriage and six with outriders. The government were uneasy at this display of force. The Parliament eyed with suspicion the unconstitutional body which had come to sit side by side with it; and were much relieved when Lord Charlemont was elected chairman, and not the Bishop of Derry. Lord Northington was viceroy. When the reconstructed cabinet, after Rockingham's untimely death, had given place to a coalition ministry, he had been sent to replace the Duke of Portland's successor, Lord Temple. He succeeded by a questionable intrigue in setting the ultra-Protestants in the convention against the tolerationists, with the result that the majority of the delegates determined to exclude the Roman Catholics from the scheme of reform.

Flood and the bishop prepared a Reform Bill of a moderate and sensible character. It was well calculated to strike at the corruption of the House, but as a broad scheme of reform it was ridiculous, as it left wholly unenfranchised the Roman Catholics, of whom the bulk of the population consisted, and its only effect on the franchise was to add some three hundred to the list of voters in the north of Ireland, and about one hundred in the south. The bill was submitted to and obtained the approval of the convention, and, believing that he would be able to coerce the Parliament into accepting it, on November 29 Flood carried the bill from the Rotunda to the House of Commons. The spirit of the House was aroused by the attempt of the convention to dictate its measures to them. Self-interest prompted many of the members who sat for the rotten boroughs to seize the opportunity of crushing out the spark of reform. The government threw in all its influence against the agitators, and General Burgoyne held his troops ready to act in case violence was actually resorted to. There was a fierce debate. The bill was vigorously opposed by Yelverton, Daly, and Fitzgibbon, on the text that Parliament was not a court to register the decrees of the volunteers, and that the existence of the legislature depended on a firm resistance to the demands of a rival body of men with arms in their hands. Late on the following Sunday morning, after a night of uproar, menace, and recrimination, the House divided, and leave to introduce the bill was rejected by 150 to 77. Parliament was triumphant; and the convention had two courses open. They could have launched the contest into an appeal to force, which meant neither more nor less than civil war; or they could take the determination of the House as final, and retire from the false position which they had assumed. The temperate counsels of Lord Charlemont prevailed over the mad recklessness of the Bishop of Derry, and, to the honor of the volunteers be it said, two days after the fiat of the division list they adjourned *sine die*, and retired peacefully to their respective counties.

Great popular excitement at the rejection of the Reform scheme now broke out, especially in Dublin. Indignation at the collapse of the volunteers showed itself in the outbreak of unreasoning hostility to the regular troops; and brutal ruffians among the mob made a practice of hamstringing the soldiers who unguardedly walked about the streets. The general good order preserved throughout the country while the volunteers were actively employed was interrupted. Whiteboy outrages recommenced in the south; faction fights took place in the north between the Roman Catholics and the Presbyterians; in Dublin the ignorant mob, under the belief that trade would be benefited by excluding the goods of other countries from the market, broke out into rioting, and tarred and feathered the unlucky merchants who were suspected of importing English merchandise.

The volunteer movement still lingered on, especially in the north, where it first came into being. The Bishop of Derry strove hard to raise fresh regiments. Napper Tandy, who had commanded the Dublin volunteer artillery, endeavored to organize a fresh convention, and requested the sheriffs of counties to summon their bailiwicks for the election of delegates. But the government, under the advice of Fitzgibbon, who was now attorney-general, adopted strong measures, fining and imprisoning those who attempted to carry out the design; and though a few persons met at a hole-and-corner meeting in Dublin in the autumn of 1784, and Flood was there with a plan of reform, the "congress" expired after a sitting of three days. Many of the corps, however, especially at Belfast, continued to drill, and retained their arms. But the class of persons which constituted the bulk of the members was very different from that of the original volunteers. The substantial people, the gentry and their tenantry, the merchants and their clerks, left the ranks, and were replaced by men of more daring views and of less substance. "They had originally," complained Grattan, "been the armed property of Ireland; they were becoming the armed beggary." As men of the stamp of Lord Charlemont broke away, the influence of the Protestant party grew less and less. The narrow spirit of bigotry disappeared, and Roman Catholics were freely enrolled. The stirring portion of the retiring members formed themselves into the Whig Club: the remnants of the corps held together as political associations whose aim and object were parliamentary reform and emancipation of the Roman Catholics; and with sincere aspirations for purging the Constitution, and without a shadow of disaffection towards England, formed the nucleus of the Society of the United Irishmen.

CHAPTER IX.

CONFLICTS WITH THE ENGLISH PARLIAMENT. A.D. 1783-1789.

THE coalition ministry had fallen by means of a discreditable intrigue between George III. and Lord Temple; and Pitt, at the age of twenty-three becoming first minister of the crown, had commenced his long supremacy of eighteen years' duration. According to the wondrous theories respecting the position of our colonies and the fostering of trade prevalent in the last century, Ireland had no claim beyond what England pleased to give her in the colonial trade. The colonies belonged (unless by favor or compact it were made otherwise) exclusively to this country. The suffering Ireland to send anything to them, to bring anything directly thence, was itself a favor. England had given to Ireland liberty to import directly and re-export to all the world, except to Great Britain, the produce of the colonies; but no change had taken place in the intercourse between the two kingdoms themselves. The heavy import duties laid on in England against Irish goods had caused great irritation in Ireland. An attempt had been made to retaliate, by persons binding themselves not to use English imported goods; and the tarring and feathering had been resorted to as a means of enforcing the exclusion of English merchandise. The natural consequence of such suicidal conduct was increased distress, and discontent followed in its train.

A committee of the House of Commons had been appointed to inquire into the state of Irish trade; and Mr. Joshua Pim, a Dublin merchant, had sketched out a scheme, which he submitted to Orde, the Irish secretary. Pitt, who was anxious to improve the commercial relations of the two countries, would not see that the unconditional removal of all restrictions would be for the advantage of both the one and the other, and determined to drive a bargain with Ireland. "I own to you," he wrote to the Duke of Rutland, "that the line to which my mind at present inclines is to give Ireland an almost unlimited communication of commercial advantages, *if we can receive in return some security that her strength and riches will be our benefit.*" And accordingly he drew up eleven propositions, which Orde was to lay before the Irish Parliament. The substance of them was : To allow the importation of the produce and manufacture of other countries through Great Britain into Ireland, or through Ireland into Great Britain, without any increase of duty on that account. In all cases where the duties on any article of the produce or manufacture of either country were different on importation into the other, to reduce them, in the kingdom where they were highest, to the lowest scale. And here came the price for the concession : That whenever the gross hereditary revenue of Ireland should rise above £656,000 in any year of peace [at this time the gross amount was £652,000] the surplus should be appropriated towards the support of the imperial navy.

Great exception was taken to this last clause by the Irish Parliament, as, in effect, it was an assigning away forever of all the future expansion of the customs and excise. But it was eventually agreed to with this proviso—that the appropriation should only be made when the revenue of the country was not exceeded by the expenditure. And the Irish Parliament, with the proposed commercial treaty in view, voted £140,000 additional taxes to secure a clean balance-sheet with no deficit. Pitt believed that the English Parliament would raise no objection to their side of the bargain. But he miscalculated the ignorance and selfishness of the English commercial world. As soon as the eleven propositions were laid before the House, the manufacturers took alarm. The admission of Irish fustians into England would ruin the cotton trade. The navigation laws, then considered the bulwark of British prosperity, would be rendered abortive. The monopoly of the East India Company would be gone. London, Liverpool, Manchester, Bristol, Edinburgh, Glasgow, Paisley, and some sixty of the chief trading towns petitioned against the proposed treaty. Counsel were heard and evidence was given. The petition of eighty thousand Lancashire manufacturers was so heavy that the member who presented it was fain to lay it on the floor of the House. So violent was the opposition that Pitt was compelled to make a number of modifications, additions, and explanations to his eleven propositions; and they were, in consequence, expanded into twenty, and materially altered in substance.

The principal changes were—a provision that whatever navigation laws the British Parliament should find desirable to enact, the same should, without question, be passed by the Irish Parliament—a manifest subjecting of the Irish to the English Houses; a provision that no West India merchandise, except that of the colonies, should be imported into England through Ireland; and a provision that Ireland should debar itself from trading with the countries to the east of the Cape of Good Hope and the west of the Strait of Magellan, so long as the charter of the East India Company should be in force. The alteration in the proposals was loudly denounced by the English opposition. Sheridan described the plan as "moved with duplicity and explained with equivocation." Fox declared "that he would not barter English commerce for Irish slavery." But after a fierce debate the twenty resolutions passed the House, and a bill embodying them advanced to its second stage.

When the transformed propositions were returned to Ireland, the greatest indignation prevailed. The changes were so material, and looked so like an attempt on the part of England to interfere with Ireland's newly acquired liberty of independent legislation, that the commercial advantages to be derived did not appear worth the sacrifice. Mr. Orde moved for leave to introduce a bill to convert the new proposals into law. Flood and Grattan united in opposing him. There was a large desertion of the Castle placemen; and though the government obtained a majority, it was so small a one that they looked upon the division as a defeat, and allowed the bill to drop.

Ever since the concession of independence to the Irish Parliament there had been in England an opinion forming that it would be to the advantage of Great Britain if the Irish Parliament were altogether suppressed, and a union of the legislatures effected. At the beginning of the century, when the Irish Parliament petitioned for incorporation, England was deaf to the proposal. Later on a strong feeling had grown up in Ireland inimical to the idea of a union. So fierce was the feeling in Dublin that in 1759, when the plan of a union was mooted, the mob stopped the members in the streets and compelled them to swear never to consent to such a measure. They broke into the House of Lords, when the House was not sitting, and placed an old woman on the throne, and searched for the journals, that they might commit them to the flames. Now that the Parliament had freed itself from England's veto, the idea of a union was still more obnoxious to the Irish. But in England it was otherwise. The trading classes dreaded Irish competition, and believed that if the legislatures could be amalgamated all such competition could be effectually checked. The manufacturers, who had raised the storm against the eleven propositions, resolved "that a real union with Ireland under one legislature *would take away every difficulty.*" English public men were beginning to exhibit an unworthy jealousy of Irish independence, and to grudge what had been conceded. Pitt himself looked forward with anxiety to a disagreement between the two Parliaments, and contemplated the absorption of the Irish Houses.*

A circumstance about this time occurred which afforded a convenient argument in favor of a union in the mouths of those who predicted a collision between the legislatures. His majesty, in 1788, showed symptoms of brain disease, and by the month of December it became apparent that a regency was inevitable. Thereupon there arose in England a smart party-contest about the limitations of the regent's powers. The hopes of the Whigs ran high, for the Prince of Wales had ostentatiously thrown himself into their arms. A regency meant Pitt's downfall and Fox's accession to power. Fox accordingly urged that the prince of natural right stepped as regent

---

* In writing to the Duke of Rutland, on January 5, 1785, he said that " he wanted to make England and Ireland one country in effect; though, *for local concerns,* under distinct legislatures."

into his father's shoes, unfettered by any condition. Pitt very sensibly sought to deprive him of the power to deal with the king's property, to grant offices for life, and to create peers. Grattan, who had recently been on a visit to England and cemented his friendship with the Whigs, rejoiced at the prospect of a change of ministry; Fox having engaged that, should the Whigs come in, an end should be put to Castle corruption by a pension bill and a place bill, and that the question of reform should be at once dealt with. The Whig view of the regency question was accordingly adopted by the Irish opposition, and the Irish Parliament hastened to signalize its independence by forestalling the English Parliament in the choice of a regent.

Pitt was delaying matters in England, in hopes the king's illness might take a more favorable turn. Grattan seized the opportunity, when Parliament opened in February, to move that the Irish Parliament should vote an immediate address to the prince, inviting him to an unrestricted regency. Vainly did the government urge delay till the course of the English Houses should be determined; vainly did Fitzgibbon threaten a union as the consequence of a divergence of opinion in the two Parliaments, and vainly did he insist that the appointment of the prince should be with limitations, and argue that a collision might be serious if each country were to choose a different regent. The king's recovery was not contemplated. Fitzgibbon and the government were believed to be a falling house. The rats of placemen rushed from it and filled the ranks of the opposition. The motion was carried without a division. The House of Lords, led by the Duke of Leinster, Lord Charlemont, and Lord Pery, followed the example of the Commons, forty-five out of seventy-one peers voting for the address. When the address was carried up to the viceroy, Lord Buckingham, he refused to transmit it to England; and the Houses then appointed a deputation to cross the Channel and present it to the prince in person.

To the confusion of the opposition, the king got well, and then the government turned upon them, threatening to make every deserter "the victim of his vote" by prompt dismissal from office. Fifty-five of the opposition, among whom were seventeen peers, endeavored to protect themselves by entering into a mutual engagement with each other not to accept any office or pension of which any of the party should be deprived, and to withhold their support from the government. The government determined that "the aristocracy, which had been broken once before under his majesty's direction, and had combined again against English authority, must be broken again." Lord Townshend had spent half a million in the accomplishment of this honorable undertaking, and Fitzgibbon shamefully threatened a repetition of the process. Rewards and punishments were dealt out with an unsparing hand. The combination of fifty-five was broken up. Temptation was too great for some, though many held by their determination. Fifteen unfaithful placemen were summarily dismissed from office or lost their pensions. The faithful were rewarded with promotion. Some were bought back with steps in the peerage, or fresh offices of emolument. The wholesale corruption was appalling. To swell the number of the rewards at their disposal, the government revived dormant employments, raised salaries, and increased commissionerships and seats at the revenue board. They even divided the lucrative office of weighmaster of butter at Cork into three sections, the duties of which were performed by deputies at a salary of £200 a year, and gave them to three of their supporters. The pension list, which amounted to £100,000 a year, was augmented by the addition of a further annual sum of £13,040, given in annuities of various sums to purchased peers or members of the Commons and their wives. Three earls became marquesses; four viscounts became earls; two barons became viscounts; and seven commoners, including Fitzgibbon, who was appointed lord chancellor, were raised to the lowest grade in the peerage. George Ponsonby asserted that the crown now held in its pay 110 placemen, and that one eighth of the gross revenue of the country was divided among members of Parliament.

CHAPTER X.

LOCAL RIOTS AND AGRARIAN DISTURBANCES. A.D. 1784–1790.

MEANWHILE the country was in a very disturbed state, both in the north and in the south. In the north a religious war had broken out between the Protestants and the Roman Catholics. Originating in a quarrel between two Presbyterian peasants, one of whom was joined by a Roman Catholic, the feud grew into a village brawl, which rapidly spread in the surrounding country until the counties of Armagh and Louth were divided into two contending camps. Both parties were composed of the lowest and most brutal of the peasantry. They met and fought, and lives were lost. The Protestants were more numerous and better armed. By law the Roman Catholics were not entitled to possess arms, and the Protestants took upon themselves to make domiciliary visits to their houses to search for arms in the early hours of the morning, and hence obtained the name of "Peep-o'-day Boys." The Roman Catholics associated themselves for self-protection, and went by the name of "Defenders." So serious were the riots that bodies of volunteers were revived for the purpose of keeping order; but this only made matters worse, as they simply took the side of the Protestant combatants, and occupied themselves in disarming the Defenders; while the Protestant magistracy showed a corresponding partiality. A party of Roman Catholic ruffians retaliated by committing a brutal outrage on an unoffending Protestant schoolmaster, and the feeling of the two parties rapidly grew into one of intense exasperation.

In the south the Whiteboys had again appeared in Munster under the name of "Rightboys;" an invisible Captain Right being the nominal head-centre, like Ever Joyce and Captain Dwyer. The disorders were repetitions of what had gone before, and arose from the same causes. Government, instead of removing the mischief which culminated in the agrarian outrages of 1761, crushed out the flames of lawlessness by coercion, and left the disease to grow and spread in silence until a fresh outbreak was inevitable. The condition of the tenantry in Munster was very miserable. The rent of potato ground had risen to £6 an acre, which was paid in labor at the rate of 6d. a day. There was hardly an estate which was not let at a rack-rent, or even above its value. Even Fitzgibbon admitted in the House of Commons that "it was impossible for human wretchedness to exceed that of the miserable tenantry of that province;" that "they were ground to powder by relentless landlords;" that "they had not food and raiment for themselves, but the landlord grasped the whole;" and that "they lived in a more abject state of poverty than human nature could be supposed able to bear."

Over and above the exactions of the landlords, the Church demanded tithe. The pasture-land was exempted;* only the cultivable land bore the burden. The wretched cottier's acre of potato ground had, in addition to the rent, hearth-money, smoke-money, and dues to the Roman Catholic priest, to pay from 12s. to 20s. to the rector for tithe. The beneficed clergy, with dwindling flocks, lived away, absentee-fashion, and drew their tithe-tribute as the absentee landlord drew his rack-rent; and like him, to save the difficulty and risk of gathering it, farmed their tithes to a middleman, or collected it through the agency of a needy and unscrupulous tithe-proctor, who paid over to his employer two thirds or three quarters of the sum collected, and made his profits by extracting the last penny from the unfortunate peasant. When the peasant could not pay, he took his bond, and charged him interest; and when the bond fell due he took his debtor's labor for nothing, and reduced him to little better than a slave.

It was not surprising that the down-trodden wretches sought to help themselves by acts of violence. The followers of Captain Right attended the Roman Catholic chapels, and swore the members of the congregations to pay no greater amount

---

* Resolution of the House of Commons, 1735: 8 Geo. II.

of tithe than Captain Right allowed. They even went so far as to prescribe the limit to the dues which should be paid to the Roman Catholic parish priests. Those who refused the oath lost their ears, and were buried in a pit full of thorns. Contributions were levied to support the movement, and sentence went forth against the tithe-proctors. Some were murdered; some were "carded;" others sought safety in flight. Nor were the proctors the only victims. The bishops were absentees, so were the incumbents of parishes; but the unfortunate, ill-paid, hard-working curate, whom the absentee incumbent put in on a wretched pittance of £40 or £50 a year, to perform the duties he had himself deserted, was on the spot to bear all the odium for which his superiors were responsible. These unoffending men were attacked by the Rightboys, and driven out of their homes. Their wives and children endured the same fate. Many fled to the towns; the few who remained lived under military protection.

Fitzgibbon's remedy was a terrific Coercion Bill; Grattan's, a motion for a committee to inquire into the system of collecting tithes, with a plan for commuting the tithes for an annual charge calculated upon an average of years. The former passed into law,* and, with the assistance of General Luttrel and the army, the first tithe war was trampled out in its infancy. "Laws of coercion," said Grattan, " perhaps necessary, certainly severe, you have already put forth. But your great engine of power you have hitherto kept back—the engine which, armed with physical and moral blessing, comes forth and overlays mankind by services — *the engine of redress.*" That engine was still to be kept back. Grattan's motion was lost by 121 to 49.

---

* 27, 28 Geo. III. c. 15.

CHAPTER XI.

THE AGITATION FOR REFORM AND ROMAN CATHOLIC EMANCIPATION. A.D. 1790-1792.

LORD BUCKINGHAM'S success in reducing the Parliament to obedience was complete. But the system of corruption was so notorious and his unpopularity so marked that the government thought it best to recall him; and, in order to escape the demonstration of popular hatred which was prepared for his final departure, he secretly slipped away to a friend's house at Blackrock, and thence sailed for England.

He was succeeded on January 5, 1790, by Lord Westmoreland; but, though the viceroy was changed, the system was unaltered. The government was unassailable. All the assaults of the opposition were met by an unbroken phalanx of 140 on the government benches. A Pension Bill and a Place Bill— that is, bills to prohibit revenue officials and holders of pensions or places from sitting in Parliament—a Barren Lands Bill, a Responsibility Bill for the appointment of persons responsible to Parliament for the disbursement of public moneys, were in vain brought in and supported by Forbes, George Ponsonby, Curran, and Grattan. The Castle sat calmly on its money-bags, with the fate of five-score hirelings in its hand. Some of the pensions were large sums paid to members of the royal family, and certain peers, and others of the deserving poor. The Dukes of Gloucester and Cumberland, for instance, each had pensions of £3000. The Princess Amalie had £1000, and the Princess Augusta £5000. Ferdinand, Duke of Brunswick, pocketed £5200; the representatives of the Countess of Yarmouth, £4000; the executors of Lords Grantham and Shannon, £2000 respectively. Lord Pery had secured £3000, and Lord Mayo £1033. The Countess of Bellamount was the happy recipient of £1500; "Single Speech" Hamilton, of £2500;

Mr. Secretary Orde, of £1700. Only Lord Rodney and the representatives of Lord Hawke received £2000 as a reward of real merit.

But the bulk of the pension list was made up of small annuities, all *terminable at the king's pleasure*, and ranging from £300 to £50 each, to wives, daughters, nieces, sisters, brothers, sons, friends, dependants, of members of either the Upper or the Lower House. A vote given against the Castle, and the pensioner's living was gone: perhaps five old maiden sisters, receiving £50 apiece, were reduced to beggary; or a son or daughter comfortably provided for out of the revenue found his or her income suddenly straitened—so sharply could the screw be put on by the chief secretary. The pension list increased by leaps and bounds: in 1784 it amounted to £86,176; in 1786, to £95,154; in 1788, to £97,689; in 1790, to £100,800. "The system was a conspiracy," said Grattan, "against the laws of the land, and had established, instead of a limited monarchy, a corrupt despotism."

It was clear to every one who had hopes of the future of the Irish Parliament that the only way to save it was to introduce a strong measure of reform—not the meagre scheme of Flood and the Bishop of Derry, but a broad measure, which would give the people of Ireland a real voice in the elections.

Grattan, the Duke of Leinster, and Lord Charlemont had instituted the "Whig Club," and kept up a correspondence with the English Whig party. Their avowed object was to purge the Augean stable on College Green, and to withstand any attempt to carry a union. The bulk of the people—more even than their political leaders—looked earnestly to reform as an urgent necessity. The Irish, like the other nations of Europe, but to a far greater degree, were at this time agitated by the momentous events which were taking place in France. They had seen a bankrupt and effete autocracy compelled to call its misgoverned subjects to its assistance. They had seen an enthusiastic national assembly come to the rescue, and take the government into its own hands; and the king, but lately an absolute monarch, obliged to make the best of his position and consent to govern by the will of the people. The highest hopes for France were entertained by Fox and the English Whigs, who were ardent sympathizers in her nascent efforts.

In Ireland, where a bloodless revolution had already taken place, the progress of the French constitutional struggle was followed with breathless interest. The Northern Whig Club— among whom were Lord Charlemont, Lord Moira, Lord de Clifford, and Robert Stewart, better known as Lord Castlereagh, who had begun his political career as a burning patriot, and had defeated the Castle candidate in the last Down election— celebrated the 14th of July, the anniversary of the destruction of the Bastile, with processions, reviews, and a banquet, where the toasts drunk were "The Revolution," "The National Assembly of France," and "The Rights of Man." But the new ideas launched by the French revolution had penetrated further than the leaders of the opposition. They were canvassed by the people, by the Dublin traders, and the Belfast manufacturers, and especially by the younger members of the Irish bar. They were eagerly seized upon by the remnant of the Ulster volunteer corps, and the political clubs which had risen from their ashes. The steady sympathy exhibited for the United States by the Presbyterian population had led to the growth of republican ideas in the manufacturing towns of the north. Belfast was full of advanced politicians; the democratic spirit was rapidly spreading to Newry and Downpatrick; and associations were formed with the express object of promoting reform and the extending of the franchise to the whole Roman Catholic population.

There had for some years been a revived Roman Catholic Committee sitting in Dublin, whose object it was to obtain the repeal of the penal laws. It represented two interests: the aristocratic Roman Catholic families, such as the Fingals, the Kenmares, the Gormanstons, with the Roman Catholic hierarchy; and the Roman Catholic trading classes, whose leaders were John Keogh, Edmund Byrne, Richard McCormack, and John Sweetman. The growing feeling of toleration had enabled Mr. Gardiner, in 1782, to pass his two bills for the relief of Roman Catholics: the first of which enabled them, on taking the oath of allegiance, to purchase, inherit, and dispose of land,

and incorporeal hereditaments, with the exception of advowsons, manors, and boroughs; it also permitted them to reside in Limerick city and the town of Galway.* The second allowed Popish schoolmasters "to teach school," and repealed the obnoxious clauses relating to the guardianship of children.† There was an increasing public opinion that further relaxation might reasonably be made in the penal code, though this indeed was counterbalanced by the most fanatical opposition from the Protestant ascendency party.

Pitt, who had repealed the most oppressive of the English penal laws, was inclined to toleration; the more so, that among the Roman Catholics themselves the aristocratic and the democratic elements were rapidly diverging, and the latter were showing signs of entertaining the more advanced ideas which had been imported from France. The point of difference was the elective franchise, which the aristocratic party were content to forego. A struggle ensued in the Roman Catholic Committee, which resulted in the victory of the advanced party by a majority of six to one, and the secession of sixty-eight of the minority from the committee itself. This action on the part of the minority was believed to have been taken at the instigation of the government, which held out to them the prospect of a partial repeal of the remaining penal laws. The support of the moderate Roman Catholics was to be purchased by concessions, and it was hoped that, after conciliating them and buying the House of Commons, the growing democratic party might be easily disposed of.

Theobald Wolfe Tone was a young barrister of considerable ability. By his own account of himself he had always been incurably idle—never settling to any occupation. After wasting his time at the university, he married a young lady, whose parents were well off, but who did not altogether seem to have approved of the match. He lived with her for a year, and then, leaving her with his father, went over to England to study law at the Temple. He spent two years there without opening a book; and, being without means, would, but for a mere acci-

---

* 21, 22 Geo. III. c. 24. † Ib. c. 62.

dent, have run away to India to try his fortune there. In 1788, however, he returned to Dublin and rejoined his wife. He was called to the bar and made a fair start, but was too lazy to persevere. He then took up politics, and conceived the idea of uniting the Roman Catholic interest with the democratic reformers of the north. He accordingly wrote a pamphlet embodying this scheme, went to Belfast, and started an association which he called the "Society of the United Irishmen."

Tone's next step was to plant a branch of the society at Dublin. Keogh, who had read his pamphlet, was bitten with the idea, and adopted his suggestions. The Dublin branch was formed under the auspices of the reconstructed Roman Catholic Committee. James Napper Tandy, a Protestant Dublin trader of very advanced opinions, an old volunteer, and a member of the Dublin Common Council, who had recently dealt the government a blow by securing the defeat of the Castle candidate for lord mayor, was appointed secretary; and the Hon. Mr. Simon Butler, a brother of Lord Mountgarret, and a member of the bar, was the first chairman.

The cause of the Roman Catholics had always been steadily advocated by Edmund Burke. Burke hated republicanism; he viewed with dislike the alliance of the Roman Catholics with the northern Radicals. He had taken a fanatically violent line against the French reformers; in consequence of which he had quarrelled with Fox, and was willing to support the government. The government, in their turn, were inclined to accept his views upon the Roman Catholic question. The Roman Catholic Committee, in order to disarm all suspicion of allying itself with Republicanism, appointed Burke's son Richard to be their agent. Keogh had been over to England and had had an interview with Pitt in September; and it was concerted by Burke and Dundas, secretary of state and a cabinet minister, that Sir Hercules Langrishe, one of the government supporters in the Irish Commons, should bring in a Roman Catholic Relief Bill at the commencement of the ensuing session.

This was accordingly done in January, 1792, and another instalment of long-delayed justice was dealt out to the Roman

Catholics. The substance of the measure* was to open to them both branches of the legal profession; to permit them to keep schools; to permit barristers and attorneys to have Roman Catholic wives, and to allow Roman Catholic solicitors to educate their children in their own faith. It also provided for the repeal of the laws prohibiting the intermarriage of Roman Catholics with Protestants, so long as the ceremony was performed by a clergyman of the Established Church; and for the binding of apprentices to a Roman Catholic tradesman or craftsman without limit to their number.

Petitions were addressed to the House, both by the Roman Catholic Committee and by the Protestants of Belfast, in favor of conferring a £20 franchise upon the Roman Catholics in counties. But the petitions were both refused after a stormy debate. The government bill was warmly supported by Grattan and the opposition, and was passed into law by an unwilling House in deference to the policy of the English cabinet.

---

32 Geo. III. c. 21.

CHAPTER XII.

PARTIAL EMANCIPATION OF THE ROMAN CATHOLICS.
A.D. 1792–1793.

The United Irishmen were meanwhile growing in importance. Branches were pushed into different parts of Ulster, and affiliated to the parent society. In this way the nucleus of an extensive organization was set on foot. Though Tone and many of his friends were theoretically in their hearts republicans, the aim of the society at this time was unobjectionable, and extended no further than a thorough reform in the House of Commons, based on the extension of the franchise to all citizens. The main planks in their reform platform were equal electoral districts, household suffrage, vote by ballot, payment of members, and annual Parliaments. The test of admission to the society was as follows: "I, A. B., in the presence of God, do pledge myself to my country that I will use all my abilities and influence in the attainment of an impartial and adequate representation of the Irish nation in Parliament; and, as a means of absolute and immediate necessity in the establishment of this chief good for Ireland, I will endeavor as much as lies in my ability to forward a brotherhood of affection, an identity of interests, a communion of rights, and a union of power among Irishmen of all religious persuasions, without which every reform in Parliament must be partial, not national, inadequate to the wants, delusive to the wishes, and insufficient for the freedom and happiness of the country."

Tone, though the originator of the movement, had hitherto not had much personal influence in the society; but after the failure of the petition of the Roman Catholic Committee, Keogh took him up and made him assistant secretary to the committee, with a salary of £200 a year—a very important addition to his means, which were extremely slender. From that time he became an accredited agent, both of the Roman Catholics and of his friends at Belfast; and the ranks of the United Irishmen were considerably reinforced from the Roman Catholic body.

Keogh, under the inspiration of the opposition leaders, started a plan, in imitation of the course pursued by the volunteers, of summoning a convention of Roman Catholics at Dublin, to give public expression to their wishes. The Ascendency party were greatly agitated by this new move. The grand juries at the ensuing assizes and the close corporations published furious addresses against the proposed convention and its authors. The magistrates denounced it from the bench. Even the Roman Catholic hierarchy, who were dependent on the government for toleration, at first were ranged in opposition. Tone obtained counsel's opinion that the convention would not be illegal, and published it in the newspapers and by handbills. The bishops were either won over or induced to remain neutral. Public meetings were held by both parties; manifestoes and counter-manifestoes were issued; and the United Irishmen's organ, *The Northern Star*, was started, at the cost of £3000, to advocate the principles of the society.

The convention met in Taylor's Hall, in Back Lane, Dublin, on December 2, 1792. Many of the sixty-eight seceders had rejoined the committee; and a petition was drawn up professing the loyalty of the king's Roman Catholic subjects, and praying that they might be restored to the rights and privileges of the Constitution. Five delegates were chosen to present it to the king—Sir Thomas French, and Messrs. Byrne, Keogh, Bellew, and Devereux.

George III. had by this time become thoroughly alarmed at the progress of the French Revolution. Louis, after having endeavored to escape from France, had been captured by his own subjects and imprisoned in the Temple. The Austrians and Prussians had unjustifiably interfered in the quarrel, and had undertaken his restoration by force of arms. The Duke of Brunswick's threat to pillage Paris had driven the people mad and led to the "September massacres." All France had risen as one man to repel the German invader. Brunswick's failure to force the passes at Valmy, and subsequent retreat, had grievously disappointed the hopes of those who had made sure of a triumphal march to Paris; and then had followed Dumouriez's brilliant victory at Jemappes, which had laid all Belgium at the mercy of France. The growing war-spirit in England was rapidly forcing Pitt into antagonism with the French government. The frantic dread of the rising democracy was driving England into an unreasoning panic. And the Tory party and the weak-kneed Whigs, lashed up by Burke's philippics, could see safety in nothing short of the forcible suppression of French republicanism.

A war with revolutionary France, who boasted that she was prepared to assist all oppressed nations to regain their liberty, could not fail to be a source of anxiety, so long as there was a discontented Ireland on England's flank. England's trouble with America had been Ireland's opportunity twelve years since; a French war might prove the same. The Irish were greatly excited; the spread of French principles in Dublin and Belfast, and the open sympathy shown for the Revolution, were a terror to the king and the government; and they clutched at the policy of winning the support of the Roman Catholics, whose faith was being cruelly persecuted by the Jacobins, by flinging the penal code overboard piece by piece. For the present the Roman Catholics were to be conciliated—the Protestant ascendency must shift for itself. But Pitt saw a way to restore the old balance; Roman Catholic Ireland was to be swamped by Protestant England, and a union to be carried at any cost. The emancipation of the Roman Catholics would force the hand of the independent Protestants.

On January 2, 1793, the five delegates were presented to his majesty by Dundas; and their petition was graciously accepted. Dundas afterwards had an interview with them, in which they told him that they looked not only for the franchise, but for total emancipation; that is, admission to the corporations and to seats in Parliament. Dundas expressed himself as convinced of the necessity of emancipation, informed them that their claims should be recommended to Parliament in the next king's speech, and said that he looked to them to support order in return. They left under the belief that the government was willing to abolish all the religious disabilities of his majesty's Roman Catholic subjects. The success of the mission appeared to be complete. The thanks of the Roman Catholic Committee were voted to Tone, together with the more substantial recognition of his services in the shape of a gold medal of the value of thirty guineas, and the round sum of £1500. A resolution was also carried that a sum of £2000 should be applied to the erection of a statue to the king, " as a monument of their gratitude for the important privileges which they had obtained from Parliament through his paternal recommendation."

Parliament assembled on January 10, 1793. The viceroy, in the speech from the throne, recommended the situation of the Roman Catholic subjects of his majesty to the attention of Parliament; and Mr. Secretary Hobart, on the 18th, brought in a bill for their further relief. The proposed measure gave to all who were 40s. freeholders in the counties and the few open cities and boroughs the right of voting for members of Parliament, and it also gave them the municipal franchise in the cities and corporate towns. It admitted them to the University of Dublin, and enabled them, under certain restrictions, to fill almost all civil and military offices, including those of grandjuryman and justice of the peace. It permitted all Roman Catholics possessed of freehold property to the amount of £100 per annum, and personal property to the amount of £1000 per annum, to bear arms, and empowered them to found colleges * to be affiliated to Dublin University, provided they should not be exclusively Roman Catholic.

It was, however, provided that no person should have the benefit of the act who did not take and subscribe the revised

---

* In consequence of the provisions of the penal code, the Roman Catholic clergy were accustomed to resort to the Continent for their education. The French Revolution had put a stop to this practice; and the government were desirous of cutting off all communication with revolutionary France. Accordingly, in 1795, by the 35th Geo. III. c. 21, Maynooth College was founded " for the education exclusively of persons professing the Roman Catholic religion," and an annual sum of £8000 was granted for its support out of the Consolidated Fund.

Oath of Allegiance,* which denied the Pope's temporal jurisdiction; and comprehended a declaration denying his infallibility and his power to absolve unconditionally.

The dismay of the Protestant ascendency party at the course adopted by the government was complete. Lord Farnham and the Archbishop of Cashel were utterly disconcerted; Dr. Dugenan raved with frantic indignation. Ogle protested that even an act of Union would be preferable to such a bill; and Fitzgibbon, now Lord Clare, who had not been consulted by the ministers, spoke with bitter hostility against the proposed measure. The government was, of course, supported by the opposition; and the bill passed both Houses, and received the royal assent on April 9.†

Yet another portion of the pitiless penal code had become a thing of the past. But, when the government gave relief with one hand, it launched a Coercion Bill with the other. The same Parliament which had so grudgingly passed the Roman Catholic Relief Bill hastened cheerfully to arm the Castle with three Coercion Acts: the Convention Act,‡ to prohibit "unlawful assemblies," which was intended to enable the government to prevent the recurrence of such an event as the "Back Lane Parliament;" the Gunpowder Act,§ imposing severe penalties on the importation and transporting of munitions of war, and giving magistrates unlimited powers of search; and an act to raise sixteen thousand militia, and to increase the regular army from twelve thousand to seventeen thousand men. ‖

The session was not unfruitful in other directions. The government gave way upon some other long-demanded reforms. Grattan's Barren Land Bill was passed, ¶ exempting from tithes for seven years all waste land which should be reclaimed. Mr. Forbes's continued efforts to carry a Pension and Place Bill were rewarded with a limited amount of success. The hereditary revenue was exchanged for a civil list of £145,000 a year for the payment of salaries, and other charges of the civil establishment. The pension list was to be provided for by an

---

* 13, 14 Geo. III. c. 35.   † 33 Geo. III. c. 21.   ‡ Ib. c. 29.
§ Ib. c. 2.   ‖ Ib. c. 22.   ¶ Ib. c. 25.

annual grant, until it should be reduced by deaths to the amount of £80,000. At this figure it was then to stand limited, and the sum of £80,000 transferred to the civil list, making it in the whole £225,000, out of which the pensions would thereafter be defrayed. In future no pension was to be given of more than £1200 a year, except to one of the royal family, or on an address by either of the Houses of Parliament. The fund for secret service was limited to £5000 a year, unless the chief secretary required it "for the purpose of detecting, preventing, or defeating treasonable or other dangerous conspiracies against the State," in which case the expenditure was to be unlimited.*

An act was also passed declaring that persons holding places of profit under the crown created after the passing of the act, or holding pensions, or having wives who held pensions, should be incapable of sitting in the next House of Commons, exceptions only being made in favor of commissioners of the treasury and their secretaries.† These three last-mentioned acts were sops thrown to the opposition by the English cabinet. Where the corrupt Irish Commons were left to take their own course, all idea of concession was thrown to the winds. William Ponsonby's two motions for reform were summarily rejected by majorities of two to one.

---

* 33 Geo. III. c. 34. † Ib. c. 41.

CHAPTER XIII.

PROSECUTIONS. A.D. 1792-1794.

THE plea upon which the government based their demand for coercion bills was the continued state of disturbance prevailing in many parts of the country. This unfortunate condition of things was due to the fanatical antagonism of the Defenders and the Peep-o'-day Boys, or Wreckers. The object of the Protestant faction was to expel from the country those Roman Catholics who were scattered about among the Protestants of the north, and to occupy their holdings. Both parties, owing to the negligent indifference of the local magistrates, had greatly increased in numbers. The Defenders especially had become extremely formidable; so that they had begun to turn the tables upon the Wreckers, and were the terror of the country-side. They retaliated fiercely on their persecutors, extending their operations to the attacking of country-houses, for the purpose of obtaining arms. Roving bands appeared in Meath and Cavan, and fought with the Protestant population settled there. They spread through all the midland counties, parties springing up right and left, plundering houses of arms, and committing other enormities. In the south and west the Rightboys reappeared under the name of Defenders, with the old system of swearing the people not to pay tithes and hearth-money. Scattered parties of soldiery were despatched by the government to restore order. In many cases the Defenders ventured to resist, and considerable loss of life ensued. A secret committee of the House of Lords, consisting of Lord Clare and eight other peers, sat to inquire into the causes of the disturbances, and published a report in which they endeavored to show that the Defenders were encouraged by the respectable Roman Catholic population, and insinuated that both the one and the other were disaffected and imbued with the spirit of French republicanism. Defenderism, however, does not appear to have been a political movement. It was a lawless outbreak of the lowest and most ignorant of the peasantry, induced by miserable poverty and harsh treatment, while the better class of the Roman Catholics was fairly content with the repeal of the penal laws; and the Roman Catholic Convention was dissolved.

Tone and the United Irishmen, however, were determined to continue the agitation, and to rest satisfied with nothing short of parliamentary reform and the admission of the Roman Catholics to seats in Parliament. The antagonism between the Defenders and the Peep-o'-day Boys was a great trouble to Tone, whose plan had been to unite Protestant with Roman Catholic in one common cause. He endeavored to induce them to accept the teaching of the United Irishmen, but only with the result that many of the Defenders joined that society, and so connected it with the party of violence. Napper Tandy, who was engaged in the attempt to bridge over the gulf between the two factions, was detected by the government in correspondence with the Defenders at Castle Bellingham, and, receiving timely warning of his intended arrest, escaped to America.

The United Men had grown rapidly in boldness and activity. They were constantly employed in distributing handbills and circulars of a semi-seditious character. They affected the French fashion of calling each other "citizen;" though Tone told them that they might as well try to make themselves "peers and noblemen by calling each other 'my lord.'" The government determined to take strong measures with the society. Mr. Simon Butler, their chairman, and Mr. Oliver Bond, a Dublin merchant, had published an address to the people of Dublin, condemning the conduct of the secret committee of the House of Lords in examining witnesses upon oath as to their own conduct and opinions. They were summoned before the committee and sentenced, without trial, to six months' imprisonment, and to pay a fine of £500. Dr. Reynolds, who had been called before the secret committee as a witness, was committed to jail for refusing to answer some questions which were put to him. Hamilton Rowan, a gentleman of family and fortune in the north of Ireland, and the secretary of the United Irishmen, had, two years before (in 1792), published a bombastic and rather violent address to the volunteers, written by Dr. Drennan, calling them to arms for the preservation of the liberties of the people. He was prosecuted for libel, and sentenced to two years' imprisonment, and to pay a fine of £500.

But a more subtle stroke was in preparation. An English clergyman named Jackson, who had resided some years in France, had formed a friendship with an Irish exile named Madget, who held an appointment in the French Foreign Office. England and France had now been at war some twelve months. The French government was anxiously canvassing the possibility of making a successful descent on the Irish coast. They had received exaggerated reports of the Defender disturbances, and believed that a general rising was imminent. Jackson was accordingly commissioned to go over and sound the popular leaders. He arrived in London, and incautiously confided his secret to an attorney of the name of Cockayne, who at once communicated the whole story to Pitt. Instead of dealing with Jackson's treason at once, Pitt took the tortuous course of permitting him to proceed to Dublin, and sending Cockayne with him as a spy, with the view of entrapping those with whom Jackson should be found to communicate in Ireland. Jackson succeeded, through Mr. McNally, a barrister in the pay of the government, in obtaining introductions to Tone, Simon Butler, and others of the leaders of the United Irishmen, and also to Hamilton Rowan, who was then in Newgate. Cockayne was always at Jackson's elbow, and Tone appears to have at first looked upon the latter as a government spy, but subsequently talked with him openly about the prospects of a French alliance, and drew up, for his instruction, a paper upon the condition of Ireland, of which Rowan made a copy while he was in prison, for Jackson's use. Then, finding that Jackson was a vain and indiscreet person, Tone and his friends dropped all communication with him; and the government, finding nothing more was to be gained by leaving Jackson at liberty, arrested him

14*

on a charge of treason. Rowan, on hearing of his apprehension, and fearing that his having copied Tone's document might be used to involve him in the charge, managed to escape from Newgate and fled to America. He was proclaimed as a traitor and outlawed, though no further offence than the one for which he had been convicted was ever proved against him. Tone, boldly admitting that he was the author of the paper found in Jackson's possession, remained in Dublin. His friends, Mr. Marcus Beresford (a nephew of Lord Clare), Mr. George Knox, and Wolfe, the solicitor-general, used their influence to deter a crown prosecution; and no steps were taken against him, upon the understanding that he would leave the country as soon as he could arrange his private affairs. He sailed for America, with his wife and children, about a twelvemonth later. Shortly after Jackson's arrest, having now successfully connected the United Irishmen with a treasonable design, the government struck another blow at the society. Taylor's Hall, their place of meeting, was broken into by the sheriffs and a body of constables, and all their papers seized.

CHAPTER XIV.
BLIGHTED HOPES. A.D. 1794, 1795.

IN the summer of 1794, the moderate Whigs in England, alarmed at the violent course of the Jacobin oligarchy, which had usurped the control of the French Convention, deserted the opposition benches and formed a coalition with Pitt. Among the number were the Duke of Portland, Lord Spencer, Lord Fitzwilliam, Edmund Burke, and William Wyndham. The price of their adhesion on the question of the French war was the adoption of Burke's policy on the Roman Catholic question in Ireland. Burke and Fitzwilliam were for total emancipation of the Roman Catholics: liberty to sit in Parliament; liberty to enter the corporations; liberty to bear arms. It was upon their exclusion from these privileges that the Protestant ascendency had rested. It had been shored up by artificial means for a hundred years. Burke believed that the time had come when it could run alone, and that the admission of the Roman Catholics to equal rights with the Protestants would unite the Irish into one nation, which would thenceforth become a source of strength to England instead of being a thorn in her side.

This was not the opinion of the Ascendency party, who were violently opposed to concession in any shape. Grattan and the opposition held with Burke. Pitt was half convinced, and was willing to try the experiment; as, in the event of failure, he calculated on carrying out his darling scheme of the union.

In August, Grattan, George and William Ponsonby, and Sir John Parnell, the chancellor of the exchequer, came over to England to arrange matters with Pitt. Pitt was undecided for many weeks. The difficulty was about the dismissal of Lord Clare, a due provision for Lord Westmoreland, and the powers to be allowed to the new viceroy. It was eventually decided that Lord Westmoreland should be recalled if an office of fitting dignity could be found for him in England, and Lord Fitzwilliam appointed lord-lieutenant in his place. Pitt clung to Lord Clare, but the old system was to be changed, and coercion laid aside. As to the question of emancipation, Pitt told Grattan that "it would not be brought on as a government measure; but if government were pressed, they would yield."

The Duke of Portland was appointed a third secretary of state, with special care for Irish affairs. He accepted office, according to what he told Mr. Burke, on the express terms "that the administration of Ireland was left wholly to him." Lord Fitzwilliam, according to the same authority, was under a similar belief as to his own powers. He himself says, in his letter to Lord Carlisle, that "he would never have taken office unless the Roman Catholics were to be relieved from every disqualification." He was not "to be the instrument of the junto," as Burke denominated the clique of Castle officials who battened on the Irish Establishment; "the set of men in Ireland who, by their innumerable corruptions, frauds, oppressions, and follies, were opening the back door to Jacobinism to rush in and take us in the rear;" the men who were the direct successors of the corrupt Protestant oligarchy who misgoverned and plundered Ireland in the reign of James I. There was to be a complete change of men and measures, and the government was to be intrusted to the leaders of the Irish opposition.

Fitzwilliam reached Dublin on January 4, 1795. There was general rejoicing, and he was received with the utmost enthusiasm. Addresses and petitions poured in from the Roman Catholics from every part of Ireland. "Not to grant cheerfully," wrote the new viceroy to the Duke of Portland, "all the Catholics wish will not only be exceedingly impolitic, but perhaps dangerous. In doing this no time is to be lost. The disaffection among the lower orders is universal; though the violences now committing are not from political causes, but the outrages of banditti, they are fostered by that cause. The higher orders are firmly to be relied on. The wealthy of the second class hardly less so, because they are fearful of their property. Yet the latter, at least, have shown no forwardness to check these outrages. And this can only arise from there being something left which rankles in their bosom."

Fitzwilliam's first act was to break up "the junto." John Beresford, the chief commissioner of customs, who had filled the civil establishment with his friends and relations, was at once compelled to retire on his full official income. So was Edward Cooke, the under-secretary of state in the civil department, with a pension of £1200 a year. The attorney-general, Wolfe, and the solicitor-general, Toler, were told that they would have to make room for George Ponsonby and Curran, Wolfe being consoled with a peerage, and Toler otherwise provided for. Grattan still held his retainer from the people. He refused office, but gave his general support to the ministry.

Some rumblings of the coming storm were already heard. Beresford had hurried over to England and raised a howl over his dismissal. Pitt, on February 9, intimated his displeasure at the viceroy's precipitancy, and forbade the change of law-officers, though Wolfe's elevation had already been approved by him, and the king's consent to the projected peerage given on the 13th of January. Still Fitzwilliam had no suspicion that all was not right. The cabinet was constantly informed of every step which was taken, and no hint was thrown out in reply that his conduct was not entirely approved of.

On February 12, Grattan, by arrangement with the viceroy, moved for leave to bring in a bill for the admission of Roman Catholics to Parliament. Meanwhile, there was a factor to be considered on which Pitt and Dundas had not fully reckoned. George III. had not hitherto grasped the importance of the change of policy. Fitzwilliam's dismissals had opened his eyes. Beresford had followed the king to Weymouth, and had had a private audience with him, in which he worked upon his fears for the safety of the Protestant religion. On February 6 he sent Pitt a memorandum, after the receipt of which there was no course open to the cabinet but to resign or reverse all that they had initiated. The king declared that he had heard of the Duke of Portland's "total change of the principles of government" with "the greatest astonishment." He spoke of his "surprise at the idea of admitting Roman Catholics to vote in Parliament." He feared "religion was but little attended to by persons of rank, and that the word *toleration* or rather *indifference* to that sacred subject has been too much admitted by them." "Yet the bulk of the nation had not been spoiled by foreign travel and manners," and he is certain that "it would be safer even to change the new ministry in Ireland if its continuance depends on the success of this proposal." Pitt had but recently said, in reference to emancipation, "that he would not risk a rebellion in Ireland on such a question." He was fully aware of the critical condition of the country, but he did not venture to remonstrate, when his master was obstinate; and he did not resign. All sorts of excuses were framed for the change of front. Fitzwilliam had misconceived and exceeded his instructions. He had dismissed the servants of the crown without consulting the cabinet. He had omitted to forward to the Duke of Portland the heads of Grattan's proposed bill. Emancipation was never intended. "It led to consequences which could not be contemplated without horror and dismay;" and, lastly, "the king had the right to remove and dismiss whom he pleased."

On February 23, the Duke of Portland wrote to Fitzwilliam, "by the king's command," that he was "authorized to resign." Lord Clare, Foster (the speaker), and the primate were appointed lords justices. Beresford was restored in triumph to the revenue board; and Lord Camden, son of the chief-justice, was despatched to succeed Fitzwilliam, with Mr. Pelham for chief-secretary.

"If the Irish administration," said Sir Lawrence Parsons, in the Irish House of Commons, "has encouraged the Catholics in their expectations without the countenance of the British cabinet, they have much to answer for. If the British cabinet has assented, and afterwards retracted, the demon of darkness could not have done more mischief had he come from hell to throw a firebrand among the people." The language was hardly exaggerated. The mass of Roman Catholics had been led on to believe that the bill on which their highest hopes were concentrated would be carried by the government. The Irish Commons had been led to believe that Lord Fitzwilliam with a changed system would repeal Lord Clare's obnoxious Dublin Police Act,* which, instead of having the effect of promoting order, had simply been a means to the late government for jobbery and waste. A Reform Bill, it was on all hands admitted, would be the necessary corollary to emancipation; and, on the strength of these promises, the House had rejected Parsons's cautious proposal to grant a short Money Bill, and had voted the unprecedented sum of £250,000 for the purposes of his majesty's navy, and an additional forty-one thousand men for home defences. The country felt it had been duped; the cup which had been placed to its lips had been dashed to the ground; and the hopelessness of despair settled down upon the hearts of all those who had fondly believed that a new order of things was about to prevail. Roman Catholics and Dissenters alike deplored the act of the cabinet. The Roman Catholic Committee hurriedly met, and drew up a petition to the king against the recall of Fitzwilliam. Addresses were poured in to the viceroy, the Parliament, even to private individuals who were supposed to be possessed of influence, importuning them to prevent the threatened catastrophe. It was all of no avail. Lord Fitzwilliam left Ireland on March 25. It was a day of general gloom. The shops in Dublin were shut. Business was stopped. The whole city put on mourning. The departing viceroy's carriage was drawn to the water's edge by some of the leading citizens. Lord Camden's arrival was correspondingly ominous. He was sworn in by the lords justices on the 31st. On leaving the Castle, the primate's carriage was stoned. Fitzgibbon's was followed by a threatening mob. Stones were flung, and he with difficulty escaped with a cut on the head from one of the missiles. The mob then turned to attack the houses of Beresford and the speaker, and were only dispersed by the bullets of the military.

---

* 26 Geo. III. c. 24. By the 5 Edw. IV. c. 5, the peace was kept in the "English towns" by constables chosen by the burgesses. A regular system of police for the city of Dublin was introduced by the 17, 18 Geo. III. c. 43.

Grattan's Emancipation Bill was of course doomed. There was a fierce debate, in which Mr. Arthur O'Connor, a nephew of Lord Longueville, made an able maiden speech attacking the government. But the venal crew of Castle placemen changed sides with the change of viceroys; and the bill was thrown out by 155 to 48. All hope, either of Roman Catholic emancipation or of reform, had vanished. Lord Clare and Protestant Ascendency had won the day; and the old coercive system was set upon its legs again.

CHAPTER XV.
NEW DEPARTURES. A.D. 1795.

JACKSON's trial for treason took place in April. The case against him was clear. The wretched Cockayne, in abject terror of assassination, was kept under guard until the trial, and gave conclusive evidence against him. The miserable Jackson, on the final morning of the trial, to anticipate judgment and sentence, and so save his little property for his widow, took arsenic on his way to the court, and died in agonies in the dock. Tone shortly afterwards sailed for America; and passed thence to France, with avowed intentions of enlisting the sympathies of the French Directory.

The United Irishmen had been suppressed; but the more desperate members of that body, now that all legitimate means of carrying out their schemes of reform had failed, reorganized the society as a secret association. The branches were reconstructed and multiplied. Each branch was to consist of twelve members, who chose out of their own number a secretary. Five of such secretaries formed a committee, called "the lower baronial." Ten lower baronials chose each a member to form the "upper baronial committee;" and each upper baronial in like manner sent a delegate to the "district" or "county committee." Two or three delegates from each county committee formed a "provincial committee," and the provincial committees elected five of the number to constitute the "executive committee" or "directory," which formed the apex of the system. In this way a subtle organization was built up, which spread its ramifications through two provinces; and was so constructed that in a short space of time it could be converted, according to its later development, from a civil to a military organization. The secretary of every twelve was their petty officer. The delegate of the lower baronial was a captain of sixty men. The delegate of the upper baronial was colonel of a battalion of six hundred; and so on, until a formidable force was enrolled on paper, numbering, in 1797, nearly 280,000 men. The reconstructed society bound each member by an oath of secrecy; and their avowed object was the wresting of Ireland from English control, and the erection of a republican form of government, if necessary by force; if necessary also, by the help of foreign intervention. The organization of Ulster was completed in May, 1795; but it does not seem to have been extended further till the autumn of 1796, when emissaries were sent to form branches in Leinster. It was not till it was well established in Leinster that the military system was grafted on the civil. Russell, Neilson, Sims, and Keogh were the early reconstructors of the society. Tone was privy to their designs before his departure from Ireland. Thomas Addis Emmet, an eminent barrister; Lewines, an attorney; McCormick, a Dublin manufacturer; and Dr. McNevin, were prominent members. Mr. Oliver Bond became one of the directory. Most of the leaders of the society were Protestants. Many of them were Ulster men.

Tone's plans for uniting the Protestants and the Roman Catholics had not resulted in the reconciliation of the two religious factions in Armagh. There the disgraceful civil strife was unabated. The authorities appeared content to permit the two fanatical parties to fight it out. Whenever they did interfere, strong partiality was shown to the Protestants. In September, 1795, a large body of Defenders came across a number of armed Peep-o'-day Boys at a village called the Diamond, where a regular battle took place, in which the Defenders were driven off with a loss of forty-eight killed and many wounded. The Protestants then set on foot a counter-organization to Defenderism, forming themselves into associations which they called Orange lodges, and demanding an oath of secrecy from all who were enrolled. This organization grew rapidly. It acted promptly and with terrible effect. It declared war against the Defenders, and openly professed as its object the complete expulsion of all Roman Catholics from Ulster. The Roman Catholics were attacked indiscriminately.

Masters were compelled to dismiss Roman Catholic servants, landlords to dismiss Roman Catholic tenants. Decent farmers, quiet peasants, hard-working weavers, quite unconnected with the Defenders, received notices "to go to hell, Connaught would not receive them." Their houses were burned, their furniture broken up, and they and their families driven from their holdings.

Lord Gosford, the governor of Armagh County, in addressing the magistrates at quarter sessions in December, 1795, publicly declared that "neither age nor sex, nor even acknowledged innocence as to any guilt in the late disturbances, is sufficient to excite mercy, much less to afford protection. The only crime which the objects of this ruthless persecution are charged with is simply a profession of the Roman Catholic religion. A lawless banditti have constituted themselves judges of this new species of delinquency, and the sentence they have pronounced is nothing less than a confiscation of all property, and an immediate banishment." The persecution was bad enough as it was; but report magnified it until the awful rumor spread among the people, and was of course believed, that seven thousand persons had been driven from their dwellings. No protection could be obtained from the magistrates, whose sympathies were all with the Orangemen, and of whom many were themselves members of Orange lodges. When at last the soldiers were sent down under General Craddock to restore order, it was found next to impossible to secure the bands of Orange depredators by reason of the timely information given to them of the movements of the troops, which enabled them to elude pursuit.

General Henry Luttrell, Lord Carhampton, had been sent into the west to suppress those of the Defenders who were creating disturbances on that side of the country. The jails were full of persons awaiting their trial. Carhampton preceded the judges of assize with his troops, and, without any form of trial or under any warrant, drew out the prisoners and sent them on board a tender, which sailed along the coast to receive them, and shipped them on board the British fleet for compulsory naval service. The local magistrates followed his example, arresting and transporting without a pretence of legality. Upwards of a thousand persons were the victims of this aristocratic press-gang. When Parliament met in January, 1796, one of the first acts of the government was to bring in an Indemnity Bill for the protection of those "justices of the peace and other officers and persons" who had "apprehended suspected persons without due authority, and had sent suspected persons out of the kingdom for his majesty's service, and had also seized arms, and entered houses, and done divers other acts not justifiable by law." *

Having effectually protected Carhampton and his imitators from the consequences of their high-handed illegality, and deprived all persons of any remedy against them, the next step was to arm the executive with the tremendous powers of a fresh Coercion Act. An Insurrection Bill was brought in. It provided that all persons convicted of administering unlawful oaths for seditious purposes should suffer death as felons; all persons taking such oaths should be transported; that all persons should be compelled to register the arms in their possession under penalties of fine and imprisonment; that magistrates might break into and enter houses to search for arms, might apprehend strangers and examine them on oath, and commit them to the house of correction till they could find sureties for their good behavior. It gave power to the viceroy to proclaim counties which the magistrates reported to him were in a state of disturbance. In a proclaimed county the inhabitants were commanded to keep within doors between sunset and sunrise, under pain of being brought before the justices, who were thereupon empowered, unless they were satisfied with the reasons given for such person being abroad, at once to send him to serve on board the British navy. The magistrates were also empowered to break open houses to see if the occupiers were out-of-doors at unlawful times. Persons who could not prove that they either had means of their own or "industriously followed some lawful trade or employment" were liable to the same penalties." †

---

* 36 Geo. III. c. 6.   † Ib. c. 20.

This "bloody code," as Curran called it, passed into law with little opposition. Even Grattan's effort to obtain the insertion of a special reference to the insurgent Orangemen and a clause to enable the ruined peasants and weavers of Armagh to obtain compensation from the county was summarily rejected. Lord Edward Fitzgerald was the only person who had the courage to vote against the government.

The United Irishmen now rapidly increased in number. The ignorant Defenders of Kildare, Meath, Westmeath, Longford, Leitrim, and Roscommon were swept into their ranks. The persecuted Roman Catholics of Armagh, Down, and Louth, hopeless of protection from the law, turned to this daring association for redress. The disappointed Roman Catholics of the middle classes in Dublin were infected with the same spirit. Even some of the advanced and ardent reformers in Parliament itself, having lost all hope of constitutional reform, took the desperate and fatal resolution of appealing to force and the enemies of England, in the vain expectation of being able to establish a new order of things. "The friends of liberty were gradually, but with a timid step, advancing towards republicanism."

CHAPTER XVI.
FRANCE AT "ENGLAND'S BACK DOOR." A.D. 1796.

Mr. Arthur O'Connor, the member for Philipstown, a borough belonging to his uncle, Lord Longueville; and Lord Edward Fitzgerald, the member for Kildare County, joined the society in the early part of the year 1796. Lord Edward Fitzgerald was brother to the Duke of Leinster. He had served with distinction under Lord Rawdon in the American war, and at the conclusion of peace had entered the Irish Parliament. He had attached himself to the opposition, was an ardent supporter of reform, and a strong opponent of the coercive system in governing Ireland. He was in Paris in the autumn of 1792, before war had broken out between France and England, when he made himself conspicuous at a banquet given by the English in that city to celebrate the triumph of the French arms against the invaders, by adopting the prefix of "citizen," and drinking the toast of " a speedy abolition of all hereditary and feudal distinctions;" in consequence of which the English government dismissed him from the army along with Lord Semple and Captain Gawler, who had also shown sympathy with the French republic. Shortly afterwards he was married at Paris to Paméla, the beautiful daughter of Philip Égalité and Madame de Genlis; and returned to Dublin with his wife, to attend to his parliamentary duties. Frank, open, and chivalrous, of simple habits, unaffected, intensely affectionate, and of a tenderly compassionate disposition, Lord Edward was a man of most lovable nature. The numerous loving letters which remain, written by him to his mother, of whom he was extremely fond, display a touching picture of warm-hearted domestic simplicity—a devoted husband, dividing his time between his wife, his babies, and his flowers. No better proof could be found of the despair which all liberal politicians felt for the future of Ireland than the fact that such a man, with such surroundings, should have convinced himself that it was his paramount duty to plunge into a dark conspiracy for the overthrow of the English government.

The enterprise was not so hopeless as it seems to us now, looking back upon its failure near a century ago. England was engaged in a desperate conflict with France. Her military efforts in the Low Countries had been the reverse of successful; and she could ill spare troops for service in Ireland. Moreover, there was good reason to believe that there was considerable disaffection in the Irish militia, and even in the regular army. If the French had succeeded in landing an expeditionary force upon the island, and a general rising had been effected, the course of history might have been very different. No one knew better than Lord Edward that an undisciplined multitude, without arms, artillery, or camp equipage, though it might be formidable, would eventually be trampled out by the soldiers. A French contingent was the hinge upon which the chances of success hung, and, having once made up his mind to resort to force, he instantly turned his attention to a French alliance.

In May, 1796, he and Arthur O'Connor with Lady Edward passed over to Hamburg, and the two former moved on to Basel, where they entered into communication with the Directory. The latter refused to negotiate with Fitzgerald, "lest the idea should get abroad, from his having married Paméla, that his mission had some reference to the Orleans family;" so, leaving O'Connor to interview General Hoche, Lord Edward rejoined his wife at Hamburg. The indefatigable Tone had come from America to Paris in February. He had managed to introduce himself to Carnot, the ablest of the Directory, and had been for six months working hard to induce the French government to send a strong force to Ireland. Tone's representations, confirmed by O'Connor's authority, satisfied Carnot of the importance of the scheme. Hoche supported it enthusiastically, and undertook to organize and command the expedition. England was threatened with the greatest peril in Ireland since the battle of Kinsale.

On the 16th of December, a French fleet of forty-three sail, consisting of seventeen ships of the line, eleven frigates and corvettes, and fifteen transports, eluded the English squadron, which was cruising off Ushant, and with a fair wind bore down upon the coast of Munster. This formidable fleet carried an army of fifteen thousand picked French troops, with twenty guns, a heavy siege-train, and forty-five thousand stand of arms, to be put into the hands of the expected insurgents. Hoche was in command, and Tone accompanied the expedition with a commission in the French army. The weather was foggy and the fleet parted company, so that but thirty-six sail were in sight on the morning of December 22, off Cape Clear; and of the missing vessels one was the *Fraternité*, with General Hoche on board.

In Ireland all was commotion. The island was utterly defenceless. Not a single ship of war guarded the coast. Cork was the only place in the south which had any fortifications towards the sea. Every town was open on the land side. General Dalrymple, who commanded in the southern province, had but four thousand men under him. With these he was doing his best to cover Cork, and was determined to fight before being compelled to fall back. Troops were being pushed on from Dublin and the other garrisons to join him, and large bodies of militia were gathering to his support. There was no sign of a rising, no sign of disaffection. The peasantry worked with a will to clear the roads for the baggage-wagons, and showed the troops the utmost hospitality. The militia and the yeomanry were enthusiastic; Limerick and Galway "vied with each other in demonstrations of loyalty." Whatever progress the United Irishmen had made in Ulster, they had not influenced the south and west.

The chances of resistance depended on time. If the French should land at once, nothing could stop them, and Cork must fall, where were stores for the British navy worth a million and a half. The French were waiting for Hoche to rejoin them. On the evening of the 22d the wind swung round to the east. A furious gale sprang up, accompanied by a heavy fall of snow, which made it impossible to land. The French ships beat up against it to Bear Island and cast anchor; but the gale increased been with difficulty restrained from committing atrocities on the Protestant inhabitants, gathered a band of ruffians and got possession of the town and prison. He dragged a number of unfortunate Protestants, who had been confined there, to the bridge, where he held a mock court-martial, and then put them to death one by one, and flung their bodies into the river. Ninety-seven had perished, when he was induced to desist by a priest named Father Corrin, who insisted, at the risk of his own life, that the butchery should cease. News of the beleaguering of Vinegar Hill and the defeat at Goff's Bridge was now brought in, and the surviving captives were hurried back to prison. Next day the fugitive army passed through the town and fled to the north, and the evacuated city was shortly afterwards occupied by General Moore.

The various bodies of rebels dispersed rapidly about the country. Some found a refuge in the Wicklow mountains, where a few predatory bands had already established themselves. Others broke into Kilkenny, and were cut to pieces by Sir Charles Asgill. Others pushed northward into Meath and Louth, and were finally destroyed at Swords, while attempting to cut their way back to the protection of the hill country in Wicklow. They played the part of a dangerous and destructive banditti for a few weeks; so that order was not finally restored in the disturbed counties till the end of July.

CHAPTER XXI.

TRAMPLING OUT THE FIRE. A.D. 1798.

The neck of the insurrection was broken by the capture of Vinegar Hill and the recovery of Wexford, and then ensued a reign of terror of the most merciless character. The brutality of the militia and yeomanry had been bad enough before the outbreak: now that the rising was crushed, their ferocity knew no bounds. The rebels had slaughtered Protestants who refused to be baptized into the Roman Catholic Church, and burned their houses, in the brief hour of triumph which they had enjoyed. The Protestants, when their turn came, showed less mercy and exacted a more terrible retribution. When the rebels had fled from Vinegar Hill, their hospital at Enniscorthy was burned, and the wounded shot as they lay there in their beds. The same scene was repeated at Wexford. The soldiers, especially a regiment of imported Hessians, scoured the country, shooting all whom they came across, outraging women, destroying the Roman Catholic chapels, and completing the general desolation by burning and plundering the remaining homesteads. Loyalist and rebel suffered alike indiscriminately, without even the benefit of a court-martial. There was no stay to inquire whether the victim were friend or foe. It was enough that he was found at large in the disaffected county. In the towns courts-martial were held, and executions quickly followed. Too often the innocent suffered with the guilty. The local magistrates, who had fled before the storm, returned to resume the old coercive system, and to wreak their vengeance upon the inhabitants.

General Lake remained for a few days in Wexford to start the execution of martial law, and then left for Dublin, leaving General Hunter to finish the work. The executions took place upon the bridge where Dixon and his myrmidons had massacred the prisoners. There Father Roche was hanged, with John Hay and Matthew Keogh alongside of him. So was Kelly, the leader of the rebel column which had penetrated into New Ross on the day of the battle. So was Bagenal Harvey, too late regretting the stirring of the fire which he had been unable to control. So was Colclough, another gentleman of considerable fortune, who had been confined with Harvey just before the outbreak, and whose only crime was that, having by the persecution of the government become an object of interest with the rebels, he was unable to escape from the disaffected country, and compelled by his unwelcome admirers to take a command in Wexford. Cornelius Grogan, a timid old gentleman, and the owner of an estate worth £8000 a year, who had been compelled for his own safety to act as commissary to their forces, was hanged with Bagenal Harvey. Father John, the rebel chief, had escaped with the roving bands which had broken into Kilkenny. He was caught and hanged at Tullow. Father Redmond, a harmless priest, who seems to have been wholly innocent of any connection with the insurgents, was put to death at Gorey. To be a priest was proof of guilt.

In Dublin the disaffected were terrified by the reckless use of the lash. The suspected were flogged under the direction of John Claudius Beresford, in the riding-house in Marlborough Street, where his corps of yeomanry assembled for parade; and in the prison at the royal barracks, by command of Major Sandys. The triangles were set up in the Royal Exchange, which had been converted into a military depot, and was the headquarters of the yeomanry; and even at the entrance of Upper Castle Yard. Judkin Fitzgerald, the Sheriff of Tipperary, continued his indiscriminate floggings, careless whether his victims were innocent or guilty. A wretched man, named O'Brien, cut his throat to avoid the sheriff's cat-o'-nine-tails. One of Fitzgerald's own captains of yeomanry gave his evidence in an action afterwards brought against the sheriff by a man whom he had flogged, named Wells; and said that "he had feared that, owing to Fitzgerald's conduct, the yeomen would not bear arms, and that his cruelty exercised in inflicting the torture would infuse a spirit of rebellion even into the most loyal." The authorities deliberately shut their eyes to these proceedings. Fitzgerald himself produced a letter in his defence, from Brigade-Major Bagwell, dated June 6, 1798, saying that "if he found any good to arise from flogging he might go on with it, *but let it not reach his ears.*" Fitzgerald was afterwards rewarded by the government for his services with a baronetcy, and the damages recovered against him by Bernard Wright, amounting to £500, were reimbursed to him out of the public treasury.

In the meantime, public opinion had shown itself so hostile to Lord Camden's government that Pitt, though he had steadily supported him all along, found it necessary to sacrifice him and to adopt a policy of greater moderation. Camden was recalled, and Lord Cornwallis was sent to replace him and to supersede Lake, combining in his own person the offices both of viceroy and commander-in-chief. Lord Castlereagh, once a delegate at the volunteer convention, and late member of the opposition loud in demanding reform, whose father had in 1797 married Lord Camden's sister, and who had thereupon been appointed keeper of the privy seal, had been for some weeks performing Mr. Pelham's duties, during the illness of the latter. By the new viceroy's desire, he continued to act, and in the following November, on Pelham's retirement, he was promoted to the post of chief secretary. This remarkable young man had just completed his twenty-ninth year.

Lord Cornwallis arrived in Dublin on the 20th of June—the day before the capture of Vinegar Hill. The new viceroy was well aware of the difficulties of his position. He had refused the viceroyalty on Lord Fitzwilliam's resignation, and it was only at the earnest request of Mr. Pitt, and from a strong sense of duty, that he agreed to accept an office which he described as "coming up to his idea of misery." On his arrival at the Castle he was shocked at the sanguinary spirit with which he found the Ascendency imbued. "The principal persons of this country," he writes, "and the members of both Houses of Parliament are, in general, averse to all acts of clemency, . . . and would pursue measures that could only terminate in the extermination of the greater number of the inhabitants, and in the utter destruction of the country. The words Papists and Priests are forever in their mouths, and by their unaccountable policy would drive four fifths of the community into irreconcilable rebellion." He says, on July 13, in reference to the depredations of the roving bands of rebels, "Our war is reduced to a predatory system in the mountains of Wicklow and the bogs of Kildare." And then he adds, "The numbers in each quarter are very small. They have very few arms, and, except as a band of cruel robbers, house-burners, and murderers, are very contemptible. Their importance, however, is purposely exaggerated by those who wish to urge the government to the continuance of violent measures."

In speaking of the reckless refusal of quarter by the troops, he says, "I am sure that a very small proportion of them [the rebels] only could be killed in battle, and I am much afraid that any man with a brown coat who is found within several miles of the field of action is butchered without discrimination." And on July 24 he writes to General Ross: "The whole country is in such a state that I feel frightened and ashamed whenever I consider that I am looked upon as being the head of it. Except in the instances of the six state-trials that are going on here, there is no law either in town or country but martial law; and you know enough of that to see all the horrors of it, even in the best administration of it. Judge, then, how it must be conducted by Irishmen heated with passion and revenge. But all this is trifling compared to the numberless murders that are hourly committed by our people without any process of examination whatever. The yeomanry are in the style of the Loyalists in America, only much more numerous and powerful and a thousand times more ferocious. These men have saved the country, but they now take the lead in rapine and murder. The Irish militia with few officers, and those generally of the worst kind, follow closely on the heels of the yeomanry in murder and every kind of atrocity; and the fencibles take a share, though much behind, with the others. The feeble outrages, burnings, and murders which are still committed by the rebels serve to keep up the sanguinary disposition on our side; and as long as they furnish a pretext for our parties going in quest of them, I see no prospect of amendment. The conversation of the principal persons of the country all tends to encourage the system of blood; and the conversation even at my table, where you will suppose I do all I can to prevent it, always turns on hanging, shooting, burning, etc.; and if a priest has been put to death the greatest joy is expressed by the whole company. So much for Ireland, and my wretched situation."

Cornwallis's first act was a proclamation promising protection to all insurgents guilty of rebellion only, who should surrender their arms and take the Oath of Allegiance. And shortly afterwards he carried an Amnesty Bill,* affecting all persons except those then in custody, those guilty of murder, those who had been officers in the Society of the United Irishmen, deserters from the yeomanry and militia, and some thirty-one Irish refugees, among whom were Tone, Tandy, Lewines, Dixon, and McCann. The strictest discipline was enjoined upon the officers, and a Highland regiment under Lord Huntley was sent to restore order in Wicklow, in place of the troops who had lately been holding the country in terror. At first the inhabitants fled at the approach of the soldiers, but the men were sternly kept from marauding, and made to pay for everything they required; and, with kind treatment and encouraging language from the officers, the people gradually returned to their homes and sought eagerly for "protections." One by one the leaders of the roving bands came in, and surrendered on the terms offered—of a new start at the antipodes. Aylmer, Luby, Ware, McCormick, and finally Joseph Holt and his Wicklow following. And the country was reported to be "full of people at work." The viceroy's firm but merciful hand was appreciated. His manly sympathy for the suffering country was received with gratitude; and as he passed along the streets of Dublin the poor people would watch for his approach and murmur, "There he goes; God bless him!"

The next step was to deal with the state prisoners, nearly

---

* 38 Geo. III. c. 55.

one hundred in number. The two Sheares were tried and convicted on July 12. They were hanged on the 14th. McCann, secretary to the Provisional Committee of Leinster, was tried and convicted on the 17th. He was hanged on the 19th. Michael Byrne, of Parkhill, a gentleman of some property in the County of Wicklow, was tried and convicted on the 21st. Oliver Bond was tried and convicted on the 23d. On the 24th sixty-four of the remaining prisoners made a proposition to the government, that if the lives of Byrne and Bond should be spared, and their own punishment limited to banishment for life, they would make a full confession. Byrne was hanged on the 28th, but Bond was respited. The prisoners' proposal pleased Cornwallis and the cabinet. They were extremely doubtful of being able to obtain convictions against the majority of the prisoners. In the trials which had already taken place the documentary evidence was overwhelming; but in a great many cases they would have to rely on the evidence of informers, and it was extremely difficult to induce the informers to go into the box. A full confession would set at rest forever the question of their guilt. Notwithstanding the howl from the attorney-general and others of the Ascendency at the bare idea of sparing a conspirator's life, the viceroy, supported by Lord Clare, who saw the great value of an admission by them of their offence, closed with the prisoners' offer. A memoir was drawn up by O'Connor, Emmett, and McNevin, and signed by them, tracing the whole history of the Society of United Irishmen; and the same men were afterwards examined by a secret committee of the House of Lords, and a report of their evidence published. There were eighty-nine prisoners affected by this compromise, but they were not all immediately released. Twenty of the leading men were sent to Fort George, where they were confined till the peace of Amiens. They were then banished. Oliver Bond died in Newgate in September, 1798.

CHAPTER XXII.
THE LAST FLICKER OF THE FLAME. A.D. 1798.

JUST when Cornwallis's policy of pacification was beginning to bear fruit, a fresh danger appeared in the west. The French government, on learning that an insurrection had actually taken place in Ireland, again turned their attention to a descent upon the Irish coast. Hoche was dead, and Bonaparte's eyes were fixed on Egypt, so that the Irish refugees had lately clamored for assistance in vain. Now their expectations again were high. General Humbert was at Rochelle with about a thousand men. General Hardi was at Brest with some three thousand more. Humbert was anxious for an opportunity to distinguish himself. He hastened to obey the orders of the Directory with the small force at his command, leaving General Hardi to follow as quickly as might be.

He embarked his troops towards the middle of August, with a few guns and a considerable stand of arms. On August 22 he anchored in Killala Bay. Having got possession of Killala, he was joined by many of the peasantry, who flocked to his standard and received the arms which the French had brought with them. Then, leaving two hundred men to hold the town, he pushed on to Ballina with about eight hundred French soldiers and a tumultuous rabble of his Irish allies. At the first news of the appearance of the French, the viceroy had sent Lake into the west. Lake had concentrated all the forces he could collect at Castlebar. He had between three and four thousand men with him, chiefly Irish militia, and several guns. Humbert, notwithstanding the disparity of numbers, attacked him on the 27th. After some desultory firing, the French charged with the bayonet. The Galway volunteers and the Kilkenny and Longford militia fled headlong. The position was lost, and Lake retreated precipitately to Tuam, leaving his guns behind him. There seems but little doubt that the two militia regiments had been tampered with, and that their flight was due to treachery. At any rate, considerable numbers of both regiments appeared in the enemy's camp after the battle, and joined the invading force.

Cornwallis was himself hurrying to the front with the troops from Dublin, and had reached Kilbeggan when he received intelligence of the disaster at Castlebar. He at once advanced to Athlone, which he found in a panic, and thence pushed on and joined Lake at Tuam. He was shortly afterwards reinforced by two regiments of the line, and felt strong enough to take the offensive. Humbert, meanwhile, with his handful of troops had not ventured to penetrate any further into the country, and, having called up the garrison he had left at Killala, moved eastward into Sligo, attended by an ever-increasing multitude of half-armed peasants, in the hope that General Hardi would soon arrive with his larger force. Lake followed him in hot pursuit, while Cornwallis moved in a parallel direction rather more to the south. Hearing that the people were "out" in the County of Longford, Humbert crossed the Shannon at Ballintra, and hurried on towards Granard. Lake was close behind him, and Cornwallis, crossing the river at Carrick, closed in upon him from the southwest. Humbert turned to bay at Ballinamuck, and, finding himself surrounded by an army of 20,000 men, surrendered at discretion. The insurgent peasantry immediately dispersed, pursued in all directions by the soldiers, and slaughtered without mercy. Castlebar and Killala, which were in the hands of the rebels under the command of French officers, were shortly afterwards reoccupied by the royal troops, not without some fighting at the latter place. Courts-martial and executions followed, and a considerable harrying of the surrounding country.

It is remarkable that in Connaught, where there had been no free-quartering, no torture, and no pitch-caps, according to the testimony of the Bishop of Killala, who was a prisoner in that town during the French occupation, "not a drop of blood was shed by the rebels except in the field of war;" and the poor ignorant peasantry appear, according to the same authority, to have joined the French more for the sake of the smart uniforms and the rations which were provided for them than from any spirit of disaffection to the government.

There was yet one more scene before the drama of '98 was closed. Hardi's expedition sailed from Brest on September 20th. It consisted of the *Hoche* (a seventy-four), eight frigates, and a schooner. Tone, the indefatigable, was on board the *Hoche*—no longer light-hearted and sanguine, but desperate and desponding. The *Hoche*, two frigates, and the schooner arrived outside Lough Swilly on October 10. On the following morning an English squadron under Admiral Warren hove in sight, and bore down upon them. The frigates and the schooner slipped away, and after a long chase the frigates were captured. The *Hoche* for six hours fought four men-of-war as big as herself, until, raked from stem to stern, she lay a disabled wreck upon the water. Tone commanded one of the batteries, fighting with desperation and courting death, but was untouched by the leaden hail which swept around him. At length the Frenchman struck and was carried into Lough Swilly. The French officers, with Tone among them, were hospitably entertained at Lord Cavan's. At his table Tone was recognized by Sir George Hill, an old college friend, and was sent in irons to Dublin.

A court-martial was held. General Loftus presided. Tone pleaded his commission in the French army, but his plea was not listened to. He begged that he might be shot like a soldier, and not hanged like a dog; but his request was refused. On the morning fixed for his execution, he cut his throat in prison. The wound was not mortal. It was dressed; and he was remorselessly ordered to the scaffold. In the meantime Curran had moved in the King's Bench for a writ of *habeas corpus* on the ground that, as the prisoner held no commission in the English army, the court-martial had no jurisdiction to try him while the courts were sitting in Dublin. The writ was granted, and arrived in time to arrest the execution. The real object of the application was gained, and Tone was allowed to die a lingering death in prison.

CHAPTER XXIII.

THE SALE OF THE CONSTITUTION. A.D. 1798–1799.

THE condition of the country towards the end of 1798 was deplorable. Trade was at a standstill. Credit was shattered. The actual losses of the Loyalists who received compensation from government, though no doubt there were many fraudulent claims, amounted to £1,023,000, of which £515,000 was claimed by the County of Wexford. The cost of the military establishment had been enormous, the expenditure for the year having been £4,815,367. The number of troops in the island was prodigious—138,000 men, of whom over 56,000 were regulars. The ordinary law was still superseded. The judges had endeavored to resume their circuits, but the military authorities refused to give up their prisoners, or send them into other districts, still professedly under martial law. Writs of *habeas corpus* were issued, but were treated with contempt, and the whole island was still practically in a state of siege.

Pitt's heart had long been set upon a legislative union of the kingdoms of Great Britain and Ireland. The opportunity had now come for its accomplishment. The scheme was propounded. Lord Clare, under the pretence that he was going to drink the waters at Harrowgate, hurried over to England to consult with the cabinet, and wrote that Pitt, the chancellor, and the Duke of Portland were of opinion that "a union only could save" what he was pleased to call his "damnable country." Edward Cooke published an anonymous pamphlet strongly upholding the proposal. The advocacy of the provincial papers was carefully secured, we are not told by what means, and Castlereagh began cautiously sounding the leading people in Dublin.

Pitt and Cornwallis were anxious that the act of Union should be accompanied by the emancipation of the Roman

Catholics, and desired "to make a union with the Irish nation instead of making it with a party;" but the Ascendency party, led by Lord Clare, were wild at the suggestion, and this more enlightened part of the plan was accordingly abandoned. This did not, however, prevent the government from bidding for the support of the Roman Catholics by leading them to suppose that emancipation should immediately follow; and their neutrality, if not their active assistance, was purchased by holding out this representation to them, when it was discovered that the Protestant party viewed the measure with abhorrence, and a counterpoise to their resistance was required.

In some parts of Ireland, particularly in the cities of Cork, Limerick, and Galway, the idea of a union was not unfavorably received. In Dublin the opposition was very strong. Both the merchant and shopkeeper class and the bar were exceedingly hostile. Of the leading public men many were hanging back to see how matters would develop. Some, however, even of the regular supporters of the Castle, at once boldly denounced the measure. Of these the most influential were Foster, the speaker; Sir John Parnell, the chancellor of the exchequer; and Fitzgerald, the prime-sergeant. The government struck heavily where they were able, and the last two were promptly dismissed from office. The viceroy had no intention of being governed by the junto. He had written to General Ross in August that he had "totally set aside the Irish cabinet." Lord Clare alone of the old set was acting with him, and Lord Castlereagh was his right-hand man. These three were the real government of Ireland; and it was their strong wills that carried out the policy which Pitt had initiated.

The Irish Parliament met on January 22, 1799. The speech from the throne contained an ambiguous reference to the desirability of a union. The opponents of the measure at once took up the glove. Sir John Parnell spoke strongly against the principle of a union. Ponsonby moved, as an amendment to the address, "that the undoubted birthright of the people of Ireland, a resident and independent legislature, should be maintained." Sir Lawrence Parsons seconded the amendment; Conolly, St. George, Daly, and the Knight of Kerry supported the government. Barrington (the notorious Sir Jonah) deserted the Castle. Castlereagh defended the proposed measure, and Plunket, in reply, made a bitter attack upon "the simple and modest youth whose inexperience was the voucher of his innocence." Frederick Trench, member for Maryborough, spoke early in the evening, on the opposition side. He presently had an interview with Cooke in the lobby, and then, alleging that he had misunderstood the meaning of Parnell's motion, voted with the government. He was created Lord Ashtown in December, 1800.

The debate was of singular vehemence, and lasted twenty-two hours. On dividing, the numbers were equal, 106 in each list. It was then discovered that Mr. Luke Fox, who had come into Parliament as a member of the nationalist party, and had voted with the opposition, had made terms with the government and accepted the "escheatorship of Munster," an office resembling the stewardship of the Chiltern Hundreds in England, shortly before the division, and his vote was disallowed. The government accordingly had a majority of one. Such a division was, however, in fact, a victory for the opposition; and, on the report of the address, Sir Lawrence Parsons moved that the objectionable paragraph should be expunged; and, after another fierce battle, the government was beaten by five—109 voting for Parsons's motion and 104 against it. Meanwhile in England all was going on swimmingly. The scheme was broached in both Houses, and hardly a voice was raised against it. In the middle of February, Pitt carried eight resolutions in the English Commons, which formed the skeleton of a bill for the effecting of a union by 120 to 16.

Great was the exultation of the Anti-unionists at the results of the first encounter in the Irish Commons, and great was the rejoicing in Dublin. The government was thrown aback for the present, but none the less was resolved to win. Prudence, however, forbade the attempt to force the question during the current session. The opposition was composed of discordant elements, and might be broken up. It was greatly reinforced in both Houses by the self-interest of those who owned the multitude of condemned rotten boroughs, which had become, by the licensing of a nefarious traffic, a source of great emolument. Lord Downshire and Lord Ely were especially hostile. The one returned no less than seven, the other no less than six, members to Parliament. In the consolidated and united Houses of Commons, two thirds of the Irish borough seats were to be disfranchised. The proprietors would not object to their disestablishment, but they looked with horror upon the prospect of disendowment. Compensation to the proprietors would disarm many of the opponents of the measure. Immoderate compensation would buy their active support. Castlereagh's arguments on this point were unanswerable.

The government programme would grow stronger as it was developed. If the Roman Catholic interest were thrown into the scale, the scheme would receive much indirect assistance. The Roman Catholic nobility and gentry were sounded. Lord Fingal was favorable; so was Lord Kenmare, with the promise of an earldom. The Roman Catholic bishops were solicited. Dr. Troy was propitious, and they were ready to stand by the Castle and to allow the crown to have a veto in the appointment of their prelates in consideration of a fixed stipend to be paid by the crown to their clergy. The most violent of the Anti-unionists were the very people who had supported the government through the recent troubles—the Protestant nobility and gentry and the Orange lodges, among whom prevailed "universal horror and disgust at the idea of a union." It was necessary to conciliate these by the most solemn assurances that the Established Church of Ireland should be maintained inviolable by statute, and its continuance should be a fundamental article of the Union. Desertion by placemen was punished by immediate dismissal. Colonel Foster, commissioner of the revenue, was the first victim. Mr. George Knox, and Mr. Wolfe, also commissioners, followed. Mr. Neville lost the commissionership of accounts; Mr. A. Hamilton, the cursitorship in chancery; Mr. John Claudius Beresford, the sinecure office of inspector-general of exports and imports; and Major C. Hamilton was dismissed from the barrack board. Colonel Cole, whose regiment was at Malta, was ordered to rejoin; and when he desired to vacate his seat, which would inevitably have been refilled by an Anti-unionist, the government refused him the escheatorship of Munster.

Parliament was prorogued in June. The government, after the adverse reception of the Union scheme at the beginning of the session, set themselves steadily to work to secure a sufficient majority in the session following. The members were corrupt enough as it was; but they were slaves to the borough-owners, who had sent them to Parliament. The first thing to do was to purchase the borough-owners, chiefly members of the Upper House; and then, either by the help of the latter to compel recalcitrant and honest members to resign their seats in favor of people who would vote for the Union; or, by means of the bait of pensions, places, and promotions, to buy the support of the venal.

In the United House of Commons there were, according to the proposed bill, to be one hundred members from Ireland; and, as the Irish Commons consisted of three hundred members, it necessarily followed that two thirds of the seats would disappear. Each of the thirty-two counties was to return two members, making sixty-four; and the remaining thirty-six were to be disposed of as follows: Two each to the cities of Dublin and Cork, one to the University, and one each to the cities of Waterford, Limerick, and Cashel, and the twenty-eight boroughs which escaped extinction. All the remaining boroughs, eighty-five in number, and each returning two members, were consigned to perdition. These eighty-five boroughs were one and all of them in the hands of private owners. No less than fifty-six of them were possessed by members of the Upper House. Castlereagh saw the way to the pockets and consciences of members of both branches of the Irish legislature through these eighty-five boroughs. He proposed to compensate every one of the proprietors at the rate of £15,000 apiece. And where, as in many cases it was so, one person possessed three or four seats, the figure at which the compensation would stand was a very large one. Lord Ely eventually received no less than £45,000 for his six seats, and Lord Downshire £52,500 for his seven. The sum required amounted in the whole to £1,260,000! and this enormous bribe to the men who sold their country was in the event actually paid, and added to the debt of Ireland.

This master-stroke in corruption was supplemented by wholesale and reckless bribery of a different description. Irish peerages, English peerages, steps in the peerage, baronetcies, bishoprics, livings, judgeships, regiments; places and preferments, legal, civil, and military; social advancements, Castle patronage, flattering condescension, even direct bribes in hard cash, were lavished with an unsparing hand according to the character and weakness of the individual to be secured. Twenty-two Irish peerages were conferred, six English peerages, and twenty-two promotions were made in the Irish peerage—forty-eight patents of nobility as a reward for dirty work.

All through the year 1799, Castlereagh and the viceroy, assisted by the Castle under-secretaries—Edward Cooke and Colonel Littlehales—were employed on their unholy mission; Cornwallis in the summer making a tour through the island, and staying at the country-houses of the nobility to complete his canvass. How vile was the traffic appears from the contemptuous loathing with which he regarded the recipients of Castle favors. "It is a sad thing," he writes to Ross, "to be forced to manage knaves, but it is ten times worse to deal with fools. . . . I am kept here to manage matters of a most disgusting nature to my feelings." And on June 8, 1799, "My occupation is now of the most unpleasant nature, negotiating and jobbing with the most corrupt people under heaven. I despise and hate myself every hour for engaging in such dirty work." And again, "The political jobbing of this country gets the better of me. It has ever been the wish of my life to avoid all this dirty business; and I am now involved in it beyond all bearing, and am consequently more wretched than ever. I trust I shall live to get out of this most accursed of all situations, and most repugnant to my feelings. How I long to kick those whom my public duty obliges me to court!" It is sad to think to what vile uses so gallant a soldier was put. Lord Castlereagh does not appear to have been so fastidious. He despised the venal crew with whom he had to deal, but he does not appear to have felt the debasing nature of the higgling.*

* For a list of peerages given in consideration of support upon the question of the Union, see Appendix 5

CHAPTER XXIV.

ANNEXATION. A.D. 1800.

On January 15, 1800, the Irish Parliament met for the last time. The opposition had striven with desperation to strengthen their party, and had obtained Anti-union petitions from twenty-six out of the thirty-two counties. They even went so far as to suggest opposition by force, and to propose the calling of the yeomanry to arms. Such was the consistency of the Protestant Ascendency, who had just trampled out in blood the armed resistance of the United Irishmen to a detested government. Lord Downshire obtained a petition against the Union from the officers and men of his regiment — the Downshire militia. He was deprived of his command and dismissed from the privy council and the lord-lieutenancy of his county. Ireland was too well garrisoned with troops to admit of active resistance.

The work of the government had been done effectually. One result of their negotiations had been that some sixteen members had accepted the escheatorship of Munster, in favor of supporters of the government; and Lord Castlereagh was reckoning on having a majority of sixty in the service of the crown.

The outline of the bill was as follows:

1. The kingdom to be united, and the succession to remain as fixed by the existing laws.

2. The United Kingdom to be represented in one Parliament. The British part to be unchanged. The Irish portion to consist in the Lower House of one hundred commoners; and in the Upper, of four lords spiritual taken in rotation, and twenty-eight temporal to be elected for life by the peers of Ireland.

3. Irish peers to be eligible for election in a constituency in Great Britain.

4. All members of the United Parliament to take the oaths which excluded Roman Catholics.

5. The continuance of the Irish Church establishment to be a fundamental article of the Union.

6. Subjects of Great Britain and Ireland to be on the same commercial footing.

7. The charges for the national debt of the two countries to be separate accounts. The contribution of Ireland towards the general expenditure to be two fifths of the whole for the first twenty years, when fresh arrangements should be made. Moneys raised after the Union to be a joint debt.

8. The courts of justice to be untouched. A final appeal to the House of Lords of the United Kingdom.

No mention of the Union was made in the address, upon which Sir Lawrence Parsons made a violent attack on the government, and moved an amendment to the effect that it was desirable to maintain the independence of the Irish Parliament, as settled in 1782. In the midst of the fierce debate which followed, Grattan walked from a sick-bed into the House, supported by William Ponsonby and Mr. Arthur Moore.

When Grattan had resigned his seat in 1797, he retired almost broken-hearted to his seat in Wicklow. He was roused from his retirement to go over to England to give evidence as to character in favor of Arthur O'Connor, on his trial at the Maidstone assizes. This accident fortunately kept him in England till the insurrection had broken out, and he did not return to Ireland until the various risings had been put down. He was so hated by the Ascendency party that, had he been in Ireland at the time of the outbreak, his life might hardly have been safe in times when the lawless soldiery too often gratified the vengeance of party spite. As it was, great efforts were made to connect Grattan's name with the disaffected. One of the Castle spies, Hughes by name, had, earlier in the year, gone with Neilson to Grattan's house at Tinnehinch, to try and obtain an interview with him; and Hughes now swore, before the secret committee, that Neilson had told him that he had enlisted Grattan as a United Irishman. Lord Clare insisted on having this libel inserted in the report made by the House of Lords; but the speaker struck it out of the report of the Commons. Nevertheless, so fierce was the rancor of the Ascendency against Grattan that they spared no pains to blacken his character; and so successful had they been that Cornwallis had removed his name from the privy council. The miserable condition of the country preyed greatly on Grattan's mind, and he lived in complete retirement. When, however, the sound of the Union battle was heard in the air, he yielded to the pressure of his friends and sought for a seat in Parliament. A seat was difficult to obtain. At length, a vacancy occurring for the town of Wicklow, Grattan gave £2400 to the patron, and was at once returned.

The debate on the address showed only too clearly how the Castle influence had debauched the House. The division was— for the amendment, 96; against it, 138: majority for the government, 42. On February 6, upon the question of taking into consideration his majesty's message for a legislative union, the government, notwithstanding the desertion of seven of their supporters who had yielded to the pressure of their constituents, had a majority of 49 in a House of 278 members. And on February 17 the chancellor of the exchequer moved the order of the day passing into committee on the resolutions of the British Parliament.

Grattan's reappearance in the House of Commons had given strength to the opposition, and was a source of anxiety to the Castle. Corry, once a patriot, now a hireling, had succeeded Parnell as chancellor of the exchequer, and was deputed to attack Grattan in the House. He had already done so more than once with great bitterness. On the occasion of his moving the order of the day, he attacked him again, repeated the old slanders about Grattan's alleged connection with the United Irishmen, and called him "an unimpeached traitor." When he sat down, Grattan rose, and gave him a fiercer castigation than he had once given Flood. "The right honorable gentleman," he said, "has called me an unimpeached traitor. I ask why not traitor unqualified by any epithet? I will tell him. It was because he dare not. It was the act of a coward, who has raised his arm to strike and has not the courage to give the blow. I will not call him villain, because it would be unparliamentary, and he is a privy-councillor. I will not call him fool, because he happens to be chancellor of the exchequer. But I say he is one who has abused the privilege of Parliament and freedom of debate to the uttering language which, if spoken out of the House, I should answer only with a blow. He has charged me with being connected with the rebels. The charge is utterly, totally, and meanly false. Does the right honorable gentleman rely on the report of the House of Lords for the foundation of his assertion? If he does, I can prove to the committee that there was a physical impossibility of that report being true. But I scorn to answer any man for my conduct. . . . Here I stand, ready for impeachment or trial. I dare accusation. I defy the honorable gentleman. I defy the government. I defy the whole phalanx. Let them come forth. I tell the ministers I will neither give them quarter nor take it."

The words "villain," "fool," and "coward" admitted of nothing but a challenge from Corry. Next morning they met at daylight in the Phœnix Park. General Craddock, Corry's second, pinioned the sheriff, who endeavored to prevent a breach of the peace, and had him held down in a ditch while the duel proceeded. At the first fire Grattan's shot struck Corry in the arm. The seconds ordered them to fire a second time. Grattan fired in the air, and Corry's shot did not take effect. Their friends then withdrew them from the ground. So ended the attempt to bully Grattan.

In the meantime the first resolution, "That a legislative union of the two kingdoms was desirable," was carried by a majority of forty-six; and one by one the remainder passed through committee, and were sent up to the Lords, where the supporters of the government were in an immense majority. When the resolutions were laid before the English Houses, the government met with as little opposition as they had in the previous year; and on May 21 Lord Castlereagh introduced into the Irish Commons a bill embodying the resolutions. The opposition could only muster 100 votes against 160 for the government. The second reading was carried on May 26, by

117 to 73. The report of the committee was carried by 153 to 88. When the House adjourned, the speaker walked out, followed by forty-one members. The populace outside uncovered, and in deep silence accompanied them to the speaker's house in Molesworth Street. On reaching it, the speaker turned round, bowed to the crowd, entered his house; and then the whole assemblage dispersed without uttering a word. All was now over. The decision of the Upper House, under the stern dominion of Lord Clare, was a foregone conclusion; and the bill received the royal assent on August 1.*

Thus ended the Parliament of the English Colony in Ireland. It was never in any sense representative of the nation. It was the corrupt embodiment of a dominant race. It sold the birthright of the nation for its own selfish ends. There had not even been a dissolution to test the opinion of the constituencies, the proposal to consult the people upon a question so vital to their interests having been sternly condemned by Pitt as "rank Jacobinism." The most remarkable and creditable thing about the whole transaction was that so many as one hundred members of the Lower House were found whose integrity the government was unable to corrupt, and whose honor it was powerless to purchase.

---

* 40 Geo. III. c. 38.

APPENDIX I.

LIST OF THE CHIEF GOVERNORS OF IRELAND FROM 1173 TO A.D. 1800.

HENRY II.

1173. *Hugh de Lacy, Earl of Meath, Lord Justice.*
Richard de Clare, Earl of Pembroke, Lord Justice.
1177. Raymond le Gros, Lord Deputy.
JOHN, EARL OF MORTON, LORD OF IRELAND.
William Fitzaldelm, Lord Justice.
1179. Hubert de Burgh, Earl of Meath, Lord Deputy.
1181. *John de Lacy,* } *Lords Justices.*
Richard de Peche,
William Fitzaldelm, Lord Deputy.
1184. Philip de Braosa, Lord Deputy.
1185. JOHN, EARL OF MORTON, LORD OF IRELAND.
John de Courcy, Earl of Ulster, Lord Deputy.

RICHARD I., 1189.

1189. *Hugh de Lacy, the younger, Lord of Meath, Lord Justice.*
1191. *William Le Petit, Lord Justice.*
William, Earl of Pembroke, Earl Marshal, Lord Justice.
Peter Pipard, Lord Justice.
1194. *Hamo de Valois, Lord Justice.*

JOHN, 1199.

1199. *Meiler FitzHenry, Lord Justice.*
1203. Hugh de Lacy, the younger, Lord Deputy.
1205. *Meiler FitzHenry, Lord Justice.*
1208. Hugh de Lacy, Earl of Ulster, Lord Deputy.
1210. KING JOHN IN PERSON, LORD OF IRELAND.
William, Earl of Pembroke, Lord Deputy.
John de Grey (*Bishop of Norwich*), *Lord Justice.*
1213. *Henry de Londres, Archbishop of Dublin, Lord Justice.*
1215. *Geoffrey de Marisco* (Mountmorres), *Lord Justice.*

HENRY III., 1216

1219. *Henry de Londres, Lord Justice.*
1224. *William, Earl of Pembroke, the younger, Lord Justice.*
1226. *Geoffrey de Marisco, Lord Justice.*
1227. *Hubert de Burgh, Earl of Kent, Lord Justice.*
Richard de Burgh, Lord of Connaught, Lord Deputy.
1229. *Maurice Fitzgerald, Lord Justice.*
1230. Geoffrey de Marisco, Lord Deputy.
1232. *Maurice Fitzgerald, Lord Justice.*
1245. Sir John de Marisco, Lord Deputy.
1247. *Theobald Walter, Lord of Carrick,* } Lords Justices.
John de Cogan,
1248. *Sir John de Marisco, Lord Justice.*
1252. *Prince Edward Plantagenet, Lord Justice.*
1255. *Alan de la Zouche, Lord Justice.*
1259. *Stephen Longespee, Lord Justice.*
1260. *William Dene, Lord Justice.*
1261. *Sir Richard de Rupella (Roche), Lord Justice.*
1266. *Sir John de Marisco, Lord Justice.*
1267. *Sir David de Barry, Lord Justice.*
1268. *Sir Robert de Ufford, Lord Justice.*
1269. *Richard de Exeter, Lord Justice.*
1270. *Sir James Audley, Lord Justice.*
1272. *Maurice Fitzmaurice Fitzgerald, Lord Justice.*

EDWARD, 1272.

1273. *Sir Geoffrey de Geneville, Lord Justice.*
1276. *Sir Robert de Ufford, Lord Justice.*
1277. Stephen de Fulburn, Bishop of Waterford, Lord Deputy.
1280. *Sir Robert de Ufford, Lord Justice.*
1282. *Stephen de Fulburn, Lord Justice.*
1287. *John de Saunford, Archbishop of Dublin, Lord Justice.*
1290. *William de Vesci, Lord Justice.*
1293. *William de la Haye, Lord Justice.*
1294. *William de Odinsele, Lord Justice.*
1295. *Thomas Fitzmaurice Fitzgerald, Lord Justice.*
Sir John Wogan, Lord Justice.
1302. Sir Maurice Rochfort, Lord Deputy.
Sir John Wogan, Lord Justice.

EDWARD II., 1307.

1308. Sir Piers Gaveston, Earl of Cornwall, Lord Deputy.

1308. Sir William Bourke, Lord Deputy.
1309. *Sir John Wogan, Lord Justice.*
1312. Sir Edmund Butler, Lord Deputy.
1314. Sir Theobald de Vardon, Lord Deputy.
1315. Sir Edmund Butler, Lord Deputy.
1317. *Sir Roger Mortimer, Earl of March, Lord Justice.*
1318. William Fitzjohn, Archbishop of Cashel, Lord Deputy.
Alexander Bicknor, Archbishop of Dublin, Lord Deputy.
1319. *Sir Roger Mortimer, Lord Justice.*
1320. Thomas Fitzjohn Fitzgerald, Earl of Kildare, Lord Deputy.
1321. *Sir John de Bermingham, Earl of Louth, Lord Justice.*
1322. Ralph de Gorges, Lord Deputy.
Sir John Darcy, Lord Deputy.
1323. Sir Thomas Burke, Lord Deputy.
1324. *Sir John Darcy, Lord Justice.*
1326. *Thomas, Earl of Kildare, Lord Justice.*

EDWARD III., 1327.

1328. Roger Outlawe, Lord Chancellor, Lord Justice.
Sir John Darcy, Lord Justice.
1329. JAMES BUTLER, EARL OF ORMONDE, LORD LIEUTENANT.
1330. Roger Outlawe, Lord Deputy.
1331. SIR ANTHONY LUCY, LORD LIEUTENANT.
1332. *Sir John Darcy, Lord Justice.*
1333. Sir Thomas de Burgh, Lord Deputy.
1334. *Sir John Darcy, Lord Justice.*
1337. *Sir John Charlton, Lord Justice.*
1338. Thomas Charlton, Archbishop of Hereford, Lord Deputy.
1340. *Roger Outlawe, Lord Justice.*
Sir John Darcy, Lord Justice.
1341. Sir John Morice, Lord Deputy.
1344. Sir Ralph Ufford, Lord Deputy.
1346. *Sir Roger Darcy, Lord Justice.*
Sir Walter Bermingham, Lord Justice.
1347. John le Archer, Prior of Kilmainham, Lord Deputy.
1348. *Sir Walter Bermingham, Lord Justice.*
1349. *Sir John de Carew,* } *Lords Justices.*
Sir Thomas Rokeby,
1351. Maurice de Rochfort, Bishop of Limerick, Lord Deputy.
1353. *Sir Thomas Rokeby, Lord Justice.*
1354. *Maurice FitzThomas Fitzgerald, Earl of Desmond, Lord Justice.*
1356. *Sir Thomas Rokeby, Lord Justice.*
1357. *Sir Almeric de St. Amand, Lord Justice.*
1359. *James Butler, Earl of Ormonde, Lord Justice.*

1360. Maurice FitzThomas Fitzgerald, Earl of Kildare, Lord Deputy.
James, Earl of Ormonde, Lord Justice.
1361. LIONEL, DUKE OF CLARENCE, EARL OF ULSTER, LORD OF CONNAUGHT, LORD LIEUTENANT (till 1369).
1364. James, Earl of Ormonde, Lord Deputy.
1365. Sir Thomas Dale, Lord Deputy.
1367. Gerald Fitzmaurice, Earl of Desmond, Lord Justice.
1369. SIR WILLIAM DE WINDSOR, LORD LIEUTENANT.
1371. Maurice, Earl of Kildare, Lord Deputy.
1372. Sir Robert Assheton, Lord Justice.
Ralph Cheney, Lord Deputy.
William Tany, Prior of Kilmainham, Lord Justice.
1374. SIR WILLIAM DE WINDSOR, LORD LIEUTENANT.
1375. Maurice, Earl of Kildare, Lord Deputy.
1376. James, Earl of Ormonde, Lord Justice.

RICHARD II., 1377.

1378. Alexander Balscot, Bishop of Ossory, Lord Justice.
1379. John de Bromwich, Lord Justice.
1380. EDMUND MORTIMER, EARL OF MARCH AND ULSTER, LORD LIEUTENANT (till 1383).
1381. John Colton, Dean of St. Patrick's, Lord Justice.
1383. PHILIP DE COURTENAY, LORD LIEUTENANT (till 1385).
1384. James, Earl of Ormonde, Lord Deputy.
1385. ROBERT DE VERE, EARL OF OXFORD, MARQUIS OF DUBLIN, AND DUKE OF IRELAND, LORD LIEUTENANT. (Never came over; attainted 1388.)
Sir John Stanley, Lord Deputy.
1386. SIR PHILIP DE COURTENAY, LORD LIEUTENANT (till 1389).
1387. Alexander Balscot, Bishop of Meath, Lord Justice.
1389. SIR JOHN STANLEY, LORD LIEUTENANT.
Richard White, Prior of Kilmainham, Lord Deputy.
1391. Alexander Balscot, Bishop of Meath, Lord Justice.
1392. James, Earl of Ormonde, Lord Justice.
1393. THOMAS OF WOODSTOCK, DUKE OF GLOUCESTER, LORD LIEUTENANT. (Never came over.)
THE KING IN PERSON, LORD OF IRELAND.
1394. Sir Thomas le Scrope, Lord Deputy.
1395. ROGER MORTIMER, EARL OF MARCH AND ULSTER, LORD LIEUTENANT.
1398. Roger Gray, Lord Justice.
THOMAS DE HOLLAND, EARL OF KENT, LORD LIEUTENANT.
1399. THE KING IN PERSON, LORD OF IRELAND.

HENRY IV., 1399.

1399. *Alexander Balscot, Lord Justice.*
SIR JOHN STANLEY, LORD LIEUTENANT.
1401. THOMAS DE LANCASTER, LORD LIEUTENANT (till 1413).
Sir Stephen Scrope, Lord Deputy.
1405. *James, Earl of Ormonde, Lord Justice.*
Earl of Kildare, Lord Justice.
1406. Sir Stephen Scrope, Lord Deputy.
1407. James, Earl of Ormonde, Lord Deputy.
1409. William de Botiller, Prior of Kilmainham, Lord Deputy.

HENRY V., 1413.

1413. SIR JOHN STANLEY, LORD LIEUTENANT.
1414. *Thomas Cranley, Archbishop of Dublin, Lord Justice.*
SIR JOHN TALBOT, LORD LIEUTENANT.
1419. Richard Talbot, Archbishop of Dublin, Lord Deputy.
1420. JAMES, EARL OF ORMONDE, LORD LIEUTENANT.

HENRY VI., 1422.

1423. EDMOND MORTIMER, EARL OF MARCH AND ULSTER, LORD LIEUTENANT.
Ed. Dantsey, Bishop of Meath, Lord Deputy.
LORD TALBOT, LORD LIEUTENANT.
1424. JAMES, EARL OF ORMONDE, LORD LIEUTENANT.
1426. *James, Earl of Ormonde, Lord Justice.*
1427. SIR JOHN DE GREY, LORD LIEUTENANT.
1428. SIR JOHN SUTTON, LORD DUDLEY, LORD LIEUTENANT.
1429. Sir Thomas Scrope, Lord Deputy.
1430. Richard Talbot, Archbishop of Dublin, Lord Deputy.
1431. SIR THOMAS STANLEY, LORD LIEUTENANT.
1432. Sir Christopher Plunket, Lord Deputy.
1435. SIR THOMAS STANLEY, LORD LIEUTENANT.
1436. Richard Talbot, Lord Deputy.
1438. LORD WELLES, LORD LIEUTENANT. (Never came over.)
1440. James, Earl of Ormonde, Lord Deputy.
1442. William Welles, Lord Deputy.
1443. JAMES, EARL OF ORMONDE, LORD LIEUTENANT.
1445. Richard Talbot, Lord Deputy (till 1449).
1446. JOHN TALBOT, EARL OF SHREWSBURY, LORD LIEUTENANT.
1449. RICHARD PLANTAGENET, DUKE OF YORK, EARL OF MARCH AND ULSTER, LORD LIEUTENANT.
Richard Nugent, Lord Delvin, Lord Deputy.

1450. James, Earl of Ormonde, Lord Deputy.
1452. Sir Edward Fitz-Eustace, Lord Deputy.
1453. JAMES, EARL OF ORMONDE, LORD LIEUTENANT.
    John Mey, Archbishop of Armagh, Lord Deputy.
1454. Sir Edward Fitz-Eustace, Lord Deputy.
1459. RICHARD PLANTAGENET, LORD LIEUTENANT.
1460. Thomas, Earl of Kildare, Lord Deputy.

EDWARD IV., 1461.

1461. *Thomas, Earl of Kildare, Lord Justice.*
    GEORGE, DUKE OF CLARENCE, LORD LIEUTENANT.
1462. Roland Fitz-Eustace, Lord Deputy.
    William Sherwood, Bishop of Meath, Lord Deputy.
1463. Thomas, Earl of Desmond, Lord Deputy.
1467. John Tiptoft, Earl of Worcester, Lord Deputy.
1468. Thomas, Earl of Kildare, Lord Deputy.
1475. William Sherwood, Bishop of Meath, Lord Deputy.
1478. RICHARD OF SHREWSBURY, DUKE OF YORK (second son to the King), LORD LIEUTENANT (till 1783; he never came over).
    Sir Robert Preston, Lord Gormanston, Lord Deputy.
    Gerald, eighth Earl of Kildare, Lord Deputy (till 1492).

EDWARD V., 1483.

RICHARD III., 1483.

1480. EDWARD, PRINCE OF WALES, LORD LIEUTENANT. (Never came over.)
1484. JOHN DE LA POLE, EARL OF LINCOLN, LORD LIEUTENANT.

HENRY VII., 1485.

1485. JASPER TUDOR, EARL OF PEMBROKE AND DUKE OF BEDFORD, LORD LIEUTENANT.
1492. Walter Fitz-Simon, Archbishop of Dublin, Lord Deputy.
1493. Lord Gormanston, Lord Deputy.
    William Preston, Lord Deputy.
1494. HENRY, DUKE OF YORK (second son to the King), LORD LIEUTENANT. (He never came over.)
    Sir Edward Poynings, Lord Deputy.
1495. *Henry Deane, Bishop of Bangor, Lord Justice.*
1496. Gerald, eighth Earl of Kildare, Lord Deputy (till 1513).

HENRY VIII., 1509.

1513. *Gerald, ninth Earl of Kildare, Lord Justice.*
Gerald, ninth Earl of Kildare, Lord Deputy (till 1520).
1515. *Lord Gormanston, Lord Justice.*
1520. THOMAS HOWARD, EARL OF SURREY, LORD LIEUTENANT.
1521. Sir Piers Butler, Earl of Ormonde, Lord Deputy.
1524. Gerald, Earl of Kildare, Lord Deputy.
1526. Lord Delvin, Lord Deputy.
1528. *Sir Piers Butler, Earl of Ossory, Lord Justice.*
1529. HENRY FITZROY, DUKE OF RICHMOND (natural son to the King), LORD LIEUTENANT. (Never came over.)
1530. Sir William Skeffington, Lord Deputy.
1532. Gerald, Earl of Kildare, Lord Deputy.
1535. Lord Leonard Gray, Lord Deputy.
1540. *Sir William Brereton, Lord Justice.*
Sir Anthony St. Leger, Lord Deputy (till 1546).
1543. *Sir William Brabazon, Lord Justice.*
1546. Sir William Brabazon, Lord Deputy.
Sir Anthony St. Leger, Lord Deputy.

EDWARD VI., 1547.

1547. *Sir William Brabazon, Lord Justice.*
1548. *Sir Edward Bellingham, Lord Justice.*
1549. *Sir Francis Bryan,* } *Lords Justices.*
Sir William Brabazon,
1550. Sir Anthony St. Leger, Lord Deputy.
1551. *Sir James Croft, Lord Justice.*
1552. *Sir James Cusacke, Lord Chancellor,* } *Lords Justices.*
Sir Gerald Aylmer, Lord Chief Justice, K. B.,

MARY, 1553.

1553. Sir Anthony St. Leger, Lord Deputy.
1556. Thomas Radclyffe, Lord Fitzwalter, Lord Deputy (till 1560).
1557. *Hugh Curwen,* } *Lords Justices.*
Sir Henry Sidney,
1558. *Sir Henry Sidney, Lord Justice.*

ELIZABETH, 1558.

1560. Sir William Fitzwilliam, Lord Deputy.
Thomas Radcliffe, Lord Fitzwalter, Earl of Sussex, Lord Deputy.

1561. Sir William Fitzwilliam, Lord Deputy.
EARL OF SUSSEX, LORD LIEUTENANT.
Sir William Fitzwilliam, Lord Deputy.
1564. *Sir Nicholas Arnold, Lord Justice.*
1565. Sir Henry Sidney, Lord Deputy.
1567. *Robert Weston, Lord Chancellor,* } *Lords Justices.*
Sir William Fitzwilliam,
1568. Sir Henry Sidney, Lord Deputy.
1571. *Sir William Fitzwilliam, Lord Justice.*
1575. Sir Henry Sidney, Lord Deputy.
1578. *Sir William Drury, Lord Justice.*
1579. *Sir William Pelham, Lord Justice.*
1580. Lord Grey de Wilton, Lord Deputy.
1582. *Adam Loftus, Archbishop of Dublin and Lord*
   Chancellor, } *Lords Justices.*
   Sir Henry Wallop,
1584. Sir John Perrott, Lord Deputy.
1588. Sir William Fitzwilliam, Lord Deputy.
1594. Sir William Russell, Lord Deputy.
1597. Lord Burgh, Lord Deputy.
Sir Thomas Norris, Lord Justice.
1598. *Adam Loftus,*
Sir Robert Gardiner, C.J.K.B., } *Lords Justices.*
Earl of Ormonde,
1599. ROBERT DEVEREUX, EARL OF ESSEX, LORD LIEUTENANT.
Adam Loftus, } *Lords Justices.*
Sir George Carew,
1600. Sir Charles Blount, Lord Mountjoy, Lord Deputy.

JAMES I., 1603.

1603. LORD MOUNTJOY, LORD LIEUTENANT.
Sir George Carew, Lord Deputy.
1604. Sir Arthur Chichester, Lord Deputy (till 1616).
1613. *Sir Richard Wingfield,* } *Lords Justices.*
Thomas Jones, Archbishop of Dublin,
1615. *Archbishop Jones,* } *Lords Justices.*
Sir John Denham,
1616. Sir Oliver St. John (Lord Grandison), Lord Deputy.
1622. Lord Falkland, Lord Deputy (till 1629).
1623. *Sir Adam Loftus, Viscount Ely, Lord Chancellor,* } *Lords*
Sir Richard Wingfield, Viscount Powerscourt, } *Justices.*

CHARLES I., 1625.

1629. *Sir Adam Loftus, Viscount Ely, Lord Justice.*

APPENDIX I. 391

1629. Richard Boyle, Earl of Cork, Lord Justice.
1632. Sir Thomas Wentworth, Lord Deputy (till 1641).
1636. Sir Adam Loftus, Viscount Ely, } *Lords Justices.*
Christopher Wandesford,
1639. Lord Dillon, } *Lords Justices.*
Christopher Wandesford,
1640. SIR THOMAS WENTWORTH, EARL OF STRAFFORD, LORD LIEUTENANT.
Sir Christopher Wandesford, Lord Deputy.
Lord Dillon, } *Lords Justices.*
Sir William Parsons,
1641. ROBERT, EARL OF LEICESTER, LORD LIEUTENANT. (Never came over.)
Sir William Parsons, } *Lords Justices.*
Sir John Borlase,
1643. Sir John Borlase, } *Lords Justices.*
Sir Henry Tichborne,
1644. JAMES BUTLER, MARQUIS OF ORMONDE, LORD LIEUTENANT.
1647. PHILIP SIDNEY, LORD LISLE, LORD LIEUTENANT (appointed by the Parliament).

THE REPUBLIC, 1649.

1649. OLIVER CROMWELL, LORD LIEUTENANT.
1650. General Henry Ireton, Lord Deputy.
1651. General Lambert, Lord Deputy.
1653. *General Charles Fleetwood,*
General Edmund Ludlow,
General Miles Corbet, } *Commissioners.*
John Jones,
John Weever,

THE PROTECTORATE, 1653.

1654. General Charles Fleetwood, Lord Deputy.
1655. *Henry Cromwell,*
Matthew Tomlinson,
Miles Corbet, } *Commissioners.*
Robert Goodwin,
William Steel,
1657. HENRY CROMWELL, LORD LIEUTENANT.
1659. *Edmund Ludlow,*
John Jones,
Matthew Tomlinson, } *Commissioners.*
Miles Corbet,
Major Bury.

CHARLES II., 1660.

1660. GEORGE MONCK, DUKE OF ALBEMARLE, LORD LIEUTENANT. (Never came over.)
John, Lord Robarts, Lord Deputy. (Never came over.)
1660. *Sir Maurice Eustace,*
Sir Charles Coote, Earl of Montrath, } *Lords Justices.*
Roger Boyle, Earl of Orrery,
1661. *Sir Maurice Eustace,* } *Lords Justices.*
Roger Boyle, Earl of Orrery,
1662. JAMES BUTLER, DUKE OF ORMONDE, LORD LIEUTENANT.
1664. Thomas Butler, Earl of Ossory, Lord Deputy.
1669. JOHN, LORD ROBARTS, LORD LIEUTENANT.
1670. JOHN, LORD BERKELEY, LORD LIEUTENANT.
1671. *Michael Boyle, Archbishop of Dublin,* } *Lords Justices* (till 1685).
Sir Arthur Forbes,
1672. ARTHUR CAPEL, EARL OF ESSEX, LORD LIEUTENANT.
1677. JAMES, DUKE OF ORMONDE, LORD LIEUTENANT (till 1685).
1682. Richard Butler, Earl of Arran, Lord Deputy.

JAMES II., 1685.

1685. HENRY HYDE, EARL OF CLARENDON, LORD LIEUTENANT.
RICHARD TALBOT, EARL OF TYRCONNEL, LORD LIEUTENANT.
Sir Alexander Fitton, Lord Chancellor, } *Lords Justices.*
William, Earl of Clanricarde,
1689. KING JAMES in person.

WILLIAM III., 1689.

1690. KING WILLIAM in person.
Henry, Viscount Sydney,
Sir Charles Porter, Lord Chancellor, } *Lords Justices.*
Thomas Coningsby,
1692. HENRY, VISCOUNT SYDNEY, LORD LIEUTENANT.
1693. *Henry, Lord Capel,*
Sir Cyril Wyche, } *Lords Justices.*
William Duncombe,
Sir Charles Porter, } *Lords Justices.*
Sir Cyril Wyche,
1695. Lord Capel, Lord Deputy (d. 1696).
1696. *Sir Charles Porter, Lord Justice.*
Sir Charles Porter,
Earl of Montrath, } *Lords Justices.*
Earl of Drogheda,
1697. *Earl of Galway, Lord Justice.*

1697. *Marquess of Winchester,*
Earl of Galway, } *Lords Justices.*
Viscount Villiers,
1699. *Duke of Bolton,*
Earl of Galway, } *Lords Justices.*
Narcissus Marsh, Archbishop of Dublin,
Duke of Bolton,
Earl of Berkeley, } *Lords Justices.*
Earl of Galway,
1701. EARL OF ROCHESTER, LORD LIEUTENANT.
1702. *Narcissus Marsh, Archbishop of Dublin,*
Earl of Drogheda, } *Lords Justices.*
Earl of Mount Alexander,

ANNE, 1702.

1702. *Earl of Mount Alexander,*
General Earl, } *Lords Justices.*
Thomas Keightley,
1703. JAMES, DUKE OF ORMONDE, LORD LIEUTENANT.
Sir Richard Cox, Lord Chancellor,
Earl of Mount Alexander, } *Lords Justices.*
General Earl,
1705. *Sir Richard Cox,*
Lord Cutts of Gowran, } *Lords Justices.*
1707. *Narcissus Marsh, Archbishop of Armagh,*
Sir Richard Cox, } *Lords Justices.*
EARL OF PEMBROKE, LORD LIEUTENANT.
Narcissus Marsh,
Richard Freeman, Lord Chancellor, } *Lords Justices.*
1709. EARL OF WHARTON, LORD LIEUTENANT.
Richard Freeman, Lord Chancellor,
General Ingoldsby, } *Lords Justices.*
1710. JAMES, DUKE OF ORMONDE, LORD LIEUTENANT.
Narcissus Marsh,
General Ingoldsby, } *Lords Justices.*
1711. *Sir Constantine Phipps, Lord Chancellor,*
General Ingoldsby, } *Lords Justices.*
1712. *Sir Constantine Phipps,*
John Vesey, Archbishop of Tuam, } *Lords Justices.*
1713. CHARLES TALBOT, DUKE OF SHREWSBURY, LORD LIEUTENANT.
1714. *Thomas Lindsay, Archbishop of Armagh,*
John Vesey, Archbishop of Tuam, } *Lords Justices.*
Sir Constantine Phipps, Lord Chancellor,

GEORGE I., 1714.

1714. *William King, Archbishop of Dublin,*
John Vesey, Archbishop of Tuam, } *Lords Justices.*
Earl of Kildare,
EARL OF SUNDERLAND, LORD LIEUTENANT. (Never came over.)
1715. *Duke of Grafton,*
Earl of Galway, } *Lords Justices.*
1716. CHARLES, VISCOUNT TOWNSHEND, LORD LIEUTENANT. (Never came over.)
Alan Brodrick, Lord Chancellor,
William King, Archbishop of Dublin, } *Lords Justices* (till 1719).
William Conolly, Speaker,
1717. DUKE OF BOLTON, LORD LIEUTENANT.
1719. *Alan Brodrick, Viscount Midleton,*
William Conolly, Speaker, } *Lords Justices.*
1721. DUKE OF GRAFTON, LORD LIEUTENANT.
1722. *William King, Archbishop of Dublin,*
Viscount Shannon, } *Lords Justices.*
William Conolly, Speaker,
1723. *Viscount Midleton, Lord Chancellor,*
William King, Archbishop of Dublin,
Viscount Shannon, } *Lords Justices.*
William Conolly,
1724. *Viscount Midleton,*
Viscount Shannon, } *Lords Justices.*
William Conolly,
LORD CARTERET, LORD LIEUTENANT.
1726. *Hugh Boulter, Archbishop of Armagh,*
Richard West, Lord Chancellor, } *Lords Justices.*
William Conolly, Speaker,

GEORGE II., 1727.

1731. LIONEL SACKVILLE, DUKE OF DORSET, LORD LIEUTENANT.
1732. *Hugh Boulter, Archbishop of Armagh,*
Lord Wyndham, Lord Chancellor, } *Lords Justices.*
Sir Ralph Gore, Speaker,
1733. *Hugh Boulter, Archbishop of Armagh,*
Lord Wyndham, Lord Chancellor, } *Lords Justices* (till 1740).
Henry Boyle, Speaker,
1737. DUKE OF DEVONSHIRE, LORD LIEUTENANT.
1740. *Archbishop Boulter,*
Robert Jocelyn, Lord Chancellor, } *Lords Justices.*
Henry Boyle, Speaker,

APPENDIX I.

1742. John Hoadley, Archbishop of Armagh,
Robert Jocelyn, Lord Chancellor,
Henry Boyle, Speaker,
} Lords Justices (till 1747).
1745. EARL OF CHESTERFIELD, LORD LIEUTENANT.
1747. George Stone, Archbishop of Armagh,
Robert Jocelyn, Lord Newport, Lord Chancellor,
Henry Boyle, Speaker,
} Lords Justices (till 1754).
EARL OF HARRINGTON, LORD LIEUTENANT.
1754. George Stone, Archbishop of Armagh,
Lord Newport, Lord Chancellor,
Earl of Bessborough,
} Lords Justices.
1755. MARQUIS OF HARTINGTON, LORD LIEUTENANT.
1756. Robert, Lord Jocelyn, Lord Chancellor,
Earl of Bessborough,
Earl of Kildare,
} Lords Justices.
1757. JOHN, DUKE OF BEDFORD, LORD LIEUTENANT.
1758. George Stone, Archbishop of Armagh,
Henry Boyle, Earl of Shannon,
John Ponsonby, Speaker,
} Lords Justices (till 1765).

GEORGE III., 1760.

1761. EARL OF HALIFAX, LORD LIEUTENANT.
1763. EARL OF NORTHUMBERLAND, LORD LIEUTENANT.
1765. LORD WEYMOUTH, LORD LIEUTENANT. (Never came over.)
John, Lord Bowes, Lord Chancellor,
John Ponsonby, Speaker,
} Lords Justices.
EARL OF HERTFORD, LORD LIEUTENANT.
1766. Lord Bowes, Lord Chancellor,
Earl of Drogheda,
John Ponsonby, Speaker,
} Lords Justices (till 1767).
EARL OF BRISTOL, LORD LIEUTENANT. (Never came over.)
1767. GEORGE, VISCOUNT TOWNSHEND, LORD LIEUTENANT.
1772. EARL HARCOURT, LORD LIEUTENANT.
1777. EARL OF BUCKINGHAMSHIRE, LORD LIEUTENANT.
1780. EARL OF CARLISLE, LORD LIEUTENANT.
1782. DUKE OF PORTLAND, LORD LIEUTENANT.
EARL TEMPLE, LORD LIEUTENANT.
1784. DUKE OF RUTLAND, LORD LIEUTENANT.
1787. Richard Rutland, Archbishop of Armagh,
Viscount Lifford, Lord Chancellor,
Right Honorable John Foster, Speaker,
} Lords Justices.
MARQUIS OF BUCKINGHAM, LORD LIEUTENANT.
1789. Lord Fitzgibbon, Lord Chancellor,
Right Honorable John Foster, Speaker,
} Lords Justices.

1790. EARL OF WESTMORELAND, LORD LIEUTENANT.
1794. EARL OF FITZWILLIAM, LORD LIEUTENANT.
   John Fitzgibbon, Earl of Clare, Lord Chancellor, } *Lords*
   Right Honorable John Foster, Speaker, } *Justices.*
1795. EARL OF CAMDEN, LORD LIEUTENANT.
1798. MARQUIS OF CLANRICARDE, LORD LIEUTENANT.

APPENDIX II.
LIST OF THE ORIGINAL PLANTERS IN MUNSTER
(According to Sir Richard Cox and the Carew Manuscripts).

CORK.	ACRES.
Arthur Robins	18,000
Fane Beecher	12,000
Hugh Worth	12,000
Sir Arthur Hyde	5,574
Arthur Hyde	11,766
Sir W. St. Leger	6,000
Hugh Cuffe	6,000
Sir Thomas Norris	6,000
Thomas Say	5,775
Sir Richard Beacon	1,600
Edmund Spenser	3,028
Sir George Bouchier	1,300
Sir Edward Fitton	16,902
Francis Fitton	3,780
Thomas Fleetwood.	
Marmaduke Edmunds.	
Sir John Stowell.	
Sir John Clifton.	

CORK AND WATERFORD.	
Sir Walter Raleigh	42,000

WATERFORD.	
Sir Christopher Hatton	10,910
Sir Edward Fitton	600
Sir R. Beacon	4,400

TIPPERARY.	
Earl of Ormonde	3,000
Sir Edward Fitton.	

LIMERICK.	ACRES.
Sir George Bouchier	12,880
William Trenchard	12,000
Sir Henry Billingsley	11,800
Sir William Courtenay	10,500
Francis Barkly	7,250
Ed. Mainwaring	3,747
Richard Alexander } Fitton	3,026
Sir Edward Fitton	11,500
William Carter	3,661
Sir George Thornton	1,500
Robert Annesley	2,599
Sir Henry Ughtred	2,000
Robert Strowde	10,000
Robert Collum	2,500
Rowland Stanley.	

KERRY.	
Sir William Herbert	13,276
Charles Herbert	3,768
Sir Valentine Brown	6,560
Sir Edward Denny	6,000
John Hollis	4,422
Captain Conway	5,260
John Champion } George Stone	1,434
John Crosbie.	
Captain Thomas Spring.	
Stephen Rice.	
Luke Morrice.	

APPENDIX III.

LIST OF THE ORIGINAL PLANTERS IN ULSTER
(According to the Carew Manuscripts).

ENGLISH.

ARMAGH.   ACRES.
Earl of Worcester.
Lord Say.................... 3,000
Powell...................... 2,000
Sacheverel.................. 2,000
John Heron.................. 2,000
Stanhawe.................... 1,500
John Dillon................. 1,500
Brownlowe................... 1,000
Machett..................... 1,000
Rolleston 1,000
                           _____
                           16,500

TYRONE.
Earl of Salisbury.
Sir Thomas Ridgway..... 2,000
Thomas Roch............ 2,000
Francis Willoughbie.... 2,000
Sir John Ashborncham... 2,000
Captain and Thomas Edney................... 1,500
George Ridgway......... 1,000
William Parsons........ 1,000
William Turvine........ 1,000
                      _____
                      12,500

TYRONE.
Lord Audley............ 3,000
Sir Mervin Audley...... 2,000
Fernando Audley........ 2,000
Sir John Davis......... 2,000
William Blunt.......... 2,000
                      _____
                      11,000

DONEGAL.
Lord Chamberlaine.
William Wilson......... 2,000
Sir Norris Barkley..... 2,000

Sir Robert Remington.... 2,000
Sir Thomas Cornwall..... 2,000
Sir William Barnes...... 1,500
Sir Henry Clare......... 1,500
Captain Coach........... 1,500
Edward Russell.......... 1,500
Captain Mansfield....... 1,500
                      _____
                      15,000

FERMANAGH.
Earl of Shrewsburie.
Sir Edward Blennerhassett................... 2,000
Thomas Blennerhassett... 2,000
Sir Hugh Woorall........ 1,000
                      _____
                       5,000

FERMANAGH.
Earl of Shrewsburie.
Thomas Flowerden....... 2,000
Edward Ward............ 1,000
Henry Hunings.......... 1,000
Thomas Barton.......... 1,000
John Ledborough........ 1,000
Robert Calvert......... 1,000
Robert Boggas.......... 1,000
John Archdale.......... 1,000
                      _____
                       9,000

CAVAN.
Earl of Northampton.
Richard Waldron......... 2,000
John Fish............... 2,000
Stephen Butler.......... 2,000
Sir Nicholas Lusher..... 2,000
Sir Hugh Wirrall........ 1,500
John Taylor............. 1,500
W. Lusher............... 1,500
                      _____
                      12,500

Total........81,500 acres.

APPENDIX III.

SCOTTISH.

ARMAGH.	ACRES.
Sir James Douglass	2,000
Claude Hamilton	1,000
William Lauder	1,000
James Craig	1,000
Henry Acheson	1,000
6,000

TYRONE.
Lord Uchiltrie | 3,000
Sir Robert Hepburne | 1,500
L. Lochnories | 1,000
Barnard Lyndsey | 1,000
Robert Stewart of Hilton | 1,000
Robert Lindsey | 1,000
Robert Stewart of Rotton | 1,000
| 9,500

TYRONE.
Earl of Abercorne | 3,000
Sir Claude Hamilton | 2,000
James Clapen | 2,000
Sir George Hamilton | 1,500
Sir Thomas Boyd | 1,500
James Haig | 1,500
Sir John Drumond of Bordland | 1,000
George Hamilton | 1,000
| 13,500

DONEGAL.
Duke of Lenox | 3,000
Lord of Minto | 1,000
John Stewart | 1,000
Alex. McAulla of Durling | 1,000
L. Glengarnock | 2,000
John Cuningham of Cranfield | 1,000
Cuthbert Cunningham | 1,000
L. Dundulf | 1,000
James Cunningham | 1,000
| 12,000

DONEGAL.
L. Bomby | 2,000
L. Brougham | 1,500
William Stewart | 1,500
Sir Patrick McKee | 1,000
Alexander Cuningham | 1,000

	ACRES.
James McCullock	1,000
Alexander Dombar	1,000
Patrick Wans	1,000
	10,000

FERMANAGH.
L. Burley | 3,000
L. Pittarre | 1,500
L. Mountwhany, jun. | 1,500
L. Kinkell | 1,000
James Traill | 1,000
George Smelhome | 1,000
| 9,000

FERMANAGH.
Sir John Horne | 2,000
Robert Hamilton | 1,500
William Fowler | 1,500
James Sibb | 1,000
Jehue Lyndsey | 1,000
Alexander Home | 1,000
John Dombar | 1,000
| 9,000

CAVAN.
Sir Alexander Hamilton | 2,000
John Auchmootie | 1,000
Alexander Auchmootie | 1,000
Sir Claude Hamilton | 1,000
John Broune | 1,000
| 6,000

CAVAN.
L. Obignye | 3,000
William Dowmbar | 1,000
William Baylie | 1,000
John Ralston | 1,000
| 6,000

Total........81,000 acres.

SERVITORS.

ARMAGH.
Sir Gerald Moore | 1,000
Sir Oliver St. John | 1,500
Lord Audley | 500
Sir Thomas Williams | 1,000
Captain Bourchier | 1,000
Captain Cooke | 1,000
Lieutenant Pomes | 200

400　HISTORY OF THE KINGDOM OF IRELAND.

ARMAGH (continued).	ACRES.
Marmaduke Whitchurch.	120
Captain Atherton	300
	6,620

TYRONE.	
Sir A. Chichester	1,320
Sir Thomas Ridgway	2,000
Sir Richard Wingfield	2,000
Sir Toby Caulfield	1,000
Sir Francis Roe	1,000
	7,320

FERMANAGH.	
Sir John Davis	1,500
Captain Samuel Harrison.	500
Piers Mostyn	246
	2,246

DONEGAL.	
Captain Stewart	1,000
Captain Craffoord	1,000
Captain John Vaughan	1,000
Captain Kinsmell	1,000
Captain Brookes	1,000
Sir Richard Hansard	1,000
Lieutenant Parkins and Ensign Hilton	300
Sir Thomas Chichester	500
Captain Hart	1,000
Sir Raffe Binglie	1,128
Lieutenant Ellyes	400
Captain Henry Vaughan.	1,000
Captain Richard Bingley.	500
Lieutenant Gale	100
Charles Grimsditch	240
Lieutenant Browne	400
	11,568

FERMANAGH.	
Sir Henry Folliott	1,500

	ACRES.
Captain Atkinson	1,000
Captain Coale	1,000
Captain Goare	1,000
	4,500

CAVAN.	
Sir George Greame and Sir Richard Greame	2,000
Captain Coolme and Walter Talbott	1,500
Captain Pinner	1,000
Lieutenant Rutlidg	800
Serjeant Johnes	150
	4,950

CAVAN.	
Sir Oliver Lambart	2,000
Captain Lyons and Joseph Jones	1,500
Lieutenant Atkinson and Lieutenant Russell	1,000
	4,500

CAVAN.	
Sir John Elliott	400
Captain John Ridgeway	1,000
Sir William Taaff	1,000
Lieutenant Garth	500
Sir Edmond Fetiplace	1,000
	3,900

CAVAN.	
Sir Thomas Ashe and John Ashe	750
Archibald More and Brent More	1,500
Captain Tirrell	2,000
	4,250

Total........39,914 acres.

APPENDIX IV.
LIST OF THE ORIGINAL PLANTERS IN WEXFORD
(According to the Carew Manuscripts).

	ACRES.
Sir Richard Cooke	1,500
Sir Lawrence Esmond	1,500
Sir Edward Fisher	1,500
Francis Blunden	1,000
Conway Brady	600
Sir Roger Jones	1,000
Sir James Carroll	1,000
John Wingfield	1,000
Sir Adam Loftus	1,000
Fergus Græmes	300
Sir Richard Wingfield	1,000
William Marwood	1,000
Francis Blondell	1,500
John Leghorn	1,000
Captain Trevillian	2,000
Captain Fortescue	2,000
Thomas Hibbets	1,000
The Bishop of Waterford	1,000
Total	20,900 acres.

The following also received grants amounting together to 12,000 acres:

Captain Dorrington.
" Meares.
" Pikeman.
" Cawell.
" Ackland.
" Henry Fisher.
Lieutenant John Fisher.

Lieutenant Burroughs.
" Stratford.
Mr. Gillet.
" Waldrond.
" Sherlock.
" Hashwell.

APPENDIX V.

LIST OF ENGLISH AND IRISH PEERAGES AND STEPS IN THE IRISH PEERAGE CONFERRED IN A.D. 1800, IN CONSIDERATION OF A SUPPORT OF THE UNION BILL.

I. CREATIONS.

IRISH PEERAGES.

Earl of Montrath to be Baron of Castlecoote with remainder to Mr. Charles Coote, M.P. for Maryborough.
Lord Langford (the Hon. William Clotworthy Rowley).
" De Blaquiere (the Right Hon. Sir John Blaquiere).
" Frankfort (the Right Hon. Lodge Morris).
Baroness Dufferin, with remainder to her son Sir James Blackwood.
Lord Henniker (Sir John Henniker).
Baroness Newcomen, wife of Sir W. Newcomen, with remainder to her heirs male.
Lord Adare (Sir Richard Quin).
" Ventry (Sir Thomas Mullins).
" Ennismore (William Hare, Esq.).
" Wallscourt (John Henry Blake, Esq.).
" Mountsandford (Henry Moore Sandford).
" Donalley (Henry Prittie, Esq.).
" Tara (John Preston, Esq.).
" Hartland (Maurice Mahon, Esq.).
" Clanmorris (John Bingham, Esq.).
" Lecale (Right Hon. Lord Charles Fitzgerald).
" Norbury (John Toler, Attorney-General).
" Ashtown (Frederick Trench, Esq.).
" Clarina (Eyre Massey, Esq.).
" Erris (Hon. Robert King).
Earl of Clanricarde to be Earl of Clanricarde with remainder to his daughters and to their heirs male.

ENGLISH PEERAGES.

Earl of Clare to be Lord FitzGibbon.
Marquis of Drogheda to be Lord Moore.
" Ely " " Loftus.
Earl of Ormonde " " Butler.
" Carysfort " " Carysfort.
Marquis of Thomond " " Thomond.

II. PROMOTIONS IN THE IRISH PEERAGE.

Earl of Inchiquin to be Marquis of Thomond.
" Bective " " Headfort.
" Altamount " " Sligo.
" Ely " " Ely.
Viscount Castlestewart to be Earl of Castlestewart.
" Bandon " " Bandon.
" Donoghmore " " Donoghmore.
" Caledon " " Caledon.
" Kenmare " " Kenmare.
" O'Neil " " O'Neil.
Lord Glentworth to be Viscount Limerick.
" Somerton " " Somerton.
" Yelverton " " Avonmore.
" Longueville " " Longueville.
" Bantry " " Bantry.
" Monck " " Monck.
" Kilconnell " " Dunlo.
" Tullamore " " Charleville.
" Kilwarden " " Kilwarden.

APPENDIX VI.

Illustrating the Relationship of the Leading Members of the O'Neil Family during the Sixteenth and Seventeenth Centuries.

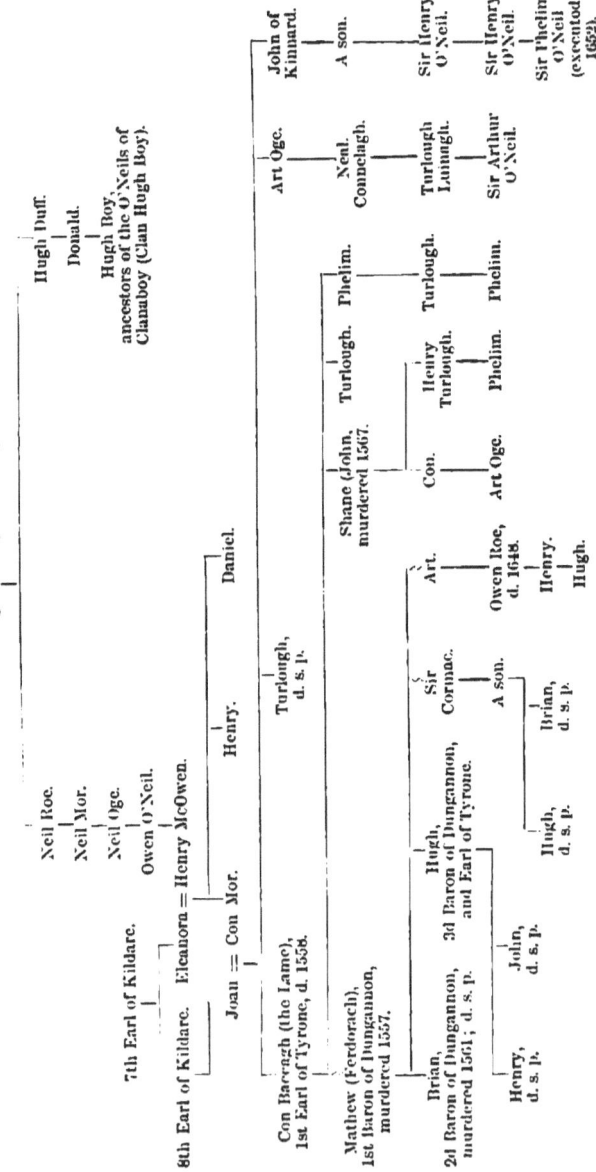

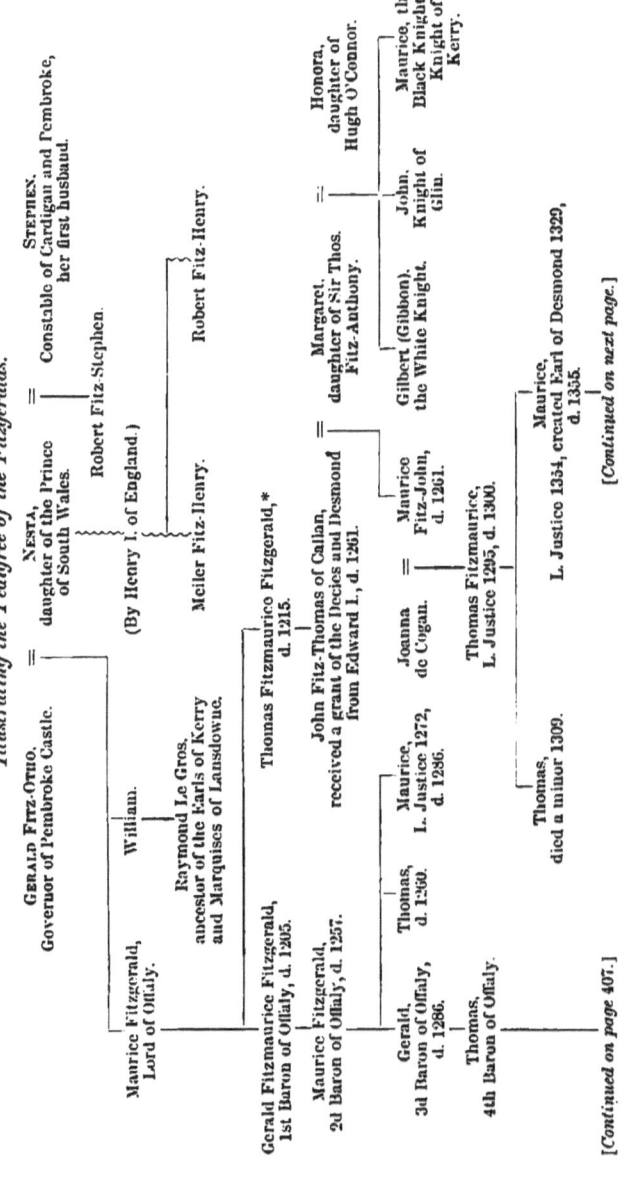

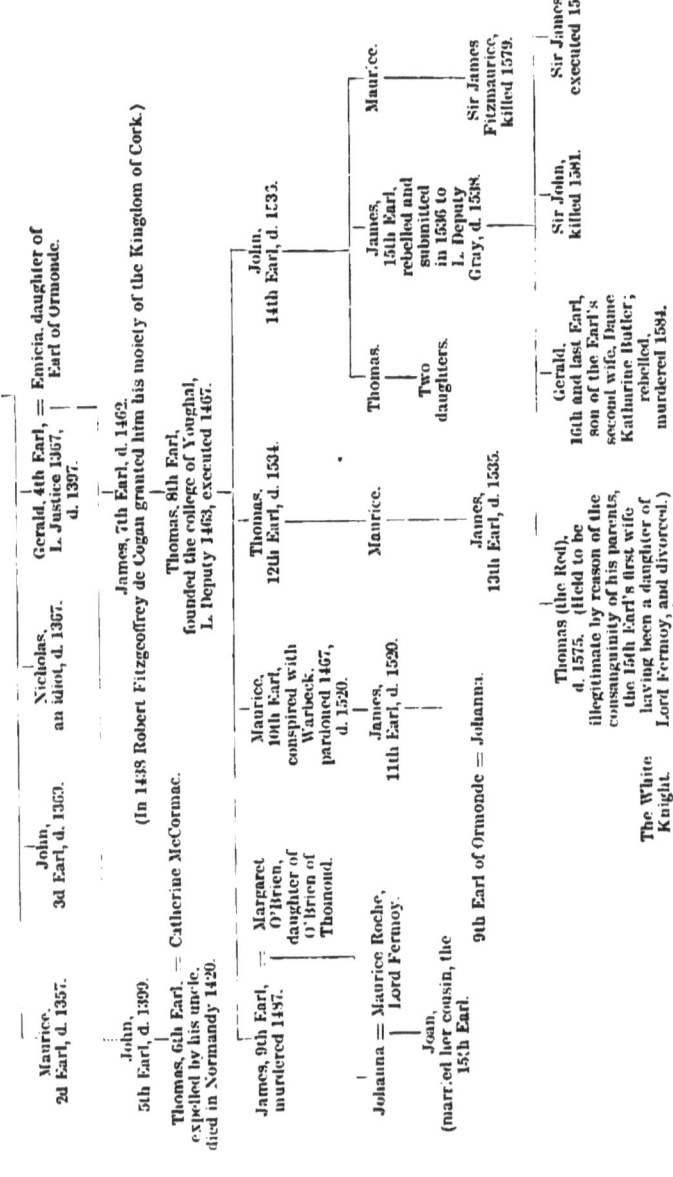

APPENDIX VI.

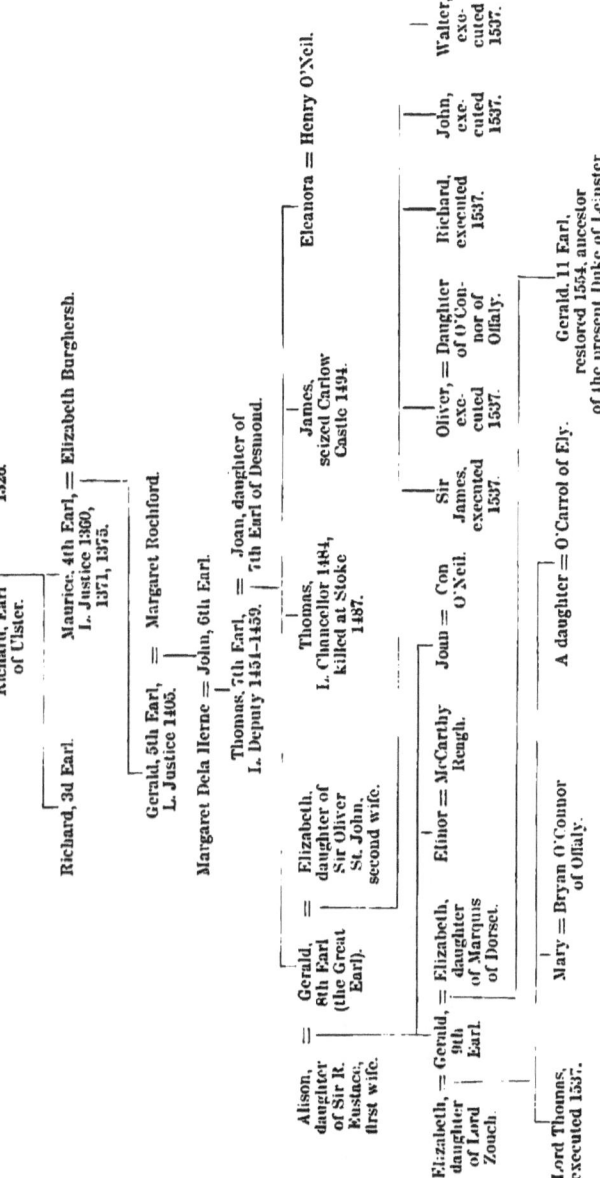

408   HISTORY OF THE KINGDOM OF IRELAND.

Illustrating the Pedigree of the De Burghs.

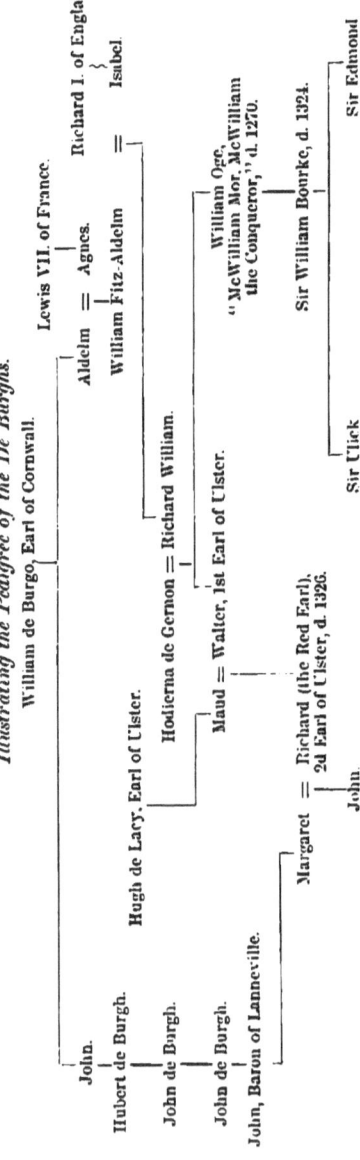
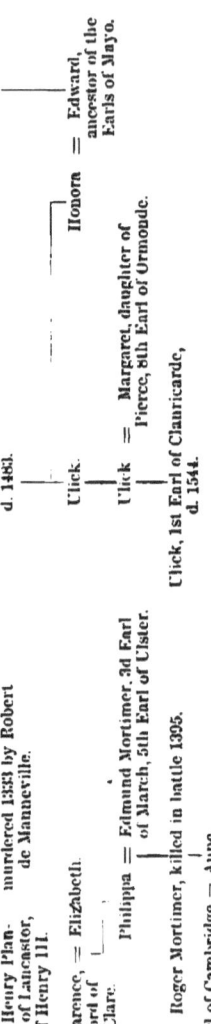

INDEX.

A.

Abbeys, suppression of the, 66, 69.
—— state of, at the Reformation, 75.
Abercromby, Sir Ralph, 344–346.
Abjuration, oath of, 239, 247.
Absentees, 140, 141, 270, 272, 284.
—— statute against, 46.
—— their estates resumed, 66.
Adrian IV. grants Ireland to Henry II., 23.
Adventurers, the, 195, 199, 206, 208, 209.
Agar, Archbishop, 345.
Agrarian disturbances, 271–273, 304–306, 319, 320.
Agriculture, improvement in, 206.
Aicill, the Book of, 5.
Allegiance, oath of, 233, 241, 317, 366.
Allen, Dr., lands at Smerwick, 97.
—— death of, 98.
Allen, murder of Archbishop, 61, 76.
American colonies, the, 281, 282.
American war, the, 282, 285, 334.
"Ancient Britons," the, 339, 351.
Anglo-Irish, the, 141, 208.
—— rebellion of, in 1641, 170.
—— conflict between, and the old Irish, 183.
—— transplantation of, 196.
—— in James's parliament, 221, 222.
Antrim, Lord, 170, 210.
Arklow, battle of, 358, 359.
Armagh, archbishopric of, founded, 14.
—— council held at, 27.
—— primacy transferred from, to Dublin, 77.
Armagh, primacy restored to, 78.
Armstrong, Captain, the spy, 342, 343, 349, 350.
Army, increase of, 275, 282.
—— Augmentation bill, 277, 278.

Ashton, Sir Arthur, 188, 190.
Ashtown, Lord, 373.
Athenry, battle of, 41.
Athlone, siege and capture of, 230, 231.
Aughrim, battle of, 231.

B.

Back Lane parliament, the, 314, 317.
Baculus Jesu, the, 77.
Bagnal, Sir Henry, 108, 109, 111, 112, 115.
—— his sister marries Tyrone, 111.
—— —— his defeat and death, 115.
Bagnal, Sir Samuel, 118.
Bagnal, Colonel, is shot, 195.
Bale, Bishop of Ossory, 77.
Ballinamuck, surrender of the French force at, 369.
Ballyan, the Baron of, 70.
Ballybogan, the rood of, burned, 77.
Baltinglass, Lord, 100, 101, 104.
Bantry, the French fleet at, 336, 337.
Barnewell, Sir Patrick, sent to the Tower, 126.
Barrons of Burnchurch, the, 210.
Beachy Head, the battle of, 227.
Belahoe, the battle of, 63.
Bellingham, Sir Edward, lord deputy, 76.
—— reduces Leix and Offaly, 82.
Benburb, the battle of, 184.
Beresford, John, 325, 326, 345.
Beresford, John Claudius, 327, 363, 374.
Beresford, Marcus, 322.
Berkeley, Lord, 214, 215.
Berwick, the Duke of, 221, 224.
Bessborough, Lord, 265, 294.
Bingham, Sir Richard, 107, 110, 111.
Bishops, Irish, 12, 13, 212, 259, 260.
"Black rent," 48, 49.
Blackwater fort, the, 115.

18

Blacquiere, Sir John, 280.
Blaney, murder of Mr., 169.
Blaney, Lord, 220.
Blood's plot, 209, 210, 214.
"Bloods, the five," 39.
Blount, Charles. *See* Mountjoy.
Bodkin, Archbishop of Tuam, 79.
Boisseleau, General, 221, 228.
Bonaght, 16, 83.
Bond, Mr. Oliver, 330, 348, 349, 367.
Borlase, Sir John, 165.
Boroughs, creation of, by James I., 137, 293.
—— condition of the, 261, 293, 294.
—— purchase of, by the government, 373-375.
Boulter, Archbishop, 208, 261, 264.
Bourke, the family of, 36, 43.
Bows, the use of enjoined, 62.
Boyle, Sir Richard, first Earl of Cork, 143, 147, 153, 157, 160, 161, 175.
—— his plantation in Cork and Waterford, 143.
Boyle. *See* Lord Shannon.
Boyne, battle of the, 226.
Bramhall, Bishop of Derry, 160, 212.
Brehon law, the, 4.
—— abolition of, 126, 127.
Brehons, the, 4.
Brian Borumha, 17.
—— defeats the Northmen, 17.
—— King of Ireland, 18.
—— death of, 18.
Bristol, Henry, Earl of Bristol, Bishop of Derry, 294-296.
Broghill, Lord, 175, 191, 192, 200, 206, 207.
Brotherhood of St. George, the, 49.
Brown, Archbishop of Dublin, 76, 77.
Bruce, Edward, 41, 42.
Bruce, Robert, 42.
Buckingham, Lord, Viceroy, 302, 307.
Buckinghamshire, Lord, Viceroy, 286.
Burgh, Hussey, 286, 287.
Burgh, Lord, 114, 115.
Burgoyne, General, 282, 296.
Burke, Edmund, 212, 286, 311, 315, 323, 324.
Burke, Richard, 311.
Butler, the family of, 35.
— rebellion of Sir Edward, 93.

Butler, Sir Edward, defends Kilkenny, 192.
Butler, Mr. Simon, 311, 320, 321.
Byrne, Edmund, 309, 314.
Byrne, Michael, execution of, 367.

C.

Calvagh O'Donnell, seizure of, by Shane, 85.
—— his release, 86.
Camden, Lord, Viceroy, 326, 327, 345, 346.
—— recall of, 364.
Camperdown, the battle of, 341.
Carew, Sir Peter, 92, 93, 100.
Carew, Sir George, 119, 120, 122, 123, 136, 148.
Carhampton, Lord, 306, 340, 344.
Carlisle, Lord, Viceroy, 289, 290, 324.
Cashel, the Synod of, 27.
Castle chamber, the, 141, 155, 160-162.
Castlebar, the battle of, 368, 369.
Castlehaven, the Earl of, 187, 193, 194, 197, 210.
Castlereagh, Lord, 309, 360, 364, 372-377, 380.
Cathal of the Bloody Hand, submission of, 32, 36.
Caulfield, Sir Toby (Lord Caulfield), 149, 167-169.
Cavan, county of, constituted, 107.
Celtic immigrations, 3.
Cessation, the, 179.
Charlemont, Lord, 289, 294-296, 302, 308, 309.
Charlemont, the fort of, 121, 226.
Charles I., accession of, 153.
—— his treatment of the Connaught land-owners, 154.
—— his arbitrary conduct in England, 163.
—— his attitude towards the rebels of 1641, 172, 178, 181.
—— makes a truce with them, 179.
—— negotiates at Oxford, 181.
—— his duplicity, 183.
—— makes a treaty with the rebels, 183.
—— execution of, 187.
Charles II. proclaimed at Kinsale, 187, 206.
—— restoration of, 206.

INDEX. 411

Charles II., his declaration for a settlement of the land question, 207.
—— his toleration of the Roman Catholics, 214.
—— his plots with Louis XIV., 214-216.
—— his death, 217.
Charter Schools, the, 261.
Chateau Renard, 234.
Chatterton's plantation, 91.
Chesterfield, Lord, 267, 274.
Chichester, Sir Arthur, 118, 122, 125, 149, 208.
—— superintends the plantation of Ulster, 130.
—— House, 208, 236.
Church lands, confiscation of the, 64, 78.
—— redistributed in Ulster, 131.
—— restored, 207.
—— misappropriated, 149.
Church, the foundation of, 12.
—— missionary spirit in, 13.
—— recast by the Pope's legate, 14.
—— harassed by the Northmen, 16.
—— Wentworth's conduct with respect to, 159-61.
—— re-established by Charles II., 206.
—— persecutes the Presbyterians, 212, 258, 260, 261.
—— the establishment of, a fundamental article in the Act of Union, 374, 378.
—— state of, at the Reformation, 74.
—— —— under Mary, 78.
—— —— at the beginning of James I.'s reign, 126.
—— —— in the time of Charles I., 159.
—— —— after Restoration, 212, 213.
—— —— in the eighteenth century, 258.
Claims, the Court of, 374, 377.
Clancarty, earldom of, granted, 84.
—— Earl of, his estates confiscated, 237.
Clanricarde, earldom of, granted, 36, 70.
—— fifth Earl of, harassed by Wentworth, 161, 162.
—— sixth Earl of, 172-174, 186, 193, 194, 196, 210.

Clare, Lord, 296, 297, 302-304, 306, 308, 316-318, 321-324, 326, 327, 345, 367, 371, 372, 378, 381.
Clare, the county of, constituted, 90.
Clare's regiment, 235.
Clarendon, Earl of, Viceroy, 217, 218.
Clergy, the state of, at the Reformation, 75, 80.
—— tithe war against, 306.
Clifford, Sir Conyers, 117.
Clonmacnoise, destruction of the Abbey of, 77.
Clonmel, the siege of, 192.
Co-arbs, the, 12.
Coercion Acts, 317, 352.
Coleraine. See Derry.
Columba, Saint, 13.
Columbanus, Saint, 13.
Commercial resolutions, the, 298-300.
Commission to inquire into defective titles, 140, 162.
—— for the repair of churches, 160.
Commissioners of plantation in Connaught, 161.
—— in Wexford, 144.
Commons, the House of, its composition, 54, 262.
Con O'Neil, 70, 84.
Confederation of Kilkenny, the, 177.
—— of the North, the, 114.
Confiscation of the Church lands, 64, 78.
—— of Leix and Offaly, 81.
—— of Munster, 104.
—— of Ulster, 130.
—— of Leinster, 140.
—— of three provinces, 195, 210.
—— of the Irish towns, 197, 208.
—— projected in 1641, 172.
—— by James's Parliament, 230.
Congé d'élire, the writ of, abolished, 79.
Connaught, treatment of the land-owners in, by James I., 145.
—— by Charles I., 154, 161, 162.
Contraband trade, the, 257, 258.
Convention Act, the, 317.
Convention, the, at Dublin, 294-296.
—— dissolved, 296.
—— of Kilkenny, 45.
—— the Roman Catholic, 313, 314.
Convocation coerced by Wentworth, 160.

Cooke, Edward, 325, 348, 345, 373, 376.
Coote, Sir Charles (the elder). 149, 173.
—— (the younger), 182, 187, 191, 192–194, 206, 207, 210.
Cork, Earl of. *See* Boyle.
Cormac Ulphada, 10.
Cornwallis, Lord, 290, 364–366, 368, 369, 371, 376.
Corporations packed by Charles II., 208.
—— reconstructed by James II., 218.
Corruption of public men, 263, 264, 275, 278, 279, 303, 375, 376, 379.
Corry, Chancellor of the Exchequer, 379.
—— his duel with Grattan, 380.
Cosbie, Francis, 97, 100.
Cosherings, commutation of, 127.
Counties palatine, 33.
Coyne and livery, 42.
—— prohibited, 46, 56.
Craddock, General, 331, 380.
Cromer, Archbishop of Armagh, 76.
Cromwell, Henry, Lord-lieutenant, 205.
Cromwell, Oliver, 181, 186–191, 205, 255.
—— captures Drogheda and Wexford, 189, 190.
—— besieges Clonmel, 192.
—— returns to England, 192.
Cromwell, Richard, 206.
Cromwellian settlement, the, 195.
—— soldiers, the, 200, 202, 206, 208, 218, 222, 223.
Crosby, Sir Piers, 162.
Curlew mountains, the fight in the, 117.
Curran, 307, 325, 333, 370, 371.
Curry, Dr., 267.
Curwin, Archbishop of Dublin, 79.
Cusacke, Sir Thomas, his report on the state of Ireland, 71.

D.

Dalrymple, General, 336.
Davis, Sir John, Attorney - General, 126, 132, 237.
—— his account of the state of the Irish Church, 126.
—— his alteration of the land laws, 127.
—— his system of espionage, 128.

Davis, Sir John, superintends the plantation of Ulster, 109, 132.
—— packs the Parliament, 136.
—— elected speaker, 138, 139.
D'Avaux, Comte, 221, 224, 226.
Debentures, the, 195, 200.
De Burgh, death of William, 48.
De Burgos, the, their wars with the Geraldines, 33.
Declaratory Act, the, 253.
—— repeal of, 290.
De Clare, Earl of Pembroke. *See* Strongbow.
De Clare, Thomas, Earl of Gloucester, invades Thomond, 33.
De Courcy, grants made to, 26, 30, 36.
Defenders, the, 304, 305, 319–321, 330–333.
De Lacy, grants made to, 35.
Del' Aguila, Don Juan, 113, 119, 120.
Delvin, Lord, 128, 129.
Dermot, McMurrough, king of Leinster, 23, 24.
De Rosen, 221, 224–226.
Derry, the county of, constituted, 107.
—— the town of, fortified by the London companies, 132, 134.
—— defended by the Protestants, 219, 220, 224.
Desmond, the earldom of, granted, 35.
—— the state of, in 1569, 90.
—— rebellion in, 95, 98.
Desmond, Gerald, sixteenth earl of, 94, 96, 98, 99, 101, 104.
Desmond, James, fifteenth earl of, his treason, 95.
Desmond, Sir James of, 102.
Desmond, Sir John of, 94, 96, 98, 100, 101.
Devereux, Bishop of Kildare, 80.
Devereux, Walter, Earl of Essex, 91.
De Vesci, his quarrel with Lord Offaly, 33, 34.
Diamond, the battle of the, 330.
Digby, Lord, 183.
Dillon, Lord, 173, 187, 232.
Dillon, Sir James, 166.
Dillon's regiment, 235.
Discoverers, the, 141.
Dixon, the rebel, 360, 363, 366.
Dockra, Sir Henry, occupies Derry, 118.

INDEX.   413

Donald, O'Lochlin, King of Ireland, 19.
Donchad, King of Ireland, 19.
Donegal, county of, constituted, 107.
—— the Earl of, 272, 273.
Dorset, the Duke of, viceroy, 265.
Doubling ordinance, the, 209, 217.
Dover, the treaty of, 215.
Dowdall, Archbishop, 76-79.
Drapier, the, letters of, 262.
Drogheda, the capture of, 189.
Drury, Sir William, President of Munster, 96, 97.
—— his campaign in Desmond, 98.
Dublin, captured by Strongbow, 24.
—— besieged by Rory O'Connor, 25.
—— granted to the citizens of Bristol, 26.
—— University, 108, 126.
—— plot to seize the castle of, 166.
—— besieged by O'Neil and Preston, 184, 185.
—— surrendered to the parliament, 185.
—— besieged by Ormonde, 187.
—— seized by Coote and Broghill, 206.
—— occupied by William III., 226, 227.
Duncan, Admiral, 340, 341.
Dundalk, battle of, 42.
Dundaniel, plantation at, 143.
Dundas, General, 315, 325.
Dungan Hill, battle of, 186.
Dungannon, barony of, 70.
—— convention of the volunteers at, 290, 294, 295.
—— the Baron of, his feud with Shane, 71, 84.
—— —— the death of, 84.
Dunsany, Lord, imprisoned by the lords-justices, 173.

E.

Elizabeth, accession of, 79.
—— her Church policy, 79.
—— her treaty with Shane O'Neil, 86.
—— state of her army, 116.
—— her efforts to crush Tyrone, 117.
—— death of, 121.
Ely, the plantation of, 81.
Emancipation of the Roman Catholics, 323, 324, 326.
—— bill for the, 325, 328.
Embargo, the, 282-284.

Emigration to America, 260, 273, 277.
Emmett, Thomas Addis, 330, 349, 367.
Enniskillen, held by the Protestants, 219, 220, 224.
Esmond, Lord, a Wexford planter, 144, 145.
—— deserts Charles I., 181.
Essex, the Earl of (the elder), his plantation, 91, 109.
—— his treatment of the natives, 92.
—— his death, 92.
Essex, the Earl of (the younger), 116.
—— his campaigns in Munster, 117.
—— his conference with Tyrone, 118.
—— recall of, 118.
Eustace, Sir Maurice, lord-justice, 206.
" Ever Joyce," 238, 304.
Everard, Sir John, his contest for the speakership, 138, 139.
Explanation, the Act of, 210, 236.

F.

Falkland, Lord, lord deputy, 153, 155, 156.
Famines, 121, 122, 238, 239, 257.
Farney, the territory of, granted to Essex, 91, 109.
Fenton, Sir Geoffrey, surveyor-general, 148.
Fercal, the plantation of, 151.
Fermanagh, the county of, constituted, 107.
—— harassed by the Binghams, 110.
Feudal system, introduction of the, 28, 29.
Fingal, 10.
Firbolgs, the, 3.
Fitzaldelm receives grants of land, 27, 30, 36.
Fitton, Sir Edward, 91.
—— his grants in Munster, 105.
Fitzgerald, Lord Edward, 333, 334, 335, 348-350.
Fitzgerald, James, seizes Carlow, 56.
Fitzgerald, Sir James Fitzmaurice, 94.
—— his first rebellion, 94.
—— his second rebellion, 97.
—— his death, 98.
Fitzgerald, Sir James FitzPiers, 144.
Fitzgerald, Judkin, 346, 363, 364.
Fitzgerald, Maurice, 24.
—— — his grants of land, 27.

Fitzgerald, Lord Thomas, 61, 62, 95.
Fitzgibbon. See Lord Clare.
Fitzmaurices, the, 34, 43.
Fitzstephen, Robert, 24.
—— his grants of land, 27.
—— his estates pass to the Earl of Desmond, 35, 93.
Fitzwilliam, Lord, viceroy, 323–326.
—— breaks up the junto, 325.
—— is recalled, 326, 327, 364.
Fitzwilliam, Sir William, lord deputy, 96, 108.
Flax, the growth of, encouraged by Wentworth, 158.
Fleetwood, lord deputy, 195, 206.
Flood, Henry, 275, 279, 283, 292, 297, 300, 308, 379.
—— accepts a vice-treasurership, 280.
—— supports free trade, 286.
—— attacks Poynings's Act, 289.
—— agitates for reform, 293–295.
—— brings in a Reform bill, 295, 296.
Foster, the Right Hon. John, 326, 345.
Fosterage, the practice of, 39, 40.
—— prohibited, 45.
Fox, Charles James, 290, 300, 302, 309.
Free trade, the demand for, 283–287.
—— conceded, 286, 287.
French expedition to Bantry, the, 335–337.
—— from the Texel, 341.
—— to Killala, 368.
—— to Lough Swilly, 369.
French Revolution, the, 308, 309, 314.
French, Sir Thomas, 314.

G.

Galway, Lord, 235.
Galway, the county of, constituted, 90.
Gardiner, Mr., his Roman Catholic Relief bills, 309.
Geilfine system, the, 7.
George III., 301, 325, 326.
—— illness of, 301, 302.
—— recalls Lord Fitzwilliam, 326, 327.
Geraldines, the, 34.
—— the Munster, 35.
—— rebellion of the, 61.
—— they combine against the planters, 93.
Gilbert, Sir Humphrey, 92, 94.
Ginkel, General, 228, 230-236.

Glamorgan, the Earl of, 182.
—— his mission, 181.
—— his treaty, 182, 183.
Glenmalure, the fight in the valley of, 101.
Godwin, the agent of the Parliament, 177–179.
Goff's Bridge, the battle of, 361.
Goodacre, archbishop of Armagh, 77.
Gorges, Dr., 225.
Gosford, Lord, his address, 331.
Grace, Colonel, defends Athlone, 227.
"Graces, the," 154, 155, 159.
Grants made by Henry II. to his followers, 27, 28.
—— made to Ormonde, 207, 208.
—— of confiscated land in Munster, 105.
—— —— in Ulster, 133.
—— —— in Leinster, 142.
—— —— made by William III., 236.
Grattan, Henry, 283, 288–302, 307–312, 317, 324–326, 333, 338–340, 379, 380.
—— his resolutions on free trade, 286.
—— —— legislative independence, 288, 290.
—— his measures relating to tithes, 313, 314.
—— his bill for the relief of the Roman Catholics, 325.
—— retires into private life, 340.
—— his reappearance in the House of Commons, 378.
—— his duel with Corry, 380.
Gray, Lord Leonard, 63, 66.
Gray, Nele, suborned to murder Shane O'Neil, 85.
Gray, de Wilton, Lord, 100.
Grogan, Cornelius, execution of, 363.
Gunpowder Act, the, 317.

H.

Habeas Corpus Act, the, 291.
—— suspended, 338.
Hamilton, Richard, deserts to James II., 220.
Harcourt, Lord, Viceroy, 279.
Hardi, General, 368-370.
Hartington, Lord, Viceroy, 265.
Harvey, Bagenal, of Barrycastle, 356, 357.
—— execution of, 363.

INDEX. 415

Hay, John, execution of, 363.
Hearts-of-steel Boys, the, 272, 273.
Heber and Heremon, 10.
Henry II. lands in Ireland, 25.
—— constitutes a government in Dublin, 26.
—— his dealings with the Church, 74.
Henry VII., 55, 58.
Henry VIII., his Irish policy, 59.
—— his quarrel with the Pope, 64.
—— his Church policy, 64, 65, 73.
—— his treaties with the chieftains, 70, 71.
Hoadly, Archbishop, 264.
Hoche, General, 336, 337, 341, 368.
Hollowblade Company, the, 237.
Holt, Joseph, the rebel, 355, 366.
Howth, Lord, 129.
Humbert, General, 368, 369.
Hutchinson, Hely, 279.

I.

Ibrackan, the barony of, 70.
—— the Baron of, 70, 71.
Inchiquin, Lord, 180, 187, 192, 210.
—— deserts Charles I., 180.
—— captures Cahir, 186.
—— defeats Lord Taaffe at Knocknanos, 186.
—— deserts the Parliament, 186, 200.
Independence, legislative, granted, 290.
Informers, the, 342, 343.
Innishowen, the rising in, 129.
—— granted to Sir Arthur Chichester, 149.
Insurrection Act, the, 331, 333.
Insurrection, the, of 1641, 167.
—— its consolidation, 177.
—— the, in Wexford, 350.
Ireton, General, 191, 193-195.
Irish Bishops, the, 12-14, 212.
—— Brigade, the, 235, 258.
—— cattle, export of, prohibited, 256.
—— Church. *See* Church.
—— contingent in England, 180.
—— forfeitures, 236.
—— kingdoms, 15.
—— members in the English Parliament, 205, 206.
—— officers at Culloden, 251.
—— soldiers enlisted in foreign service, 197, 234, 235.

Irish women and boys shipped to the West Indies, 197.
—— the, condition of, after the war with Tyrone, 123.
—— the, condition of, in the eighteenth century, 269 271, 304, 305.
—— extension of English law to, 139.
—— the early, 3.
—— laws and customs of the early, 4.
—— progress of, 56, 57.
—— rise against Prince John, 31.
—— submission of, to Henry II., 25.
—— Statutes against, 40, 49, 50.

J.

Jackson, 321, 322, 329.
James I., accession of, 125.
—— his proclamation against the Roman Catholics, 126.
—— his policy in Ulster, 126, 127.
—— his plantations in Ulster, 130.
—— packs the Parliament, 136.
—— compromises with the recusants, 138.
—— his plantations in Leinster, 140.
—— his extravagant government, 145.
—— his project to confiscate the towns, 145.
—— his project to plant Connaught, 146.
—— his death, 146.
James II., his Irish policy, 216, 217.
—— his flight from England, 219.
—— arrives in Ireland, 221.
—— holds a Parliament, 221, 222.
—— his new peers, 221, 222.
—— debases the coinage, 224, 238.
—— his flight from Ireland, 227.
Jones, Dr., 149.
—— Colonel Michael, 185-188.
—— Paul, 283, 285.
Judges, bill to render their tenure of office perpetual, 277, 291.

K.

Kavenaghs, the, 112.
Kells, the Synod of, 14.
Kendal, the Duchess of, 262, 263.
Kenny, Nicholas, escheator-general, 144, 148.
Keogh, John, 309-314, 330.

INDEX.

Keppel, Earl of Albemarle, grants to, 236.
Kidnapping, 197.
Kildare, the earldom of, 33, 34.
—— the great Earl of, 53, 57, 60.
—— the ninth Earl of, 60–62.
—— the tenth Earl, restored, 78.
Kilkenny, the confederation of, 177, 196.
—— the convention of, 45.
—— the statute of, 45, 56.
Killala, the French at, 368.
Kimbaoth, King of Ireland, 10.
King's county constituted, 82.
Kinsale, the battle of, 120.
Knight of Glin, the, 35, 115.
Knight of Kerry, the, 35.
Knocknanos, the battle of, 186.
Knoctow, the battle of, 58.

L.

Lake, General, 346, 360, 362–364, 369.
—— in Ulster, 338, 340.
—— Commander-in-chief, 346, 360.
—— defeated at Castlebar, 368, 369.
Lambeth Articles, the, 154, 160.
Lancaster, Bishop of Kildare, 77.
Land, change in the tenure of, by Henry VIII., 28, 29.
—— by James I., 126, 127.
—— the law relating to the tribal, 6, 7.
—— policy of the Normans in relation to, 28, 29.
—— question, the, 206, 210. 211, 222, 223.
—— sale of coarse and barren, 236, 237.
—— the tribal, 3.
—— confiscation of, in Connaught, 162.
—— —— Leinster, 140.
—— —— —— Leix and Offaly, 81.
—— —— —— Munster, 103.
—— —— three provinces, 195, 200, 201, 210, 211.
—— —— —— Ulster, 133.
" Landlordism," league against, 273.
Langrishe, Sir Hercules, 311.
Laud, Archbishop, 156, 159, 160, 163, 212.
Lauzun, the Comte de, 226–229.
Le Poer, grants of land to, 31.

Leinster, the plantation of, 140.
Leinster, the Duke of, 286, 294, 302, 308, 340.
Leitrim, the county of, constituted, 90.
—— the plantation of, 142.
Leix, the plantation of, 81, 131.
—— ravaged, 119.
Leoghaire, King of Ireland, 11.
Leslie, Henry, 212.
Leslie, John, 212.
License of the soldiery, 339, 340, 344–347, 354, 355, 362–365.
Limerick, Articles of, 233, 234, 239–243.
—— burned by Brian Borumha, 17.
—— first siege of, 227, 228.
—— second siege of, 232.
Linen trade, the, 157, 282, 283.
Lionel, Duke of Clarence, 37, 45.
Loftus, Adam, Archbishop of Armagh, 79, 80, 107, 108, 114, 115, 149.
—— Lord Chancellor, 153, 156.
—— deprived of his office, 162.
—— prosecuted for treason, 179.
Loftus, General, 357–360, 370.
London Companies undertake land in Ulster, 133.
Long Parliament, the, 163, 175.
Longford, county of, constituted, 90.
—— plantation of, 142.
Lorraine, the rebels offer the crown of Ireland to the Duke of, 193.
Louis XIV., 215, 220, 221, 226.
Lucas, Dr., 264–266, 275, 288.
Lucy, Sir Anthony, 44.
Ludlow, General, 195, 205.
Luttrell, General. *See* Carhampton.
Luttrell, Henry, 221.
Luttrell, Simon, 221.

M.

McCabe, William Putnam, 354.
McCarthy, Col. Justin, 221–226, 235.
McCarthy Mor, created Earl of Clancarty, 81.
McCarthys, the, 15, 32, 114.
McCracken, Henry Joy, 353.
McDermots, the, 112.
McGennis, Sir Con, 168.
McGinnusses, the, 37, 112, 167, 168.
McGuire, Lord, 166, 167.
McGuire, Rory, 169.
McGuires, the, 37, 110, 112, 167.

INDEX. 417

McGeoghans, the, 44, 68.
McGilapatrick, of Upper Ossory, 68–70.
McGilapatricks, the, 140.
Melbrien of Ara, 98.
McMahon, Rossa, 108.
McMahons, the, 112, 167.
McMurrough, Art, 47, 48, 50, 140, 141.
McMurroughs, the, 15, 43, 46, 141.
McNally, Leonard, 321, 342.
McNevin, Dr., 330, 342, 349, 367.
McWilliam, Iochtar, 43.
McWilliam, Uachtar, 43.
Malachy, Bishop, 14.
Malby, Sir Nicholas, 97, 98, 142.
Malone, Anthony, 265.
Marlborough, the Duke of, captures Cork, 229.
Marston Moor, the battle of, 181.
Martial law, 338, 346.
Mary, her accession, 78.
—— her church policy, 78.
Massacre in Armagh, 169.
—— of Drogheda, 189.
—— of Island McGee, 171.
—— of Mullaghmast, 97.
—— of the Northmen, 17.
—— of Rathlin Island, 92.
—— of Scullabogue, 357.
—— of Torry Island, 129.
—— at Vinegar Hill, 359.
—— at Wexford, 361.
Maynooth, capture of, 61.
—— College of, 316.
Mayo, the county of, constituted, 90.
Mayo, Lord, 166, 173, 174, 177, 195.
Meath, the kingdom of, granted to De Lacy, 26, 35.
Melachlin, king of Meath, 17, 18.
Michael O'Clery, 10.
Middlemen, the, 270, 271, 305.
Militia, act for establishing, 285.
Milo de Cogan invades Connaught, 30.
—— grants made to, 31.
Moinmor, the battle of, 19.
Moira, Lord, 309, 343.
Molyneux, 252, 266, 288.
Monaghan, the county of, constituted, 107.
—— confiscation of, 180.
Monasteries, the, 65.
—— confiscation of, 66, 69, 70.

Money bills, conflicts upon the, 278, 279, 288, 289.
Monk, General, 187, 206.
Moore, General, 360, 361.
Mortimer, Edmund, 37.
Mortimer, Roger, 37, 47.
Moryson, President of Munster, 122, 137.
Mountcashel. *See* Col. McCarthy.
Mountcashel's regiment, 235.
Mountgarret, Lord, 174, 177, 184, 216.
Mountjoy, the fort of, 121.
Mountjoy, Lord, reforms the army, 118.
—— besieges Kinsale, 119.
—— crushes Tyrone's rebellion, 121.
—— created Earl of Devonshire, 125.
Mountmorres, Hervey, 23, 27.
Mountnorris, Lord, court-martialed, 162.
Mullaghmast, the massacre of, 97.
Munroe, General, 176–181, 213.
—— defeated at Benburb, 184.
Munster, the kingdom of, 15.
—— the plantation of, 103, 115.
—— the rebellion in, 95, 115.
Murkertach, king of Ireland, 19.
Murphy, Father John, 356, 359.
Murphy, Father Michael, 359.
Murtough O'Lochlin, king of Ireland, 20.
Muskerry, Lord, 174, 184, 195.
Mutiny Act, 291.
—— bill, 289.

N.

Nantwich, the Irish contingent cut off at, 180.
Naseby, the battle of, 181.
National debt, the, 263, 275, 289.
Navigation Acts, the, 255.
Needham, General, 358–360.
Neilson, Samuel, 330, 348–350, 379.
Nemedians, the, 3.
Nevill, the surveyor-general, 265.
New interest, the, 146, 149, 208, 209, 222, 223.
New Ross, the battle of, 357.
Newbury, the battle of, 181.
Newhaven, Lord, supports free trade, 284.
Newtown Butler, the battle of, 224.
Nial of the Nine Hostages, 11.

18*

Normans, the invasion of the, 23, 29.
—— endow the Church, 74.
Norris, Sir John, 112-114.
Norris, Sir Thomas, 112, 115.
North, Lord, 278, 284, 285, 287, 289, 290.
"Northern Star," the, 314, 338.
Northington, Lord, viceroy, 295.
Northmen, invasions of the, 16.
—— settlements of the, 17.
—— conversion of the, 18.
—— defeats of the, 17.
—— the, driven out of Dublin by Strongbow, 25.
Nugent, Lord, supports free-trade, 283.

O.

Oakboys, the, 272, 273.
Oates, Titus, 216.
O'Briens, the, 46, 174.
O'Byrne of Glenmalure, death of, 114.
O'Byrne, Phelim, treatment of, 144.
O'Byrnes, the, 43, 68, 100, 112, 140, 144, 148, 173.
O'Carrols, the, 60, 81.
O'Connor, Arthur, 328, 334, 335, 338, 348, 367, 378.
O'Connors of Sligo, 112.
O'Connors, the, 43, 61, 68, 81, 82.
Octennial Act, the, 277.
—— bill, the, 265, 266.
O'Dempseys, the, 68, 81.
O'Dogherty, Sir Cahir, 129, 130.
O'Donnel, Con, 92.
O'Donnel, Hugh, defeats Shane O'Neil, 87.
O'Donnel, Hugh Roe, 109-113, 117, 120.
O'Donnel, Sir Neal, 129.
O'Donnel, Rory, Earl of Tyrconnel, 128, 129, 139.
O'Donoghues, the, 115.
O'Dowds, the, 112.
O'Doynes, the, 140.
O'Driscol rebels, 120.
O'Duns, the, 68, 81.
O'Farrels, the, 141, 142, 167.
Offaly, the Baron of, quarrels with De Vesci, 33, 34.
—— plantation of, 81, 130, 131.
—— recovered by the O'Connors, 43.
O'Hanlons, the, 167.

O'Kane, his dispute with Tyrone, 84, 129, 167.
O'Kanes, the, 37, 167.
O'Kellys, the, 97, 112.
Ollam, Fohdla, 10.
O'Melaghlins, the, 44, 68, 140.
O'Molloys, the, 68, 81, 140.
O'Moore, Rory, the outlaw, 97.
—— the contriver of the rebellion of 1641, 166, 168, 171, 174, 176, 178.
O'Moores, the, 43, 61, 68, 81, 97, 142, 166.
O'Neil, Con. *See* Con O'Neil.
O'Neil, Sir Brian, of Clanaboy, 92.
O'Neil, Hugh, the defender of Limerick, 192, 194.
O'Neil, Hugh, Earl of Tyrone, 110-114, 120, 121, 128, 129, 139.
O'Neil, Col. Owen, 176-179, 184-188, 192, 195.
O'Neil, Sir Phelim, 166-171, 175-178, 195.
O'Neil, Shane. *See* Shane O'Neil.
O'Neil, Turlough Luinagh, 88, 93, 111, 113.
Opposition, the, 261-263, 276, 288, 294, 302-304, 339, 373, 377, 379-381.
—— secession of the, 339, 340.
O'Quins, the, 167.
Orange, the Prince of, 219, 223.
Orange Lodges, formation of, 330, 331.
Orangemen, the, 331-333, 339, 353-355, 374.
Orde, Mr. Secretary, 299, 300.
O'Reilly, 69.
O'Reilly, the, created Baron of Cavan, 85.
O'Reillys, the, 167.
Orkney, grants to the Countess of, 236.
Ormonde, the family of, 35.
Ormonde, James, twelfth Earl of, 163, 170-172, 174, 178-182, 187, 192, 197, 207, 208, 210, 214, 223.
—— created a marquis and lord-lieutenant, 181.
—— is besieged in Dublin, 184, 185.
—— surrenders Dublin to the parliament, 185.
—— heads the rebels in the royal cause, 186.
—— defeated at Rathmines, 188.
—— retires to France, 193.

Ormonde, grants made to, 207-209.
O'Rourke of Brefny, 23.
O'Rourkes, the, 110, 140.
Orr, William, 343, 344.
Ossory, the Baron of Upper, 70.
O'Sullivan of Beare rebels, 120, 121.
O'Tooles, the, 43, 68, 112, 140, 173.

P.

Pale, 48, 89.
—— the reign of terror in the, 101.
Paparo, Cardinal, 14.
Parliament, the origin of the, 54.
—— limitation of the, 276.
—— King James II.'s, 222.
—— state of the, in the reign of George II., 261, 262.
—— subjection of the, 253.
Parnell, Sir John, 324, 372, 379.
Parsons, Sir Lawrence, 326, 327, 372, 373, 378.
Parsons, Sir William, 144, 145, 148, 153, 165, 167, 179.
Patrick, Saint, 11, 12.
"Patriots, the," 261, 264-263, 276-279, 283, 288, 289, 291.
Paul Jones, 283, 285.
Peep-o'-day Boys, the, 304, 319, 320, 330.
Peerages, the sale of, 279, 280, 283, 303, 375, 376.
Pelham, Sir William, 99, 103.
Pelham, Mr., chief secretary, 326, 364.
Penal laws, the, 238.
Pension bill, the, 302, 317, 318.
Pension list, the, 262, 263, 275, 279, 283, 303, 307, 308.
Perrot, Sir John, 94, 105, 107-109, 146.
Perry, Anthony, the rebel, 355.
Pery, Mr., 275, 279, 302, 307.
Petty, Sir William, 199-201, 210, 237.
Pim, Mr. Joshua, 298.
Pirates, the, suppressed by Wentworth, 157.
Pitt, William, 298-302, 310, 315, 323-326, 344, 361, 365, 371-373, 381.
Plantation, a, projected in Wicklow by Richard II., 47.
—— made by the Earl of Cork, 143.
—— made by the East India Company, 143.

Plantation policy of Elizabeth, the, 91.
—— of the Irish Council, the, 59.
—— the Cromwellian, 200.
—— the, of Connaught, 162.
—— of Leinster, 139.
—— of Leix and Offaly, 81, 131.
—— of Munster, 104.
—— of Ulster, 130.
—— of Wicklow, 144.
Plunket, Dr., execution of, 216, 217.
Police Acts, the, 327.
Ponsonby, George, 303, 307, 323, 325, 339, 372.
Ponsonby, John, the Speaker, 265, 276, 279, 294.
Ponsonby, William, 318, 323.
Popish plot, the, 216.
Portland, the Duke of, 290, 295, 323-327.
Potwallopers, the, 293.
Poynings, Sir Edward, 55, 56.
Poynings's Acts, 56, 158, 159, 167, 181, 222, 239, 252, 253, 278, 288, 289.
—— the practice under, 253.
—— the repeal of, 290.
Presbyterians, the, 206, 209, 296.
—— clergy, the, inducted into Ulster livings, 153.
—— persecution of the, 212-214, 260, 261.
—— flight of, to America, 213, 273, 281.
—— their marriages acknowledged, 291.
Presidential courts established, 90.
Preston, Colonel, 176-178, 184-186, 193.
Priests, the hunting down of the, 201.
—— condition of the, 267, 268.
Proctors, the, 54.
—— are silenced, 66.
Protestant ascendency, the, 138, 150, 251, 255.
Protestants, the, disarmed, 219, 220.
—— disturbances of the, with the Roman Catholics, 304, 305, 330, 331.
—— flight of the, 219.

Q.

Queen's County, formation of, 82.
Quin, Bishop, 77.

R.

Raleigh, Sir Walter, in Munster, 100, 101.
—— his grant of land, 105.
—— his grant passes to Boyle, 143, 144, 148.
Ranelagh, Lord, President of Connaught, 173.
Rapparees, the, 219, 229.
Rath Bresail, the synod of, 13.
Rathlin Island, the massacre at, 92.
Rathmines, the battle of, 188.
Raymond le Gros, 24, 30, 34.
Reform of the parliament, 290, 294, 297.
Reform bill, brought in by Flood, 295.
—— brought in by Grattan, 339.
Regency question, the, 301, 302.
Regicides, the estates of the, 207, 208.
Regium donum, the, 260.
Renunciation, the Act of, 292.
Reprisal ground, the, 207, 208.
Resumption bill, the, 236.
Reynolds, the agent of the parliament, 178, 179.
Reynolds, Dr., 320.
Reynolds, Thomas, the spy, 342, 348.
Richard II., 46, 47.
Rightboys, the, 304, 306, 319.
Rinuccini, 183–187.
Ripon, the treaty of, 163.
Risings, the, of 1798, 349–353, 355, 362, 369.
"Robin Hoods, the," 106.
Roche, Father, 358, 359–361, 363.
Rockingham, Lord, 290, 295.
Roman Catholic clergy, the, 259, 267, 268.
—— Committee, the, 267, 309–311, 316, 327.
—— Convention, the, 313, 314.
—— hierarchy, the, established, 125.
Roman Catholics, James I.'s proclamation against the, 126.
—— petition James I., 126, 158.
—— outnumbered in James's parliament, 138.
—— harassed by the New Interest, 153.
—— their treatment by James I. and Charles I., 153, 154.
—— their lands confiscated, 201, 210.
Roman Catholics contest the Act of Settlement, 209.
—— toleration of, 214, 215.
—— persecution of, 215, 216, 330.
—— in James II.'s parliament, 221, 222.
—— exile of, 235.
—— penal laws against, 238.
—— disfranchisement of, 247.
—— condition of, in the eighteenth century, 251. 267–269.
—— loyalty of the, 267, 268.
—— riots of, with the Protestants, 304, 330.
—— bills for the relief of, 284, 285, 309–317.
—— emancipation of, 324.
—— support the Union, 374.
Romney, Lord, grants of land to, 236.
Rory O'Connor, 19, 20, 24, 30, 31.
Roscommon, the county of, constituted, 90.
Ross, the battle of, 179.
Rowan, Hamilton, 320–322.
Russell, Sir William, 110, 112–114.
Rutland, the Duke of, 299, 301, 302.
Ruvigny, grants of land to, 236.
Ryan, death of Captain, 349, 350.

S.

Saint George, the brotherhood of, 49.
St. John, Sir Oliver, 137, 143, 153.
St. Leger, Sir Anthony, 68, 77, 78.
St. Leger, Sir Wareham, 173, 179.
St. Patrick. *See* Patrick.
St. Ruth, 230, 231.
Sanders, Dr. Nicholas, 97, 99–102.
Saratoga, the surrender at, 282.
Sarsfield, Patrick, 221, 224–229, 232, 234.
Scandinavian invasion, the, 16.
Schomberg, General, 224, 225.
Scoti, the, 3.
Scots, the invasion of the, 41.
—— the immigration of the, 84, 85.
—— the murder Shane O'Neil, 87.
Scotus, Joannes, 13.
Secret Committee of the House of Lords, the, 319, 320, 378.
Secret-service money, 317, 318, 343.
Senchus Mor, the, 4.
Septennial Act, the, 276.

INDEX.

Servitors, the, in Longford, 142.
—— in Ulster, 132-134.
Settlement, the Act of, 209, 217, 218, 223, 236.
—— the petition to reconsider, 215.
—— repealed by James's Parliament, 223.
Shane O'Neil, 71, 84-87.
Shane, Sir Francis, his claim on the County of Longford, 142.
Shannon, the first Earl of, 265.
—— second Earl of, 278, 279, 294, 307.
Sheares, the brothers, 349, 350.
—— executed, 367.
Shelburne, Lord, 284, 286, 290, 292.
Sidney, Sir Henry, his report of the state of the Church, 80.
—— his interview with Shane, 84, 85.
—— his league against Shane, 87.
—— his exactions on the Pale, 89, 97, 100.
—— his campaign in Munster, 94.
"Silken Thomas," 61.
Simnel is crowned in Dublin, 53.
Simple repeal, 292.
Sirr, Town Major, 343, 349.
Skeffington, Sir William, 61.
Sligo, the county of, constituted, 90.
Smerwick, 97-101.
Smith's plantation, 91.
Smugglers, the, 258.
Spaniards, the, land at Smerwick, 100.
—— massacred, 100, 101.
—— land at Kinsale, 119.
Spenser, Edmund, the poet, in Munster, 100.
—— his account of the state of Munster, 103, 104.
—— receives a grant of land in Cork, 105.
Spies, the, 342, 343.
Staples, Bishop of Meath, 76, 77.
Stewart, Robert. *See* Castlereagh.
Stone, Archbishop, 264, 265.
Strafford, Lord. *See* Wentworth.
Strongbow, 24.
—— grants of land made to him, 33.
—— the inheritors of his estates, 34.
Stukeley, 97.
Subinfeudations, 36, 37.
Sugan Earl, the, 115.
Sulchoid, the battle of, 17.

Supremacy, the Act of, 66, 69.
—— the oath of, 125, 126, 131, 132, 153, 155, 161, 162, 182, 183, 238, 239.
—— —— a test of loyalty, 96.
Survey of Ulster made by James I., 127, 132.
—— Connaught made by Strafford, 199.
—— Ireland made by Sir W. Petty, 199.
Sussex, the Earl of. 83, 85, 86.
Swift, Jonathan, Dean of St. Patrick's, 261, 262, 266.
Sydney, Lord, his quarrel with the Irish Commons on the Money bills, 278.
Synod at Kells, the, 14.
—— at Cashel, the, 27.
—— at Rath Bresail, the, 13.

T.

Taaffe, defeat of Lord, at Dungan hill, 186.
Talbot, Peter, 215, 216, 227-229.
Talbot, Richard, 209, 215, 217-221, 232.
Tandy, James Napper, 297, 311, 320, 366.
Tanist, the, 4.
Tanistry, the law of, 4.
—— disturbances concerning, 71, 72, 84.
—— abolished, 127.
Taylor, Jeremy, 212-214.
Temple, Lord, 295.
Test clause, the, 260, 298.
Teutonic immigrations, 3.
Thomond, the earldom of, granted, 69.
Thonory, Bishop of Ossory, 80.
Thurot's attack on Carrickfergus, 267.
Tichborne, Sir Henry, 171, 179.
Tillage Act, the, 257, 258, 271-273.
Tithe proctors, the, 305, 306.
Tithes, 305, 306.
—— the institution of, 14.
—— regulations as to, of King James's parliament, 222, 223.
—— disturbances arising out of the collection of, 271-273, 305.
Toler, the attorney-general, 325, 345.
Toleration Act, the, 260.
Tom the Devil, 355.
Tone, Theobald Wolfe, 310-316, 320-322, 329, 330, 335, 341, 366, 370, 371.

422   INDEX.

Tories, the hunting-down of the, 195, 238, 239.
—— depredations by, 214, 229, 238, 239.
—— acts against, 238, 239.
Torry Island, the massacre of, 129.
Torture of the peasantry and farmers, 346, 354, 363, 364.
Townshend, Lord, 276–280, 303.
Trade, 222, 223, 251, 252, 283.
—— the destruction of, 255, 282, 283.
—— the, with England, 298.
Transplantation, 130, 131.
Travers, bishop of Leighlin, 77.
Tribal system, the, 3, 4.
—— decay of the, 16.
Trinity College, Dublin, 126.
Troy, Dr., 374.
Tuath da Danaan, the, 3.
Tuathal, 10, 11.
Turanian Irish, the, 3.
Turges, 16.
Turlough O'Brien, king of Ireland, 19.
Turlough O'Connor, king of Ireland, 19.
Tyrconnel, the earldom of, 70, 128.
—— the Earl of. *See* Richard Talbot.
Tyrone, the county of, constituted, 107, 108, 111.
—— the earldom of, 70.
—— Hugh, Earl of. *See* Hugh O'Neil.
—— Hugh, third Earl of, an exile, 166.
Tyrrel, Captain, 112, 113, 115, 119, 120.

U.

Ufford, Sir Ralph, 45.
Ulster, incorporation of the new towns in, 138.
—— the plantation of, 130.
—— the risings in, in 1641, 167.
—— tenant-right in, 135.
Undertakers, the, in Leinster, 143.
—— in Munster, 106.
—— in Parliament, 131, 132.
—— in Ulster, 131, 133, 134.
Uniformity, the Act of, 79, 95, 126, 153, 213, 214.
Union, the Act of, 380, 381.
—— a, proposed by the Irish parliament, 179, 300, 301.
—— unpopular, 301.

Union projected, 315, 371.
—— the debates on the, 372, 373, 378–381.
—— the proposed, defeated in the Irish House of Commons, 373.
—— resolutions in favor of, passed by the English House of Commons, 373, 380.
—— resolutions in favor of, passed by the Irish House of Commons, 380, 381.
—— outline of the bill for the, 377, 378.
"United army of Wexford," the, 354.
United Irishmen, the Society of, 297, 313, 319, 320, 336, 338, 339, 343, 351, 352, 354–356, 366, 367, 378, 379.
—— formation of the, 310, 311.
—— oath of the, 313.
—— suppression of the, 321, 322.
—— reorganization of the, 329, 330.
—— increase of the, 333, 340.
—— cruelties upon the, 346, 347.
—— rising of the, 350.
—— trial of the leaders of the, 366, 367.
University of Dublin, the, 108, 126.
Upton, Mr., 272, 273.
Usher, Archbishop, 153, 160, 212.

V.

Verois, M. de, his pension, 275.
Vinegar Hill, the rebel camp at, 357, 359.
—— capture of, 360–362.
Virgilius, bishop of Salzburg, 13.
Volunteers, the, 285, 286, 289, 290, 296, 297.
—— formation of, 285.
—— pass resolutions at Dungannon in favor of legislative independence, 289, 290.

W.

Waller, Sir Hardress, sent prisoner to England, 206.
Walpole, Col., 358, 359.
Walsh, Bishop of Meath, 79.
Walter, Theobald, 29.
—— grants made to him, 29.
Warbeck, Perkin, 54.
Wards, the Court of, 155.

Waterford captured by Strongbow, 24.
—— granted to the Northmen, 27.
—— besieged by the Earl of Desmond, 54.
—— surrendered by Preston, 192, 193.
Wentworth, Sir Thomas, 156, 181.
—— his policy, 157.
—— his arbitrary conduct, 158, 160, 161.
—— is made Earl of Strafford, 163.
—— is executed, 163, 164.
Westmeath divided from Meath, 82, 83.
—— plantation of, 140.
Westmoreland, Lord, viceroy, 307, 323.
Wexford, the plantation of the county of, 141, 142.
—— capture of the town of, by Cromwell, 190.
—— —— by the rebels in 1798, 356.
—— recovery of the town of, 361.
Whig Club, the, 297, 308, 309.
—— the Northern, 309.
Whiteboys, the, 271-274, 276, 282.
—— Acts, the, 273, 296, 305.
White Knight, the, 35, 43.
—— restored to his lands, 105.
—— rebellion of the, 115.
—— betrays the Sugan Earl, 119.

Wicklow, the county of, constituted, 137.
—— the plantation of, 137.
William III., 226-229.
—— his terms to the Irish, 230.
—— confirms the Treaty of Limerick, 233.
—— his grants of the confiscated estates, 236.
Wilmot, Lord, 162.
Wingfield, Sir Richard, 149.
Wolfe, attorney-general, 325.
Wolves, increase of, 201.
Wood's patent, 262.
Woollen trade, the, crippled by Wentworth, 157, 158.
—— destroyed, 256, 257.
—— repeal of the laws against, 287.
Wreckers, the, 319.
Wright, Bernard, 346, 364.
Wyse, Mr., 267.

Y.

Yellow Ford, the battle of the, 115.
Yelverton, 296.
York, the Duke of, receives a grant of the estates of the regicides, 208.
—— resigns the post of High Admiral, 215.
—— his Irish policy, 217.
Yorktown, the surrender at, 290.

THE END.

www.ingramcontent.com/pod-product-compliance
Lightning Source LLC
Chambersburg PA
CBHW051859300426
44117CB00006B/460